Intermediate Examination Paper 5

ACCOUNTING

23305

Published March 1991 by Financial Training Publishing and Distance Learning, 151 Freston Road, London, W10 6TH

ISBN 1 85179 295 3

Past examination questions have been reproduced by kind permission of the Association of Accounting Technicians.

Answers have been prepared by our team of specialist authors.

Printed in England.

CONTENTS

0041V

INTRODUCTION

This Revision Pack provides students with sufficient practice at questions to ensure confidence in the exam. The aim is to cover all areas of the syllabus and give a balanced range of questions, most of which are from recent past exams.

HOW TO USE THIS REVISION PACK

The Revision Pack is split into two sections: a bank of questions with answers and a mock exam. The questions are organised by topic to ensure you cannot forget any of the areas on which you may be examined.

Do questions without reference to your notes and time yourself strictly; it is better to know your weaknesses now than on the day itself! Nothing is more infuriating than wasting months of hard work by mistiming an answer in the exam.

The model answers are there to help you; learn from their structure and content and check your answers against them carefully.

The Revision Pack ends with a mock exam which, if attempted under exam conditions, is an excellent opportunity to develop your exam technique.

STUDENTS ENROLLING ON REVISION COURSES

This Revision Pack provides the material for the revision course. Students enrolling on these courses should not use the questions in this Pack before attending the course.

THE EXAMINATION

FORMAT OF THE EXAMINATION

There are **seven** questions on the paper. Candidates are to answer the **two** compulsory questions in Section A and **two** questions from the five in Section B.

SYLLABUS

Aims

To develop:

(a)   a comprehension of accounting concepts and methods;
(b)   a competence in the collection and use of accounting data; and
(c)   a base for more advanced technical studies.

Syllabus

10%   **Accounting concepts:** the entity – distinction between the entity and its owner. Monetary measurement, going concern, consistency, conservatism and matching, and their application to the recording of transactions and drafting of accounting statements.

25%   **Accounting records:** the nature of the more usual forms of business transactions and their documentation. The techniques of double entry book keeping to record transactions and process entries through to trial balance. The location of errors and the use of suspense accounts; adjustments to correct errors, internal control; bank reconciliations; the purpose and operation of control accounts.

50%   **Accounting statements:** the significance of the capital/revenue distinction. The accounting treatment of stocks, fixed assets, depreciation and VAT. The adjustment of the trial balance for accruals, prepayments, provisions for depreciation, doubtful debts and stock profits; the production of manufacturing, trading, profit and loss and appropriation accounts and balance sheets for sole traders, partnerships and companies.

Partnership accounts; entries on the formation of a partnership, the appropriation of partnership profits, current and capital accounts. Partnership and company, compared and contrasted, as forms of business structure.

Preparation of accounts from incomplete records, and the use of incomplete records techniques to calculate stock losses and defalcations. Receipts and payments accounts and the accounting statements of non commercial undertakings.

15%   **Interpretation of financial statements:** the significance and limitations of financial ratios, the definition and application of basic financial ratios and the selection and application of appropriate accounting concepts and methods to simple business problems.

A knowledge of the disclosure requirements of the Companies Acts will not be required at this level.

EXAM TECHNIQUE

Common failings

- Poor time allocation: some candidates fail to attempt all the questions because they run out of time.

- Failure to produce what is asked for in the 'required' section of the question.

- Failure to present organised proformas: there is evidence, for example, that some students do not know the order of presentation of 'current assets'.

- Obsession with the difficult points (eg, suspense accounts) rather than the easy marks.

- Lack of professionalism in written questions.

Helpful tips

(1)   Time allocation is vital in accounting, you **must** move on to the next question when your time is up.

(2)   If you are confident about a particular written question, do it first.

(3)   Read the **'required'** at the foot of each question carefully; if you produce anything other than what is asked for, you will score zero.

(4)   Lay out proformas first; make sure you know them before the exam.

(5)   Go for the easy marks; you can slot some figures into the proformas immediately.

(6)   If you get stuck on a point in the question, ignore it: you may lose two marks, but you only need forty!

(7)   Try and complete each question in the time allowed; you will have missed some of the difficult points, but produced a finished product.

(8)   Be professional: 'joke addresses' in a report question, for example, are suicidal.

(9)   Do not get bogged down in minor parts of questions. If you are stuck, **leave it** and get on with the rest of the question.

(10)   Remember if it is a hard question, it is hard for **everybody** so keep going.

(11)   Do not panic! You only need half marks. Passing exams is based on **getting the easy marks** in every question.

(12)   Please read this again the night before the exam.

0041V

ANALYSIS OF THE LAST SIX PAPERS

0041V

REVISION TOPICS

1   **Year-end adjustments**

    (a)   **Accruals and prepayments** – In constructing the profit and loss account of a business you must be aware of the importance of the 'trading period'.

           This area tests whether you understand the principle that the profit or loss a business makes is calculated by deducting the expenses incurred within a defined period from the income earned within that same period.

    (b)   **Depreciation and stocks** – The depreciation charge is a provision or estimate of the use of the asset for the year. The pre-requisites to calculation are:

           (i)   the cost of the asset;
           (ii)   the life of the asset;
           (iii)   any residual or scrap value.

           You must know the different methods of calculating depreciation charge particularly straight-line and reducing-balance method. You must be able to deal with the accounting treatment relating to additions and disposals and the balance sheet presentation especially where there is a large category of assets.

           Revise the different methods of stock valuation particularly:

           (i)   FIFO;
           (ii)   LIFO;
           (iii)   Weighted average.

           You should be able to deal with the valuation of stock issues to production and the balance at the end of period. Be able to justify the rule of 'lower of cost or net realisable value'.

    (c)   **Bad and doubtful debts** – You must be able to distinguish between bad debts, ie, those debts written off from the debtor's account to the profit and loss account and doubtful debts which require a provision the likelihood of the debt not being settled in the coming period.

           Be certain as to the accounting treatment of specific and general provisions as well as bad debts now recovered.

2   **Accounting concepts and principles**

In this area you should expect a number of examination questions which normally require in part a written answer outlining the normal accounting treatment of items and the reasons for such treatment, followed by the application of these rules to specific examples. It often helps to read through the examples before attempting the written part of the question, particularly if you are uncertain as to how best to describe the relevant concept and its application.

Pay particular attention to:

(a)   the four fundamental accounting concepts, accruals, going concern, prudence and consistency;

(b)   the treatment of accruals and prepayments;

(c)   fixed assets and depreciation, and particularly the purpose of depreciation;

(d)   provisions for bad and doubtful debts;

(e)   the valuation of stock and work in progress.

3   Correction of errors, journal entries and suspense accounts

These questions are concerned with testing your grasp of double entry. Work out, for each item in the question, firstly the entries that have been made and secondly those which should have occurred. Prepare a journal entry changing the first to the second and remember that every journal entry requires a description, without which you can gain no more than half marks.

Be very careful – not all journal entries have two sides – those correcting errors made in recording items sometimes have only one, but those for unrecorded items must have both a debit and a credit.

4   Control accounts and bank reconciliation

Remember the 'golden rule' that governs the use of control assets:

'Whatever is entered in the individual debtors/creditors accounts must be entered in the control account.' The debtors/creditors accounts are effectively the memorandum accounts unless otherwise told.

The bank reconciliation statement is not part of double-entry but is necessary to check the accuracy of the postings in the cash book. There are basically three reasons why the bank statement balance and the cash book balance do not balance:

(a)   items in the cash book but not on the bank statement;
(b)   items on the bank statement but not in the cash book; or
(c)   errors, normally in the cash book.

It is practical to start with the balance per bank statement. It may be necessary to write up/adjust the cash book for (b) and (c) before proceeding.

5   The accounts of clubs and societies

Remember clubs and societies are non-trading organisations and therefore have income and expenditure accounts instead of profit and loss accounts.

Revise the layout of the accounts and pay particular attention to the treatment of:

(a)   subscriptions (sometimes income is treated on a cash basis, a 'receipts and expenditure' account),

(b)   the treatment of small trading activities within the club, eg, bar,

(c)   the accumulated fund: remember the excess of income over expenditure is added to this on the balance sheet.

6   Incomplete records – the accounts of sole traders

Learn the layout of the accounts of sole traders: remember no appropriation account is required for the profit and loss account.

Approach questions requiring final accounts in a logical manner. Try to prepare both the balance sheet and profit and loss account together on two pieces of paper. (A large number of errors arise from failure to complete the double entry on an accrual and prepayment. If you can make entries in both the profit and loss account and the balance sheet at the same time, your mistakes are reduced.)

The preparation of accounts from incomplete records requires a methodical approach in order to to prepare a 'full set of accounting records' with the minimum of effort. Don't forget that the opening balance sheet is often required to identify starting capital. The closing balance sheet may need profit inserted as the balancing figure. Remember to put all difficult figures into workings and to solve the missing figures on your working accounts one by one starting with those workings where only one figure is missing.

This approach to questions is often adopted where records are lost, eg, after a fire or flood or where a defalcation has occurred, eg, cash or goods stolen and in these circumstances the gross profit percentage is normally given.

7 Manufacturing accounts

It is important that you know the layout, so revise this and make sure that you know the critical subtotals, ie:

(a) prime cost;
(b) total cost of manufacturing;
(c) cost of goods transferred.

Remember this application could well be extended to include sole-trader, partnership and company accounts.

8 The accounts of partnerships

Revise the layout of partnership accounts. Pay particular attention to the profit and loss appropriation account and the use of partners' capital and current accounts.

Make sure you know the rules regarding:

(a) salaries to partners;
(b) interest on capital;
(c) profit sharing ratio;
(d) interest on advances in excess of agreed capital (loans).

Remember interest on loans is a profit and loss account charge while all the rest appear in the appropriation account if the agreement specifies them.

Ensure that you can deal with the situation where a new partner is admitted to the partnership. In particular, the calculation of goodwill is vital here.

9 The accounts of limited companies

Learn the difference between sole trader and partnership accounts and those of companies. Pay particular attention to:

(a) taxation;
(b) dividends paid and proposed;
(c) share capital;
(d) reserves.

Remember that reserves normally belong to the ordinary shareholders and are treated as part of their capital for calculating ratios.

10   Accounting ratios and interpretation

Ensure that you know how to calculate ratios dealing with profitability, financial stability, liquidity and gearing, all have appeared in past exams.

Note: Some ratios relate to more than one of the areas given above.

Also make sure that you know how to prepare a source and application of funds statement. Be prepared to explain the significance of a change in any of the ratios above.

11   VAT

Make sure that you understand how to deal with:

(a)   VAT on purchases and sales;
(b)   VAT control account including amounts to/from HMC&E;
(c)   VAT with discounts for sales and purchases.

0041V

INDEX TO QUESTIONS AND ANSWERS

0041V

0041V

0041V

QUESTIONS

1   YEAR-END ADJUSTMENTS

1.1   HALE

Hale owns a fleet of motor vehicles. He prepares his accounts to 31 December
each year. He writes off the cost of vehicles on the straight line basis over a
period of five years and charges a full year's depreciation for the year in which a
vehicle is acquired and none in the year of sale.

Examination of the books gives you the following information:

(1)   The balance on the motor vehicles account on 31 December 19X4 showed
motor vehicles at cost, £18,093.

(2)   Expenditure on motor vehicles over the last six years had been:

		£
Before	19X0	4,273
During	19X0	2,480
During	19X1	2,350
During	19X2	6,890
During	19X3	–
During	19X4	2,100
During	19X5	2,260

(3)   Two vehicles were sold during 19X5:

(i)   one for £215, bought before 19X0 for £980; and
(ii)   the other for £420, bought in 19X2 for £1,150.

No vehicles were sold before 19X5.

Required

(a)   Prepare a schedule showing the computation of the balance on the motor
vehicles depreciation account on 1 January 19X5, and the charge for
depreciation for the year ended 31 December 19X5.

(b)   Write up the ledger accounts for the year ended 31 December 19X5 showing
the charge for depreciation and the profit or loss on each vehicle sold.

(20 marks)

0042V

1.2 ROE LTD

The following information relates to the acquisition and issue of Material 2XA by Roe Ltd, a small manufacturing company, for the three months to 31 March 19X3:

Material 2XA

Date	Acquisitions quantity kg	Price per kg £	Issues quantity kg
1.1.X3	100	3.00	
15.1.X3	200	4.00	
29.1.X3			150
17.2.X3	400	4.50	
5.3.X3			450
16.3.X3	100	5.00	
31.3.X3			50

Note: There was no material in stock at 1 January 19X3.

Required

(a)   Calculate the closing stock value of Material 2XA using each of the following methods of pricing the issue of stock to production:

(i)   first–in, first–out (FIFO);
(ii)   last–in, first–out (LIFO);
(iii)   periodic simple average;
(iv)   periodic weighted average;
(v)   weighted average.

(b)   Examine the effect on gross profit of using the first–in, first out (FIFO) and last–in, first–out (LIFO) methods of pricing the issue of stock to production assuming that price levels are rising.

(15 marks)

1.3 STOCK VALUATION

You are the accountant to a medium–sized engineering company, and are presented with the following information relating to the valuation of part of the stock held by the company at the year–end.

	Historic cost £	Replacement cost £	Net realisable value £
Sheet steel	8,000	9,500	8,600
Iron bars	7,600	6,750	7,000
Electrical circuits	12,400*	16,000	13,100
	28,000	32,250	28,700

*The historic cost valuation of the electrical circuits has been reached as follows:

Purchases during the year:	£
250 at £30	7,500
300 at £35	10,500
200 at £40	8,000
	26,000

	Issues £
200 at £40 =	8,000
160 at £35 =	5,600
	13,600
Closing stock	12,400

Required

(a)   What principles should be applied to the valuation of the stock?

(b)   Explain clearly what value you, as the accountant, would place on the stock.

(20 marks)

1.4   **EXPRESS TRANSPORT LTD (D86)**

The following information has been extracted from the motor lorry records of Express Transport Ltd:

Lorry	Date bought	Cost £	Method of payment
B393KPQ	1 October 19X3	22,000	Cash transaction
B219BXY	1 January 19X4	25,000	Cash transaction
C198TKL	1 October 19X5	34,000	Cash transaction
C437FGA	1 April	28,000	B393KPQ given in part exchange plus cheque for £18,000

Express Transport Ltd, which was incorporated in 19X3, has only owned the vehicles mentioned above during its existence.

Up to 30 September 19X5, the company used the reducing balance method for depreciating its motor lorries; the rate of depreciation being 25% per annum.

However, as from 1 October 19X5 it has been decided to change to the straight line method for depreciating the motor lorries; the rate of depreciation to be used is 20% per annum and it is assumed that all vehicles will have a nil residual value. As a result of this decision, it will be necessary for appropriate adjustments to be made in the company's accounts so that the balance of the motor lorries provision for depreciation account at 1 October 19X5 will be on the basis of the straight line method.

Required

(a) Prepare the journal entry (or entries) necessitated by the charge of depreciation policy on 1 October 19X5 from the reducing balance method to the straight line method. **Note:** Journal entries should include narratives.

(9 marks)

(b) Prepare the following accounts for the year ended 30 September 19X6 in the books of Express Transport Ltd:

(i) motor lorries at cost;
(ii) motor lorries provision for depreciation;
(iii) motor lorry B393KPQ disposal.

(16 marks)
(Total 25 marks)

1.5 FINE SPINDLES LTD (J87)

The accounts of Fine Spindles Ltd are prepared on a quarterly basis.

Owing to very severe staff shortages at 31 March 19X7, the usual stock-taking was not undertaken.

However, the following information has now been produced:

(1) The accounts for the quarter ended 31 December 19X6 showed stock in trade, at cost, at that date of £16,824.

(2) An error, only now discovered, in the stock sheets for 31 December 19X6 shows an overcast of £2,000.

(3) Goods invoiced to customers during the quarter ended 31 March 19X7 totalled £54,210; however this includes goods sold for £1,040 despatched to customers in December 19X6.

(4) Goods invoiced to customers at £3,900 in April 19X7 were despatched by Fine Spindles Ltd in March 19X7.

(5) Goods purchased by the company during the quarter ended 31 March 19X7 amounted to £46,680, at invoice prices.

(6) A burglary at the company's stores in March 19X7 resulted in stock costing £8,000 being stolen.

(7) In March 19X7, it was decided that a quantity of stock, which would normally be sold for £1,950 will only realise half cost price. This stock was unsold at 31 March 19X7.

(8) Credit notes totalling £4,550 were issued to customers for returns inwards during the quarter ended 31 March 19X7.

(9) The company normally obtains a gross profit of 30% on cost price on all sales.

Required

(a)   Prepare a computation of the stock valuation at 31 March 19X7.   (16 marks)

(b)   Prepare the trading account for the quarter ended 31 March 19X7.   (9 marks)
(Total 25 marks)

1.6   JOHN BROWN AND PARTNERS (D87)

In November 19X6, John Brown and Partners, building contractors, decided to build a new workshop for the manufacture of window frames. The workshop, built on freehold land already owned by the partnership, was constructed mainly by the firm's own workforce. The building was completed and came into use on 1 May 19X7.

During the year ended 31 October 19X7, the following expenditure was incurred in connection with the new workshop.

19X7		£
January – April	Construction costs:	
	Direct materials	15,000
	Direct labour	9,000
	Variable overheads	3,000
February	Central Electrics Ltd – supply of electric installation	2,400
March	Central Electrics Ltd – repair of electric installation following vandalism	1,000
August	Redecoration costs following fire:	
	Direct materials	2,000
	Direct labour	1,600
	Variable overheads	300

The firm's policy is to apportion budgeted fixed overheads to contracts or jobs done in proportion to the cost of direct labour. The firm's budgeted fixed overheads and budgeted total direct labour costs for the year ended 31 October 19X7 were £450,000 and £225,000 respectively.

The firm's insurers paid the following amounts in full and complete settlement of insurance claims made during the year ended 31 October 19X7:

		£
June 19X7	March 19X7 vandalism claim	800
October 19X7	August 19X7 fire claim	4,000

Depreciation is provided on the straight-line basis on the firm's buildings at the rate of 5% per annum assuming nil residual values.

Required

(a)   Prepare the following accounts for the year ended 31 October 19X7 in the books of John Brown and Partners:

New workshop at cost;
New workshop provision for depreciation;
Workshop repair.

(16 marks)

(b)   Explain why it is necessary to distinguish in accounting between revenue expenditure and capital expenditure.

(9 marks)
(Total 25 marks)

1.7 THOMAS DART (J88)

Thomas Dart, builders' merchant, is now completing his stock valuation at 31 May 19X8. He fears that his financial results for the year ended 31 May 19X8 will be poor as compared with recent years, but nevertheless wishes his accounts to show a favourable view of his business so that his bank manager will approve a renewal of the business bank overdraft.

The stock at 31 May 19X8 includes the following items:

	Unit cost price £	Expected sales price £	Replacement price £
200 'Padgetts'	200	340	260
100 'Wodgetts'	110	280	140

Thomas Dart has now decided that the above items should be valued on the following bases:

	Unit valuation £	Reason
200 'Padgetts'	340	An important customer has written saying he hopes to buy all the stock of 'Padgetts' on 10 June 19X8.
100 'Wodgetts'	140	Anticipating a growing demand for 'Wodgetts', Thomas Dart bought a large quantity before the price rose to £140. Most competitors' stocks were bought at a price of £140.

As far as other items of stock are concerned, Thomas Dart proposes to use the last in first out basis of stock valuation instead of the first in first out basis used in previous years.

Required

As the accounting technician employed by Thomas Dart, prepare a report addressed to him, commenting on his proposed bases for valuing his stock at 31 May 19X8. In your report make reference to appropriate accounting concepts.

(25 marks)

1.8 JOHN GAUNT (J89)

John Gaunt commenced trading on 1 January 19X6 as a distributor of the Red Diamond Mark 1 Farm Tractor with an initial capital of £50,000 used to open a bank account.

Upon commencing trading, John Gaunt bought fixtures and fittings costing £10,000 which he installed in his rented premises.

Overhead expenses, including rent of premises but excluding depreciation, have been incurred as follows:

	£
Year ended 31 December 19X6	24,000
Year ended 31 December 19X7	26,000
Year ended 31 December 19X8	31,000

Depreciation on fixtures and fittings is to be provided at the rate of 20% per annum using the reducing-balance method. Purchases and sales of the Red Diamond Mark 1 Farm Tractor up to 31 December 19X8 were as follows:

	Purchases	Sales
19X6	6 at £25,000 each	4 at £30,000 each
19X7	8 at £25,000 each	(3 at £30,000 each
19X8		(4 at £32,000 each
February		1 at £34,000
March	4 at £28,000 each	
May		3 at £37,000 each
July	5 at £30,000 each	
September		4 at £38,000 each
October	2 at £32,000 each	
December		2 at £38,000 each

John Gaunt has accepted, with some reluctance, his accountant's advice to use the first in first out basis for stock valuation as from 1 January 19X8 instead of the last in first out basis which he claims to have used in earlier years.

All John Gaunt's business transactions are on a cash (non-credit) basis.

John Gaunt does not intend to take any drawings from the business until 19X9.

Required

(a) Prepare, in as much detail as possible, John Gaunt's trading and profit and loss account for **each** of the years ended 31 December 19X6, 19X7 and 19X8 using:

    (i)   the last in first out basis of stock valuation; and
    (ii)   the first in first out basis of stock valuation. (13 marks)

(b) Prepare John Gaunt's capital account for the year ended 31 December 19X8.
    (5 marks)

(c) A concise report to John Gaunt in support of the accountant's advice concerning the stock valuation basis. (7 marks)
    (Total 25 marks)

1.9   DOCKS LTD

Docks Ltd, a window replacement company, offers fairly generous credit terms to its high risk customers. Provision is made for bad debts at a varying percentage based on the level of outstanding trade debtors, and an assessment of general economic circumstances, resulting in the following data for the last three accounting periods:

Year to 31 March	19X0 £	19X1 £	19X2 £
Trade debtors at the year-end (before allowing for any bad debts)	186,680	141,200	206,200
Estimated bad debts (companies in liquidation)	1,680	1,200	6,200
Provision for bad debts	10%	12.5%	15%

The provision for bad debts at 1 April 19W9 amounted to £13,000.

7

Required

(a) Prepare the provision for bad debts account for each of the three years to 31 March 19X0, 19X1 and 19X2 respectively, showing how the balances would appear on the balance sheets as at these dates.

(b) Assuming that a debt of £1,000 written off as bad in 19X0 was subsequently recovered in cash in 19X1, state briefly how this would have affected the profit for the year to 31 March 19X0, and also how it would be treated in the accounts for the year to 31 March 19X1. (20 marks)

1.10 J ROYAL

J Royal commenced business on 1 April 19X1. The following information relates to the first three years that he is in business:

Year to 31 March	19X2 £	19X3 £	19X4 £
Sales (all credit)	458,400	567,600	537,200
Cash received	355,300	512,700	481,200
Discounts allowed	45,800	47,300	48,600
Specific bad debts at 31 March (to be written off)	2,200	4,900	2,500
	%	%	%
Provision to be made for bad debts	5	10	7½
Provision to be made for discounts on trade debtors	10	12½	15

Required

Write up the following accounts to the nearest £, for each of the three years to 31 March 19X2, 19X3 and 19X4 respectively:

(a) trade debtors;
(b) bad debts;
(c) bad debts provision; and
(d) discounts allowed provision.

1.11 ZOOM PRODUCTS LTD (J87)

(a) The balance sheet as at 31 December 19X5 of Zoom Products Ltd included:

Trade debtors £85,360

The accounts for the year ended 31 December 19X5 included a provision for doubtful debts at 31 December 19X5 of 3% of the balance outstanding from debtors. During 19X6, the company's sales totalled £568,000 of which 90%, in value, were on credit and £510,150 was received from credit customers in settlement of debts totalling £515,000. In addition, £3,000 was received from K Dodds in settlement of a debt which had been written off as bad in 19X5; this receipt has been credited to K Dodd's account in the debtors' ledger.

On 30 December 19X6, the following outstanding debts were written off as bad:

J Sinder	£600
K Lambert	£2,000

Entries relating to bad debts are passed through the provision for doubtful debts account whose balance at 31 December 19X6 is to be 3% of the amount due to the company from debtors at that date.

Required

(i)   Write up the provision for doubtful debts account for the year ended 31 December 19X6 bringing down the balance at 1 January 19X7.

(10 marks)

(ii)   Prepare a computation of the amount to be shown as 'trade debtors' in the company's balance sheet at 31 December 19X6.   (4 marks)

(b)   On 1 January 19X5, J Cort Ltd purchased the following fixed assets upon the opening of a new department producing cakes:

Cake mixing machine	£20,000
Delivery vehicle	£25,000

Provision for depreciation for these assets were made as follows:

Cake mixing machine	10% per annum reducing balance method;
Delivery vehicle	20% per annum straight line method.

On 1 January 19X7, the company closed the cake department and sold the cake mixing machine and delivery vehicle to Creamy Cakes Ltd for £23,000, payment to be made on 1 March 19X7. The accounting year end of J Cort Ltd is 31 December. A sale of cake department fixed assets account is to be opened in the books of J Cort Ltd.

Required

Prepare the journal entry (or entries) recording the disposal of the cake department fixed assets on 1 January 19X7.   (11 marks)

Note: Journal entries should be supported by narratives.   (Total 25 marks)

1.12   JOHN PEACOCK LTD (D88)

(a)   On 1 April 19X8, John Peacock Ltd, a recently formed transport company, bought a second-hand lorry at a cost of £40,000. The lorry required immediate repairs costing £5,000 to make it roadworthy; these repairs were completed by 1 May 19X8 when the lorry was brought into service by the company.

Upon acquiring the lorry, John Peacock Ltd insured it at an annual premium of £1,200 which was paid immediately.

On 1 July 19X8 the lorry was damaged slightly in a road accident necessitating repairs costing £600; the company decided not to make a claim against the insurance company.

John Peacock Ltd has decided to provide for depreciation on the motor lorry on the straight-line basis from 1 May 19X8 assuming an expected useful economic life in the business of five years and an estimated nil residual value at the end of that period.

Required

Prepare the following accounts in the books of John Peacock Ltd for the year ended 31 October 19X8:

motor lorry at cost;
motor lorry provision for depreciation;
motor lorry insurance.

(13 marks)

(b)   The accounts for the year ended 30 November 19X7 of Springboard Ltd included a provision for doubtful debts at that date of £900.00.

During the year ended 30 November 19X8, the company received £500.00 from James Lyon towards the settlement of a debt of £700.00 which had been written off as irrecoverable by the company in 19X5. There is no evidence that James Lyon will be able to make any further payments to the company. Trade debtors at 30 November 19X8 amounted to £22,000.00 which includes the following debts it has now been decided to write off as bad:

Mary Leaf	£800
Angus Way	£300

In its accounts for the year ended 30 November 19X8, the company is to continue its policy of maintaining a provision for doubtful debts of 5% of debtors at the year-end.

Note: Bad debts written off or recovered are not to be recorded in the provision for doubtful debts account.

Required

(i)   Prepare the journal entry (or entries) in the books of the company necessitated by the receipt of £500.00 from James Lyon.

Notes

(1)   Journal entries should include narratives.

(2)   For the purposes of this question, assume cash receipts are journalised.

(6 marks)

(ii)   Prepare the provision for doubtful debts account in the books of the company for the year ended 30 November 19X8. (4 marks)

(iv)   The entry for debtors which will be included in the balance sheet as at 30 November 19X8 of the company.

(2 marks)
(Total 25 marks)

1.13   SHARP EDGE (D89)

Since 1 October 19X7, the Sharp Edge Engineering Co Ltd has been building up its own customers' delivery service and accordingly has purchased the following vehicles:

19X7	1 October	van	E676TVX	costing	£28,000.00
19X8	1 January	lorry	E438CBA	costing	£36,000.00
19X9	1 February	van	E779GMS	costing	£16,000.00
	1 July	van	F934KTA	costing	£24,000.00

Additional information

(1) Lorry E438CBA proved to be unsuitable for the company's trade and was therefore sold on 31 December 19X8 to John Kerry for £21,680.00

(2) Van E779GMS was bought second hand. Before joining the company's transport fleet on 1 April 19X9, this van was converted to meet the company's requirements. The conversion work was carried out in the company's own workshops, the following costs being incurred:

	£
Direct labour	1,880.00
Direct materials	3,200.00
Variable overheads	1,370.00

Fixed overheads apportionment added at 25% of prime cost.

(3) It is the company's policy to provide depreciation on motor vehicles at the rate of 20% per annum on cost.

(4) The company has a contract with the Fairdeal Insurance Co Ltd under which each vehicle in the transport fleet is insured at an annual premium of £5,000.00; the first premium for each vehicle is paid the day the vehicle is bought.

(5) The company's accounting year–end is 30 September.

Required

Prepare the following accounts where relevant for each of the years ended 30 September 19X8 and 19X9 in the books of the Sharp Edge Engineering Co Ltd:

Motor vehicles at cost;
Motor vehicles provision for depreciation;
Lorry E438CBA disposal;
Motor vehicles insurance.

(25 marks)

1.14 MARY SMITH (D90)

Mary Smith commenced trading on 1 September 19Y0 as a distributor of the Straight Cut garden lawn mower, a relatively new product which is now becoming increasingly popular.

Upon commencing trading, Mary Smith transferred £7,000 from her personal savings to open a business bank account.

Mary Smith's purchases and sales of the Straight Cut garden lawn mower during the three months ended 30 November 19Y0 are as follows:

19Y0	Bought	Sold
September	12 machines at £384 each	–
October	8 machines at £450 each	4 machines at £560 each
November	16 machines at £489 each	20 machines at £680 each

Assume all purchases are made in the first half of the month and all sales are in the second half of the month.

At the end of October 19Y0, Mary Smith decided to take one Straight Cut garden lawn mower out of stock for cutting the lawn outside her showroom. It is estimated that his lawn mower will be used in Mary Smith's business for eight years and have a nil estimated residual value. Mary Smith wishes to use the straight-line basis of depreciation.

Additional information

(1) Overhead expenses paid during the three months ended 30 November 19Y0 amounted to £1,520.

(2) There were no amounts prepaid on 30 November 19Y0, but sales commissions payable of 2½% of the gross profit on sales were accrued due on 30 November 19Y0.

(3) Upon commencing trading, Mary Smith resigned a business appointment with a salary of £15,000 per annum.

(4) Mary Smith is able to obtain interest of 10% per annum on her personal savings.

(5) One of the lawn mowers not sold on 30 November 19Y0 has been damaged in the showroom and is to be repaired in December 19Y0 at a cost of £50 before being sold for an expected £400.

(**Note**: Ignore taxation.)

Required

(a) Prepare, in as much detail as possible, Mary Smith's trading and profit and loss account for the quarter ended 30 November 19Y0 using:

(i)   the first-in, first-out basis of stock valuation; and
(ii)   the last-in, first-out basis of stock valuation.   (14 marks)

(b) Using the results in (a)(i) above, prepare a statement comparing Mary Smith's income for the quarter ended 30 November 19Y0 with that for the quarter ended 31 August 19Y0.   (5 marks)

(c) Give one advantage and one disadvantage of each of the bases of stock valuations used in (a) above.   (6 marks)
          (Total 25 marks)

1.15   QUICKMEAL PRODUCTS LTD (D90)

Quickmeal Products Ltd commenced business on 1 April 19X8 as manufacturers of high-class confectionery products.

Immediately on commencing business, the company took delivery of a specialised food mixing machine (number FM1) which cost £80,000 plus installation costs of £10,000. At the time of purchase, it was estimated that this machine would have an estimated net residual value of £5,000.

In response to a rapidly increasing demand for its products, Quickmeal Products Ltd acquired a second specialised food mixing machine (number FM2) on 1 October 19X9 at a cost of £120,000 plus installation costs of £24,000. At the same time, it is estimated that machine FM2 will have an estimated net residual value of £4,000.

During December 19X9, machine FM1 suffered a series of breakdowns which resulted in the machine being operational for only four hours each day.

On 1 January 19Y0, the manufacturers of machine FM1 agreed to accept it in part exchange for a new food mixing machine FM3 with a list price of £96,000. Quickmeal Products Ltd paid £60,000 in full settlement of the purchase of machine FM3. In addition machine installation costs totalled £16,000. The net residual value of machine FM3 is £6,000.

Upon acquisition, all food mixing machines have estimated lives within the business of ten years.

It is the policy of Quickmeal Products Ltd to use the straight-line method in providing for depreciation covering the actual period fixed assets are owned by the company.

During the year ended 31 March 19X9 Quickmeal Products Ltd sent two supervisory members of staff on training courses for the operation of the food mixing machines as follows.

For the operation of machine FM1 – John Smith – course in April 19X8 at a cost of £2,000.

For the operation of machine FM2 – Audrey Jones – introductory course in March 19X9 at a cost of £1,000 followed by a second and final course in August 19X9 at a cost of £3,000.

Required

(a)   The following accounts for each of the years ended 31 March 19X9 and 19Y0 in the books of Quickmeal Products Ltd:

   food mixing machines at cost;
   food mixing machines provision for depreciation.   (13 marks)

(b)   The disposal of food mixing machine FM1 account.   (6 marks)

(c)   Indicate how the training course costs for John Smith and Audrey Jones should be dealt with in the accounts of Quickmeal Products Ltd.   (6 marks)

Note: Answers should make reference to relevant accounting concepts.
(Total 25 marks)

2   ACCOUNTING CONCEPTS AND PRINCIPLES

2.1   NATURE OF A BALANCE SHEET

Critically analyse the statement that 'a balance sheet is a list of all assets owned by an enterprise and all liabilities owed by it. It therefore shows the net worth of the business at any particular date'.

(10 marks)

2.2   H GEE

An acquaintance of yours, H Gee, has recently set up in business for the first time as a general dealer.

The majority of his sales will be on credit to trade buyers but he will sell some goods to the public for cash.

He is not sure at which point of the business cycle he can regard his cash and credit sales to have taken place.

After seeking guidance on this matter from his friends, he is thoroughly confused by the conflicting advice he has received. Samples of the advice he has been given include:

The sale takes place when:

(1)   'you have bought goods which you know you should be able to sell easily';
(2)   'the customer places the order';
(3)   'you deliver the goods to the customer';
(4)   'you invoice the goods to the customer';
(5)   'the customer pays for the goods';
(6)   'the customer's cheque has been cleared by the bank'.

He now asks you to clarify the position for him.

Required

(a)   Write notes for Gee, setting out, in as easily understood a manner as possible, the accounting conventions and principles which should generally be followed when recognising sales revenue.

(b)   Examine each of the statements (a) to (f) above and advise Gee (stating your reasons) whether the method advocated is appropriate to the particular circumstances of his business.

(15 marks)

2.3   A, B AND C (D89)

The following accounting problems have arisen in separate companies all of which are clients of the same firm of practising accountants.

(1)   Company A, suppliers of building materials, are very confident of receiving an order for the sale of a large quantity of specialised building materials of £50,000 sales value early in January 19Y0. Virtually all the negotiations for the order were undertaken in the year ended 30 November 19X9 and all the materials involved have been obtained in that year and are currently held in stock by Company A.

The company considers that the stock concerned should be valued at 30 November 19X9, the company's year-end, at net realisable value, ie January 19Y0 sales value £50,000 less £300 for delivery charges; the cost of the goods was £32,000.

(2)   Although Company B has a very good trading and profit record, some of its competitors have gone out of business in recent years. The company's directors therefore consider it would be prudent not to base stock valuations at 30 November 19X9, the company's year-end, on the assumption that the company is a going concern.

(3) During the past year, Company C has introduced a programme of high quality fixed asset machine maintenance. In the words of the maintenance manager 'the machines are now kept as good as new'. The directors are now arguing for depreciation not to be provided in the accounts.

Required

Prepare concise replies to the submissions by each of the three companies.

(25 marks)

2.4 JOHN ABEL (J90)

John Abel, an accounting technician, has been asked by his employer to reply to a departmental manager with very limited accounting knowledge who has submitted the following queries.

(1) What is the difference between accounting reserves and accounting provisions? (Answers should be supported by one example of an accounting reserve and one of an accounting provision.)

(2) Why is it possible for a company which has made a greatly increased profit to be unable to pay dividends to its shareholders? (Two distinct possible reasons are required.)

(3) Why is it necessary to provide for depreciation in accounts when it does not guarantee the necessary resources for the replacement of fixed assets?

Required

Prepare a report, in the name of John Abel, addressed to the departmental manager, answering the queries outlined above. (25 marks)

2.5 HILLSIDE PRODUCTS LTD (D90)

The draft final accounts of Hillside Products Ltd for the year ended 31 August 19Y0 have been prepared by a keen, but relatively inexperienced, accounts clerk. In the course of examining these accounts, Thomas Harvey, an accounting technician, makes the following discoveries.

(1) A quantity of timber in stock at 31 August 19Y0 has been included in the stock valuation at £5,400, its expected selling price less £100 for future advertising expenses; the timber cost Hillside Products Ltd £4,600 when bought in June 19Y0.

(2) The fixtures and fittings, at cost, account has been debited on 1 February 19Y0 with £2,100 for new workshop shelving made and installed by the company's own work people.

The charge has been arrived at as follows:

	£	
Materials at cost	400	)
Workshop labour	800	) See Note 1
Overheads – Variable	300	) below
– Fixed	100	)
Profit margin	500	See Note 2 below
	2,100	

Notes

1 These items have also been credited to the relevant expense accounts.

2 The profit and loss account has been credited with the profit margin.

(3) Depreciation has been provided on the company's motor vehicles at 20% per annum on the reducing–balance method instead of 20% per annum on cost as previously used.

In supporting the change the company's transport manager has pointed out that the mileage covered by the company's fleet of vehicles is greatly reduced compared with earlier years.

(4) Value added tax on the sales of a new product has been credited to sales since the total charged to customers for this product during the year ended 31 August 19Y0 only amounted to £20,010.

(**Note:** The company is registered for VAT.)

The company's chief accountant has asked Thomas Harvey to report upon any adjustments which may now be necessary to the draft accounts under review.

Required

Prepare a report, in the name of Thomas Harvey, addressed to the chief accountant, concerning the accounting treatment of any **three** of the four discoveries made, giving your reasons in support of all recommendations made.

(**Note:** Reports should make reference to relevant accounting concepts and practices affecting each discovery.)   (25 marks)

3   CORRECTION OF ERRORS, JOURNAL ENTRIES AND SUSPENSE ACCOUNTS

3.1   BAKER AND JONES

Baker and Jones, partners in a manufacturing business, prepared the following rough balance sheet at 30 June 19X7, after their first 9 months' trading:

	Baker £	Jones £	£		£
Capital accounts:				Plant and machinery	4,200
Cash introduced	2,000	2,000		Motor vehicle	360
Profit for the period	1,500	1,500		Stock on hand	2,100
	———	———		Book debts	2,430
	3,500	3,500		Payments in advance	90
Less: Drawings for				Cash in hand	10
the period	1,500	2,500			
	———	———			
	2,000	1,000			

	Baker £	Jones £	£	£
			3,000	
Current liabilities:				
Trade and other creditors		1,308		
Amounts due under hire				
purchase agreement		2,262		
Bank overdraft		2,620		
			6,190	
			9,190	9,190

During the course of your examination of the books, the following facts were disclosed:

(1) Stock on hand (£2,100) included raw material costing £160 which was on approval only and had not been recorded in the books.

(2) Bad debts amounting to £120 were considered to be irrecoverable and others totalling £60 doubtful.

(3) Plant and machinery and the motor vehicle had been acquired on 1 October 19X6, and were included at cost. It was agreed that depreciation should be provided at 10% and 20% per annum on cost respectively.

(4) Goods costing £40 had been supplied to Jones from stock but not recorded in the books.

(5) No adjustment had been made in the accounts for the unexpired portion of an insurance premium of £60 paid for the year ended 30 September 19X7.

(6) £100, interest on the bank overdraft to 30 June 19X7, had not been taken into account.

(7) Interest amounting to £262 had been charged to the profit and loss account in respect of payments under the hire purchase agreement falling due after 30 June 19X7.

(8) Trade creditors included £200 for goods which had been returned to the suppliers before 30 June 19X7, and for which credit notes had not been received or recorded.

Required

(a) Prepare a summary of the adjustments to the profit and loss account for the period.

(b) Prepare a revised balance sheet at 30 June 19X7. (18 marks)

3.2 ABC LTD

After completing a draft profit and loss account for the year ended 30 April 19X3 of ABC Ltd the following balances remained and a suspense account entry was required for the difference which had arisen:

	£	£
Fixed assets, at cost	60,000	
Provision for depreciation		31,000
Ordinary share capital		35,000
Retained earnings		12,000
Stock in trade, at cost	14,000	
Sales ledger control account	9,600	
Purchases ledger control account		6,500
Balance at bank	1,640	
Difference on balances suspense account		740
	85,240	85,240

After investigation the following discoveries were made.

(a) A rent payment of £350 in March 19X3 has been debited in the sales ledger control account.

(b) Although instructed to do so, the accounts clerk had not set a debt due from B Bell of £1,560 in the sales ledger control account against an amount due to B Bell in the purchases ledger control account.

(c) Discounts allowed of £500 during the year ended 30 April 19X3 had not been recorded in the company's accounts.

(d) No entry had been made for the refund of £2,620 made by cheque to L Green in March, 19X3, in respect of defective goods returned to the company.

Note: The correct entries had been made previously for the return of the goods to ABC Ltd.

(e) The purchases day book for February 19X3 had been undercast by £300.

(f) A payment of £1,000 to K Bloom in January 19X3 for cash purchases had been debited in the purchases ledger control account.

Note. The company does not maintain a credit account with K Bloom.

(g) No entries had been made in the company's books for cash sales of £2,450 on 30 April 19X3 and banked on that date.

(h) No entries had been made in the company's books for bank charges of £910 debited in the company's bank account in December 19X2.

(i) The company's cash book (bank debit column) had been overcast by £1,900 in March 19X3.

(j) A cheque payment of £8,640 for new fixtures and fittings in April 19X3 had not been recorded in the company's books.

(k) A payment by cheque of £1,460 in June 19X2 for stationery had not been posted to the appropriate nominal account.

Required

(a) The journal entries for items (a), (f) and (i) above.

   Note: Narratives are required.

(b) The corrected list of balances at 30 April 19X3.

(c) Explain briefly the reasons for preparing bank reconciliation statements.

(30 marks)

3.3   JOHN BOLD (J86)

Allan Smith, an inexperienced accounts clerk, extracted the following trial balance, as at 31 March 19X6, from the books of John Bold, a small trader.

	£	£
Purchases	75,950	
Sales		94,650
Trade debtors	7,170	
Trade creditors		4,730
Salaries	9,310	
Light and heat	760	
Printing and stationery	376	
Stock at 1 April 19X5	5,100	
Stock at 31 March 19X6		9,500
Provision for doubtful debts	110	
Balance at bank	2,300	
Cash in hand	360	
Freehold premises:		
At cost	22,000	
Provision for depreciation	8,800	
Motor vehicles:		
At cost	16,000	
Provision for depreciation	12,000	
Capital at 1 April 19X5		23,096
Drawings		6,500
Suspense		21,760
	160,236	160,236

In the course of preparing the final accounts for the year ended 31 March 19X6, the following discoveries were made:

(1) No entries have been made in the books for the following entries in the bank statements of John Bold:

19X6	Payments	£
March 26	Bank charges	16
March 31	Cheque dishonoured	25

   Note: The cheque dishonoured had been received earlier in March from Peter Good, debtor.

(2) In arriving at the figure of £7,170 for trade debtors in the above trial balance, a trade creditor (Lionel White £70) was included as a debtor.

(3) No entries have been made in the books for a credit sale to Mary Black on 29 March 19X6 of goods of £160.

19

(4) No entries have been made in the books for goods costing £800 withdrawn from the business by John Bold for his own use.

(5) Cash sales of £700 in June 19X5 have been posted to the credit of trade debtors' accounts.

(6) Discounts received of £400 during the year under review have not been posted to the appropriate nominal ledger account.

(7) The remaining balance of the suspense account is due to cash sales for January and February 19X6 being posted from the cash book to the debit of the purchases account.

Required

(a) The journal entry necessary to correct for item 7 above.

Note: A narrative should be included. (8 marks)

(b) Prepare a corrected trial balance as at 31 March 19X6. (17 marks)
(Total 25 marks)

3.4 TIMBER PRODUCTS LTD (J87)

The trial balance as at 30 April 19X7 of Timber Products Ltd was balanced by the inclusion of the following debit balance:

Difference on trial balance suspense account £2,513.

Subsequent investigations revealed the following errors:

(1) Discounts received of £324 in January 19X7 have been posted to the debit of the discounts allowed account.

(2) Wages of £2,963 paid in February 19X7 have not been posted from the cash book.

(3) A remittance of £940 received from K Mitcham in November 19X6 has been posted to the credit of B Mansell Ltd.

(4) In December 19X6, the company took advantage of an opportunity to purchase a large quantity of stationery at a bargain price of £2,000. No adjustments have been made in the accounts for the fact that three quarters, in value, of this stationery was in stock on 30 April 19X7.

(5) A payment of £341 to J Winters in January 19X7 has been posted in the personal account as £143.

(6) A remittance of £3,000 received from D North, a credit customer, in April 19X7 has been credited to sales.

The draft accounts for the year ended 30 April 19X7 of Timber Products Ltd show a net profit of £24,760.

Timber Products Ltd has very few personal accounts and therefore does not maintain either a purchases ledger control account or a sales ledger control account.

Required

(a) Prepare the difference on trial balance suspense account showing, where appropriate, the entries necessary to correct the above accounting errors.

(8 marks)

(b) Prepare a computation of the corrected net profit for the year ended 30 April 19X7 following corrections for the above accounting errors.

(11 marks)

(c) Outline the principal uses of trial balances. (6 marks)

(Total 25 marks)

3.5 **LESLIE RIVERS LTD (D87)**

The draft balance sheet as at 31 August 1987 of Leslie Rivers Ltd is as follows:

Fixed assets	Cost	Aggregate depreciation		Capital and reserves	
	£	£	£		£
Freehold property	20,000	11,550	8,450	Ordinary shares	
Motor vehicles	19,000	11,400	7,600	of £1 each issued	
				and full paid	25,000
	39,000	22,950	16,050	Profit and loss	
				account	5,100
Current assets					
Stock		12,000			
Debtors		9,200			
Balance at bank		2,360			
		23,560			
Less Creditors:					
Amounts falling due within one year					
Trade creditors	3,800				
Accrued charges	710	4,510	19,050		
			35,100		
Less Charges:					
Amounts falling due after more than one year					
Bank loan			5,000		
			30,100		30,100

Notes

(1) The stock at 31 August 19X7 includes goods received in July 19X7 from Worldwide Products Ltd on a sale or return basis. These goods, which remained unsold at 31 August 19X7, had been recorded as purchased from the supplying company at the pro forma invoice price of £1,000.

(2) A debt of £300 due to the company from Cable Products Ltd is now regarded as irrecoverable. However, this debt has been included in the debtors in the above draft balance sheet.

(3)   The company's directors have decided that a provision for doubtful debts of 3% of debtors at 31 August 19X7 is to be created.

(4)   A payment in August 19X7 of £900 to K Bream, trade creditor, has been posted from the cash book to the printing and stationery expenses account.

(5)   Provision is to be made for a proposed dividend for the year ended 31 August 19X7 on the ordinary shares of 10p per ordinary share.

(6)   It can be assumed that a purchases ledger control account is not maintained.

Required

(a)   Prepare the corrected balance sheet as at 31 August 19X7 of Leslie Rivers Ltd.   (18 marks)

(b)   Prepare the journal entry (or entries) necessary for any corrections required for Note 1 above.

Narratives are required.   (7 marks)
(Total 25 marks)

3.6   THOMAS SMITH (J88)

(a)   Thomas Smith, a retail trader, has very limited accounting knowledge. In the absence of his accounting technician, he extracted the following trial balance as at 31 March 19X8 from his business' accounting records:

	£	£
Stock in trade at 1 April 19X7		10,700
Stock in trade at 31 March 19X8	7,800	
Discounts allowed		310
Discounts received	450	
Provision for doubtful debts	960	
Purchases	94,000	
Purchases returns	1,400	
Sales		132,100
Sales returns	1,100	
Freehold property: at cost	70,000	
provision for depreciation	3,500	
Motor vehicles: at cost	15,000	
provision for depreciation	4,500	
Capital – Thomas Smith		84,600
Balance at bank	7,100	
Trade debtors		11,300
Trade creditors	7,600	
Establishment and administrative expenditure	16,600	
Drawings	9,000	
	239,010	239,010

Required

Prepare a corrected trial balance as at 31 March 19X8.   (10 marks)

(b)   After the preparation of the above trial balance, but before the completion of the final accounts for the year ended 31 March 19X8, the following discoveries were made:

(1)   The correct valuation of the stock in trade at 1 April 19X7 is £12,000; apparently some stock lists had been mislaid.

(2)   A credit note for £210 has now been received from J Hardwell Ltd; this relates to goods returned in December 19X7 by Thomas Smith. However, up to now J Hardwell Ltd had not accepted that the goods were not of merchantable quality and Thomas Smith's accounting records did not record the return of the goods.

(3)   Trade sample goods were sent to John Grey in February 19X8. These were free samples, but were charged wrongly at £1,000 to John Grey. A credit note is now being prepared to rectify the error.

(4)   In March 19X8, Thomas Smith painted the inside walls of his stockroom using materials costing £150 which were included in the purchases figure in the above trial balance. Thomas Smith estimates that he saved £800 by doing all the painting himself.

Required

Prepare the journal entries necessary to amend the accounts for the above discoveries. (**Note:** Narratives are required.)   (15 marks)
    (Total 25 marks)

3.7   HIGHWAY PRODUCTS LTD (D88)

The following trial balance as at 31 October 19X8 has been extracted from the books of Highway Products Ltd.

	£	£
Freehold land and buildings		
At cost	120,000	
Provision for depreciation		25,000
Plant and machinery		
At cost	60,000	
Provision for depreciation		29,000
Motor vehicles		
At cost	43,000	
Provision for depreciation		34,400
Stock	27,000	
Trade debtors	13,000	
Balance at bank	6,000	
Trade creditors		19,000
Long-term loan: J Baker		20,000
Capital: Ordinary shares of £1.00 each fully paid		100,000
Retained earnings		52,600
Suspense account	11,000	
	280,000	280,000

The above trial balance was prepared after the preparation of the draft final accounts of the company for the year ended 31 October 19X8.

Subsequently, the following discoveries were made:

(1)   Bank charges of £410 accrued due at 31 October 19X8 have not been recorded in the company's books.

(2)   The following cheque payment has been recorded twice in the company's cash book and relevant ledger account:

10 October 19X8 Wages   £120

(3)   A receipt of £2,700 from J Prince in August 19X8 has been posted to the relevant personal account as £7,200.

(4)   Provision has not been made in the accounts for interest for the year ended 31 October 19X8 at the rate of 10% per annum on the loan from J Baker; this interest is paid annually, in arrear, on 1 November.

(5)   No entries have been made in the company's books for:

–   the supply of goods of sales value £5,100 to Central Garages Ltd on 30 September 19X8;

–   the purchase on 31 October 19X8 of a motor vehicle costing £5,000 from Central Garages Ltd.

These are the only transactions the company has had with Central Garages Ltd.

(6)   The balance of the suspense account arises from a payment in September 19X8 to John Gray, trade creditor, not being posted from the cash book to the personal account.

Note: Highway Products Ltd does not keep either a sales ledger total or control account or a purchases ledger total or control account.

Required

(a)   Prepare the journal entries necessary for item (5) above; narratives are required.   (5 marks)

(b)   Prepare the corrected balance sheet as at 31 October 19X8 of Highway Products Ltd.   (20 marks)
                                                                        (Total 25 marks)

3.8   JANE SIMPSON (J89)

Jane Simpson, a retail trader, has been trying to keep her own accounting records and has extracted the following list of balances as at 30 April 19X9 from her accounts prior to the preparation of the annual accounts and balance sheet by James Lang, an accounting technician:

	£
Fixtures and fittings	
At cost	8,000
Provision for depreciation at 1 May 19X8	3,000
Motor vehicles	
At cost	9,600
Provision for depreciation at 1 May 19X8	5,600
Stock in trade	12,000
Trade debtors	7,000
Balance at bank	1,700
Trade creditors	6,900
Sales	132,000

	£
Cost of sales	79,200
Establishment and administrative expenses	11,800
Sales and distribution expenses	33,500
Drawings	9,700
Capital	30,000

In preparing the annual accounts, James Lang made the following discoveries:

(1)   The trial balance as at 30 April 19X9 prepared from the above list of balances did not balance.

(2)   The stock in trade at 30 April 19X8 should have been valued at £16,000 not £13,000 as included in the accounts for the year ended 30 April 19X8.

(3)   Provision is to be made for a commission for sales staff of 2% of gross profit in the accounts for the year ended 30 April 19X9.

(4)   An entry in the cash book for the purchase of fixtures and fittings on 1 February 19X9 costing £4,500 has not been posted to the ledger.

(5)   Depreciation is to be provided for the year ended 30 April 19X9 as follows:

| Fixtures and fittings | 10% per annum on cost |
| Motor vehicles | 25% per annum on cost |

(6)   A credit sale of £4,700 in March 19X9 was included correctly in the posting to the sales account but recorded as £4,200 in the debtor's account.

(7)   Goods costing £600 withdrawn by Jane Simpson for her own use have not been recorded in the accounts.

Required

(a)   Prepare Jane Simpson's uncorrected trial balance as at 30 April 19X9.

(4 marks)

(b)   Prepare Jane Simpson's trading and profit and loss account for the year ended 30 April 19X9 and balance sheet as at that date.   (21 marks)

(Total 25 marks)

3.9   AUDREY PRINGLE (D89)

Audrey Pringle, the owner of a small trading business, has been experiencing some difficulty in completing her annual accounts for the years ended 31 October 19X8 and 19X9. However, the draft accounts for those years are now available and are summarised as follows:

Trading and profit and loss accounts for the years ended 31 October 19X8 and 19X9

	19X7/X8 £	19X8/X9 £
Sales	126,000	136,000
Less: Cost of sales	92,000	100,000
Gross profit	34,000	36,000
Less: Overhead expenses	13,000	24,000
Net profit	21,000	12,000

0042V

Balance sheets as at 31 October 19X8 and 19X9

		19X8 £	19X9 £
Fixed assets:	At cost	84,000	36,000
	Provision for depreciation	62,000	68,000
		22,000	28,000
Current assets			
	Stock	14,000	12,000
	Debtors	9,000	10,000
	Balance at bank	8,000	1,000
		31,000	23,000
Less:	Current liabilities		
	Creditors	6,000	3,000
		25,000	20,000
Net assets		47,000	48,000
Represented by:			
Capital account			
Balance brought forward		40,000	47,000
Net profit		21,000	12,000
		61,000	59,000
Less: Drawings		14,000	11,000
		47,000	48,000

Since the above accounts were prepared, it has been revealed that:

(1) The stock at 31 October 19X8 has been valued at net realisable value in the accounts; the cost of the stock at that date was £12,600.

(2) No adjustment has been made in these accounts for goods withdrawn from Audrey Pringle's own use as follows:

Year ended 31 October 19X8 £2,000 at cost;
Year ended 31 October 19X9 £4,000 at cost.

(3) There are no entries in the accounts for fixtures and fittings scrapped during the year ended 31 October 19X9; the cost of the items scrapped was £10,000 and the related provision for depreciation at the date of scrapping was £7,000. It was not possible to sell the scrapped items.

(4) In preparing these accounts, account has not been taken of a loss of stock owing to fire damage during the year ended 31 October 19X9; the cost of the stock concerned was £5,000. The stock loss was not covered by insurance.

Required

(a) Prepare corrected summarised trading and profit and loss accounts for each of the years ended 31 October 19X8 and 19X9 and corrected summarised balance sheets as at 31 October 19X8 and 19X9. (14 marks)

(b) Prepare the journal entry/entries required for the scrapping of the fixtures and fittings during the year ended 31 October 19X9.

Note: Each journal entry should include a narrative. (5 marks)

(c) Using three distinct financial ratios indicate aspects of Audrey Pringle's business which have improved or deteriorated during the year ended 31 October 19X9 as compared with the previous year.

Note: In answering part (c), use the corrected accounts prepared for (a) above. (6 marks)
(Total 25 marks)

3.10 ALLSQUARE ENGINEERS LTD (J90)

The trial balance as at 31 March 19X0 of Allsquare Engineers Ltd did not balance and therefore a suspense account was opened showing a credit balance of £549. Unfortunately, the errors in the accounts were only traced after the completion of the draft final accounts for the year ended 31 March 19X0 which showed the following results:

	£
* Profit on manufacturing	12,760
Gross profit	23,410
Net profit	9,746

* Manufactured goods are transferred to the trading account at wholesale prices.

The following errors were discovered.

(1) 2 January 19X0 Credit sales to T Sparkes of £1,200 not recorded in the sales day book.

(2) 15 January 19X0 A receipt of £500 from K Dodds, debtor, was recorded in the cash book only.

(3) February 19X0 Discounts received of £376 have been recorded correctly in the purchases ledger control account and then debited in the discounts allowed account.

Discounts allowed of £224 have been recorded correctly in the sales ledger control account and then credited in the discounts received account.

(4) 31 March 19X0 Payments to suppliers totalling £21,257 have been debited in the purchases ledger control account as £21,752.

(5) Depreciation for the year ended 31 March 19X0 on manufacturing equipment was correctly recorded in the provision for depreciation account but not posted to the manufacturing account. The correction of this error cleared the suspense account.

Required

(a) The suspense account as it would appear after the correction of all the accounting errors. (8 marks)

(b) A statement showing the effects, if any, of the correction of the errors upon each of the following results in the draft accounts for the year ended 31 March 19X0:

(i) profit on manufacturing;
(ii) gross profit;
(iii) net profit.

(17 marks)
(Total 25 marks)

4 CONTROL ACCOUNTS AND BANK RECONCILIATIONS

4.1 CHARLES POOTER

Charles Pooter runs two hardware shops, one in the City of London and one in Holloway. He makes substantial credit purchases and sales, and at 31 December 19X5 there were the following balances in the books of his business:

	Dr £	Cr £
Cash book	427	
Creditors' ledger control account	42	13,876
City debtors' ledger control account	9,240	
Holloway debtors' ledger control account	11,785	235

Charles had tried to prepare reconciliations at 31 December 19X5 between the cash book and the bank statement, and between the control accounts and the respective lists of individual balances, but none of them agreed. The control accounts are taken as part of the double entry.

He asks for your assistance, and on investigation you discover the following:

(1) The bank had incorrectly charged Charles's account with a payment of £400 to the Thames Water Authority, which had been made by another customer with a similar name. Without realising that this was an error, he had entered the amount as a payment in his cash book and posted it to Thames Water's account in the creditors' ledger; he had not entered it in the creditors' ledger control account.

(2) Receipts from City debtors amounting to £1,827 had been incorrectly analysed in the cash book as receipts from Holloway debtors.

(3) Unpresented cheques amounting to £5,884 at 31 December 19X5 included:

(i) cheques for suppliers totalling £2,100 which had been entered in the cash book in December but not signed or sent out until January 19X6 (these had also been posted to the creditors' ledger and its control account);

(ii) a cheque for £235 in respect of a refund to Huttle Ltd, a Holloway debtor, which had been posted to Huttle Ltd's account in the creditors' ledger.

(4) Lodgements of £12,840 were paid into the bank on 30 December 19X5. They did not appear on the bank statement at 31 December 19X5, nor had they been entered in the cash book at that date.

The amount of £12,840 included £2,800 received from City debtors and £1,020 received from Holloway debtors, the balance being cash sales.

(5) Cash book receipts had been overcast by £4,000. The cross-cast of the analysis columns agreed because an overcast of £4,000 had also been made in the column showing receipts from City debtors.

(6) A debit balance of £42 in the creditors' ledger had been transferred to the same supplier's account in the City debtors' ledger. This entry had been made correctly in the debtors' ledger control account, but no corresponding entry had been made in the creditors' ledger control account.

Required

(a) Draft the journal entries required to correct the above matters (narrative is not required).

(b) Prepare a bank reconciliation statement at 31 December 19X5, showing the necessary adjustments to the cash book.

(c) State the correct figures which should appear in Charles's balance sheet for debtors and creditors at 31 December 19X5, showing the necessary adjustments to the control accounts. (Total 17 marks)

4.2 **ARGO LTD**

The following transactions relate to a sales ledger of Argo Ltd for the year ended 31 December 19X4:

	£
Balance on sales ledger control 1 January 19X4	8,952
Sales as per posting summaries	74,753
Receipts from debtors	69,471
Discounts allowed	1,817

The clerk in charge had prepared from the ledger cards a list of balances outstanding on 31 December 19X4 amounting to £9,663 but this did not agree with the balance of the sales ledger control account. There were no credit balances on the ledger cards.

Investigation of the differences revealed:

(1) The bank statement showed credit transfers of £198 which had been completely overlooked.

(2) Journal entries correctly posted to the ledger cards had been overlooked when posting control account: debts settled by set-off against creditors' accounts £2,896, bad debts £640.

(3) When listing the debtor balances three ledger cards with debit balances of £191 had been incorrectly filed and consequently had not been included in the list of balances.

(4) The machine operator when posting a ledger card had incorrectly picked up an old balance of £213.50 as £13.50 and had failed to check her total balances.

(5) £1,173 entered in the cash book as a receipt from J Spruce had not been posted as no account under that name could be traced. Later it was discovered it was in payment for a car which had been used by the sales department and sold to him second-hand.

Required

(a) Prepare the sales ledger control account for the year ended 31 December 19X4 taking into account the above adjustments.

(b) Reconcile the clerk's balance of £9,663 with the corrected balance on the sales ledger account.

(c) Explain the benefits that accrue from operating control accounts.

(25 marks)

4.3 MAINWAY DEALERS LTD (J86)

Mainway Dealers Ltd maintains a debtors (sales) ledger and a creditors (purchases) ledger.

The monthly accounts of the company for May 19X6 are now being prepared and the following information is now available:

		£
Debtors' ledger as at 1 May 19X6:	Debit balances	16,720
	Credit balances	1,146
Creditors' ledger as at 1 May 19X6:	Debit balances	280
	Credit balances	7,470
Credit sales May 19X6		19,380
Credit purchases May 19X6		6,700
Cash and cheques received May 19X6:	Debtors' ledger	15,497
	Creditors' ledger	130
Cheques paid May 19X6:	Debtors' ledger	470
	Creditors' ledger	6,320
Credit notes issued May 19X6 for goods returned by customers		1,198
Credit notes received from suppliers May 19X6 for goods returned by Mainway Dealers Ltd		240

*Cheques received and subsequently dishonoured May 19X6:

	Debtors' ledger	320
Discounts allowed May 19X6		430
Discounts received May 19X6		338
Bad debts written off May 19X6		131
*Bad debt written off in December 19X5 but recovered in May 19X6 (R Bell)		142

* Included in cash and cheques received May 19X6 £15,497.

Debtors' ledger as at 31 May 19X6:	Debit balances	(to be determined)
	Credit balances	670
Creditors' ledger as at 31 May 19X6:	Debit balances	365
	Credit balances	(to be determined)

It has been decided to set off a debt due from a customer, L Green, of £300 against a debt due to L Green of £1,200 in the creditors' ledger.

The company has decided to create a provision for doubtful debts of 2.5% of the amount due to Mainway Dealers Ltd on 31 May 19X6 according to the debtors' ledger control account.

Required

(a)   Prepare the debtors' ledger control account and the creditors' ledger control account for May 19X6 in the books of Mainway Dealers Ltd.   (20 marks)

(b)   An extract of the balance sheet as at 31 May 19X6 of Mainway Dealers Ltd relating to the company's trade debtors and trade creditors.

(5 marks)
(Total 25 marks)

4.4   **JOHN HENRY LTD (1) (D86)**

The bank reconciliation statement as at 19 September 19X6 for the account number 0439567 of John Henry Ltd with Industrious Bank plc showed that the difference between the cash book and bank statement was due entirely to four unpresented cheques, numbers 765417 to 765420 inclusive.

The cash book, bank columns, for the period from 19 September to 30 September 19X6, of John Henry Ltd is as follows:

B/F   671·30

19X6		£	19X6		Cheque	£
23 Sept	B Main	692.30	19 Sept	Balance b/f		21.00
23 Sept	T Patrick	27.24	22 Sept	S Salter Ltd	765421	25.67
25 Sept	S Saunders	410.00	22 Sept	Sway District Council	765422	275.10
26 Sept	P King	400.00	23 Sept	North South	Direct	
26 Sept	K Plunket	39.60		Electricity Authority	debit	316.50
28 Sept	J Lim	324.92	23 Sept	John Peters Limited	765423	18.34
30 Sept	S Balk	220.39	24 Sept	Furniture Trade	Standing	
				Association	order	45.00
			24 Sept	K Patel	765424	19.04
			25 Sept	Cash (petty cash)	765425	50.00
			26 Sept	J Green Limited	765426	45.00
			26 Sept	G Glinker	765427	174.00
			29 Sept	Deposit account		600.00
			29 Sept	Wages	Transfer	390.00
			30 Sept	Balance c/f		134.80
		2,114.45				2,114.45

1 Oct   Bal b/fwd   134.80

Early in October 19X6, John Henry Ltd received the following statement from Industrious Bank plc.

Statement of account with Industrious Bank plc
East Road, Streamly

Account number 0439567:

Date 19X6	Particulars	Payments £	Receipts £	Balance £
19 Sept	Balance			453.26
22 Sept	765419	138.35		314.91
23 Sept	Sundry credits		719.54	1,034.45
23 Sept	Direct debit	316.50		717.95
24 Sept	765421	25.67		692.28
24 Sept	Standing order	45.00		647.28
25 Sept	765420	160.04		487.24
26 Sept	765422	275.10		212.14
26 Sept	Sundry credits		400.00	612.14
26 Sept	Bank Giro credit		410.00	1,022.14
29 Sept	Bank Giro credit		334.92	1,357.06
29 Sept	765418	21.69		1,355.37
29 Sept	765424	19.04		1,316.33
29 Sept	Transfer to deposit account	600.00		716.33
29 Sept	Transfer	390.00		326.33
29 Sept	765425	50.00		276.33
29 Sept	As advised		65.00	341.33
29 Sept	Bank Giro credit		39.60	380.93
30 Sept	Loan account interest	41.25		339.68
30 Sept	Bank charges	16.70		322.98

The following additional information is given.

(1) The amount received from J Lim on 28 September 19X6 was £334.92 not £324.92.

(2) The amount credited in the bank statement on 29 September 19X6 and shown as 'As advised £65.00' concerned dividends received.

(3) John Henry Ltd has written to the bank complaining concerning the bank charges of £16.70; the company's view is that no charges should arise for the month of September. The bank has a reputation for not cancelling bank charges.

Required

(a) Prepare a bank reconciliation statement as at 30 September 19X6.

Note: Indicate the amount which should be included in the balance sheet as at 30 September 19X6 of John Henry Ltd for the company's account number 0439567 with Industrious Bank plc. (20 marks)

(b) What are the major uses of a bank reconciliation statement? (5 marks)
(Total 25 marks)

4.5 JAMES SWIFT LTD (D87)

A sales ledger control account and a purchases ledger control account were maintained as integral parts of the accounting records of James Swift Ltd.

The following information is relevant to the business of James Swift Ltd for the year ended 30 November 19X7.

(1) Balances at 1 December 19X6:   £

Sales ledger   10,687 debit
                                                                   452 credit
Purchases ledger   1,630 debit
                                                                 9,536 credit

(2) Sales totalled £130,382 whilst sales returns amounted to £1,810.

(3) £127,900 was received from debtors in settlement of accounts totalling £130,650. In addition, £1,200 was received for a debt which had been written off as irrecoverable in the year ended 30 November 19X6.

(4) A debt of £350 due from J Hancock was transferred to the purchases ledger and set off against a debt of £1,100 due to J Hancock.

(5) An amount of £560 due to James Swift Ltd for goods supplied to T Dick was written off as bad in November 19X7.

(6) Purchases amounted to £99,000 at list prices and purchases returns totalled £600 at list prices. All purchases and purchases returns were subject to a trade discount of 10%.

(7) £83,500 was paid to suppliers in settlement of debts due of £85,000.

(8) Balances at 30 November 19X7 included:

                                                                     £
Sales ledger   1,008 credit
Purchases ledger   760 debit

Required ·

Prepare the following accounts for the year ended 30 November 19X7 in the books of James Swift Ltd:

(a) Sales ledger control   (14 marks)
(b) Purchases ledger control   (11 marks)
                                                          (Total 25 marks)

4.6 CENTRAL MANUFACTURERS (J88)

(a) On 1 May 19X7, the account of John Banks, furniture retailer, showed a debit balance of £3,100 in the books of Central Manufacturers Ltd.

During the year ended 30 April 19X8, the following transactions took place between the company and John Banks:

(1) John Banks bought goods whose list prices totalled £86,360 and which were subject to a trade discount of 10%.

(2) Goods, which had been invoiced at £160 to John Banks were returned to the company as unsuitable; an appropriate credit note was issued.

(3) Remittances totalling £75,000 were received by Central Manufacturers Ltd in settlement of debts amounting to £76,100.

(4) On 30 April 19X8, Central Manufacturers Ltd sold John Banks a second hand photocopier at the written down book value of the machine in the company's books at that date. The photocopier had been bought by the company for £5,000 on 1 November 19X6; depreciation was provided in the company's books at the rate of 25% per annum on the straight–line basis. On the day of the sale, the company received from John Banks a cheque for £3,000 in part settlement of the transaction.

(5) Central Manufacturers Ltd bought furniture from John Banks costing £1,200.

Required

Prepare the ledger accounts of John Banks for the year ended 30 April 19X8 in the books of Central Manufacturers Ltd.

(**Note:** The company does not maintain total or control accounts for debtors or creditors.) (13 marks)

(b) The balance sheet as at 31 May 19X7 of Forest Traders Ltd included a provision for doubtful debts of £2,300.

The company's accounts for the year ended 31 May 19X8 are now being prepared.

The company's policy now is to relate the provision for doubtful debts to the age of debts outstanding. The debts outstanding at 31 May 19X8 and the required provisions for doubtful debts are as follows:

Debts outstanding	Amount £	Provision for doubtful debts %
Up to 1 month	24,000	1
More than 1 month and up to 2 months	10,000	2
More than 2 months and up to 3 months	8,000	4
More than 3 months	3,000	5

Customers are allowed a cash discount of 2½% for settlement of debts within one month. It is now proposed to make a provision for discounts to be allowed in the company's accounts for the year ended 31 May 19X8.

Required

Prepare the following accounts for the year ended 31 May 19X8 in the books of Forest Traders Ltd to record the above transactions:

(i) provision for doubtful debts;
(ii) provision for discounts to be allowed on debtors. (12 marks)
(Total 25 marks)

4.7 JANE BANKS (D88)

Jane Banks, who is in business as a car dealer, prepares a bank reconciliation statement weekly. The bank reconciliation statement as at 5 November 19X8, in addition to bank charges of £25.60 not then recorded in the cash book, included only the following unpresented cheques:

Cheque number	£
162358	95.10
162361	147.64 ✓
162362	16.00 ✓
162364	38.90

The cash book, bank columns only, of Jane Banks for the week ended 12 November 19X8 is as follows:

19X8		£	19X8		Cheque no	£
7 Nov	Balance b/f	2,823.28	7 Nov	K Supplies	162365	16.41 ✓
8 Nov	Sun Blinds Ltd	110.00 ✓	7 Nov	J Bay	162366	273.69 ✓
8 Nov	John Bell	210.80	8 Nov	L Simms	162367	116.20 ✓
9 Nov	Thomas Jones Ltd	169.00	8 Nov	M Dint	162368	1,399.38 ✓
9 Nov	Jean Hill	1,921.00	8 Nov	D Feint	162369	200.00 ✓
10 Nov	Andrew Wall –		9 Nov	W Young	162370	70.00
	Cheque	710.00	9 Nov	S M Hotels	162371	47.00 ✓
	Discount	6.00	10 Nov	Bank charges		25.60 ✓
11 Nov	Direct Dealers Ltd	29.00	10 Nov	H Meng	162372	139.10 ✓
12 Nov	Balance c/f	312.20	10 Nov	F Grundy	162373	17.20 ✓
			11 Nov	P Waters	162374	101.00
			11 Nov	V Neall	162375	385.70
			12 Nov	H Dent	162376	3,500.00
		6,291.28				6,291.28
			14 Nov	Balance b/f		312.20

The following bank statement has been received by Jane Banks:

Central Bank plc, Northtown Branch
Jane Banks, Account number 547892

Statement of account

19X8		Payments £	Receipts £	Balance £
8 November	Opening balance			3,095.32
8 November	162366	273.69 ✓		2,821.63
8 November	162362	× 16.00 ✓		2,805.63
8 November	Bank giro credit		110.00 ✓	2,915.63
9 November	162368	1,399.38 ✓		1,516.25
9 November	162361	× 147.64 ✓		1,368.61
9 November	162365	16.41 ✓		1,352.20
10 November	Bank giro credit		379.80 ✓	1,732.00
10 November	162369	200.00 ✓		1,532.00
10 November	162367	116.20 ✓		1,415.80
11 November	162373	17.20 ✓		1,398.60
11 November	Car Dealers' Association –			
	Standing order	25.00 ✓		1,373.60
11 November	162372	139.10 ✓		1,234.50
11 November	Bank giro credit		2,631.00 ✓	3,865.50

The cheque prepared in favour of S M Hotels on 9 November was not despatched and has now been cancelled; a proposed visit of Jane Banks to the Central Hotel owned by S M Hotels is not now to take place.

Required

(a)   Prepare a bank reconciliation statement as at 12 November 19X8.

(19 marks)

(b)   Explain why it is necessary to prepare bank reconciliation statements.

(6 marks)
(Total 25 marks)

4.8   HIGHGROUND DEALERS LTD (J89)

The trial balance as at 31 December 19X8 of Highground Dealers Limited included the following items:

	Debit £	Credit £
Purchases ledger control account	245	152,498

The following relevant information has been provided by the company for the first three months of 19X9:

19X9	Purchases at list prices £	Purchases returns at list prices £	Cash paid £	Discounts received £	Purchases ledger debit balances at month–end £
January	142,000	4,200	157,760	2,510	180
February	98,000	5,700	126,150	1,870	276
March	112,000	6,500	85,700	1,430	355

The company's stock in trade increased from £30,000 at 31 December 19X8 to £38,000 at 31 March 19X9.

Highgrou d Dealers Ltd normally obtains a gross profit of 40% on the cost of all goods sold; however in February 19X9 the company sold at half the normal sales price, a quantity of goods which it had bought for £10,000.

The company obtains its purchases at list prices less 10%.

On 28 February 19X9 the following account in the sales ledger was closed by the transfer of the balance to K Marden's account in the purchases ledger:

K Marden   £3,000 debit

Required

(a)   Prepare the purchases ledger control account of Highground Dealers Ltd for each of the three months to 31 March 19X9.   (19 marks)

(b)   Prepare a computation of the gross profit for the three months ended 31 March 19X9 of Highground Dealers Ltd.   (6 marks)

(Total 25 marks)

4.9   MARY SAUNDERS (D89)

The following balances as at 1 November were extracted from the books of Mary Saunders Ltd:

	Debit £	Credit £
Purchases ledger control account	1,436	16,892
Sales ledger control account	35,975	874
Provision for doubtful debts		1,100
Provision for discounts allowable		640

The following transactions took place during the year ended 31 October 19X9.

	£
Credit sales	417,920
Cash sales	91,210
Credit purchases	289,439
Cash purchases	12,960
Amounts received from credit customers	392,710
Paid to credit suppliers	264,360
Returns outwards to credit suppliers	9,400
Returns inwards from credit customers	11,556
Bad debts written off	1,927
Bad debt recovered (relevant bad debt written off in 19X7)	518

Additional information

(1)   The provision for doubtful debts at 31 October 19X9 is to be 5% of amounts due to the company according to the sales ledger control account.

(2)   The provision for discounts allowable at 31 October 19X9 is to be 2½% of the relevant amount derived from the sales ledger.

(3)   A despatch of goods in October 19X9 to a credit customer has been charged out at the list price of £2,000 without adjusting for the trade discount due of 10%.

(4)   It is the company's policy to record bad debts recovered in the sales ledger control account.

(5)   The trial balance as at 31 October 19X9 of Mary Saunders Ltd included the following:

	Debit £	Credit £
Purchases ledger control account	937	
Debtors' ledger control account		572

Required

(a)   Prepare the following accounts for the year ended 31 October 19X9 in the books of Mary Saunders Ltd:

(i)   purchases ledger control;
(ii)   sales ledger control.   (19 marks)

(b) A computation of the amounts to be included in the balance sheet as at 31 October 19X9 of Mary Saunders Ltd for the following items:

(i) trade debtors;
(ii) trade creditors. (6 marks)

(Total 25 marks)

4.10 THOMAS P LEE (D89)

In the draft accounts for the year ended 31 October 19X9, of Thomas P Lee, garage proprietor, the balance at bank according to the cashbook was £894.68 in hand.

Subsequently the following discoveries were made:

(1) Cheque number 176276 dated 3 September 19X9 for £310.84 in favour of G Lowe Ltd has been correctly recorded in the bank statement, but included in the cashbook payments as £301.84.

(2) Bank commission charged of £169.56 and bank interest charged of £109.10 have been entered in the bank statement of 23 October 19X9, but not included in the cashbook.

(3) The recently received bank statement shows that a cheque for £29.31 received from T Andrews and credited in the bank statements on 9 October 19X9 has now been dishonoured and debited in the the bank statement on 26 October 19X9. The only entry in the cashbook for this cheque records its receipt on 8 October 19X9.

(4) Cheque number 177145 for £15.10 has been recorded twice as a credit in the cashbook.

(5) Amounts received in the last few days of October 19X9 totalling £1,895.60 and recorded in the cashbook have not been included in the bank statements until 2 November 19X9.

(6) Cheques paid according to the cashbook during October 19X9 and totalling £395.80 were not presented for payment to the bank until November 19X9.

(7) Traders' credits totalling £210.10 have been credited in the bank statement on 26 October 19X9, but not yet recorded in the cashbook.

(8) A standing order payment of £15.00 on 17 October 19X9 to Countryside Publications has been recorded in the bank statement, but is not mentioned in the cashbook.

Required

(a) Prepare a computation of the balance at bank to be included in Thomas P Lee's balance sheet as at 31 October 19X9. (11 marks)

(b) Prepare a bank reconciliation statement as at 31 October 19X9 for Thomas P Lee. (8 marks)

(c) Briefly explain why it is necessary to prepare bank reconciliation statements at accounting year-ends. (6 marks)

(Total 25 marks)

4.11   JOAN SEAWARD (J90)

The following information relates to the trading affairs of Joan Seaward, retailer:

		£
As at 1 January 19X0	Stock in trade, at cost	121,000
	Trade creditors	84,000
	Trade debtors	93,000
Three months ended	Returns inwards	9,800
31 March 19X0	Returns outwards	16,500
	Gross profit	124,240
	Bad debts written off	5,000
	Discounts allowed	2,300
	Discounts received	4,100
	Paid to suppliers	410,000
	Received from cash and credit customers	575,306
As at 31 March 19X0	It is estimated that:	

(a) bad debts of £3,800 may arise from the outstanding trade debtors;

(b) £60,000 of the amount due from trade debtors will be settled by 30 April 19X0 and therefore qualify for a cash discount of 2½%.

Additional information relating to the three months ended 31 March 19X0

(1)   The average of the opening and closing stocks in trade has been used to determine the rate of stock turnover for the period at 5.

(2)   With the exception of a quantity of stock costing £100,000 in January 19X0 which was sold at half the normal selling price, a gross profit of 40% has been obtained on the cost of all goods sold.

(3)   Forty percent of the net turnover arose from cash sales.

(4)   There were no sales returns arising from cash sales.

(5)   As expected, all amounts due from trade debtors at 1 January 19X0 have been received.

(6)   Joan Seaward did not allow cash discounts prior to 1 January 19X0.

Required

(a)   Prepare the following accounts for the three months ended 31 March 19X0 in as much detail as possible in the books of Joan Seaward:

(i)   trading;
(ii)   purchases ledger control;
(iii)   sales ledger control.

Note: The trading account should show the closing stock.   (22 marks)

(b)   Prepare a computation of the amount to be included for trade debtors in the balance sheet as at 31 March 19X0 of Joan Seaward.   (3 marks)
(Total 25 marks)

5   THE ACCOUNTS OF CLUBS AND SOCIETIES

5.1   SCOTT SOCIAL CLUB

The following is a summary of the receipts and payments for the year to 31 March 19X3 of the Scott Social Club:

	£
Receipts	
Club subscriptions	17,000
Donations	1,500
Christmas dance	850
Bar takings	27,000
Payments	
Rates	900
General expenses	26,200
Bar purchases	18,500
Christmas dance expenses	150

Other relevant information at the beginning and end of the year is as follows:

	1.4.X2 £	31.3.X3 £
Subscriptions due	900	600
Subscriptions paid in advance	50	100
Rates owing	450	500
Bar stock	2,000	2,500
Club premises (cost £50,000)	20,000	18,000
Furniture (cost £10,000)	3,000	2,000
Bank and cash in hand	1,600	2,200

Required

(a)   Prepare the club's bar trading account for the year to 31 March 19X3.

(b)   Prepare the club's income and expenditure account for the year to 31 March 19X3, and a balance sheet as at that date.   (15 marks)

5.2   BUNBURY COUNTRY CLUB

You have been asked to assist in preparing accounts for the Bunbury Country Club at 30 June 19X6. The treasurer has been chronically sick for most of the year, and no detailed records of receipts and payments are available. On investigation, however, you discover the following:

(1) **Balance sheet at 30 June 19X5**

Fixed assets	£ Cost	£ Dep'n	£
Fixtures and fittings	10,340	2,840	7,500
Investments at cost			6,000
			13,500
Current assets			
Bar stocks		2,180	
Subscriptions in arrears		2,000	
Bank – Deposit a/c		5,000	
– Current a/c		7,345	
		16,525	
Current liabilities			
Creditors for bar purchases		3,180	
Subscriptions in advance		300	
		3,480	
			13,045
Total net assets			26,545
Balance on accumulated fund at 30 June 19X5			26,545

(2) Bar stocks had not been counted at 30 June 19X6, but it is known that:

(i) bar takings accounting to £29,348 had been banked during the year ended 30 June 19X6;

(ii) there was £2,800 in the bar till on that date;

(iii) £27,330 had been paid to bar suppliers during the year;

(iv) those suppliers were owed £4,634 at 30 June 19X6;

(v) the mark–up on cost is consistently 30%.

(3) The club has 500 members, each paying a subscription of £50 per annum. By 30 June 19X6, 4 members had paid in advance for the year to 30 June 19X7. £24,100 had been received in subscriptions during the year ended 30 June 19X6.

(4) Certain investments had been sold during the year for £1,800, producing a profit on sale of £850.

(5) Fixtures and fittings are to be depreciated at the rate of 20% per annum on the reducing instalment method, calculated on a month–by–month basis.

On 1 July 19X5 fixtures originally bought for £1,000 on 1 January 19X4 were sold for £800, and on 31 March 19X6 additional fixtures were bought for £500.

(6)   There were no changes to the bank deposit account during the year apart from interest credited on 30 September, 31 December, 31 March and 30 June at the rate of 10% per annum compounded on those dates.

(7)   The bank current account showed a balance (in hand) of £9,388 on 30 June 19X6.

Required

Prepare a balance sheet for the club at 30 June 19X6, and calculate the surplus of income and expenditure for the year ended on that date.

(18 marks)

5.3   CAWDOR SOCIAL CLUB

The following is a receipts and payments account prepared from the bank statements by the treasurer of the Cawdor Social Club for the year ended 31 December 19X8.

19X8	Receipts	£	19X8	Payments	£
1 Jan	Cash in hand	24	31 Dec	Bar purchases	3,584
	Balances at bank as per bank statements:			Purchase of billiards equipment	60
	Deposit account	210		Rates, water and insurance	92
	Current account	86		Wages	340
31 Dec	Bar takings	4,521		Repairs	64
	Subscriptions	62		Printing, stationery etc	86
	Billiards takings	58		Balances at bank as per bank statements:	
	Bank interest on Deposit account	6		Deposit account	160
				Current account	581
		4,967			4,967

You are given the following information.

	On 1.1.X8 £	On 31.12.X8 £
Subscriptions due but not paid	8	6
Rates and insurance paid in advance	22	25
Amounts owing for printing, stationery, etc	12	14
Cost of billiards equipment	240	300
Value of bar stock	210	226
Unpresented cheques being payment for bar purchases	60	80
Amounts due to brewery	230	390

(being invoices for which cheques had not yet been written)

You are also informed that:

(1)   a barrel of beer costing £12 had been given to the local flower show during the year;

(2)   the billiards equipment and additions thereto are to be depreciated by £30 on 31 December 19X8;

(3)   an amount of £75, being the bar takings on New Year's Eve, was in the hands of the steward on 31 December 19X8 and was not paid into the bank until 2 January 19X9;

(4)   the steward is to be paid a commission of 10% on the gross profit made by the bar, before charging wages and excluding billiards takings.

Required

(a)   Prepare a computation showing the balance of the club's accumulated fund at 1 January 19X8.

(b)   Prepare an income and expenditure account for the year ended 31 December 19X8.

(c)   Prepare a balance sheet at that date.   (20 marks)

5.4   WOODLANDS HOCKEY CLUB

The secretary of the Woodlands Hockey Club gives you the following summary of his cash book for the year ended 31 May 19X7:

	£		£
Balance at commencement		Rent	234
of year:		Printing and stationery	18
At bank	63	Affiliation fees	12
In hand	10	Captain's and secretary's	
Subscriptions:		expenses	37
Supporters	150	Refreshments for visiting teams	61
Supporters 19X7/X8 season	20	Annual social	102
Game fees	170	Equipment purchased	26
Annual social	134	Balances at close of year:	
		At bank	49
		In hand	8
	—		—
Carried forward	547		547
	—		—

The secretary also gives you the following information.

	31.5.X6	31.5.X7
	£	£
Amounts due to the club:		
Supporters' subscriptions	14	12
Game fees	78	53
Re annual social	6	–
Amounts owing by the club:		
Rent	72	54
Printing	–	3
Secretary's expenses	4	8
Refreshments	13	12

On 31 May 19X6 the club's equipment appeared in the books at £150. It is desired that 12.5% be written off the book value of the equipment as it appears on 31 May 19X7.

Required

(a)   Show your computation of the club's accumulated fund as on 31 May 19X6.

(b)   Prepare the income and expenditure account showing the result for the year ended 31 May 19X7, and the balance sheet on that date.   (20 marks)

5.5 SPRINGTIME GARDENERS CLUB (J87)

The following receipts and payments account for the year ended 31 December 19X6 of the Springtime Gardeners Club has been prepared by the club's treasurer:

	£		£
Opening bank balance	876	National Gardening Show –	
Seed sales	1,684	purchase of tickets and	
National Gardening Show –		brochures	3,600
ticket sales to non-members	400	Seed purchases	1,900
Lawn mower sales	3,800	Lawn mower purchases	5,400
Subscriptions received	7,190	Coaches to National	
Closing bank overdraft	270	Gardening Show	490
		Club premises – rent	500
		Gardening magazines for	
		members' use	390
		Secretarial expenses	940
		Proposed new club building	
		plans – architect's fees	1,000
	14,220		14,220

The club's executive committee has now decided that members should receive an income and expenditure account for the year ended 31 December 19X6 and a balance sheet as at that date.

Accordingly, the following additional information has been given.

(1) Club assets and liabilities, other than bank balances or overdrafts

As at	1 January 19X6	31 December 19X6
	£	£
Plot of land for proposed new club building, bought 1 January 19X0 for £2,000; current market value	5,000	5,500
Stock of seeds, at cost	250	560
Debtors – lawn mower sales	400	1,370
Membership subscriptions received in advance	240	390
Creditors – lawn mower supplier	800	170
seed growers	110	340

(2) The club sells lawn mowers at cost price to members; however the club never holds any stocks of unsold lawn mowers.

(3) Membership benefits include a ticket and transport to the National Gardening Show.

Required

(a) Prepare the club's accumulated fund as at 1 January 19X6.　(8 marks)

(b) Prepare the club's income and expenditure account for the year ended 31 December 19X6.　(10 marks)

(c) Prepare the club's balance sheet as at 31 December 19X6.　(7 marks)
(Total 25 marks)

5.6   PHOENIX MODEL ENGINEERING SOCIETY (J89)

The following account has been prepared by the treasurer of the Phoenix Model Engineering Society.

Receipts and payments statement for the year ended 31 March 19X9

	£		£
1 April 19X8 opening balance b/f	894	Purchase of building land	8,000
Subscriptions received	12,000	Purchase of machinery and tools	17,500
Sales of machinery and tools	21,000	Rent of temporary office meeting room	600
Sale of wooden hut	1,100	Printing, stationery & postages	860
Sales of tickets for annual national exhibition	300	Deposit in building society investment account	7,500
		Secretary's honorarium	150
		Coach to annual national exhibition	110
		Admission charges to annual national exhibition	220
		31 March 19X9 closing balance c/f	354
	35,295		35,295

The following additional information has been obtained from the Society's records.

(1) In addition to the balances at bank shown in the above receipts and payments statement, the Society's assets and liabilities were:

As at	1 April 19X8 £	31 March 19X9 £
Stocks of machinery and tools at cost	1,200	600
Subscriptions due to the Society	150	250
Wooden hut at valuation	1,300	–
Subscriptions prepaid by members	300	To be determined
Outing to annual national exhibition	–	See note 4 below

(2) The annual subscription for the year ended 31 March has been £50 per member since 1 April 19X7.

All subscriptions due at 1 April 19X8 have now been paid.

The Society's membership as 238 during the year ended 31 March 19X9.

(3) All sales of machinery and tools are to members on a strictly cash basis.

(4) **Annual national exhibition,** £40 for tickets was owing by a member to the Society on 31 March 19X9 and at that date the Society owed £45 for the purchase of exhibition programmes distributed to members without charge.

(5) Since preparing the above receipts and payments statement, the treasurer has received a bank statement showing bank charges of £14 debited in the Society's bank account on 30 March 19X9; no adjustment was made for these charges in the above statement.

(6)   Since the sale of the wooden hut on 1 July 19X8, the Society has rented a temporary office and meeting room at an annual rent of £600 payable in advance.

Required

Prepare an income and expenditure account for the year ended 31 March 19X9 and a balance sheet as at that date for the Society.   (25 marks)

Note: The income and expenditure account should show clearly the overall result of the trade in machinery and tools and the profit or loss of the visit to the annual national exhibition.

6   INCOMPLETE RECORDS – THE ACCOUNTS OF SOLE TRADERS

6.1   A HIGHTON

A Highton is in business as a general retailer. He does not keep a full set of accounting records; however it has been possible to extract the following details from the few records that are available.

Balances as at:	1.4.X1	31.3.X2
	£	£
Freehold land and buildings, at cost	10,000	10,000
Motor vehicle (cost £3,000)	2,250	
Stock, at cost	3,500	4,000
Trade debtors	500	1,000
Prepayments:		
Motor vehicle expenses	200	300
Property insurance	50	100
Cash at bank	550	950
Cash in hand	100	450
Loan from Highton's father	10,000	
Trade creditors	1,500	1,800
Accrual		
Electricity	200	400
Motor vehicle expenses	200	100

Extract from a rough cash book for the year to 31 March 19X2

	£
Receipts	
Cash sales	80,400
Payments	£
Cash purchases	17,000
Drawings	7,000
General shop expenses	100
Telephone	100
Wages	3,000

Extract from the bank pass sheets for the year to 31 March 19X2

	£
Receipts	
Cash banked	52,850
Cheques from trade debtors	8,750

	£
Payments	
Cheques to suppliers	47,200
Loan repayment (including interest)	10,100
Electricity	400
Motor vehicles expenses	1,000
Property insurance	150
Rates	300
Telephone	300
Drawings	1,750

Note: Depreciation is to be provided on the motor vehicle at a rate of 25% per annum on cost.

Required

Prepare a trading and profit and loss account for the year to 31 March 19X2, and a balance sheet as at that date. (25 marks)

6.2 **PILTDOWN**

Piltdown, a dealer in fancy goods, has produced the following draft balance sheet at 31 December 19X8, his first year of trading.

	£	£
Fixed assets		
Leasehold premises		25,000
Motor vehicles		7,200
		32,200
Current assets		
Stocks	9,630	
Debtors	5,250	
Cash at bank	3,060	
Cash in hand	375	
	18,315	
Current liabilities		
Creditors	4,920	
Accrued charges	2,295	
	7,215	
		11,100
		43,300
Loan from T Keating		5,000
		38,300
Representing:		£
Capital introduced		30,000
Profit for the year		13,500
		43,500
Less: Drawings		5,200
		38,300

0042V

On examining the business's records, you discover the following.

(1) No depreciation had been charged on fixed assets. It is agreed that the premises should be amortised equally over the period of the lease (10 years), and that the motor vehicles should be depreciated at 25% per annum on cost. A full year's depreciation is to be charged in all cases, irrespective of the date of purchase.

(2) At stocktaking on 31 December 19X8 one of the stock sheets had been undercast by £2,000.

(3) Piltdown had drawn goods from stock for his own use during the year, but had not recorded this in the books. The sales value of these goods was £300; Piltdown consistently makes a gross profit of 25% on selling price.

(4) Debtors were shown in the balance sheet after deducting a doubtful debt of £150. It was agreed that this debt should be considered bad and should be written off. It was also agreed to make a further provision of £125 against doubtful debts.

(5) The charge which had been made against profit for rates of £2,000 covered the period from the acquisition of the premises on 1 April 19X8 up to 31 March 19X9.

(6) An amount of £400 included in sundry expenses should have been included in purchases.

(7) The loan from T Keating carries interest at 12% per annum, calculated on a monthly basis from the start of the loan on 1 June 19X8. No interest has yet been paid, and none has been charged in the accounts.

Required

(a) A statement showing the adjustments which should be made to the profit for the year. (15 marks)

(b) A revised balance sheet at 31 December 19X8. (10 marks)
(Total 25 marks)

6.3 JEAN SMITH (J86)

Jean Smith, who retails wooden ornaments, has been so busy since she commenced business on 1 April 19X5 that she has neglected to keep adequate accounting records. Jean's opening capital consisted of her life savings of £15,000 which she used to open a business bank account. The transactions in this bank account during the year ended 31 March 19X6 have been summarised from the bank account as follows:

	£
Receipts:	
Loan from John Peacock, uncle	10,000
Takings	42,000
Payments:	
Purchases of goods for resale	26,400
Electricity for period to 31 December 19X5	760
Rent of premises for 15 months to 30 June 19X6	3,500
Rates of premises for the year ended 31 March 19X6	1,200
Wages of assistants	14,700
Purchase of van, 1 October 19X5	7,600
Purchase of holiday caravan for Jean Smith's private use	8,500
Van licence and insurance, payments covering a year	250

According to the bank account, the balance in hand on 31 March 19X6 was £4,090 in Jean Smith's favour.

Whilst the intention was to bank all takings intact, it now transpires that, in addition to cash drawings, the following payments were made out of takings before bankings:

	£
Van running expenses	890
Postages, stationery and other sundry expenses	355

On 31 March 19X6, takings of £640 awaited banking; this was done on 1 April 19X6. It has been discovered that amounts paid into the bank of £340 on 29 March 19X6 were not credited to Jean's bank account until 2 April 19X6 and a cheque of £120, drawn on 28 March 19X6 for purchases was not paid until 10 April 19X6. The normal rate of gross profit on the goods sold by Jean Smith is 50% on sales. However, during the year a purchase of ornamental gold fish costing £600 proved to be unpopular with customers and therefore the entire stock bought had to be sold at cost price.

Interest at the rate of 5% per annum is payable on each anniversary of the loan from John Peacock on 1 January 19X6.

Depreciation is to be provided on the van on the straight–line basis; it is estimated that the van will be disposed of after five years' use for £100.

The stock of goods for resale at 31 March 19X6 has been valued at cost at £1,900.

Creditors for purchases at 31 March 19X6 amounted to £880 and electricity charges accrued due at that date were £180.

Trade debtors at 31 March 19X6 totalled £2,300.

Required

Prepare a trading and profit and loss account for the year ended 31 March 19X6 and a balance sheet as at that date.   (25 marks)

6.4   **SKYMASTER (J87)**

The following trial balance as at 31 March 19X7 has been extracted from the books of the Skymaster Manufacturing Co Ltd:

	£	£
Market value of goods manufactured	80,000	
Profit on goods manufactured		14,000
Provision for unrealised profit on goods manufactured at 31 March 19X6		1,365
Stock of raw materials at 31 March 19X7	5,000	
Stock of finished goods at 31 March 19X6	7,800	
Work in progress at 31 March 19X7	9,100	
Plant and machinery:		
At cost	29,000	
Provision for depreciation at 31 March 19X7		16,400
Shop fixtures and fittings:		
At cost	49,000	
Provision for depreciation at 31 March 19X6		9,800
Sales		130,000
Debtors/creditors	12,700	8,000
Shop rent and rates	3,900	
Shop light and heat	7,600	
Shop salaries	11,700	
Balance at bank	4,300	
Share capital: ordinary shares of 50p each, fully paid		30,000
Retained earnings		10,535
	220,100	220,100

Additional information

(1)   The stock of finished goods at 31 March 19X7 has been valued, at market value, at £6,600. **Note:** The company only sells goods it manufactures.

(2)   The provision for unrealised profit on goods manufactured at 31 March 19X7 is to be £1,155.

(3)   Depreciation is to be provided on shop fixtures and fittings at the rate of 10% of the cost of assets held at the accounting year end.

(4)   Provision is to be made for a proposed dividend of 10p per ordinary share.

Required

(a)   Prepare a trading and profit and loss account for the year ended 31 March 19X7 of the Skymaster Manufacturing Co Ltd.   (15 marks)

(b)   Prepare a balance sheet as at 31 March 19X7 of the Skymaster Manufacturing Co Ltd.   (10 marks)
(Total 25 marks)

6.5   JEAN BLACK (D87)

The following summary for the year ended 31 October 19X7 has been prepared from the cash book of Jean Black, a retailer.

19X6	Receipts	Cash £	Bank £
November 1	Balances brought forward	142	2,830
	Cash sales	390	9,200
	Credit sales	110	37,500
	Cash from bank	748	
	Legacy from late aunt's estate		8,000
	Sale of motor vehicle		500
19X7			
October 31	Balance carried forward		1,400
		1,390	59,430

	Payments	Cash £	Bank £
	Purchases of goods for resale		24,300
	Wages		7,400
	General expenses	240	6,510
	Cash from bank		748
	Drawings	900	10,600
	Purchase of motor vehicle		9,872
19X7			
October 31	Balance carried forward	250	
		1,390	59,430

Unfortunately Jean Black does not keep a full set of accounting records. However the following additional information has been obtained for the accounting year ended 31 October 19X7:

(1)   Jean Black's assets and liabilities, other than cash and bank balances, were:

As at		1 November 19X6 £	31 October 19X7 £
Motor vehicle valued at		300	7,404
Stock valued at		1,900	2,500
Trade debtors		3,100	3,900
General expenses	– prepaid	390	–
	– accrued due	82	36
Wages: accrued due		–	810
Trade creditors		2,100	5,400

(2)   During the year ended 31 October 19X7, Jean Black withdrew goods costing £800 from the business for her own use.

(3)   The above cash book summary does not include bank charges of £40 debited to Jean Black's account by the bank on 31 October 19X7.

Required

(a)   Prepare Jean Black's trading and profit and loss account for the year ended 31 October 19X7.   (13 marks)

(b)   Prepare Jean Black's balance sheet as at 31 October 19X7.   (12 marks)
                                                                    (Total 25 marks)

6.6   MARK BEAN (J88)

The balance sheet as at 29 February 19X8 of Mark Bean, retailer, is as follows:

	£	£	£
Fixed assets:			
Fixtures and fittings:			
At cost		76,000	
Less: Provision for depreciation		18,000	
			58,000
Current assets:			
Stock	16,000		
Trade debtors	13,000		
Balance at bank	10,000		
		39,000	
Less: Current liabilities:			
Trade creditors		11,000	
			28,000
			86,000
Mark Bean: Capital account			86,000

The unexpected opportunity to acquire new business premises has necessitated 'final accounts' being required for the three months ended 31 May 19X8. Accordingly the following information has been prepared from the business' bank account.

		19X8	
	March £	April £	May £
Receipts:			
Sales – Cash	6,000	9,000	8,000
Credit	15,500	11,500	13,000
Sales of surplus display cabinet		500	
Payments:			
Purchases	11,000	11,900	10,900
General expenses	4,600	3,700	2,700
Drawings	1,200	1,400	1,500

Additional information

(1)   All receipts and payments are passed through the business bank account.

(2)   A half of credit sales are paid for in the month sales take place and the balance of the cash due is received in the following month.

(3)   Purchases are paid for in the month following the receipt of the goods; all general expenses are paid on a cash basis. Purchase creditors at 31 May 19X8 amounted to £9,600.

(4)   A gross profit of 30% is obtained on all sales.

(5)   During March, April and May 19X8, Mark Bean withdrew from the business goods for his own use of £600 at cost price.

(6)   The display cabinet sold in April 19X8 cost £2,000 when bought in 19X5 and had a written down book value in fixtures and fittings at 29 February 19X8 of £1,400.

(7) The depreciation charge for fixtures and fittings for the three months to 31 May 19X8 is £1,850.

Required

(a) Prepare a computation of the business bank account balance at 31 May 19X8 of Mark Bean.   (5 marks)

(b) Prepare Mark Bean's trading and profit and loss account for the three months ended 31 May 19X8.   (10 marks)

(c) Prepare Mark Bean's balance sheet as at 31 May 19X8.   (10 marks)
                                                               (Total 25 marks)

6.7 **MARY GRIMES (D88)**

Mary Grimes, retail fruit and vegetable merchant, does not keep a full set of accounting records. However, the following information has been produced from the business' records:

(1) **Summary of the bank account for the year ended 31 August 19X8**

	£		£
1 Sept 19X7 balance b/f	1,970	Payments to suppliers	72,000 ✓
Receipts from trade		Purchase of motor van	
debtors	96,000 ✓	(E471 KBR)	13,000
Sale of private yacht	20,000	Rent and rates	2,600
Sale of motor van		Wages	15,100
(A123 BWA)	2,100	Motor vehicle expenses	3,350
		Postages and stationery	1,360
		Drawings	9,200
		Repairs and renewals	650
		Insurances	800
		31 Aug 19X8 balance c/f	2,010
	_____		_____
	120,070		120,070
	_____		_____

1 Sept 19X8 balance b/f   2,010

(2) **Assets and liabilities, other than balances at bank**

	31 Sept 19X7	31 Aug 19X8
Trade creditors	4,700	2,590
Trade debtors	7,320	9,500
Rent and rates accruals	200	260
Motor vans:		
A123 BWA – At cost	10,000	–
Provision for depreciation	8,000	–
E471 KBR – At cost	–	13,000
Provision for depreciation		To be determined
Stock in trade	4,900	5,900
Insurances prepaid	160	200

(3) All receipts are banked and all payments are made from the business bank account.

(4) A trade debt of £300 owing by John Blunt and included in the trade debtors at 31 August 19X8 (see (2) above), is to be written off as a bad debt.

(5) It is Mary Grimes' policy to provide depreciation at the rate of 20% on the cost of motor vans held at the end of each financial year; no depreciation is provided in the year of sale or disposal of a motor van.

(6) Discounts received during the year ended 31 August 19X8 from trade creditors amounted to £1,100.

Required

(a) Prepare Mary Grimes' trading and profit and loss account for the year ended 31 August 19X8. (13 marks)

(b) Prepare Mary Grimes' balance sheet as at 31 August 19X8. (12 marks)

(Total 25 marks)

6.8 HAROLD WEBB (D88)

The following draft trading and profit and loss account for the three months ended 30 September 19X8 and draft summary of the capital account for that period have been prepared for Harold Webb, retailer.

**Draft trading and profit and loss account
for the three months ended 30 September 19X8**

		£	£
Sales			172,200
Less:	Cost of sales:		
	Opening stock	7,680	
	Purchases	102,720	
		110,400	
	Less: Closing stock	7,080	
			103,320
Gross profit			68,880
Less:	Establishment and distribution expenditure	42,480	
	Depreciation – Freehold buildings	5,000	
	Fixtures and fittings	7,000	
			54,480
Net profit			14,400

**Harold Webb, draft capital account
for the three months ended 30 September 19X8**

		£	£
As at 1 July 19X8		80,880	
Add:	Net profit for the three months to 30 September 19X8	14,400	
		95,280	
Less:	Drawings	18,280	
			£77,000

54

0042V

Harold Webb has now queried some of the figures in the above statements which have been prepared by an inexperienced clerk, James Gale. Whilst noting that the rate of gross profit on sales is what he expected and that which has been obtained in the business over several years, Harold Webb has made the following points:

(1) His drawings are all by cash and total £3,360 for each calendar month.

(2) The following analysis of establishment and distribution expenditure appears to be as expected:

	£
Fixed overheads	25,260
Variable overheads (10% of sales)	17,220
	42,480

Subsequent investigations by an independent accountant reveal:

(1) The sales figure in the draft accounts has been inflated by fictitious sales which have been posted to the debit of drawings.

(2) A quantity of stock has been stolen by James Gale.

(3) Whilst establishment and distribution fixed overheads are £25,260 and the related variable overheads incurred amount to 10% of the actual sales the variable overheads figure in the draft accounts includes an unauthorised payment for holiday expenses for James Gale.

Although Harold Webb is not insured for any stock losses or staff defalcations, James Gale has agreed, in principle, to compensate Harold Webb.

Consequently, discussions are now taking place which may result in James Gale compensating Harold Webb fully for losses suffered by him; the result will not be known until March 19X9.

The manufacture of the goods sold by Harold Webb will be restricted for the next three years.

Required

(a) Prepare a corrected trading and profit and loss account for the three months ended 30 September 19X8 on the assumption that James Gale will not compensate Harold Webb. (19 marks)

(b) Prepare a statement of the amount to be claimed for full compensation by Harold Webb from James Gale. (6 marks)
(Total 25 marks)

6.9 **HAROLD WOOD (D89)**

Harold Wood commenced trading on 1 June 19X9 as a furniture retailer. The following month by month summary of his cash receipts and payments has now been prepared.

Questions

	June £	July £	Aug £	Sept £	Oct £	Nov £
Receipts:						
Credit sales	–	–	15,522	11,973	13,494	16,419
Cash sales	949	859	1,113	893	1,083	836
Loan from T Bunn	–	–	10,000	–	–	–
	949	859	26,635	12,866	14,577	17,255
Payments:						
Purchases	–	14,270	9,443	10,543	12,100	9,850
Wages	500	1,100	1,100	1,200	1,300	1,100
Rent (paid 1 June)	12,600	–	–	–	–	–
General expenses	1,000	970	860	930	1,100	1,050
Fixtures and fittings	–	12,000	–	–	–	–
Drawings	800	840	1,100	1,300	1,300	1,300
	14,900	29,180	12,503	13,973	15,800	13,300
Opening bank balances	20,000	6,049	(22,272)	(8,140)	(9,247)	(10,470)
Closing bank balances	6,049	(22,272)	(8,140)	(9,247)	(10,470)	(6,515)

Additional information

(1) All receipts and payments have been passed through the business bank account and, except where otherwise stated, have occurred on the last day of the relevant month.

(2) Credit sale customers are given two months credit and are granted a 2½% cash discount for payment by the due date; all amounts due have been received by the due dates.

(3) All purchases have been made on a monthly credit basis.

(4) Wages and general expenses are paid in the month the debt is incurred; rent is paid annually in advance.

(5) The fixtures and fittings were acquired on 1 June 19X9.

(6) Depreciation is to be provided on the fixtures and fittings at the rate of 10% per annum on cost.

(7) Interest at the rate of 12% per annum is payable on the loan from T Bunn.

(8) Stock at 31 August 19X9 has been valued at £2,141.

Harold Wood wishes to ascertain the results of his first three months' trading.

Required

(a) Prepare a trading and profit and loss account for the three months ended 31 August 19X9 and a balance sheet as at that date. (19 marks)

(b) Briefly explain the benefits of accrual accounting in contrast to cashflow accounting. (6 marks)
(Total 25 marks)

6.10   CURRY AND GRAY (J90)

John Curry is very interested in purchasing the business of Thomas Gray who commenced trading on 1 May 19X8 as a retailer, but has now decided to retire following a serious car accident.

The summarised final accounts for the two years to 30 April 19Y0 of Thomas Gray are as follows:

Trading and profit and loss accounts year ended 30 April

	19X9 £	19X9 £	19Y0 £	19Y0 £
Sales		160,000		190,000
Cost of sales		96,000		114,000
Gross profit		64,000		76,000
Establishment and administrative expenses	14,000		16,500	
Sales and distribution expenses	25,000		29,500	
		39,000		46,000
Net profit		25,000		30,000

Balance sheets as at 30 April

	19X9 £	19X9 £	19Y0 £	19Y0 £
Fixed assets – at cost less aggregate depreciation		64,000		51,200
Current assets				
Stock in trade	15,000		24,000	
Trade debtors	18,000		21,000	
Balance at bank	13,000		21,800	
	46,000		66,800	
Less: Current liabilities – Trade creditors	5,000		8,000	
		41,000		58,800
		105,000		110,000
Capital account				
At 1 May 19X8/19X9		100,000		105,000
Add: Net profit		25,000		30,000
		125,000		135,000
Less: Drawings		20,000		25,000
		105,000		110,000

Additional information concerning Thomas Gray's business

(1)   Stock in trade as at 30 April

		19X9 £	19Y0 £
At cost		9,000	16,000
At net realisable value		15,000	24,000

(2)   The capital at 1 May 19X8 consisted of:

	£
Fixed assets	80,000
Balance at bank	20,000

There have been no subsequent additions or disposals of fixed assets.

(3)   Since preparing the above accounts, it has been discovered that stock costing £10,000 had been stolen in January 19Y0; this loss was not covered by insurance.

(4)   John Curry considers that Thomas Gray's fixed assets should be depreciated at the rate of 20% per annum on the straight-line basis.

(5)   If John Curry purchases Thomas Gray's business, he proposes to employ a manager to run the business on his behalf; it is estimated that the salary of the manager will be £12,000 per annum.

(6)   John Curry is of the opinion that bad debts of £150 will be written off in each financial year from 1 May 19Y0.

(7)   It is expected that, subject to bad debts to be written off in future years, the results achieved by Thomas Gray's business in the year ended 30 April 19Y0 can be maintained for the foreseeable future.

Required

(a)   A statement showing the net profit that John Curry may expect to earn in the forthcoming year if he purchases Thomas Gray's business.   (21 marks)

(b)   A computation of the amount John Curry may be expected to pay for the business of Thomas Gray assuming an appropriate rate of return to be 10% per annum.
(4 marks)
(Total 25 marks)

6.11   J PATEL (D90)

The assets and liabilities as at the close of business on 31 October 19X9 of J Patel, retailer, are summarised as follows.

	£	£
Motor vehicles		
At cost	9,000	
Provision for depreciation	1,800	
		7,200
Fixtures and fittings		
At cost	10,000	
Provision for depreciation	6,000	
		4,000
Stock		16,100
Trade debtors		19,630
Cash		160
		47,090
Capital – J Patel		30,910
Bank overdraft		6,740
Trade creditors		9,440
		47,090

All receipts from credit customers are paid intact into the business bank account whilst cash sales receipts are banked after deduction of cash drawings and providing for the shop till cash float. The cash float was increased from £160 to £200 in September 19Y0.

The following is a summary of the transactions in the business bank account for the year ended 31 October 19Y0.

Receipts	£	Payments	£
		C/F Balance	6740,
Credit sales	181,370	Drawings	8,500
Cash sales	61,190	Motor van	
		(bought 1 May 19Y0)	11,200
		Purchases	163,100
Proceeds of sale of		Establishment and	
land owned privately		administrative expenses	33,300
by J Patel	16,000	Sales and distribution expenses	29,100
	258560		251940

Additional information for the year ended 31 October 19Y0 is as follows.

(1)   A gross profit of 33⅓% has been achieved on all sales.

(2)   Bad debts of £530 have been written off during the year.

(3)   Trade debtors at 31 October 19Y0 were reduced by £8,130 as compared with a year earlier.

(4)   Trade creditors at 31 October 19Y0 amounted to £12,700.

(5)   Depreciation is to be provided at the following annual rates on cost:

            Motor vehicles   20%
            Fixtures and fittings   10%

(6)   Stock at 31 October 19Y0 has been valued at £23,700.

Required

A trading and profit and loss account for the year ended 31 October 19Y0 and a balance sheet as at that date for J Patel.   (25 marks)

7 MANUFACTURING ACCOUNTS

7.1 JENKINS

Jenkins carries on business as a clothing manufacturer with two managers, Owen who is responsible for the factory and Rogers who is responsible for the sales department. Each manager is entitled to a commission of 20% of the net profits of his department, before charging some commission.

Finished goods are transferred from the factory to the sales department at factory cost plus 20%.

Jenkins is to be credited with interest at the rate of 8% per annum on his fixed capital of which three quarters is to be taken as being employed by the factory, and one-quarter by the sales department.

The trial balance of the business as on 31 December 19X9 was as follows:

	£	£
Capital account – Jenkins		30,000
Freehold factory at cost (including land £4,000)	20,000	
Factory plant and machinery at cost	4,800	
Travellers' cars	2,600	
Provision for depreciation 31 December 19X8		
Freehold factory		1,920
Factory plant and machinery		1,600
Travellers' cars		1,200
Stocks at 31 December 19X8		
Raw materials at cost	6,800	
Finished goods at transfer value	2,520	
Finished goods stock provision 31 December 19X8		420
Trade debtors and creditors	3,600	4,200
Provision for doubtful debts		280
Purchase of raw materials	36,600	
Wages and salaries	19,800	
Rates and insurance (factory £1,160)	1,510	
Sundry expenses (factory £1,100)	1,500	
Motor expenses	400	
Sales		72,000
Balance at bank	11,490	
	111,620	111,620

You are given the following information.

(1) Stocks on hand as on 31 December 19X9 were as follows: £

	£
Raw materials at cost	8,400
Finished goods at transfer value	2,400

(2)   Wages and salaries included the following   £

    Owen – salary   1,400
    Rogers – salary   1,500
    Jenkins – salary   2,400
    Sales department wages and salaries   1,800

    The balance represented factory wages.

(3)   Provision is to be made for depreciation on the freehold factory, plant and machinery and travellers' cars at 2%, 10% and 25% respectively, calculated on cost.

(4)   On 31 December 19X9 £120 was owing for sundry expenses (sales department) and rates paid in advance amounted to £260 (sales department £50).

(5)   Of the trade debtors £60, for which provision had previously been made, is to be written off.

Required

(a)   Prepare accounts for the year ended 31 December 19X9 showing:

    (i)   prime cost;
    (ii)   factory cost of goods produced;

    (iii)   profit of the factory and of the sales department; and
    (iv)   appropriation of profits.

(b)   Prepare the balance sheet as on that date.   (20 marks)

7.2   **TYBALT**

Tybalt is the proprietor of a furniture manufacturing business. He makes up his accounts to 31 December each year. Set out below is Tybalt's trial balance at 31 December 19X5:

	£	£
Advertising	830	
Bad debts	605	
Bad debts provision		1,000
Bank charges	120	
Capital at 1 January		36,623
Drawings	8,000	
Discount		412
Factory power	3,614	
Fixtures and fittings	900	
General expenses – Factory	205	
– Office	346	
Insurance	902	
Light and heat	482	
Plant and machinery, 1 January	15,000	
Plant and machinery, bought 30 June	2,000	
Purchases	33,668	
Packing and transport	1,085	
Rent and rates	1,486	
Repairs to plant	785	
Salaries – Office	3,690	
Sales		79,174
Stocks etc, 1 January		
Raw materials	5,230	
Finished goods	7,380	
Work in progress (at prime cost)	1,670	
Wages – Factory	20,700	
Trade debtors and creditors	10,560	6,150
Cash at bank	3,926	
Cash in hand	175	
	123,359	123,359

The following additional information is relevant.

	£
(1) Stocks, etc at 31 December, were:	
Raw materials	3,560
Work in progress (at prime cost)	1,740
Finished goods	9,650
Packing materials	125

(2) The following liabilities are to be provided for:	
Factory power	562
Rent and rates	386
Light and heat	160
General expenses – Factory	25
– Office	40

(3) Insurance paid in advance is £170.

(4) Five–sixths of rent and rates, light and heat and insurance are to be allocated to the factory and one–sixth to the office.

(5) Depreciation is to be provided at 10% per annum on plant and machinery, and 5% per annum on fixtures and fittings.

(6) The bad debts provision is to be increased by £500.

0042V

Required

Prepare a manufacturing, trading and profit and loss account for the year ended 31 December 19X5, and a balance sheet at that date. (15 marks)

7.3 MARR

Marr was the sole proprietor of a sweets manufacturing business and the following trial balance was extracted from his books at 31 December 19X0:

	Dr £	Cr £
Capital		20,400
Freehold land and buildings, at cost	15,000	
Plant and machinery, at cost	14,500	
Plant and machinery: provision for depreciation		7,000
Travellers' cars, at cost	4,000	
Travellers' cars: provision for depreciation		2,800
Loose tools at valuation on 1 January 19X0	1,200	
Stocks, 1 January 19X0: Raw materials	3,300	
Finished goods (25 tons)	6,600	
Purchased: Raw materials	18,500	
Loose tools	800	
Sales (210 tons)	66,000	
Wages: Factory	13,640	
Administration	5,500	
Sales department	3,000	
Rates and insurance	1,600	
Repairs to buildings	1,000	
Sales expenses including vehicle running costs	1,440	
Electricity and power	6,000	
Administration expenses	2,810	
Provision for doubtful debts		1,000
Debtors	6,100	
Creditors	3,580	
Bank	3,710	
Cash in hand	100	
Provision for unrealised profit at 1 January 19X0		600
	105,090	105,090

You are given the following information.

(1) Closing stocks on 31 December 19X0: raw materials £2,800; finished goods (15 tons), £4,290 (including profit loading); loose tools £1,600.

(2) The output of manufactured goods is transferred from the factory at factory cost plus 10%.

(3) Provision is to be made for the following amounts owing on 31 December 19X0: Electricity and power £800; New machinery £500.

(4) Payments in advance on 31 December 19X0 were as follows: rates £300, vehicle licences £40.

(5) Annual depreciation on plant and machinery and travellers' cars is to be provided at the rate of 15% and 20% respectively on cost at the end of the year.

(6) Bad debts amounting to £500 are to be written off and the provision for doubtful debts reduced to £600.

(7) Expenses are to be allocated as follows:

	Works	Administration
Rates and insurance	7/10	3/10
Repairs	4/5	1/5
Electricity and power	9/10	1/10

Adjustments for bad debts and the provision for doubtful debts are attributable to selling and delivery expenses.

Required

(a) Prepare the manufacturing, trading and profit and loss accounts for the year ended 31 December 19X0, and the balance sheet at that date.

(b) Calculate the factory cost per ton produced. (20 marks)

7.4 MR WORTHING

Mr Worthing is in business as a manufacturer of fancy goods. Wishing to allocate profits fairly between the production and selling functions, he operates a system whereby finished goods are transferred from the factory to the sales department at factory cost plus 20%.

The trial balance of the business at 30 June 19X6 was as follows.

	£	£
Capital account		30,000
Freehold factory, at cost (including land £4,000)	20,000	
Factory plant and machinery, at cost	4,800	
Travellers' cars	2,600	
Provision for depreciation, 1 July 19X5:		
Freehold factory		1,920
Factory plant and machinery		1,600
Travellers' cars		1,200
Stocks, 1 July 19X5:		
Raw materials, at cost	6,800	
Finished goods, at transfer value	2,520	
Finished goods stock provision, 1 July 19X5		420
Trade debtors and creditors	3,600	4,200
Provision for doubtful debts		280
Purchase of raw materials	36,600	
Wages and salaries	19,800	
Rates and insurance (factory £1,160)	1,510	
Sundry expenses (factory £1,100)	1,500	
Motor expenses	400	
Sales		72,000
Balance at bank	11,490	
	111,620	111,620

You are given the following information.

(1)   Stocks on hand at 30 June 19X6 were as follows: £

Raw materials, at cost   8,400
Finished goods, at transfer value   2,400

(2)   Wages and salaries included the following: £

Factory manager   – salary   1,400
Sales manager   – salary   1,500
Mr Worthing   – drawings   2,400
Sales department wages and salaries   1,800

The balance represented factory wages.

(3)   Provision is to be made for depreciation on the freehold factory, plant and machinery and travellers' cars at 2%, 10% and 25% respectively, calculated on cost.

(4)   On 30 June 19X6, £120 was owing for sundry expenses (sales department) and rates paid in advance amounted to £260 (sales department £50).

(5)   Of the trade debtors £60, for which provision had previously been made, is to be written off.

Required

(a)   Prepare manufacturing, trading and profit and loss accounts for the year ended 30 June 19X6, and a balance sheet at that date.   (20 marks)

(b)   Comment briefly on the purpose and implications of the mark–up applied to goods transferred from the factory to the sales department.   (4 marks)
                                                                   (Total 24 marks)

7.5   **WILLIAM SPEED (J86)**

The following balances as at 31 December 19X5 have been extracted from the books of William Speed, a small manufacturer:

		£
Stocks at 1 January 19X5:	Raw materials	7,000
	Work in progress	5,000
	Finished goods	6,900
Purchases of raw materials		38,000
Direct labour		28,000
Factory overheads:	Variable	16,000
	Fixed	9,000
Administrative expenses:	Rent and rates	19,000
	Heat and light	6,000
	Stationery and postages	2,000
	Staff salaries	19,380
Sales		192,000
Plant and machinery:	At cost	30,000
	Provision for depreciation	12,000
Motor vehicles (for sales deliveries):		
	At cost	16,000
	Provision for depreciation	4,000
Creditors		5,500
Debtors		28,000

	£
Drawings	11,500
Balance at bank	16,600
Capital at 1 January 19X5	48,000
Provision for unrealised profit at 1 January 19X5	1,380
Motor vehicle running costs	4,500

Additional information:

(1) Stocks at 31 December 19X5 were as follows:

	£
Raw materials	9,000
Work in progress	8,000
Finished goods	10,350

(2) The factory output is transferred to the trading account at factory cost plus 25% for factory profit. The finished goods stock is valued on the basis of amounts transferred to the debit of the trading account.

(3) Depreciation is provided annually at the following percentages of the original cost of fixed assets held at the end of each financial year:

Plant and machinery	10%
Motor vehicles	25%

(4) Amounts accrued due at 31 December 19X5 for direct labour amounted to £3,000 and rent and rates prepaid at 31 December 19X5 amounted to £2,000.

Required

Prepare a manufacturing, trading and profit and loss account for the year ended 31 December 19X5 and a balance sheet as at that date.

Note: The prime cost and total factory cost should be clearly shown.

(25 marks)

7.6 JANE SEYMOUR (D86)

The following list of balances as at 31 July 19X6 has been extracted from the books of Jane Seymour who commenced business on 1 August 19X5 as a designer and manufacturer of kitchen furniture.

	£
Plant and machinery, at cost on 1 August 19X5	60,000
Motor vehicles, at cost on 1 August 19X5	30,000
Loose tools, at cost	9,000
Sales	170,000
Raw materials purchased	43,000
Direct factory wages	39,000
Light and power	5,000
Indirect factory wages	8,000
Machinery repairs	1,600
Motor vehicle running expenses	12,000
Rent and insurances	11,600
Administrative staff salaries	31,000
Administrative expenses	9,000
Sales and distribution staff salaries	13,000

	£
Capital at 1 August 19X5	122,000
Sundry debtors	16,500
Sundry creditors	11,200
Balance at bank	8,500
Drawings	6,000

Additional information for the year ended 31 July 19X6.

(1)   It is estimated that the plant and machinery will be used in the business for 10 years and the motor vehicles used for four years; in both cases it is estimated that the residual value will be nil. The straight-line method of providing for depreciation is to be used.

(2)   Light and power charges accrued due at 31 July 19X6 amounted to £1,000 and insurances prepaid at 31 July 19X6 totalled £800.

(3)   Stocks were valued at cost at 31 July 19X6 as follows:

        Raw materials   £7,000
        Finished goods   £10,000

(4)   The valuation of work in progress at 31 July 19X6 included variable and fixed factory overheads and amounted to £12,300.

(5)   Two thirds of the light and power and rent and insurances costs are to be allocated to the factory costs and one third to general administration costs.

(6)   Motor vehicles costs are to be allocated equally to factory costs and general administration costs.

(7)   Goods manufactured during the year are to be transferred to the trading account at £95,000.

(8)   Loose tools in hand on 31 July 19X6 were valued at £5,000.

Required

(a)   Prepare a manufacturing, trading and profit and loss account for the year ended 31 July 19X6 of Jane Seymour.   (18 marks)

(b)   An explanation of how each of the following accounting concepts have affected the preparation of the above accounts:

        (i)   conservatism;
        (ii)   matching;
        (iii) going concern.   (7 marks)
                                                          (Total 25 marks)

7.7   LONG MEASURES LTD (J88)

The following balances as at 31 March 19X8 have been extracted from the accounting records of Long Measures Ltd:

	£
Raw material stock at 1 April 19X7	4,100
Raw material purchases	39,200
Raw material carriage inwards	1,800
Direct labour	33,000

Questions

	£
Variable overheads	23,000
Fixed overheads	34,000
Work–in–progress at 1 April 19X7	12,600
Finished goods stock at 1 April 19X7	35,000
Finished goods purchased	67,500
Establishment expenditure	29,400
Administrative expenditure	17,100
Sales and distribution expenditure	23,500
Sales	320,000
Freehold property:	
at cost	80,000
provision for depreciation at 1 April 19X7	20,000
Plant and machinery:	
at cost	44,000
provision for depreciation at 1 April 19X7	6,000

Additional information

(1) Stock valuations at 31 March 19X8:

	£
Raw material	3,600
Finished goods	28,000

(2) The company's work in progress valuations include prime cost, variable overheads and fixed overheads; the work in progress valuation at 31 March 19X8 was £9,500.

(3) Depreciation is provided annually on the cost of fixed assets at the relevant year end at the following rates:

	%
Freehold property	2½
Plant and machinery	10

Only half the freehold property depreciation is charged to manufacturing.

(4) Direct labour charges accrued due at 31 March 19X8 amounted to £200 whilst establishment expenditure prepaid at that date was £600.

(5) The company only manufactured 2,000 Codgetts during the year ended 31 March 19X8 which were transferred to the trading account at a total market value of £150,000. In addition to Codgetts, the company sells certain ancillary goods which it buys already manufactured.

Required

Prepare the manufacturing, trading and profit and loss account for the year ended 31 March 19X8 of Long Measures Ltd and show the following:

(a) prime cost;
(b) profit or loss on goods manufactured;
(c) unit cost of manufacture.

(25 marks)

0042V

7.8 JOHN KING (D88)

The following information has been extracted from the accounting records of John King, manufacturer.

(1) Expenditure analysis

| | At 31 July 19X8 | | Payments 19X8 | | | At 31 October 19X8 | |
	Amounts prepaid £	Amounts accrued due £	August £	Sept £	October £	Amounts prepaid £	Amounts accrued due £
Raw material purchases	–	16,000	90,000	60,000	94,000	–	28,000
Operating labour	–	800	80,300	80,500	69,500	–	500
Manufacturing overheads:							
Variable	1,200	900	58,000	59,000	60,000	9,000	1,700
Fixed	–	–	24,000	24,000	24,000	1,000	–
Purchases – Goods for resale	–	2,000	15,000	14,000	11,000	–	7,000
Carriage inwards on goods purchased	–	–	2,100	1,900	2,000	–	–
Establishment expenditure	900	–	14,000	15,000	16,000	900	–
Administrative expenditure	–	1,000	9,000	10,500	11,500	2,000	–

(2) Fixed asset depreciation is to be provided for the three months ended 31 October 19X8 as follows:

	£
Manufacturing fixed assets	24,000
Showroom and administrative offices fixed assets	8,000

(3) During the three months ended 31 October 19X8, 810 units were manufactured and transferred to finished goods stock at £1,000 each.

(4) Stocks were valued as follows:

	31 July 19X8 £	31 October 19X8 £
Raw materials	21,300	16,400
Finished goods: Manufactured by John King	25,000	33,000
Bought by John King	11,000	7,000

(5)   There was no work in progress at either 31 July 19X8 or 31 October 19X8.

(6)   Sales for the three months ended 31 October 19X8 totalled £950,000.

Required

Prepare a manufacturing, trading and profit and loss account for the three months ended 31 October 19X8 of John King.

Note: Show the prime cost and manufacturing profit.   (25 marks)

7.9   FAIRDEAL MANUFACTURERS LTD (J90)

The following list of balances as at 30 April 19X0 has been extracted from the books of Fairdeal Manufacturers Ltd which commenced business on 1 May 19W9:

	£
Factory plant and machinery at cost 1 May 19W9	120,000
Motor delivery vehicles at cost 1 May 19W9	25,000
Purchases of raw materials	41,000
Factory labour: Machine operatives	36,000
Supervisory	7,000
Factory plant and machinery repairs	8,710
Heat, light and power	24,750
Rates and insurance	2,550
General administrative expenses	9,400
Administrative salaries	12,090
Trade debtors	12,000
Trade creditors	7,100
Bank overdraft	4,900
Sales	136,500
Ordinary shares of £1 each, fully paid	120,000
Share premium account	30,000

Additional information

(1)   Raw material stocks, at cost, at 30 April 19X0 were valued at £3,000.

(2)   Work in progress at 30 April 19X0 was valued at £24,000.

(3)   Depreciation is to be provided on fixed assets at the following rates on cost:

	% per annum
Factory plant and machinery	10
Motor delivery vehicles	25

(4)   Rates and insurances prepaid at 30 April 19X0 amounted to £600; heat, light and power accrued due at 30 April 19X0 was £2,300.

(5)   Rates and insurances and heat, light and power charges are to be apportioned three quarters to manufacturing and a quarter to the profit and loss account.

(6)   Manufactured goods are to be transferred from the manufacturing account to the trading account at wholesale prices; the wholesale price of goods manufactured during the year ended 30 April 19X0 was £100,000.

(7) Finished goods stock at 30 April 19X0, at wholesale prices, was valued at £10,000.

Required

(a) Prepare the manufacturing, trading and profit and loss account for the year ended 30 April 19X0 of Fairdeal Manufacturers Ltd. (15 marks)

(b) Prepare the balance sheet as at 30 April 19X0 of Fairdeal Manufacturers Ltd. (10 marks)
(Total 25 marks)

8 THE ACCOUNTS OF PARTNERSHIPS

8.1 RAY AND MOND

Ray and Mond are in partnership sharing profits and losses in the ratio 2 : 1. The following trial balance has been extracted from the books of the partnership as at 31 May 19X3:

	Dr £	Cr £
Cash at bank	400	
Accumulated depreciation on furniture (at 1.6.X2)		2,000
Furniture, at cost	4,000	
Gross profit for the year		35,000
Office expenses	10,000	
Partners' capital accounts (at 1.6.X2):		
Ray		20,000
Mond		10,000
Partners' current accounts (at 1.6.X2):		
Ray		5,000
Mond		2,000
Partners' drawings for the year:		
Ray	10,000	
Mond	9,000	
Premises, at cost	28,000	
Provision for doubtful debts		400
Rates	5,000	
Stock (at 31.5.X3)	1,500	
Trade creditors		6,000
Trade debtors	12,500	
	80,400	80,400

Notes

(1) Mond is entitled to a salary of £6,000 per annum; no interest is payable or chargeable on either the partners' capital or current accounts.

(2) Depreciation is to be charged on the furniture at a rate of 10% per annum on cost.

(3) A bad debt of £500 is to be written off.

(4) The provision for doubtful debts is to be made equal to 5% of trade debtors as at 31 May 19X3.

Required

(a) Prepare the profit and loss, and the profit and loss appropriation accounts for the year to 31 May 19X3.

(b) Compile the partners' current accounts for the year to 31 May 19X3.

(c) Prepare the partnership balance sheet as at 31 May 19X3.   (22 marks)

8.2   JACK AND FRED

The balance sheet of Jack and Fred as at 31 March 19X6 was as follows:

	£	£		£	£
Capital accounts			Land and buildings		
Jack	5,000		(cost)	8,000	
Fred	4,000		Depreciation	1,560	
		9,000			6,440
Current accounts			Machinery (cost)	9,000	
Jack	980		Depreciation	4,300	
Fred	750				4,700
		1,700	Stock		1,180
Loans (made by Jack)		2,000	Debtors		1,350
Trade creditors		830	Prepaid expenses		140
Accrued expenses		90	Cash in hand		80
Bank overdraft		270			
		13,890			13,890

The balance on the current account had been reached as shown below:

	Jack £	Fred £		Jack £	Fred £
Drawings	3,160	3,960	Opening balance	1,140	780
Closing balance	980	720	Interest on capital	500	400
			Share of profits	2,500	2,000
			Salary	–	1,500
	4,140	4,680		4,140	4,680

An accountant, carrying out an audit of the partnership records, discovered the following facts.

(1) The closing stock included items which had cost £220 at that value, but, in fact, the items were damaged and could only be sold for £80.

(2) Fred had introduced £2,000 additional capital on 1 October 19X5, but the interest on that capital had been calculated for a full year.

(3) Bank charges of £70 had not been included in the partnership records.

(4) The depreciation on machinery for the year (£450) had been omitted in error.

(5) A trade creditor for £370 had been omitted from both creditors and purchases, although the items concerned had been included in the closing stock.

(6) Rates of £600 had been charged in the profit and loss account but £80 of the sum related to the period after 1 April.

(7) Jack was entitled to interest on his loan of 7.5% per annum but this had been omitted from the accounts.

(8) Fred's salary credited at £1,500 should have been £1,400.

Required

(a) Prepare a statement to show the net profit (before appropriation) for the year, taking into account the data above.

(b) Prepare the amended current accounts of the partners.

(c) Redraft the balance sheet as at 31 March 19X6.

(d) Explain clearly in the context of a partnership the reason underlying the different treatment of

    (i) interest on a bank loan as contrasted with interest on a partner's capital account; and

    (ii) a salary to an employee as contrasted with a salary to a partner.

(25 marks)

8.3 STRONGCOLOUR FABRICS (J86)

The following trial balance as at 31 March 19X6 has been extracted from the books of John Brown, trading as Strongcolour Fabrics:

	£	£
John Brown: Capital account at 1 April 19X5		61,000
John Brown: Drawings	22,600	
Freehold property:		
At cost	40,000	
Provision for depreciation		6,000
Fixtures and fittings:		
At cost	30,000	
Provision for depreciation		5,400
Motor vehicles:		
At cost	12,000	
Provision for depreciation		5,000
Debtors	14,000	
Creditors		9,000
Balance at bank	5,700	
Sales		240,000
Cost of sales	168,000	
Stock at 31 March 19X6	5,100	
Establishment and distribution expenses	29,000	
	326,400	326,400

0042V

On 1 January 19X6, Peter Grey, a senior employee, joined John Brown in partnership trading as Allcolour Cloths.

The goodwill of Strongcolour Fabrics was valued at 31 December 19X5 at £12,000, but it has been agreed that a goodwill account will not be opened. A John Brown loan account is to be opened as from 1 January 19X6 with a transfer of £20,000 from John Brown's capital account. A capital account and a current account is to be maintained for each partner.

Peter Grey has not been paid his salary of £12,000 per annum as administrative manager since 1 April 19X5 and no adjustment has been made yet in the books for such salary in view of the impending partnership. However, it has now been agreed that the amount due to Peter Grey as an employee will form the basis of his capital as a partner of Allcolour Cloths.

It has been agreed that all assets and liabilities recorded in the books of Strongcolour Fabrics will be carried forward to Allcolour Cloths at their book values with the exception of freehold property which has been revalued at 1 January 19X6 at £50,000.

The following additional information has been given for the year ended 31 March 19X6.

(1) All sales have produced a uniform rate of gross profit.

(2) One eighth of the turnover took place in the last quarter of the year.

(3) Establishment and distribution expenses accrued due at 31 March 19X6 amounted to £1,000.

(4) Establishment and distribution expenses are to be apportioned uniformly throughout the year.

(5) Depreciation, apportioned uniformly throughout the year, is to be provided at the following rates on the original cost of fixed assets held at the year end:

Fixtures and fittings	12%
Motor vehicles	25%

No depreciation is to be provided on the freehold property for the year.

Required

(a) Prepare a trading and profit and loss account for the nine months ended 31 December 19X5 for Strongcolour Fabrics. (8 marks)

(b) Prepare a trading and profit and loss account for the three months ended 31 March 19X6 for Allcolour Cloths. (8 marks)

(c) Prepare a balance sheet as at 31 March 19X6 for Allcolour Cloths.
(9 marks)
(Total 25 marks)

8.4 PETER JAMES AND ANGUS VICTOR (D86)

The following list of balances as at 30 September 19X6 has been extracted from the books of Peter James and Angus Victor who are trading in partnership.

		£
Freehold property:	at cost at 30 September 19X5	30,000
	provision for depreciation at 30 September 19X5	6,000
Fixtures and fittings:	at cost at 30 September 19X5	18,000
	provision for depreciation at 30 September 19X5	9,600
Stock at 30 September 19X6		11,000
Debtors		4,600
Creditors		5,800
Balance at bank		2,700
Gross profit		39,000
Establishment and administrative expenses		9,100
Sales and distribution expenses		13,000

		£
Capital accounts at 30 September 19X5:	Peter James	25,000
	Angus Victor	15,000
Current accounts at 30 September 19X5:	Peter James	6,000 credit
	Angus Victor	2,300 debit
Loan from Peter James		10,000
Drawings: Peter James		15,700
Angus Victor		10,000

Additional information for the year ended 30 September 19X6:

(1) Interest at the rate of 10% per annum is payable annually in arrears on the loan from Peter James; the loan was received on 1 April 19X6.

(2) All sales produce a uniform rate of gross profit.

(3) Provision is to be made for depreciation as follows:

Freehold property	5%	per annum on cost
Fixtures and fittings	10%	per annum on cost

(4) Electricity charges accrued due at 30 September 19X6 amounted to £360.

Note: The electricity charges are included in establishment and administrative expenses.

(5) 2/3rds of sales took place in the second half of the year.

(6) No provision has been made in the accounts for a sales commission of 2% of gross profit payable to sales staff as from 1 April 19X6.

(7) Provision is to be made for a salary of £10,000 per annum to be credited to Angus Victor as from 1 April 19X6.

(8) Partners are to be credited with interest on the balances of their capital accounts at the rate of 5% per annum.

Required

(a) Prepare the profit and loss account and profit and loss appropriation partnership account for the year ended 30 September 19X6. (12 marks)

(b) Prepare the partnership balance sheet as at 30 September 19X6. (10 marks)

(c) Indicate one significant matter revealed in the accounting statements prepared which should be brought to the attention of the partners. (3 marks)
(Total 25 marks)

8.5 TWIGG AND BRANCH (J87)

The following summarised trial balance as at 31 December 19X6 has been extracted from the books of John Twigg and Raymond Branch trading as Treetop Stores.

	£	£
Fixed assets	55,000	
Current assets	30,000	
Current liabilities		17,000
Capital accounts: John Twigg at 1 January 19X6		25,000
Raymond Branch at 1 July 19X6		10,000
Net profit for the year ended 31 December 19X6		42,000
Drawings: John Twigg	4,000	
Raymond Branch	5,000	
	94,000	94,000

Raymond Branch was admitted as a partner on 1 July 19X6 when he paid into the business bank account £20,000 for the credit of his capital account. Unfortunately, only £10,000 was credited to his capital account, the balance was credited to the sales account. After the preparation of the above trial balance, it has been discovered that accounting entries have not been made for the following matters agreed upon the admission of Raymond Branch as a partner:

(1) The valuation of land owned by John Twigg and included in the business accounts should be increased by £5,000.

(2) Goodwill was valued at £17,000; however it is agreed that a goodwill account should not be opened in the business books.

(3) John Twigg's capital account balance as from 1 July 19X6 should be £35,000 credit, any excess being transferred to a John Twigg loan account.

The partnership agreement provides for:

(1) Interest at 10% per annum to be credited to partners for any loans to the business.

(2) Raymond Branch to be credited with a partner's salary of £9,000 per annum.

(3)   Interest at 5% per annum to be credited to partners on the balances of their capital accounts.

(4)   The balance of profits and losses to be divisible between John Twigg and Raymond Branch in the proportions 3/5ths and 2/5ths respectively.

Note: It can be assumed that the net profit shown in the above trial balance accumulated uniformly throughout 19X6.

Required

(a)   Prepare the capital accounts of John Twigg and Raymond Branch up to 31 December 19X6. **Note:** Assume that current accounts are being maintained for each partner.   (13 marks)

(b)   Prepare the partnership profit and loss appropriation account for the period from 1 July to 31 December 19X6.   (12 marks)
(Total 25 marks)

8.6   RIVER, STREAM AND POOL (D87)

The following trial balance as at 30 September 19X7 has been extracted from the books of River, Stream and Pool who are trading in partnership.

	£	£
Freehold land and buildings – net book value	42,000	
Fixtures and fittings – net book value	16,000	
Stock	9,000	
Debtors	6,000	
Balance at bank	2,000	
Creditors		7,000
Capital accounts as at 1 October 19X6:		
River		30,000
Stream		20,000
Pool		15,000
Current accounts as at 1 October 19X6:		
River		1,000
Stream		700
Pool		–
Drawings:		
River	21,000	
Steam	13,000	
Pool	11,000	
Net profit for the year ended 30 September 19X7 per draft accounts		46,300
	120,000	120,000

Pool joined River and Stream in partnership on 1 October 19X6 under an agreement which included the following terms.

(1)   Pool to introduce £15,000 cash to be credited to his capital account.

(2)   The goodwill of the business of River and Stream as at 1 October 19X6 to be valued at £28,000, but a goodwill account is not to be opened.

(3)   The value of the stock of River and Stream as at 1 October 19X6 to be reduced from £9,000 to £7,000.

(4)   £10,000 is to be transferred on 1 October 19X6 from Rivers' capital account to the credit of a loan account; River to be credited with interest at the rate of 10% per annum on his loan account balance.

(5)   Pool to be credited with a partner's salary of £11,000 per annum.

(6)   Interest at the rate of 5% per annum to be credited to partners in respect of their adjusted capital account balances at 1 October 19X6.

(7)   The balances of profits and losses to be shared between River, Stream and Pool in the ratio 5:3:2 respectively.

It now transpires that effect has not yet been given to the above terms 2 and 7 inclusive in the partnership books.

Up to 30 September 19X6, River and Stream had no formal partnership agreement.

Required

(a)   Prepare the partnership profit and loss appropriation account for the year ended 30 September 19X7.
(8 marks)

(b)   Prepare the partners' capital and current accounts for the year ended 30 September 19X7.
(17 marks)
(Total 25 marks)

8.7   BELL, RING AND GONG (J89)

Bell, Ring and Gong who traded separately for several years decided to form a partnership on 1 April 19X8 and transferred all the assets and liabilities of their individual businesses to the partnership at that date.

Whilst the assets and liabilities brought into the partnership have been recorded in the partnership books of account at agreed valuations, it has now been discovered that recognition has not been given in the partnership books for the goodwill as at 1 April 19X8 of the businesses transferred to the partnership, ie:

	£
Bell	8,000
Ring	12,000
Gong	16,000

At the same time, it must be noted that the partners do not want a goodwill account to be maintained in the partnership books.

The partnership agreement provides for partners to be credited with interest on their capital account balances at the rate of 10% per annum, Ring and Gong to be credited with partners' salaries of £10,000 and £13,000 per annum respectively and the balance of profits and losses to be shared between Bell, Ring and Gong in the ratio 5:3:2 respectively.

The following trial balance as at 31 March 19X9 has been extracted from the partnership accounts:

	£	£
Freehold land and buildings		
At valuation	50,000	
Provision for depreciation		1,250
Plant and machinery		
At valuation	21,000	
Provision for depreciation		2,100
Motor vehicles		
At valuation	12,000	
Provision for depreciation		3,000
Stock	9,000	
Debtors	4,000	
Balance at bank	600	
Creditors		5,250
Capital accounts		
Bell		40,000
Ring		20,000
Gong		14,000
Drawings		
Bell	13,000	
Ring	11,000	
Gong	9,000	
Net profit for the year ended 31 March 19X9		44,000
	129,600	129,600

Additional information

(1) It is agreed that a current account be opened for each partner.

(2) On 1 October 19X8, by agreement between the partners, Ring acquired from the partnership a motor vehicle at a valuation of £2,000 – this vehicle was valued at £2,400 at 1 April 19X8. Entries have not yet been made in the partnership books for this transfer which is to be debited to the partner's drawings account.

(3) There have been no additions to any fixed assets since the commencement of the partnership.

(4) The partners have decided that depreciation is to be provided on the straight–line basis as follows:

	% per annum
Freehold land and buildings	2½
Plant and machinery	10
Motor vehicles	25

Required

(a) Prepare the partnership's profit and loss appropriation account for the year ended 31 March 19X9. (13 marks)

(b) Prepare the partnership's balance sheet as at 31 March 19X9. (12 marks)
(Total 25 marks)

8.8 A ABLE AND B BAKER (D88)

The summarised balance sheet as at 30 September 19X7 of A Able, wholesaler, was as follows:

	£
Fixed assets – freehold buildings, plant and machinery, at net book value	120,000
Net current assets	60,000
	180,000
Capital – A Able	£180,000

On 1 October 19X7, B Baker joined A Able in partnership and paid £70,000 into the partnership bank account for the credit of B Baker's capital account. Whilst all the fixed and net current assets of A Able at 30 September 19X7 were transferred to the partnership at book values, the business of A Able was valued at £220,000 at that date. It has been agreed that a goodwill account will not be opened in the partnership books.

The partnership agreement between Able and Baker provides for:

(1) £50,000 to be transferred from Able's capital account to a loan account on the commencement of the partnership; interest on the loan at the rate of 12½% per annum to be credited to Able's current account annually on 30 September for the preceding financial year.

(2) Interest at the rate of 10% per annum on partners' capital account balances to be credited to partners' current accounts annually on 30 September for the preceding financial year.

(3) Partners are to be credited with salaries as follows:

		£
A Able:	Up to 31 March 19X8	12,000 per annum
	From 31 March 19X8	9,000 per annum
B Baker:	From 1 October 19X7	10,500 per annum

(4) The balance of profits and losses to be shared between the partners as follows:

A Able 3.5ths   B Baker 2/5ths

The gross profit arose uniformly throughout the year ended 30 September 19X8 and amounted to £90,000. During the year, establishment expenses totalled £15,000 and sales and distribution expenses £24,000; 2/3rds of these expenses relate to the first six months of the financial year ended 30 September 19X8.

Partners' drawings during the year ended 30 September 19X8 were:

	£
A Able	21,000
B Baker	16,000

Required

(a) Prepare the profit and loss account for the year ended 30 September 19X8.

(10 marks)

(b) Prepare the partners' capital accounts for the year ended 30 September 19X8. (6 marks)

(c) Prepare the partners' current accounts for the year ended 30 September 19X8. (9 marks)

(Total 25 marks)

8.9 CLIVE ABEL (D89)

Clive Abel, a long established sole trader, was joined in partnership on 1 April 19X9 by John McBain.

The partnership agreement includes the following provisions:

(1) The accounting records of Clive Abel are to continue in use for the partnership.

(2) The goodwill of Clive Abel's business at 31 March 19X9 was valued at £16,000; a goodwill account is not to be opened in the partnership books.

(3) On 1 April 19X9, John McBain transferred to the partnership as capital a freehold building valued at £50,000.

(4) A capital account and a current account is to be maintained for each partner.

(5) Clive Abel is to be credited with a partner's salary of £8,000 per annum.

(6) Interest at the rate of 5% per annum is to be provided on partners' capital accounts.

(7) The balance of net profits and losses is to be shared between Clive Abel and John McBain in the ratio 3.2 respectively.

(8) John McBain made a loan to the partnership of £12,000 on 1 April 19X9, interest being payable annually in arrears on 31 March at the rate of 10% per annum.

(9) The accounting year end of the partnership is to be 30 September, the same as that of Clive Abel.

The following balances, in addition to those of John McBain's capital and loan accounts, were extracted from the partnership books at 30 September 19X9.

	£
Freehold building at valuation at 1 April 19X9	50,000
Fixtures and fittings – at cost at 1 October 19X8	94,000
provision for depreciation at 1 October 19X8	28,200
Stock at 1 October 19X8	32,000
Debtors	34,410
Balance at bank	15,171
Creditors	19,380
Clive Abel – Capital account at 1 October 19X8	65,000
Drawings – Clive Abel (all after 1 April 19X9)	10,610
– John McBain	9,000
Sales	396,090
Purchases	286,500
Establishment expenses	16,450
Administrative expenses	9,310
Sales and distribution expenses	13,219

Additional information for the year ended 30 September 19X9:

(1) Establishment expenses accrued due at 30 September 19X9 amounted to £1,020 and sales and distribution expenses prepaid at that date totalled £364.

(2) Depreciation is to be provided at the following annual rates on the cost or valuation of fixed assets:

	%
Freehold buildings	2
Fixtures and fittings	10

(3) Two thirds of the turnover occurred in the first six months of the year.

(4) All sales throughout the year achieved a uniform rate of gross profit.

(5) Establishment expenses and administrative expenses were incurred uniformly throughout the year.

(6) Sales and distribution expenses were incurred in proportion to turnover.

(7) Stock at 30 September 19X9 was valued at £25,100.

Required

Prepare the following:

(a) The trading and profit and loss account for the six months ended 31 March 19X9 of Clive Abel. (5 marks)

(b) The trading and profit and loss appropriation account for the six months ended 30 September 19X9 of Clive Abel and John McBain. (8 marks)

(c) The balance sheet as at 30 September 19X9 of Clive Abel and John McBain. (12 marks)

Notes

(1) Make and state any necessary assumptions.

(2) Clive Abel's net profit or loss for the six months ended 31 March 1989 is to be transferred to his capital account which will become his partnership capital account.

(Total 25 marks)

8.10 STONE, PEBBLE AND BRICK (J90)

Owing to staff illnesses, the draft final accounts for the year ended 31 March 19X0 of Messrs Stone, Pebble and Brick, trading in partnership as the Bigtime Building Supply Company, have been prepared by an inexperienced, but keen, clerk. The draft summarised balance sheet as at 31 March 19X0 is as follows:

	£	£
Tangible fixed assets: at cost less depreciation to date		45,400
Current assets	32,290	
Less: Trade creditors	6,390	
		25,900
		71,300

Represented by:	Stone £	Pebble £	Brick £	Total £
Capital accounts: at 1 April 19W9	26,000	18,000	16,000	60,000
Capital accounts:				
Share of net profit for the year ended 31 March 19X0	12,100	12,100	12,100	
Drawings year ended 31 March 19X0	(8,200)	(9,600)	(7,200)	
At 31 March 19X0	3,900	2,500	4,900	11,300
				71,300

The partnership commenced on 1 April 19W9 when each of the partners introduced, as their partnership capital, the net tangible fixed and current assets of their previously separate businesses. However, it has not been discovered that contrary to what was agreed, no adjustments were made in the partnership books for the goodwill of the partners' former businesses now incorporated in the partnership. The agreed valuations of goodwill at 1 April 19W9 are as follows:

	£
Stone's business	30,000
Pebble's business	20,000
Brick's business	16,000

It is agreed that a goodwill account should not be opened in the partnership's books. It has now been discovered that effect has not been given in the accounts to the following provisions in the partnership agreement effective from 1 January 19X0.

(1) Stone's capital to be reduced to £20,000 the balance being transferred to a loan account upon which interest at the rate of 11% per annum will be paid on 31 December each year.

(2) Partners to be credited with interest on their capital account balances at the rate of 5% per annum.

(3) Brick to be credited with a partner's salary at the rate of £8,500 per annum.

(4) The balance of the net profit or loss to be shared between Stone, Pebble and Brick in the ratio 5:3:2 respectively.

0042V

Notes

(1)   It can be assumed that the net profit indicated in the draft accounts accrued uniformly throughout the year.

(2)   It has been agreed between the partners that no adjustments should be made for any partnership goodwill as at 1 January 19X0.

Required

(a)   Prepare the profit and loss appropriation account for the year ended 31 March 19X0.   (10 marks)

(b)   Prepare a corrected statement of the partners' capital and current accounts for inclusion in the partnership balance sheet as at 31 March 19X0.

(15 marks)
(Total 25 marks)

8.11   BRICK AND STONE (D90)

The following list of balances as at 30 September 19Y0 has been extracted from the books of Brick and Stone, trading in partnership, sharing the balance of profits and losses in the proportions 3 : 2 respectively.

	£
Printing, stationery and postages	3,500
Sales	322,100
Stock in hand at 1 October 19X9	23,000
Purchases	208,200
Rent and rates	10,300
Heat and light	8,700
Staff salaries	36,100
Telephone charges	2,900
Motor vehicle running costs	5,620
Discounts allowable	950
Discounts receivable	370
Sales returns	2,100
Purchases returns	6,100
Carriage inwards	1,700
Carriage outwards	2,400
Fixtures and fittings	
at cost	26,000
provision for depreciation	11,200
Motor vehicles	
at cost	46,000
provision for depreciation	25,000
Provision for doubtful debts	300
Drawings	
Brick	24,000
Stone	11,000
Current account balances at 1 October 19X9	
Brick	3,600 credit
Stone	2,400 credit
Capital account balances at 1 October 19X9	
Brick	33,000
Stone	17,000
Debtors	9,300
Creditors	8,400
Balance at bank	7,700

Additional information

(1)   £10,000 is to be transferred from Brick's capital account to a newly opened Brick loan account on 1 July 19Y0.

Interest at 10% per annum on the loan is to be credited to Brick.

(2)   Stone is to be credited with a salary at the rate of £12,000 per annum from 1 April 19Y0.

(3)   Stock in hand at 30 September 19Y0 has been valued at cost at £32,000.

(4)   Telephone charges accrued due at 30 September 19Y0 amounted to £400 and rent of £600 prepaid at that date.

(5)   During the year ended 30 September 19Y0, Stone has taken goods costing £1,000 for his own use.

(6)   Depreciation is to be provided at the following annual rates on the straight-line basis:

Fixtures and fittings	10%
Motor vehicles	20%

Required

(a)   Prepare a trading and profit and loss account for the year ended 30 September 19Y0.   (13 marks)

(b)   Prepare a balance sheet as at 30 September 19Y0 which should include summaries of the partners' capital and current accounts for the year ended on that date.   (12 marks)

(Note: In both (a) and (b) vertical forms of presentation should be used.)
                                                                                        (Total 25 marks)

Questions

9   THE ACCOUNTS OF LIMITED COMPANIES

9.1   IMP PLC

Imp plc makes up its accounts to 30 June in each year. The following list of balances was compiled from the company's books on 30 June 19X4.

	£	£
Ordinary share capital		250,000
General reserve		40,000
Profit and Loss Account, balance as on 30 June 19X3		93,000
Goodwill at cost	50,000	
Freehold land and buildings at cost	100,000	
Unquoted investments at cost	27,500	
Quoted investments at cost (market value, £13,492)	12,400	
Provision for doubtful debts		2,340
Provision for depreciation on motor cars, 30 June 19X3		24,250
Motor cars at cost	54,000	
Stock on hand 30 June 19X4 at cost	176,480	
Debtors	72,260	
Creditors and accrued expenses		56,492
Balance at bank	130,670	
Trading profit (before adjustments) for the year ended 30 June 19X4		153,278
Income from investments:		
Unquoted	2,750	
Quoted		1,200
	623,310	623,310

You are also given the following information.

(a)   Provision is required for:

    (i)   doubtful debts to give a total of 5% on outstanding debtors;

    (ii)   depreciation for the year on motor cars at 25% on cost;

    (iii)   directors' fees of £2,500 for the chairman and £2,000 for the managing director.

(b)   Corporation tax based on the profits for the year ended 30 June 19X4 is estimated at £70,000.

(c)   The turnover of the company for the year ended 30 June 19X4 amounted to £1,086,000.

(d)   The directors recommend payment of an ordinary dividend of 20%.

(e)   Net operating expenses (before adjustments) are made up as follows:

Distribution expenses	£50,654
Administration expenses	£56,708

Required

Prepare the company's accounts for the year ended 30 June 19X4 comprising a profit and loss account and balance sheet.

(25 marks)

0043V

9.2   MARMADUKE LTD

The following is the trial balance of Marmaduke Ltd on 31 December 19X5.

	£	£
Issued share capital		21,000
(ordinary shares of £1 each)		
Freehold properties, at cost	37,500	
Motor vans, at cost	1,250	
Provision for depreciation on motor vans to 31 December 19X4		500
Administration expenses	4,200	
Selling expenses	4,625	
Stock, 31 December 19X4	6,000	
Purchases	69,375	
Sales		103,250
Directors' remuneration (50% administration : 50% selling and distribution)	12,500	
Rents receivable		1,800
Investments, at cost	3,375	
Investment income		170
7% Debentures		7,500
Debenture interest	525	
Bank interest	291	
Bank overdraft		575
Debtors and creditors	15,500	12,050
Interim dividend paid	630	
Profit and loss account, 31 December 19X4		8,926
	155,771	155,771

You ascertain the following.

(1)   All the motor vans were purchased during 19X3. Depreciation has been, and is to be, provided at the rate of 25% per annum on cost. On 31 December 19X5 one van, purchased on 1 January 19X3, costing £450, was sold for £275, as part settlement of the price of £400 of a new van, but no entries with regard to these transactions were made in the books, and the balance was still owing to the garage at 31 December 19X5. The vans are used for deliveries.

(2)   The estimated corporation tax liability for the year to 31 December 19X5 is £6,350.

(3)   It is proposed to pay a final dividend of 10% for the year to 31 December 19X5.

(4)   Stock at the lower of cost or net realisable value on 31 December 19X5 is £8,350.

(5)   It is expected that the investments will be sold during 19X6.

Required

Prepare, without taking into account the relevant statutory provisions:

(a)   a profit and loss account for the year ended 31 December 19X5;
(b)   a balance sheet at that date.

(25 marks)

9.3 ALPHA CO LTD

The Alpha Co Ltd, a retail business, has an authorised share capital of 200,000 £1 ordinary shares and 250,000 8% £1 redeemable preference shares.

The trial balance of that company as at 31 December 19X5 (after preparing the trading and profit and loss account) was as follows.

	£
Provision for depreciation	
Fittings	75,000
Vehicles	187,000
Goodwill	60,000
Issued share capital	
100,000 £1 ordinary shares	100,000
250,000 8% £1 redeemable preference shares	250,000
Share premium account	20,000
Trade debtors and prepayments	85,400
Land and buildings at valuation (cost £220,000)	270,000
Capital redemption reserve fund	150,000
Fittings at cost	175,000
Motor vehicles at cost	397,000
10% debentures	80,000
Trade creditors and accruals	48,000
Short term investments (market value £43,000)	39,000
Stock at 31 December 19X5	148,000
Bank overdraft	27,000
Revaluation reserve	50,000
Net profit for the year	72,000
Undistributed profit at 1 January 19X5	73,000
General reserve	55,000
Provision for doubtful debts	2,400
Interim dividends paid	
Ordinary	5,000
Preference	10,000

The directors wish to:

(i)   transfer £25,000 to general reserve;
(ii)   provide for a 5% final ordinary dividend, and the final preference dividend;
(iii) write £20,000 off the goodwill account.

Required

(a)   Prepare in good form the appropriate account of the Alpha Co Limited for the year ended 31 December 19X5 and a balance sheet as at that date. (Ignore taxation.)   (15 marks)

(b)   Write a short response to the following questions based on the above accounts:

    (i)   When can the company issue the balance of its share capital?

    (ii)   What is the return on net capital employed (after making adjustment for debenture interest)? What is the significance of this figure?

    (iii) What is the company's working capital and what is the importance of this?

(iv) How could the 'goodwill' have arisen?

(v) Assuming the company had the cash, what is the maximum amount which could be distributed by way of dividend?

(vi) Why should the market value of the ordinary shares differ from their book value?

(vii) What is the significance of the 'share premium' account?   (10 marks)
(Total 25 marks)

9.4   ARAD LTD

Arad Ltd, a wholesale distributor, makes up its accounts each year to 31 March. The following balances have been extracted from the company's books as on 31 March 19X4.

	£	£
Share capital (authorised 20,000 shares of £1 each)		8,500
Cash in hand	85	
Office furniture and fittings, at cost	1,570	
Provision for depreciation to 31.3.X3		370
Purchases	85,640	
Sales		102,480
Bank overdraft		2,600
Motor vehicles, at cost	8,890	
Provision for depreciation to 31.3.X3		3,550
Stock 31.3.X3	6,900	
Rent and rates	835	
Lighting and heating	610	
Motor expenses	2,630	
Wages and salaries	6,950	
Trade expenses	1,627	
Repairs and renewals	380	
Bank charges and interest	143	
Provision for doubtful debts 31.3.X3		480
Trade debtors	14,980	
Trade creditors		7,460
Profit and loss account balance as on 31.3.X3		5,800
	131,240	131,240

You are also given the following information.

(1) Stocks in the warehouse on 31 March 19X4, at cost, amounted to £8,670.

(2) Debtors and sales include goods supplied on sale or return amounting to £480. The cost of these goods was £400 and on 31 March 19X4, half had been sold by the customer.

(3) Motor expenses include licences for the year ended 31 December 19X4: £160.

(4) Provision is to be made for:

(i) accrued repairs and renewals £100, trade expenses £95 and audit fees £180;

(ii) depreciation on motor vehicles and office equipment at 20% and 10% on written down values respectively;

(iii) a staff bonus of 10% on sales in excess of £100,000.

(5) Debts for which provision has been made amounting to £400 are to be written off and the provision for doubtful debts to be subsequently increased to 5% of the trade debtors.

(6) The estimated corporation tax liability for the year is £1,200.

Required

Prepare, for admission to management:

(a) detailed trading and profit and loss accounts for the year ended 31 March 19X4;   (12 marks)

(b) balance sheet as on 31 March 19X4.   (13 marks)
                                                                    (Total 25 marks)

9.5 **PRIME PRODUCTS LTD (D86)**

The following draft sheet as at 30 September 19X6 of Prime Products Ltd has been prepared by the company's assistant accountant:

	Cost	Aggregate depreciation	Net book value
Fixed assets	£	£	£
Plant and machinery	31,000	19,375	11,625
Motor vehicles	17,000	10,200	6,800
	48,000	29,575	18,425
Current assets			
Stock	Over-valued 6000	12,400	
Trade debtors and prepayments	400) —	9,600	
Balance at bank	9200	3,900	
		25,900	
Less: Current liabilities			
Creditors and accrued charges		5,100	
			20,800
			39,225

	£
Financed by:	
Share capital – ordinary shares of £1 each, full paid	20,000
Share premium account	5,000
Reserves – General	10,000
Retained earnings	4,225
	39,225

The following discoveries were made after the preparation of the above balance sheet:

(1) No entry has been made in the company's accounts for bank charges of £150 debited in the company's bank statements on 25 September 19X6.

(2) The draft accounts prepayments figure of £400 does not include insurance premiums of £300 prepaid at 30 September 19X6.

(3) A significant casting error has now been found in the stock valuation sheets of 30 September 19X5. As a result, the stock valuation at 30 September 19X5 should have been £16,000 not £10,000 as included in the company's published accounts for the year ended 30 September 19X5.

(4) On 1 September 19X6, the company forwarded goods costing £1,200 to John Peters of Aberdeen on a sale or return basis. None of these goods were sold by John Peters until late October 19X6. However, in preparing the draft accounts for the year ended 30 September 19X6 of Prime Products Ltd it was assumed that all the goods sent to John Peters had been sold.

Note: Prime Products Ltd obtains a gross profit of 25% on all sales.

(5) No entries have been made in the company's accounts for a bonus (scrip) issue of ordinary shares on 10 September 19X6 involving the issue of one ordinary share of £1 for every four ordinary shares previously held.

Note: It is the company's policy to maintain the maximum flexibility so far as the availability of reserves for the payment of dividends are concerned.

(6) It has now been decided to introduce a provision for doubtful debts of 2½% of trade debtors at 30 September 19X6.

(7) A bonus of 1% of gross profit is payable to the sales manager for all sales of the company on or after 1 October 19X5; the bonus is payable annually on 30 November for the immediately preceding accounting year. Provision was made for this bonus in the preparation of the draft accounts for the year ended 30 September 19X6.

Required

Prepare a corrected balance sheet as at 30 September 19X6 of Prime Products Ltd.

(25 marks)

0043V

9.6   BROADBENT LTD (D87)

Alan Smith is a director of Broadbent Ltd, for which he receives an annual salary of £15,000, and owns half the share capital of the company. Alan's brother Norman is trading in partnership with Joseph Pain; under the partnership agreement Norman receives a partner's salary of £15,000 per annum and 50% of the balance of the net profit or net loss. The partners withdraw from the partnership all partners' salaries and all shares of profits immediately these are computed on the last day of the relevant financial period. It is generally agreed that Norman Smith's services to the partnership business are worth £16,000 per annum. The summarised balance sheets as at 31 October 19X7 of the company and partnership are as follows.

Broadbent Ltd

	£
Net assets	160,000
Capital – Ordinary Shares of 50p each fully paid	100,000
Retained Profits	60,000
	160,000

Notes

(1)   Provision has been made in the accounts for the year ended 31 October 19X7 for a proposed final dividend of 10p per share.

Note: The company does not pay interim dividends.

(2)   The company's net profit, after tax, for the year ended 31 October 19X7 is £26,000.

(3)   Broadbent Ltd did not issue any shares during the year ended 31 October 19X7.

Norman Smith and Joseph Pain trading in partnership

	£
Net assets	160,000
Capital accounts	
Norman Smith	80,000
Joseph Pain	80,000
	160,000

Note: The net profit for the year ended 31 October 19X7 of the partnership is £36,000.

Required

(a)   Prepare the summarised balance sheet as at 31 October 19X6 of Broadbent Ltd.

(7 marks)

(b) Prepare statements of the financial benefits which each of Alan and Norman Smith received from their respective businesses for the year ended 31 October 19X7. (6 marks)

(c) Assuming that the partnership had been a limited company during the year ended 31 October 19X7, paying market salary rates for all its staff, prepare a statement of its net profit for that year. (6 marks)

(d) Alan Smith has the opportunity to convert his shareholding in Broadbent Ltd into £50,000 10% Loan Stock in the company.

Using appropriate computations as necessary, advise Alan Smith of the advantages and disadvantages to him of converting his shareholding to loan stock. (6 marks)

(Total 25 marks)

9.7 LOWDALE LTD (D90)

The following trial balance as at 30 November 19Y0 has been extracted from the books of Lowdale Ltd.

	£	£
Land and buildings		
At cost	100,000	
Provision for depreciation		32,000
Plant and machinery		
At cost	74,000	
Provision for depreciation		26,000
Motor vehicles		
At cost	28,000	
Provision for depreciation		15,000
Stocks		
Raw materials	19,400	
Finished goods	10,808	
Debtors		
Trade	43,800	
Prepayments and accrued income	3,092	
Cash in hand	7,900	
Trade creditors		18,900
Bank overdraft		7,300
Accrued expenditure		1,800
10% loan stock 2000/05		40,000
Ordinary share capital		
50p ordinary shares fully paid		80,000
Share premium account		20,000
General reserve		22,000
Profit and loss account		23,100
Suspense account		900
	287,000	287,000

Additional information

(1) It has now been decided to create a provision for doubtful debts as at 30 November 19Y0 of £1,500.

(2) Plant and machinery additions acquired on 1 December 19X9 at a cost of £10,000 have been debited to the land and buildings at cost account.

Notes

1   It is the company's policy to provide depreciation annually as follows:

Land and buildings
    Land   Not depreciated.
    Buildings   2% per annum on the reducing-balance basis.
Plant and machinery   12½% per annum on the straight-line basis.
Motor vehicles   25% per annum on the straight-line basis.

2   Land at cost of £20,000 is included in land and buildings at cost.

3   Depreciation for the year ended 30 November 19Y0 has been provided in all cases where necessary before the above trial balance was extracted.

(3)   Finished goods stocks are included at selling price in the above trial balance. (**Note:** A gross profit of 40% is obtained on the cost of all goods sold.)

(4)   A cheque payment of £1,300 in October 19Y0 to K Dart, a trade creditor, has been recorded correctly in the cash book but not posted to the creditors (or purchases) ledger control account.

(5)   Establishment expenses accrued charges at 30 November 19Y0 have been recorded correctly in the appropriate expenditure account but added to prepayments and accrued income instead of accrued expenditure. As a result of the correction for this item, the suspense account is cleared.

(6)   It is now proposed to recommend a final dividend of 10p per share for the year ended 30 November 19Y0.

Notes

1   The draft trading and profit and loss account for the year ended 30 November 19Y0 and draft balance sheet as at that date have been prepared already, but do not take into account any of the items of additional information above.

2   Ignore advance corporation tax.

Required

(a)   Prepare the journal entries to correct for items (3), (5) and (6) above. (**Note:** Narratives are required.)　　　　　　　　　　　　(8 marks)

(b)   Prepare the corrected balance sheet as at 30 November 19Y0. (**Note:** The balance sheet should be presented in good form, but need not comply with the requirements of the Companies Acts.)　　　　　　　　(17 marks)
　　　　　　　　　　　　　　　　　　　　　　　　　　(Total 25 marks)

10 ACCOUNTING RATIOS AND INTERPRETATION

10.1 K GEORGE

The following extracts relate to K George's accounts for the year to 31 August 19X4.

Trading and profit and loss account for the year ended 31 August 19X4

	£	£
Sales (all credit)		100,000
Less: Cost of goods sold:		
Opening stock	10,000	
Purchases	52,000	
	62,000	
Less: Closing stock	12,000	
		50,000
Gross profit		50,000
Less: Expenses		25,000
Net profit		25,000

Balance sheet at 31 August 19X4

	£	£
Fixed assets		
Machinery at cost		30,000
Less: Depreciation		12,000
		18,000
Current assets		
Stocks	12,000	
Trade debtors	7,000	
Bank	1,000	
	20,000	
Less: Current liabilities		
Trade creditors	5,000	
		15,000
		33,000
Financed by	£	£
Capital		18,000
Net profit for the year	25,000	
Less: Drawings	10,000	
		15,000
		33,000

Required

Calculate the following accounting ratios:

(a) gross profit;
(b) mark–up on cost of goods sold;
(c) net profit on sales;
(d) return on capital employed;
(e) stock turnover;
(f) debtor collection period;
(g) current ratio; and
(h) quick (or acid test).   (25 marks)

10.2 WHITE AND BLACK

White and Black are sole traders. Both are wholesalers dealing in a similar range
of goods. Summaries of the profit calculations and balance sheets for the same
year have been made available to you, as follows:

Profit and loss accounts for the year	White £'000	White £'000	Black £'000	Black £'000
Sales		600		800
Cost of goods sold		450		624
		150		176
Administration expenses	64		63	
Selling and distribution expenses	28		40	
Depreciation				
Equipment and vehicles	10		20	
Buildings	—	102	5	128
		48		48

Balance sheets as at end of the year	White £'000	White £'000	Black £'000	Black £'000
Buildings		29		47
Equipment and vehicles		62		76
Stock		56		52
Debtors		75		67
Bank balance		8		
		230		242
Creditors	38		78	
Bank balance	–		4	
		38		82
Capital		192		160

Required

Compare the performance and position of the two businesses on the basis of the
above figures, supporting your comments where appropriate with ratios and noting
what further information you would need before reaching firmer conclusions.

(25 marks)

10.3   HARCOURT LTD

The following summarised financial statements pertain to the earnings and financial position of Harcourt Co Ltd for the financial years ended 31 December 19X5, 19X6, and 19X7.

Comparative profit and loss accounts
for the year ended 31 December 19X5, 19X6 and 19X7

	19X7 £'000	19X6 £'000	19X5 £'000
Sales	10,000	9,000	8,000
Cost of goods sold	6,500	5,580	4,800
Gross profit	3,500	3,420	3,200
Selling expenses	500	450	400
Administrative expenses	1,400	860	720
Total expenses	1,900	1,310	1,120
Net profit before tax	1,600	2,110	2,080
Taxation	960	1,266	1,248
Net profit after tax	640	844	832

Comparative balance sheets as at 31 December 19X5, 19X6 and 19X7

	19X7 £'000	19X6 £'000	19X5 £'000
Assets			
Current assets	500	600	750
Long-term investment	100	200	250
Plant and equipment (net)	5,500	3,500	2,500
	6,100	4,300	3,500
Liabilities and capital			
Current liabilities	400	300	250
Long-term liabilities	1,900	1,000	500
Capital (ordinary £1 shares fully paid)	2,500	2,000	2,000
Undistributed profits	1,300	1,000	750
	6,100	4,300	3,500

Required

(a)   Compute the following for each of the three years:

   (i)   net working capital;
   (ii)   current ratio;
   (iii)   debt/equity ratio.

(5 marks)

0043V

(b)   Express the profit and loss account data in percentages of sales.

(5 marks)

(c)   Express the balance sheet data in trend percentages.   (5 marks)

(d)   Comment on the significance of the statements and ratios, and state the strengths and weaknesses revealed by your analysis.   (5 marks)
(Total 25 marks)

10.4   GORDON RAY (J86)

Gordon Ray is currently reviewing his results for the year ended 31 December 19X5 and comparing them with those of Smooth Dealers Ltd, a company engaged in the same trade.

The chairman of Smooth Dealers Ltd receives an annual salary of £12,000 for performing duties very similar to those performed by Gordon Ray in his business. The summarised final accounts for 19X5 of Gordon Ray and Smooth Dealers Ltd are as follows:

Trading and profit and loss accounts
for the year ended 31 December 19X5

Gordon Ray £'000		Smooth Dealers Ltd £'000
90	Turnover	150
48	Less: Cost of sales	80
42	Gross profit	70
12	Administrative expenses	37
15	Sales and distribution expenses	25
–	Debenture interest	3
27		65
15	Net profit	5

Balance sheets as at 31 December 19X5

Gordon Ray £'000			Smooth Dealers Ltd £'000
60	Fixed assets		50
28	Current assets:	Stock	56
22		Debtors	69
6		Balance at bank	10
56			135
16	Current liabilities:	Creditors	25
40	Net current assets		110
100	Net capital employed		160
100	Capital account		
		Ordinary share capital	80
		Retained earnings	50
		10% debenture stock	30
100			160

Required

(a) Calculate five appropriate ratios comparing the results of Gordon Ray with those of Smooth Dealers Ltd and briefly comment on each ratio.

(20 marks)

(b) Outline three distinct reasons why a comparison of the amount of profit earned by different businesses should be approached with great care.

(5 marks)
(Total 25 marks)

10.5   JAMES SIMPSON (D86)

The following are the summarised trading and profit loss accounts for the years ended 31 December 19X3, 19X4 and 19X5 and balance sheets as at 31 December 19X2, 19X3, 19X4 and 19X5 of James Simpson, a retail trader.

Trading and profit and loss accounts
years ended 31 December 19X3, 19X4 and 19X5

	19X3 £'000	19X4 £'000	19X5 £'000
Sales	100	120	140
Cost of sales	60	72	98
Gross profit	40	48	42
Expenses (including loan interest)	20 +12	30 +12	28 +12
Net profit	20 -12	18 -12	14 -12

Balance sheets as at 31 December 19X2, 19X3, 19X4 and 19X5

	19X2 £'000	19X3 £'000	19X4 £'000	19X5 £'000
Fixed assets	38	48	68	90
Current assets				
Stocks	14	16	20	29
Trade debtors	10	18	40	52
Balance at bank	9	13	39	16
	71	95	167	187
Financed by				
Capital at 1 January	51	67	87	105
Add: net profit for the year	16	20	18	14
	67	87	105	119
Loan (received 31 December 19X4)	–	–	50	50
Current liabilities – trade creditors	4	8	12	18
	71	95	167	187

Additional information

(1) James Simpson, a man of modest tastes, is the beneficiary of a small income from his grandfather and therefore has taken no drawings from his retail business.

(2) Interest of 10% per annum has been paid on the loan from 1 January 19X5.

(3) It is estimated that £12,000 per annum would have to be paid for the services rendered to the business by James Simpson.

(4) All sales are on a 30 days credit basis.

(5) James Simpson is able to invest in a bank deposit account giving interest at the rate of 8% per annum.

Required

(a) Calculate for each of the years ended 31 December 19X3, 19X4 and 19X5 the following financial ratios – return on gross capital employed:

  (i) acid or quick;
  (ii) stock turnover; and
  (iii) net profit to sales. (14 marks)

(b) Use two financial ratios (not referred to in (a) above) to draw attention to two aspects of the business which would appear to give cause for concern.
(4 marks)

(c) Advise James Simpson whether, on financial grounds, he should continue his retail business.

Note: Answers should include appropriate computations. (4 marks)

(d)   Advise James Simpson as to whether it was a financially sound decision to borrow £50,000 on 31 December 19X4.   (3 marks)

(Total 25 marks)

10.6   JOHN BRIGHT (J87)

John Bright has provided his son, Thomas, with all the capital required in the setting up of a business on 1 April 19X5 and its subsequent development. Thomas has now produced the following summarised accounts as a basis for discussing the business's progress with his father:

Trading and profit and loss accounts

Year ended	31 March 19X6 £'000	31 March 19X7 £'000
Sales	100	140
Cost of sales	60	90
Gross profit	40	50
Overheads: Variable	20	35
Fixed	12	16
	32	51
Net profit/(net loss)	8	(1)

Balance sheets

As at	1 April 19X5 £'000	31 March 19X6 £'000	31 March 19X7 £'000
Fixed assets	70	70	80
Net current assets			
Stock	5	7	8
Debtors	–	11	24
Bank balance/(overdraft)	13	2	(4)
(Creditors)	(3)	(5)	(8)
	15	15	20
Net capital employed	85	85	100

Thomas is keen for his father to increase the capital employed in the business and has drawn his father's attention to the following favourable matters revealed in the accounts.

(1)   A £15,000 increase in net capital employed can be linked with a £40,000 increase in sales during the past year.

(2)   The rate of stock turnover during the past year has been 12 as compared with 10 in the previous year.

(3) The increased fixed overheads last year is due to the renting of larger premises; however these new premises would be adequate for a turnover of £200,000.

John Bright is not pleased with the results of his son's business.

Thomas Bright can easily obtain employment offering a salary of £10,000 per annum and John Bright can obtain 10% per annum from a bank deposit account.

Required

(a) Calculate for each of the years ended 31 March 19X6 and 19X7, four financial ratios which draw attention to matters which could give John Bright cause for concern. **Note:** State clearly the formula or basis of each ratio used. (13 marks)

(b) Outline three reasons for closing the business and one reason in favour of its continuance. (6 marks)

(c) Outline the importance of distinguishing between fixed and variable overheads. (6 marks)
(Total 25 marks)

10.7 JOHN TIMPSON (D87)

John Timpson, an established retail trader, who is very pleased with the expansion of his business during the past financial year, has been warned by his accountant that he must not simply concentrate his attention on profit growth. John Timpson recognises that a legacy from his late father has made an important contribution to the recent development of his business.

The following summarised information relates to John Timpson's business during the years ended 30 September 19X6 and 19X7:

Summarised balance sheets

As at 30 September	19X6 £	19X6 £	19X7 £	19X7 £
Fixed Assets				
At cost		280,000		350,000
Less Depreciation provision		80,000		50,000
		200,000		300,000
Current Assets				
Stock	40,000		147,000	
Debtors	45,000		58,000	
Balance at bank	35,000		5,000	
	120,000		210,000	
Less: Current Liabilities Creditors	50,000	70,000	84,000	126,000
		270,000		426,000
Less: Long term loan – 10% pa		30,000		50,000
		240,000		376,000

Year ended 30 September	19X6 £	19X7 £
Sales	200,000	300,000
Gross profit	60,000	108,000
Net profit	30,000	37,600

Required

(a) Brief notes in support of John Timpson's optimistic view of the progress of his business. (12 marks)

(b) Brief notes in support of the accountant's warning concerning developments in John Timpson's business. (13 marks)

Note: Answers should be supported by the use of appropriate financial ratios.
(Total 25 marks)

10.8 JOAN STREET (J88)

The trading stock of Joan Street, retailer, has been reduced during the year ended 31 March 19X8 by £6,000 from its commencing figure of £21,000.

A number of financial ratios and related statistics have been compiled relating to the business of Joan Street for the year ended 31 March 19X8; these are shown below alongside comparative figures for a number of retailers who are members of the trade association to which Joan Street belongs:

	Joan Street %	Trade Association %
Net profit	15	16
Net capital employed		
Net profit	9	8
Sales		
Sales	$166\frac{2}{3}$	200
Net capital employed		
Fixed assets	45	35
Sales		
Working capital ratio:		
$\dfrac{\text{Current assets}}{\text{Current liabilities}}$	400	$287\frac{1}{2}$
Acid test ratio:		
$\dfrac{\text{Bank + debtors}}{\text{Current liabilities}}$	275	$187\frac{1}{2}$
Gross profit	25	26
Sales		
Debtors collection period:		
$\dfrac{\text{Debtors x 365}}{\text{Sales}}$	$36\frac{1}{2}$ days	$32\frac{17}{20}$ days
Stock turnover (based on average stock for the year)	10 times	8 times

Joan Street has supplied all the capital for her business and has had no drawings from the business during the year ended 31 March 19X8.

Required

(a) Prepare the trading and profit and loss account for the year ended 31 March 19X8 and balance sheet as at that date of Joan Street in as much detail as possible. (16 marks)

(b) Identify two aspects of Joan Street's results for the year ended 31 March 19X8 which compare favourably with the trade association's figures and identify two aspects which compare unfavourably. (4 marks)

(c) Outline two drawbacks of the type of comparison used in this question.
(5 marks)
(Total 25 marks)

10.9 GRAY PRODUCTS (J89)

John Street, who has £100,000 available for long-term investment, is very interested in purchasing an established business and wishes to receive a return on his investment comparable to the interest of 10% per annum which he obtains at present from a bank deposit account.

After much investigation, John Street is in the course of deciding which one of two businesses to purchase. The businesses are in the same trade and occupy similar premises which one of the businesses owns but the other business rents.

The following information has been obtained concerning the businesses under consideration by John Street:

	Mary Penney's business £	Gray Products Ltd's business £
Annual rent of premises (see note 2)	6,000	–
Manager's salary per annum (see note 2)	–	14,000
Directors' fees per annum (see note 2)	–	4,000
Net profit per accounts (see note 2)	28,000	22,000
Net capital employed per accounts	70,000	80,000
Premises at net book value	–	18,000
Premises at estimated current market value	–	35,000
Sale of price of business	100,000	125,000 (see note 4)

Additional information

(1) Mary Penney has been actively engaged in the running of her business.

(2) It is expected that the following items will be maintained for the foreseeable future at the amounts stated above:

> Annual rent of premise
> Manager's salary per annum
> Directors' fees per annum
> Net profit per accounts

(3) Gray's Products Ltd are able to rent premises suitable for their business at a similar rent to that paid by Mary Penney.

(4) The purchaser of the Gray's Products Ltd's business will become the owner of the share capital of the company; the company has no loan capital.

(5) John Street is currently employed as a sales representative at a salary of £16,000 per annum, and plans to continue in that employment.

Required

As financial consultant to John Street, advise him of the attractiveness of purchasing each of the two businesses mentioned above and conclude your report with a recommendation as to which business, if any, should be purchased.

Notes

(a) Reports should wherever possible be supported by computations.

(b) Ignore taxation.

(c) Make and state any necessary assumptions.   (25 marks)

10.10 JOYCE WALTERS (J90)

Joyce Walters, who has traded as a retailer since 31 March 19X8, has not kept an adequate set of accounting records.

However, after much research the following information has been obtained.

(1) Fixed assets brought into the business on 31 March 19X8:

		£
Freehold land	costing	30,000
Freehold buildings	costing	60,000
Motor vehicles	costing	12,000

(Note: The freehold land is used as a car park.)

(2) Trade debtors:

	£
As at 31 March 19X9	8,600
As at 31 March 19Y0	9,800

(3) Balance at bank:

	£
As at the commencement of the business on 31 March 19X8	4,800
As at 31 March 19X9	2,300
As at 31 March 19Y0	2,800

(4) Trade creditors:

	£
As at 31 March 19X9	13,800
As at 31 March 19Y0	3,900

(5)   Drawings:

	Cash £	Goods for own use at cost £
Year ended 31 March 19X9	9,000	8,500
Year ended 31 March 19Y0	9,400	13,000

(6)   Stock brought into the business on 31 March 19X8:

	£
At cost	14,000

(7)   Stock turnover rate, using the average of opening and closing stocks:

Year ended 31 March 19X9	8 times
Year ended 31 March 19Y0	10 times

(8)   Sales:

	£
Year ended 31 March 19X9	210,000
Year ended 31 March 19Y0	294,000

(9)   A uniform rate of gross profit of 40% on the cost of sales has been obtained throughout the two years to 31 March 19Y0.

(10) There have been no additions or disposals of fixed assets since 31 March 19X8.

(11) Depreciation is to be provided on fixed assets on the straight-line basis as follows:

Freehold building at 2½% per annum
Motor vehicles at 20% per annum

Required

(a)   Prepare Joyce Walters' balance sheets as at 31 March 19X8, 19X9 and 19Y0.
(19 marks)

(b)   Prepare a statement of Joyce Walters' net profit or loss for each of the years ended 31 March 19X9 and 19Y0.
(6 marks)
(Total 25 marks)

10.11   T CARR LTD (D90)

The summarised trading and profit and loss accounts for the three years ended 30 September 19X8, 19X9 and 19Y0 are as follows.

Trading and profit and loss accounts

Years ended 30 September	19X8		19X9		19Y0	
	£'000	£'000	£'000	£'000	£'000	£'000
Sales		120		180		270
Less: Cost of sales		80		135		216
Gross profit		40		45		54
Less: Overhead expenses						
Variable	18		27		27	
Fixed	10		10		20	
		28		37		47
Net profit		12		8		7

Balance sheets

As at 30 September	19X8		19X9		19Y0	
	£'000	£'000	£'000	£'000	£'000	£'000
Fixed assets		30		60		80
Current assets						
Stock	24		25		40	
Debtors	26		40		55	
Balance at bank	20		10		–	
	70		75		95	
Less: Current liabilities						
Creditors	20		35		45	
Bank overdraft	–		–		10	
	20		35		55	
		50		40		40
		80		100		120
Share capital						
Ordinary shares of £1		50		62		75
Retained earnings		30		38		45
		80		100		120

All the share capital of T Carr Ltd is owned by two brothers, James and Henry Carr, who have bought additional shares, at par, in the company in 19X9 and 19Y0. The company has not paid any dividends since 19X6.

The major objective of the company in each of the last two financial years has been to increase turnover by 50% on the immediately preceding year.

Questions

Required

(a) Prepare a table of four accounting ratios, each ratio showing a distinctly different aspect of changes in the company during the past three years.

Note: The ratios may be expressed as percentages. (10 marks)

(b) A brief, but reasoned, report addressed to James and Henry Carr concerning the advisability of the company continuing to concentrate on increasing turnover by 50% each year. (15 marks)
(Total 25 marks)

11 VAT

11.1 AK LTD

Using the information given below relating to AK Ltd you are required to:

(a) draft, with suitable layouts, the following analysed books of prime entry:

    (i) bank cash book;
    (ii) sales day book (net); and
    (iii) purchase day book (net);

(b) enter the balances at 31 January 19X2 in the appropriate ledger accounts;

(c) enter the undermentioned transactions for the month ended 28 February 19X2 in the books of prime entry;

(d) make the appropriate postings from the books of prime entry to the ledger accounts for the February 19X2 transactions; and

(e) list the balances on the ledger accounts and the bank cash book at 28 February 19X2, indicating whether these balances are debit or credit.

Some of the company's ledger account balances at 31 January 19X2 were:

	£
Bank cash book, balance in hand	21,831
General ledger	
Sales of product Y	20,000
Sales of product Z	30,000
Purchases of material W	10,000
Purchases of material X	15,000
Creditors for VAT	2,849
Debtors ledger control	64,000
Creditors ledger control	44,000
Salaries payroll control	–
Creditors for PAYE income tax	1,900
Creditor for National Insurance	1,240
Discount received	1,020
Discount allowed	1,118
Office salaries	10,000
National Insurance (company's contribution)	700
Plant and machinery at cost	294,000
Telephone	60

	£
Debtors ledger	
B Ltd	36,000
C and Co Ltd	28,000
Creditors ledger	
K & Sons	15,000
J Ltd	29,000

The following transactions occurred during February 19X2:

1st   Invoiced B Ltd with credit sales of £9,000 for product Y and £11,000 for product Z, plus VAT.

8th   Received a purchase invoice from K and Sons for credit purchases of £7,000 for material W and £9,000 for material X, plus VAT.

12th Invoiced C and Co Ltd with credit sales of £14,000 for product Y and £26,000 for product Z, plus VAT.

16th Received a purchase invoice from J Ltd for credit purchases of £14,000 for material W and £18,000 for material X, plus VAT.

19th Received a cheque from B Ltd for £29,318 in settlement of an account for £30,000.

20th Received a cheque from C and Co Ltd for £21,500 in settlement of an account for £22,000.

21st Drew a cheque for £14,660 payable to K and Sons in settlement of an account for £15,000.

21st Drew a cheque for £27,860 payable to J Ltd in settlement of an account for £28,500.

21st Drew cheques for:

VAT of £2,845
PAYE income tax of £1,900
National Insurance (employees' and company's contributions of £1,240)
Telephone account of £44, including VAT
A new machine costing £6,600, including VAT.

22nd Invoiced B Ltd with credit sales of £7,000 for product Y and £13,000 for product Z, plus VAT.

25th J Ltd issued a credit note to AK Ltd covering returns of material W £1,000 and material X £2,000, plus VAT.

26th Warrants totalling £14,000 were sent to the ordinary shareholders in respect of a dividend, and a cheque was drawn for £6,000 in respect of advance corporation tax.

28th Gross salaries earned in February amounted to £10,000 and employee deductions were £2,000 for PAYE income tax and £500 for National Insurance. The net salaries of £7,500 were transferred to the current accounts of the employees.

The company's contribution to National Insurance was £800, but this (and the employees' contribution) was not paid over immediately.

For the purpose of this question assume that the rate of value added tax (VAT), which applied to all relevant transactions, was 10%. There were no exempt or zero rate transactions.

11.2   JOHN HENRY LTD (2) (J86)

During the quarter ended 31 May 19X6, the raw materials purchased by John Henry Ltd, manufacturers of furniture, amounted to £181,590 before VAT at the standard rate of 15% and, in addition, the following items of expenditure occurred:

		£	£
March 12	Highway Garage Ltd		
	Motor van C478TBR	9,500.00	
	VAT @ 15%	1,425.00	
		10,925.00	
	Vehicle excise duty	100.00	
			11,025.00
March 19	Smith Motors Ltd		
	Motor car C379KTA	8,000.00	
	VAT @ 15%	1,200.00	
		9,200.00	
	Vehicle excise duty	100.00	
			9,300.00
April 23	Super Machines Ltd		
	Used drilling machine Number KXY54	8,200.00	
	VAT @ 15%	1,230.00	
			9,430.00
May 7	Highway Garage Ltd		
	Car repairs	210.00	
	VAT @ 15%	31.50	
			241.50
May 20	Machine Repairs Ltd		
	Renovation drilling machine		
	Number KXY54	500.00	
	VAT @ 15%	75.00	
			575.00

Note: This renovation was necessary before the drilling machine could be used in the factory.

The VAT due to the Customs and Excise Department on 28 February 19X6 amounting to £84,000 was paid on 20 March 19X6.

During the quarter ended 31 May 19X6, the company's turnover, before VAT, amounted to £800,000 and analysed for VAT purposes was as follows:

		Turnover £
Taxable –	Standard rate	620,000
	Zero rated	120,000
Non–taxable –	Exempt	60,000
		800,000

The company maintains an analytical purchases day book.

Required

(a) Prepare the analytical purchases day book for the three months ended 31 May 19X6 of John Henry Ltd.   (13 marks)

Note: Raw material purchases for the three months ended 31 May 19X6 should be shown as one entry in the purchases day book.

(b) Prepare the account for HM Customs and Excise – VAT for the three months ended 31 May 19X6 in the accounts of John Henry Ltd.   (12 marks)
(Total 25 marks)

11.3 HAROLD PEACOCK (D86)

(a) Harold Peacock, a retailer, is registered for VAT purposes.

During September 19X6, the following transactions took place in Harold Peacock's business:

(1) 18 September Goods bought, on credit, from T King and Sons Ltd, list price £640 subject to trade discount of 10% and also a cash discount of 2½% for payment within 30 days.

(2) 22 September New car, for use in the business, bought from XL Garages Ltd at an agreed price of £8,000.00; payment to be effected on delivery.

(3) 25 September Goods sold, on credit, to G Siddle Ltd, list price £1,200 subject to trade discount of 15% and cash discount of 2% for payment within 30 days.

Required

Record the above transactions in the ledger accounts of Harold Peacock.

Note: Harold Peacock does not maintain total or control accounts for debtors or creditors.   (14 marks)

(b) The balances at 31 October 19X6 of the sales ledger control account of Timber Products Ltd according to the draft final accounts were:

	£
Debit	21,7000
Credit	700

The account of T Bean in the sales ledger was closed in September 19X5 when the debit balance of £400 was written off as a bad debt. In August 19X6 T Bean unexpectedly received a legacy from the estate of a distant relative. T Bean's improved circumstances enabled him to pay Timber Products Ltd a cheque for £400 in early September 19X6; this receipt was credited to an account for T Bean in the sales ledger.

Note: T Bean will not be trading with Timber Products Ltd in the future.

The company's finance director has now decided that:

(1)   the following balances due to the company should be written off as bad:

K Milson	£250
T Longdon	£150

(2)   The provision for doubtful debts at 31 October 19X6 should be 3% of the amount due to the company at that date according to the sales ledger.

Note: The balance of the provision for doubtful debts account brought forward at 1 November 19X5 was £890; this balance was brought forward from the previous year's accounts.

Required

(i)   Prepare a computation of the corrected sales ledger account balances at 31 October 19X6.   (6 marks)

(ii) Write up the provision for doubtful debts account for the year ended 31 October 19X6.   (5 marks)
                                                                            (Total 25 marks)

11.4   GRANDBAY MACHINISTS LTD (J89)

(a)   During April 19X9, the credit transactions of Grandbay Machinists Ltd included the following:

10 April	Purchase of motor car F600SSS from Circle Garages Limited	£8,000
13 April	Purchase of lorry F717KBL from Heavy Goods Trucks Limited	£42,000
17 April	Repairs to motor car C123RTE by Quickservices Limited	£300
19 April	Purchase of fog lights for F600SSS from Car Supplies Limited	£80

All the above transactions were subject to the addition of value added tax (VAT) at 15%.

Required

Prepare journal entries recording the above transactions in the books of Grandbay Machinists Ltd.   (12 marks)

Notes

(1)   Narratives are not required.

(2)   Assume the company does not maintain a purchases day book or purchases ledger control account.

(b)   The trial balance as at 31 May 19X9 of Tip Top Dealers Ltd included the following:

	Debit £	Credit £
Purchases ledger control account	654	7,348
Sales ledger control account	12,360	716
Provision for doubtful debts		410
Bad debts recovered (received from K L Blaney)		970

Additional information

(1)   K L Blaney's bad debt was written off in the accounts for the year ended 31 May 19X7.

(2)   It had now been decided to write off the following debts, due to the company, as irrecoverable:

	£
L Pink	210
G Slack	50

(3)   The provision for doubtful debts account is not used for actual bad debts written off or for bad debts recovered.

(4)   The company's continuing policy is to maintain a provision for doubtful debts at 2% of outstanding debtors at each accounting year end.

Required

(i)   Prepare the provision for doubtful debts account for the year ended 31 May 19X8 in the books of Tip Top Dealers Ltd.   (7 marks)

(ii)   Prepare the entry for debtors and creditors which will be included in the balance sheet as at 31 May 19X9 of Tip Top Dealers Ltd.
(6 marks)
(Total 25 marks)

1   YEAR–END ADJUSTMENTS

1.1   HALE

(a)   **Schedule showing the balance of motor vehicles depreciation account on 1 January 19X5**

		Expenditure	Depreciation at 31.12.X4 Number of years @ 20%	Total
		£		£
Before	19X0	4,273	5	4,273
During	19X0	2,480	5	2,480
During	19X1	2,350	4	1,880
During	19X2	6,890	3	4,134
During	19X3	–	–	–
During	19X4	2,100	1	420
		18,093		13,187

Schedule showing the charge for depreciation for 19X5

		Expenditure	Sales in 19X5	Net cost	Dep'n @ 20% for 19X5
		£	£	£	£
Before	19X0	4,273	980	3,293	–
During	19X0	2,480	–	2,480	–
During	19X1	2,350	–	2,350	470
During	19X2	6,890	1,150	5,740	1,148
During	19X3	–	–	–	–
During	19X4	2,100	–	2,100	420
During	19X5	2,260	–	2,260	452
		20,353	2,130	18,223	2,490

(b)   **Motor vehicles account**

		£			£
19X5			19X5		
1 January	Balance b/f	18,093	31 December	Motor vehicles	
31 December	Cash	2,260		disposals accounts:	
				– Pre 19X0	980
				– 19X2	1,150
				Balance c/f	18,223
		20,353			20,353
19X6					
1 January	Balance b/f	18,223			

Motor vehicles – Provision for depreciation

19X5		£	19X5		£
31 December	Motor vehicles disposals accounts:		1 January	Balance b/f	13,187
	– Pre 19X0	980	31 December	Depreciation expense	2,490
	– 19X2	690			
	Balance c/f	14,007			
		15,677			15,677
			19X6		
			1 January	Balance b/f	14,007

Pre–19X0 disposals account

19X5		£	19X5		£
31 December	Motor vehicles	980	31 December	Depreciation	980
	Profit on sale	215		Cash	215
		1,195			1,195

19X2 disposals account

19X5		£	19X5		£
31 December	Motor vehicles	1,150	31 December	Depreciation	690
				Cash	420
				Loss on sale	40
		1,150			1,150

Depreciation expense

19X5		£	19X5		£
31 December	Provision for depreciation	2,490	31 December	Profit and loss account	2,490

1.2   **ROE LTD**

(a)   **Closing stock valuation**

(i)   **FIFO**

		£
100kg x £5.00		500
50kg x £4.50		225
		___
		725
		___

(ii)   **LIFO**

		£
50kg x £5.00		250
100kg x £3.00		300
		___
		550
		___

(iii)   **Simple average**

Receipts – price per kg	£
1.1.X3	3.00
15.1.X3	4.00
17.2.X3	4.50
16.3.X3	5.00
	____
	16.50 – 4
	____

= £4.125 x 150kg =   £618.75

(iv)   **Periodic weighted average**

Receipts	Quantity kg	Value £
1.1.X3	100	300
15.1.X3	200	800
17.2.X3	400	1,800
16.3.X3	100	500
	___	___
	80	3,400
	___	___

$\dfrac{£3,400}{800\text{kg}}$ = £4.25 x 150kg =   £637.50

(v) **Weighted average**

		Value £	Average price per kg
1.1.X3	100 x £3	300	£3.00
15.1.X3	200 x £4	800	
	300	1,100	£3.6
29.1.X3	(150) @ £3	(550)	
	150	550	£3.6
17.2.X3	400 @ £4.50	1,800	
	550	2,350	£4.2727
5.3.X3	(450)@ £4.2727	1,922.73)	
	100	427.27	£4.2727
16.3.X3	100 x £5	500.00	
	200	927.27	£4.6364
31.3.X3	(50) x £4.6364	(231.82)	
	150	695.45	£4.6364

Therefore closing stock

150 kg @ £4.6364 =   £695.45

(b) Under the FIFO method, issues to production are priced at the cost price of the material when it was **first** taken into the stock from which the issue was been drawn. Thus the closing stock will have a **higher** value.

Under LIFO, the issue price is the cost price of the material when it was **most recently** taken into the stock. Thus the closing stock will have a **lower** value.

The effect on gross profit during inflationary periods is that FIFO tends to result in higher levels of gross profit than does the LIFO method.

The advantage the LIFO method of pricing material issues is that production costs reflect current values of materials. In addition, in the current environment of rising prices the method results in a conservative valuation of material stocks. However when an issue exceeds the quantity of recent receipts, part of the issue will be charged to production at out-of-date prices thereby defeating the advantages stated earlier. For taxation purposes LIFO is not an acceptable method of valuing stock in the UK, probably because it results in lower profit.

1.3 STOCK VALUATION

(a) SSAP 9 requires that stock should be valued at cost or net realisable value, whichever is lower. Cost is normally arrived at by using the 'first in first out' convention, or by taking the average price. The cost and net realisable value of individual stock items are compared and the lower value adopted.

(b) In the question the LIFO (last in first out) method has been used and this is unacceptable under SSAP 9 and is also unacceptable for taxation purposes. The value which should be placed on the stock is:

	£	£
Sheet steel (cost)		8,000
Iron bars (reduced to net realisable value)		7,000
Electrical circuits:		
390 units on FIFO basis:		
200 at £40	8,000	
190 at £35	6,650	
	14,650	
Net realisable value is lower –		13,100
		28,100

1.4 EXPRESS TRANSPORT LTD

(a) 19X5 Journal

	£	£
Oct 1 Motor lorries – provision for depreciation	1,841	
Profit and loss account		1,841

Being adjustment in provision for depreciation necessary at this date following change of policy from reducing–balance method to straight–line method

Workings: Vehicle	B393KPQ	B219BXY		Total provision
Cost	22,000	25,000		–

Depreciation – reducing–balance method

	£	£		£
19X3/X4	5,500	4,688	(¾ x £6,250)	10,188
WDV 30.9.19X4	16,500	20,312		
19X4/X5	4,125	5,078		9,203
WDV 30.9.19X5	12,375	15,234		19,391

Depreciation – straight–line method

	£	£		£
19X3/X4	4,400	3,750	(¾ x £5,000)	8,150
19X4/X5	4,400	5,000		9,400
				17,550

Reduction in depreciation provision following change of policy to straight–line basis		£1,841

Answers

(b)   **Motor lorries – at cost**

19X5			£	19X6			£
Oct 1	Balance b/f		47,000	Apr 1	Motor lorry		
Oct 1	Bank (C198TKL)		34,000		B393KPQ disposal		22,000
				Sept 30	Balance c/f		87,000
19X6							
Apr 1	Motor lorry B393KPQ disposal (Re C437FGA)		10,000				
Apr 1	Bank (C437FGA)		18,000				
			109,000				109,000
Oct 1	Balance b/f		87,000				

Motor lorries – provision for depreciation

19X5			£	19X5			£
Oct 1	Profit & loss		1,841	Oct 1	Balance b/f		19,391
19X6				**19X6**			
Apr 1	Motor lorry B393KPQ disposal		11,000	Sept 30	Profit & loss (£5,000 + £6,800 + £2,800 + £2,200)		16,800
Sept 30	Balance c/f		23,350				
			36,191				36,191
				Oct 1	Balance b/f		23,350

Motor lorry – B393KPQ disposal

19X6			£	19X6			£
Apr 1	Motor lorries at cost		22,000	Apr 1	Motor lorries provision for depreciation		11,000
				Apr 1	Motor lorries at cost		10,000
				Apr 1	Profit and loss (loss on sale)		1,000
			22,000				22,000

1.5   FINE SPINDLES LTD

		£	£
(a)	Stock, at cost, at 31 December 19X6		16,824
	Less: Overcost error in stock sheets		2,000
			14,824
	Add: Purchases in quarter to 31 March 19X7		46,680
			61,504
	Less: Cost of stock lost in burglary		8,000
			53,504
	Less: Sales in quarter to 31 March 19X7		
	Goods invoiced	54,210	
	Less: Despatched December 19X6	1,040	
		53,170	
	Add: Despatched April 19X7	3,900	
		57,070	
	Less: Returns inward	4,550	
	Sales	52,520	
	Cost price of sales $\frac{10}{13}$ x £52,520		40,400
			13,104
	Less: Stock reduced $\frac{1}{2}$ x $\frac{10}{13}$ x £1,950		750
	Stock valuation at 31 March 19X7		12,354

(b)   **Trading account for the quarter ended 31 March 19X7**

		£		£
Cost of goods sold:			Sales	52,520
	Opening stock	16,824		
	Purchases	46,680		
		63,504		
Less:	Closing stock	12,354		
		51,150		
Less:	Stock stolen	8,000		
		43,150		
Gross profit		9,370		
		52,520		52,520

1.6   JOHN BROWN AND PARTNERS

(a)   (i)

New workshop at OST

19X7		£	19X7		£
Jan – April	Construction costs:				
	Direct materials	15,000			
	Direct labour	9,000			
	Variable overheads	3,000			
	Fixed overheads:				
	($\frac{450}{225}$ x £9,000)	18,000			
Feb	Supply of electric installation	2,400	Oct 31	Bal c/f	47,400
		47,400			47,400
Nov 1	Balance b/f	47,400			

(ii)

New workshop provision for depreciation

19X7	£	19X7		£
		Oct 31	Provision £47,400 x 6/12 x 5%	1,185

(iii)

Workshop repair

19X7		£	19X7		£
Mar	Repair of electric installation	1,000	June	Insurance settlement	800
Aug	Redecoration costs		Oct	Insurance settlement	4,000
	Direct materials	2,000			
	Direct labour	1,600			
	Variable overheads	300			
	Fixed overheads				
	($\frac{450}{225}$ x £1,600)	3,200	Oct	Manufacturing account	3,300
		8,100			8,100

(b)   Revenue expenditure is expenditure which maintains the operations of a business without resulting in an increase in asset values from one accounting period to the next.

Capital expenditure is expenditure which results in an increase in asset value from one accounting period to the next, excluding the purchase of assets for resale in the course of trade.

The asset value of a business would be incorrect if capital expenditure were written off on acquisition whereas revenue expenditure should be charged directly against profit to ensure that income and related expenditure are 'matched' in the same accounting period.

The asset values will decrease in the due course of time and depreciation charges (which are charged against profit in each accounting period) ensure that the diminution in asset value is properly charged against profits over the useful life of the asset.

1.7 THOMAS DART

Report

To: Thomas Dart
From: Accounting Technician
Subject: Proposed stock valuation at 31 May 19X8

Introduction

This report comments on the bases, proposed by you, for valuing the company's stock at 31 May 19X8. I have set out the relevant accounting concepts and the likely effect of the proposals.

Accounting concepts

Statement of Standard Accounting Practice (SSAP) No 2 sets out the fundamental accounting concepts on which all accounts should be based. The concepts relevant to this matter are:

(a) **Consistency** – There should be consistency of accounting policies between similar items and from one year to the next. This would cause problems in both senses with the proposed valuations. 'Padgetts' and 'Wodgetts' should both be valued on the same basis, whereas you suggest selling price for the former and replacement cost for the latter. Secondly the adoption of last in first out (LIFO) will be inconsistent with previous years when first in first out (FIFO) has been used.

(b) **Prudence** – Profits must not be accounted for unless realised whilst losses must be accounted for as soon as they are foreseeable. In this context it means that stocks must be stated at the lower of cost and net realisable value as follows:

	Cost £/unit	NRV £/unit	Valuation £/unit
Padgetts	200	340	200
Wodgetts	110	280	110

If the figures suggested of £340 and £140 are used then unrealised profits will be recognised in the accounts to 31 May 19X8.

(c) **Accruals** – Costs should be matched with revenues in the period in which they are earned. Again this gives a preference for stock valuation on a cost basis rather than expected sales price or replacement price.

LIFO basis – As outlined above this would be inconsistent with earlier years. As a valuation basis LIFO has little to commend it since it usually bears little or no relation to the actual pattern of stock movements that occur. FIFO provides the fairest approximation to actual cost and therefore comes closest to satisfying the accruals requirement.

Disclosure – Finally, you should be aware that any change in accounting policies, which this would be, would have to be disclosed in the company's annual financial statements and therefore may come to the attention of any reader of the accounts such as the bank.

(**Note:** The last point is not relevant if Thomas Dart is an unincorporated business.)

1.8   JOHN GAUNT

(a)

Trading and profit and loss accounts
years ended 31 December

	19X6 LIFO and FIFO £	19X7 LIFO and FIFO £	19X8 LIFO £	19X8 FIFO £
Sales	120,000	218,000	373,00	373,000
Less: Cost of goods sold	100,000	175,000	293,000	277,000
Gross profit	20,000	43,000	80,000	96,000
Overhead expense excluding depreciation	24,000	26,000	31,000	31,000
Fixtures & fittings depreciation	2,000	1,600	1,280	1,280
	26,000	27,600	32,280	32,280
Net profit/(loss)	(6,000)	15,400	47,720	63,720

(b)   **Capital account year ended 31 December 19X8**

			£
1 January 19X8	Capital at 1 January 19X6		50,000
	Less: Net loss year ended 31.12.19X6		6,000
			44,0000
	Add: Net profit year ended 31.12.19X7		15,400
	Balance		59,400
31 December 19X8	Net profit year ended 31.12.19X8 (see note below)		63,720
31 December 19X8	Balance carried forward		123,120

Note: The net profit for 19X8 is based on FIFO as indicated in the question.

(c)   The report to John Gaunt should mention the following points:

(i)   It is a matter of indifference whether John Gaunt used the last in first out basis or first in first out basis for stock valuation in the particular circumstances existing in 19X6 and 19X7 when there were no changes in the price of goods purchased.

(ii)   However from an operational point of view it is not practicable to be ambivalent on the choice of basis for stock valuation; it would be necessary to choose a particular method.

(iii)   The first in first out method identifies more closely with the actual stock movements in that stock issues will be of the items longest in stock and will be priced at the actual prices paid for the stock issued.

(iv)   With first in first out, the stock in hand at the end of an accounting period will be valued normally at the actual cost incurred.

(v)   The first in first out method is widely used, particularly in the United Kingdom where it is accepted for tax purposes.

(vi)   The first in first out method is more in harmony with the historical cost accounting model.

1.9   DOCKS LTD

(a)   Provision for bad debts account

		£			£
			1.4.W9	Balance b/f	13,000
31.3.X0	Balance c/f (10% x £185,000)	18,500	31.3.X0	Profit & loss	5,500
		18,500			18,500
31.3.X1	Profit & loss	1,000	1.4.X0	Balance b/f	18,500
31.3.X1	Balance c/f (12.5% x £140,000)	17,500			
		18,500			18,500
			1.4.X1	Balance b/f	17,500
31.3.X1	Balance c/f (15% x £200,000)	30,000	31.3.X2	Profit & loss	12,500
		30,000			30,000
			1.4.X2	Balance b/f	30,000

Balance sheet extract at 31 March

	19X0 £	19X1 £	19X2 £
Trade debtors	185,000	140,000	200,000
Less: Provision for bad debts	18,500	17,500	30,000
	166,500	122,500	170,000

Workings	19X0 £	19X1 £	19X2 £
Trade debtors at 31 March	186,680	141,200	206,200
Less: Bad debts	1,680	1,200	6,200
	185,000	140,000	200,000

(b) The effect on the profit for the year ended 31.3.X0 is a reduction of £1,000, the bad debt written off. As this was subsequently recovered in case the following year the entry is:

Dr Cash account   Cr Bad debt account

The effect on the profit for the year ended 31.3.X1 is increase of £1,000, the bad debt previously written off now recovered.

1.10   J ROYAL

(a)   Trade debtors account

		£			£
31.3.X2	Sales account	458,400	31.3.X2	Cash account	355,300
				Discount allowed account	45,800
				Bad debts account	2,200
				Balance c/f	55,100
		458,400			458,400
1.4.X2	Balance b/f	55,100	31.3.X3	Cash account	512,700
31.3.X3	Sales account	567,600		Discount allowed account	47,300
				Bad debts account	4,900
				Balance c/f	57,800
		622,700			622,700
1.4.X3	Balance b/f	57,800	31.3.X4	Cash account	481,200
31.3.X4	Sales account	537,200		Discount allowed account	48,600
				Bad debts account	2,500
				Ballance c/f	62,700
		595,000			595,000
1.4.X4	Balance b/f	62,700			

(b)   Bad debts account

		£			£
31.3.X2	Debtors account	2,200	31.3.X2	Profit & loss a/c	2,200
31.3.X3	Debtors account	4,900	31.3.X3	Profit & loss a/c	4,900
31.3.X4	Debtors account	2,500	31.3.X4	Profit & loss a/c	2,500

(c)   Bad debts provision account

		£			£
31.3.X2	Balance c/f (5% x £55,100)	2,755	31.3.X2	Profit & loss a/c	2,755
		2,755			2,755
			1.4.X2	Balance b/f	2,755
31.3.X3	Balance c/f (10% x £57,800)	5,780	31.3.X2	Profit & loss a/c – increase in provision	3,025
		5,780			5,780
31.3.X4	Profit & loss a/c – decrease in provision	1,078	1.4.X3	Balance b/f	5,780
31.3.X3	Balance c/f (7.5% x £62,700)	4,702	1.4.X4	Balance b/f	4,702
		5,780			

(d)   Discount allowed provision account

		£			£
31.3.X2	Balance c/f (10% x (55,100 – 2,755)	5,235	31.3.X2	Profit & loss a/c	5,235
		5,235			5,235
			1.4.X2	Balance b/f	5,235
31.3.X3	Balance c/f (12.5% x (57,800 – 5,780))	6,503	31.3.X3	Profit & loss a/c	1,268
		6,503			6,503

(d)   Discount allowed provision account (cont)

		£			£
			1.4.X3	Balance b/f	6,503
31.3.X4	Balance c/f (15% x (62,700 – 4,702),	8,700	31.3.X4	Profit & loss a/c	2,197
		8,700			8,700
			1.4.X4	Balance b/f	8,700

Answers

1.11 ZOOM PRODUCTS LTD

(a) (i)

Provision for doubtful debts account for the year ended 31 December 19X6

		£			£
19X6			**19X6**		
Dec 30	Debtors' ledger a/c:		Jan 1	Balance b/f	
	J Sinder	600		(working 1)	2,640
	K Lambert	2,000	Dec 31	Debtors ledger –	
Dec 31	Balance c/f			K Dodds	3,000
	(working 2)	2,448			
		———			
		5,048			
Dec 31	Profit and loss	592			
		———			———
		5,640			5,640
		———			———
			19X7		
			Jan 1	Balance b/f	2,448

(ii) **Zoom Products Ltd balance sheet as at 31 December 19X6**

Trade debtors (£81,600 less £2,448) = £79,152.

(b)

J Cort Ltd
Journal entries

19X7			£	£
Jan 1	Cake mixing machine provision			
	for depreciation		3,800	
	Delivery vehicle provision for			
	depreciation		10,000	
	Sale of cake department fixed assets		31,200	
	Cake mixing machine at cost			20,000
	Delivery vehicle at cost			25,000
	Being transfer of assets sold upon			
	closure of cake department			
Jan 11	Creamy Cakes Ltd		23,000	
	Sale of cake department fixed assets			23,000
	Being sale of cake department fixed assets;			
	settlement to be on 1 March 19X7			
Jan 1	Profit and loss		8,200	
	Sale of cake department fixed assets			8,200
	Transfer of loss on sale of cake department			
	fixed assets			

Workings

(1)   Debtors outstanding at 31 December 19X5

		£
£85,360 x $\frac{100}{97}$		88,000
Less: Provision for doubtful debts (3%)		2,640
Debtors at 31 December 19X5		85,360

(2)   Debtors' ledger year ended 31 December 19X6

19X6		£	19X6		£
Jan 1	Balance b/f	88,000	Dec 31	Bank	510,150
Dec 31	Sales (90% x £568,000)	511,200	Dec 31	Discounts allowed	4,850
Dec 31	Provision for doubtful		Dec 31	Bank (K Dodds)	3,000
	debts (K Dodds)	3,000	Dec 31	Provision for doubtful debts (£600 + £2,000)	2,600
			Dec 31	Balance c/f	81,600
		602,200			602,200
19X7					
Jan 1	Balance b/f	81,600			

Provision for doubtful debts at 31 December 19X6 = 3% x £81,600 = £2,448.

1.12   JOHN PEACOCK LTD

(a)

Motor lorry at cost

19X8		£
1 Apr	Bank	40,000
1 May	Bank (pre service repairs)	5,000
		45,000

Motor lorry provision for depreciation

	£	19X8		£
		31 Oct	Profit and loss (6 mths at £9,000 pa)	4,500

Motor lorry insurance

19X8		£	19X8		£
1 Apr	Bank	1,200	31 Oct	Profit and loss (7 months)	700
			31 Oct	Balance c/f	500
		1,200			1,200
1 Nov	Balance b/f	500			

Answers

(b) (i)   **Springboard Ltd**

19X8	£	£
Bank	500	
James Lyon		500

Being amount received in part settlement of
debt previously written off

James Lyon	500	
Bad debts recovered (or bad debts)		500

Being amount received for debt previously
written off in 19X5 transferred to recovered
account

(ii)   **Provision for doubtful debts account**

19X8		£	19X7		£
30 Nov	Balance c/f	1,045	1 Dec	Balance b/f	900
			19X8		
			30 Nov	Profit and loss (see note below)	145
		1,045			1,045
			1 Dec	Balances b/f	1,045

Note: Transfer to profit and loss account 30 November 19X8

	£
Debtors at 30 November 19X8	22,000
Less: Written off as bad	1,100
	20,900

	£
Provision for doubtful debts at 30 November 19X8	
5% of £20,900	1,045
Less: Already provided	900
Charge to P&L account year ended 30 November 19X8	145

(iii)   **Balance sheet as at 30 November 19X8**

Trade debtors (£20,900 less £1,045)	£19,855

1.13   SHARP EDGE

Sharp Edge Engineering Co Ltd

Motor vehicles at cost

19X7		£	19X7		£
1 Oct	Bank (E676 TVX)	28,000			
19X8			19X8		
1 Jan	Bank (E438 CBA)	36,000	30 Sept	Balance c/f	64,000
		64,000			64,000
19X8					
1 Oct	Balance c/f	64,000	31 Dec	Disposal (E438 CBA)	36,000
19X9			19X9		
1 Feb	Bank (E779 GMS)	16,000			
1 April	Direct labour	1,880			
	Direct materials	3,200			
	Variable overheads	1,370			
	Fixed overheads (25% x 1,880 + 3,200)	1,270			
1 July	Bank (F934 KTA)	24,000	30 Sept	Balance c/f	75,720
		111,720			111,720

Motor vehicles provision for depreciation

19X8		£	19X8		£
30 Sept	Balance c/f	11,000	30 Sept	Profit and loss (20% x £28,000 + 20% x £36,000 x 9/12)	11,000
		11,000			11,000
31 Dec	Disposal (E438 CBA) (20% x £36,000)	7,200	1 Oct	Balance b/f	11,000
19X9			19X9		
30 Sept	Balance c/f	14,772	30 Sept	Profit and loss (20% x £28,000 + 20% x £36,000 x 3/12 + 20% x £23,720 x 6/12 + 20% x £24,000 x 3/12)	10,972
		21,972			21,972

Answers

Lorry E438 CBA Disposal

19X8		£	19X8		£
31 Dec	Motor Vehicles at cost	36,000	31 Dec	Motor vehicles provision for depreciation	7,200
			31 Dec	Bank	21,680
			19X9		
			30 Sept	Profit and loss (loss on disposal)	7,120
		36,000			36,000

Motor vehicles insurance

19X7		£	19X7		£
1 Oct	Bank (E676 TVX)	5,000			
19X8			19X8		
1 Jan	Bank (E438 CBA)	5,000	30 Sept	Profit and loss	8,750
			30 Sept	Balance c/f (£5,000 x 3/12)	1,250
		10,000			10,000
19X8			19X8		
1 Oct	Balance b/f	1,250			
1 Oct	Bank (E676 TVX)	5,000			
19X9			19X9		
1 Feb	Bank (E779 GMS)	5,000	30 Sept	Profit and loss	10,833
1 July	Bank (F934 KTA)	5,000	30 Sept	Balance c/f (£5,000 x 4/12 + £5,000 x 9/12)	5,417
		16,250			16,250

1.14   MARY SMITH

(a)   Trading and profit and loss account for the quarter ending 30 November 19Y0

(i)   First-in, first-out basis

	£	£
Sales (2,240 + 13,600)		15,840
Less: Cost of sales (W1)		10,408
		5,432
Expenses		
Overheads	1,520	
Sales Commissions (2½% x 5,432)	136	
Depreciation (384 x 1/8 x 1/4)	12	
		1,668
Net Profit		3,764

(ii)   Last-in, first-out basis

	£	£
Sales		15,840
Less: Cost of sales (W2)		11,392
		4,448
Expenses		
Overheads	1,520	
Sales Commission (2½% x 4,448)	111	
Depreciation (450 x 1/8 x 1/4)	14	
		1,645
Net profit		2,803

(b)   Mary Smith's income quarter ending 31 August 19Y0

	£
Salary (1/4 x £15,000)	3,750
Interest on savings (£7,000 x 10% x 1/4)	175
	3,925
Net profit under (a)(i) for quarter ending 30 November 19Y0	£3,764

(c)   First-in, first-out

Advantages

–   Closing stock figures will be more likely to closely approximate to current prices.

–   Likely to be closer to pattern of actual physical movement of goods.

Answers

- If prices are rising will give lower cost of sales figure therefore higher gross profit.

Disadvantages

- In times of rising prices profit figures include 'holding gains'.

Last–in, first–out

Advantages

- The cost of goods sold will more likely reflect current price levels.
- Profit figure will contain smaller element of 'holding gains'.

Disadvantages

- The value of closing stock is less likely to equate to current price levels.

- In times of rising prices cost of sales will be higher resulting in a lower gross profit.

Workings

(1)	**Cost of sales – FIFO**	£	£
	Purchases (4,608 + 3,600 + 7,824)		16,032
	Less: Lawn mower taken as fixed asset		(384)
			15,648
	Less: Closing stock		
	September purchases (0)		
	October purchases (0)		
	November purchases (11 x 489)	5,379	
	Less: Reduction of one lawn mower to net realisable value (489 – 350)	(139)	
			5,240
			10,408

(2)	**Cost of sales – LIFO**	£	£
	Purchases		16,032
	Less: Lawn mower taken as fixed asset		(450)
			15,582
	Less: Closing stock		
	September purchases (11 x 384)	4,224	
	October purchases (0)		
	November purchases (0)		
	Less: Reduction of one lawn mower to NRV (384 – 350)	(34)	
			4,190
			11,392

1.15   QUICKMEAL PRODUCTS LTD

(a)

Mixing Machines at cost

19X8			£	19X8		£
1 April	Bank (FM1)		80,000	Balance c/f		
	Bank (FM1)		10,000	31 March 1989		90,000
			90,000			90,000
19X9						
1 April	Balance b/f		90,000			
1 October	Bank (FM2)		120,000			
	Bank (FM2)		24,000			
19Y0				**19Y0**		
1 January	Bank (FM3)		60,000	1 January Disposal Account		90,000
	Bank (FM3)		16,000			
	Disposal Account (part exchange value) (FM1)		36,000	31 March Balance c/f		256,000
			346,000			346,000
19Y0						
1 April	Balance b/f		256,000			

Mixing Machines provision for depreciation

19X9		£	19X9		£
31 March Balance c/f		8,500	31 March Depreciation Charge (FM1) (10% x (90,000 − 5,000))		8,500
		8,500			8,500
			19X9		
			1 April Balance b/f		8,500
19Y0			**19Y0**		
1 January Disposal Account (FM1) (8,500 + 6,375)		14,875	31 March Depreciation Charge FM1 (8,500 x 9/12)		6,375
			FM2 (10% x 144,000 − 4,000 x 6/12)		7,000
31 March Balance c/f		9,650	FM3 (10% x 112,000 − 6,000 x 3/12)		2,650
		24,525			24,525
			19Y0		
			1 April Balance b/f		9,650

0044V

(b)   **Disposal Account FM1**

19Y0		£	19Y0		£
1 January	Food mixing machines at cost (FM1)	90,000	1 January	Food mixing machines provision for depreciation (FM1)	14,875
				Food mixing machines at cost FM1 part exchange value 36,000	
				Profit and loss – loss on sale	39,125
		90,000			90,000

(c)   **John Smith**

The intention of the training course in April 19X8 is presumably that John Smith will be able to operate FM1 for its entire ten–year life. Therefore, under the accruals concept there might be an argument for spreading this cost over the expected 10 year life of FM1.

However the prudence concept would overrule this requiring that such training costs, revenue expenditure, should be written off immediately in the year in which they occurred.

Audrey Jones

Again the prudence concept would override the accruals concept to ensure that these costs were written off as incurred. However the accruals or matching concept could be used to argue that the introductory course in March 19X9 should be carried forward and written off in the year ended March 1990, as the course was for machine FM2 and this was not purchased until October 1989.

2   ACCOUNTING CONCEPTS AND PRINCIPLES

2.1   NATURE OF A BALANCE SHEET

The major relevant points worthy of examination:

(a)   Not all assets are necessary included in the balance sheet – for example goodwill, human resources and other intangible assets are excluded.

(b)   Adherence to historical cost means that the book value of inventories and fixed assets is quite different and usually lower than their value to the business.

(c)   'Net worth' is not a concept which is capable of precise definition. The worth of a business or the value of shares in a business may vary considerably from one person to another.

(d)   The cost figure of the various assets usually relates to varying periods of time and consequently to varying values in the purchasing power of money. This is true not only of different assets in the same balance sheet, but also within the same asset, where several items are purchased in different periods at different price levels.

2.2   H GEE

(a)   Sales revenue may be regarded as having arisen when:

    (i)   the transaction can be measured objectively in monetary terms (ie when quantity and price are known); and

    (ii)   the transaction is complete or certain to be completed; or

    (iii)   the critical event in the transaction cycle is complete (perhaps securing the order or obtaining payment).

Generally a sale is recognised when goods or services have been exchanged for cash or a legally enforceable promise to pay.

(b)   Statement (1)   is incorrect as measurement in monetary terms is not possible and no exchange has occurred.

    Statement (2)   is not appropriate as the transaction is not yet certain and the exchange has not occurred.

    Statement (3)   is appropriate for a cash sale or when invoicing takes place with delivery.

    Statement (4)   is appropriate if invoicing follows delivery.

    Statement (5)   is appropriate for cash sales but not for credit sales unless the payment is the critical event, ie, the customer was felt to be a bad risk.

    Statement (6)   Would be appropriate only when the buyer is an extremely bad risk.

2.3   A, B AND C

Company A

If Company A were to value this specialised building material stock at its sales value less delivery charges – £49,700 – then the company would effectively be taking credit for the sale in the year ended 30 November 19X9.

However confident the company is of a sale credit should not be taken until the sale takes place in January 19Y0. Therefore the stock should be valued at £32,000, the lower of its cost and net realisable value.

Company B

The problem here is whether or not the company is a going concern. The basis of the going concern concept is that the profit and loss account and balance sheet assume no intention or necessity to liquidate or curtail the scale of operations for the foreseeable future.

Therefore, from the evidence, does it appear that Company B is likely to liquidate or curtail its operations in the near future? The only indications we have are that some of Company B's competitors have gone out of business in recent years. This does not necessarily imply that Company B will go the same way. Indeed Company B may in fact benefit by picking up business from its liquidated competitors.

Company B must look to its own trading and profit record and future projections and prospects in order to come to a conclusion on its going concern position. If the company were not to base its stock valuation on a going concern basis this could in itself lead to a reduction in value of the company.

Therefore without good reason for considering that Company B was in fact not a going concern the stock should be valued at the lower of cost and net realisable value in the normal manner.

Company C

The purpose of depreciation is to charge a portion of a fixed asset's cost to the profit and loss account each year during the asset's useful life to the business. However well-maintained an asset is it is unlikely that its useful life will be infinite, indeed depreciation policy assumes that fixed assets are maintained throughout their useful life.

Again, however well-maintained an asset is, its useful life may be determined by such things as economic and technological factors. Therefore the maintenance of an asset to being kept 'as good as new' does not mean that a proportion of the asset's cost need not be charged each year as depreciation. The maintenance may well increase the estimated useful life of the asset but depreciation will still need to be charged.

2.4   **JOHN ABEL**

Report to departmental manager concerning accounting queries

Dear Sir

In reply to your queries about certain accounting matters I have set out below explanations of the three points that you raised.

(1)   A provision is an amount retained in the accounts either for a liability or loss that is likely to be incurred, for example, provision for doubtful debts or a certain future liability or loss for which the amount or timing is as yet uncertain (eg, provision for repair).

A reserve is an amount that is to be specifically retained within the business. This may be because of statutory requirements eg. share premium accounts or revaluation reserves or supply because the business wishes to retain some resources (eg, a general reserve).

(2)   When a business makes a profit this can be either distributed to the owners, for example by way of dividend, or used within the business eg for increases in stock or purchases of fixed assets. Therefore there may be occasions when a business has made a profit but is unable to distribute this as a dividend as the funds are needed within the business.

The generation of a profit does not always equate with the generation of cash and even if a company has made a large profit we may not have the cash available to pay a dividend.

(3)   The purpose of depreciation is to reflect the use of fixed assets in the business during an accounting period according to the accruals or matching concept. If a fixed asset is used in the business then some of its cost should be charged to the business in that period. By charging an amount to the

profit and loss account as depreciation the profits and thereby possible dividends are reduced. However the purpose of depreciation is not to 'save up' for the replacement of assets in this way but to accord with the accruals concept.

Yours faithfully

John Abel

2.5   HILLSIDE PRODUCTS LTD

Report to the chief accountant, Hillside Products Ltd, concerning accounting adjustments

Dear Sir

In the course of examining your draft final accounts for the year ended 31 August 19Y0 I have discovered four items which should be brought to your attention.

Timber stock

A quantity of timber stock has been included in the accounts at its selling price less a provision for future advertising expenses.

Stock should in fact be valued at the lower of cost and net realisable value. The prudence concept dictates that no credit should be taken for any profit before the stock is sold.

Therefore the timber stock should be written down to its cost in the accounts by the following adjustment.

Debit	profit and loss account	£800
Credit	stock account	£800

Fixtures and fittings

When fixed assets are made by the business itself rather than purchased in an arm's length transaction then the costs to be included need careful consideration.

It would be normal practice to include workshop labour and variable overheads in a cost valuation together with the materials used. It may also be normal accounting practice for Hillside Products Ltd to include an element of fixed overheads in such a valuation. However it must be checked that the basis for determining the fixed overheads is reasonable given the nature of the business operations and that the method used for apportioning the overhead is systematically applied throughout the business.

However what is unacceptable accounting practice is the inclusion of a profit element in the valuation. There has been no transaction with a third party therefore this profit should be eliminated as follows.

Debit	profit and loss account	£500
Credit	fixtures and fittings account	£500

This reduction in 'cost' of fixtures and fittings will also entail a reduction in the depreciation charge as follows.

Debit   fixtures and fittings provision for depreciation
Credit   profit and loss account

Motor vehicle depreciation

It is quite appropriate for a business's management to change the method of depreciation of assets if they believe that the new method would result in a fairer presentation of the results and financial position.

The management should review the assets' expected future life and estimated residual value in order to decide whether a change from straight line to reducing balance method of depreciation will give a fairer presentation of these assets and their usage.

If the change in method is considered to be reasonable then no accounting alterations are necessary. However if the effect of the change of depreciation method is material then it should be disclosed in the accounts together with the reasons for the change.

VAT

As Hillside Products Ltd is registered for VAT then all VAT collected on its sales is due to be paid over to the Customs and Excise. Therefore VAT should not be included in sales but instead credited to a customs and excise account.

Debit	sales account (£20,010 x 15/115)	£2,610
Credit	customs and excise account	£2,610

Yours faithfully

Thomas Harvey

3 CORRECTION OF ERRORS, JOURNAL ENTRIES AND SUSPENSE ACCOUNTS

3.1 BAKER AND JONES

(a) **Summary of the adjustments to profit and loss account for the nine months ended 30 June 19X7**

	£	£ +	£ −	£
Profit for the period from draft balance sheet				3,000
Adjustments				
Stock on approval included in stock on hand			160	
Bad debts	120			
Provision for doubtful debts	60			
			180	
Depreciation for nine months:				
Plant and machinery (10%)	315			
Motor vehicle (20%)	54			
			369	
Goods drawn by Jones		40		
Insurance prepaid (1/4 x 60)		15		
Interest on bank overdraft			100	
Hire purchase interest in abeyance incorrectly written off prior to 30 June		262		
Purchase returns not recorded		200		
		517		
			809	
			517	
				(292)
				2,708

	£	£
Adjusted profit for the period (shared equally)		
Baker	1,354	
Jones	1,354	
		2,708

Answers

Revised balance sheet at 30 June 19X7

		£
Capital accounts		
Cash introduced		
Baker		2,000
Jones		2,000
		4,000
Profit for the period		
Baker		1,354
Jones		1,354
		2,708
		6,708
Less: Drawings		
Baker		1,500
Jones		2,540
		4,040
		2,668

Represented by

Fixed assets	£	Cost £	Dep'n £
Plant and machinery	4,200	315	3,885
Motor vehicles	360	54	306
	4,560	369	4,191

Current assets			
Stock			1,940
Debtors, less provision for			
doubtful debts		2,250	
Payments in advance		105	
Cash in hand		10	
		4,305	
Current liabilities			
Trade and other creditors	1,108		
Amounts due under hire purchase			
agreement	2,000		
Bank overdraft	2,720		
	5,828		
		(1,523)	
		2,668	

3.2 ABC LTD

(a) Journal

		Dr £	Cr £
(a)	Rent	350	
	To sales ledger control		350
	(Being correction of error; rent payment previously debited in sales ledger control.		
(f)	Purchases	1,000	
	To purchase ledger control		1,000
	(Being correction of error; cash purchase payment previously debited to purchase ledger control.		
(i)	Suspense	1,900	
	To bank		1,900
	(Being correction of error; bank debit column of cash book overcast in March 19X3.		

(b) Opening trial balance

	£	£	Adjustments £	Adjustments £	Revised trial balance £	£
Fixed assets						
At cost	60,000		(j) 8,640		68,000	
Provision for dep'n		31,000				31,000
Ordinary share capital		35,000				35,000
Retained Earnings		12,000	(a) 350 (c) 500 (f) 1,000 (h) 910 (k) 1,460	(g) 2,450		10,230
Stock in trade						
At cost	14,000				14,000	
Sales ledger control	9,600		(d) 2,620	(a) 350 (b) 1,560 (c) 500	9,810	
Purchase ledger control		6,500	(b) 1,560	(e) 300 (j) 1,000 (h) 910		6,240
Bank	1,640		(g) 2,450	(d) 2,620 (i) 1,900 (j) 8,640		9,980
Suspense		740	(e) 300 (i) 1,900	(k) 1,460		
	85,240	85,240			92,450	92,450

(c) Reasons for the preparation of bank reconciliation statements:

(i) the establishment and verification of bank balances in the business cash book;

(ii) the assurance that all items entered in the bank account are recorded in the business cash book;

(iii) the identification of 'unpaid' cheques.

3.3   JOHN BOLD

(a)

	Dr £	Cr £
Suspense	1,900	
Sales		950
Purchases		950

Being correction of posting error; cash sales for January and February 19X6 previously posted to debit of purchases (W2).

(b)   **Trial balance as at 31 March 19X6 (corrected)**

	£	£
Purchases (£75,950 − £800 − £950)	74,200	
Sales (£94,650 + £160 + £950 + £700)		96,460
Trade debtors (£7,170 + £25 + £700 − £70 + £160)	7,985	
Discounts received		400
Trade creditors (£4,730 + £70)		4,800
Salaries	9,310	
Light and heat	760	
Bank charges	16	
Printing and stationery	376	
Stock at 1 April 19X5	5,100	
Provision for doubtful debts		110
Balance at bank (£2,300 − £16 − £25)	2,259	
Cash in hand	360	
Freehold premises: At cost	22,000	
Provision for depreciation		8,800
Motor vehicles: At cost	16,000	
Provision for depreciation		12,000
Capital at 1 April 19X5		23,096
Drawings (£6,500 + £800)	7,300	
	145,666	145,666

Workings

(1) **Trial balance redrafted** – but before taking into account errors discovered to ascertain correct amount on suspense account.

	Debit £	Credit £
Purchases	75,950	
Sales		94,650
Trade debtors	7,170	
Trade creditors		4,730
Salaries	9,310	
Light and heat	760	
Printing and stationery	376	
Stock at 1 April 19X5	5,100	
Provision for doubtful debts		110
Balance at bank	2,300	
Cash in hand	360	
Freehold premises – cost	2,200	
– depreciation		8,800
Motor vehicles – cost	1,600	
– depreciation		12,000
Capital at 1 April 19X5		23,096
Drawings	6,500	
	145,826	143,386
∴ Difference – suspense		2,440
	145,826	145,826

(2)

Suspense account

	£		£
Debtors (L White)	70	Balance b/f (W1)	2,440
Creditors (L White)	70		
Discount received	400		
Balance c/f	1,900		
	2,440		2,440
Purchases	950	Balance b/f	1,900
Sale	950		
	1,900		1,900

3.4 TIMBER PRODUCTS LTD

(a) **Difference on trial balance suspense account**

	£		£
Balance per trial balance	2,513	Wages	2,963
Discounts allowed	324	J Winters	198
Discounts received	324		
	3,161		3,161

0044V

(b) **Computation of corrected net profit for the year ended 30 April 19X7**

		£	£	£
Net profit per draft accounts				24,760
		Decreases	Increases	
1	Discounts		648	
2	Wages	2,963		
3	Remittance from K Mitcham	No effect		
4	Stationery stock		1,500	
5	Payment to J Winters	No effect		
6	Remittance from N North	3,000		
		5,963	2,148	–3,815
Corrected net profit				20,945

(c) **Principal uses of trial balances**

(i)   A trial balance provides an overall record for preparation of annual accounts.

(ii) The fact that a trial balance balances, provides some evidence that the records are accurate. The trial balance would still balance if the following errors occurred:

–   postings to wrong accounts;

–   compensating errors;

–   both sides of entry omitted.

3.5   LESLEY RIVERS LTD

(a)   **Balance sheet as at 31 August 19X7**

Fixed assets	Cost	Aggregate depreciation	
	£	£	£
Freehold premises	20,000	11,550	8,450
Motor vehicles	19,000	11,400	7,600
	39,000	22,950	16,050

Current assets			
Stock (£12,000 – £1,000)		11,000	
Debtors (W2)		8,633	
Balance at bank		2,360	
		21,993	

Less: Creditors: Amounts falling due within one year			
Trade creditors (W3)	1,900		
Accrued charges	710		
Proposed dividends (25,000 x 10p)	2,500	5,110	16,883
			32,933

Less: Creditors: Amounts falling due after more than one year			
Bank loan			5,000
			27,933

	£
Capital and reserves	
Ordinary shares of £1 each issued and fully paid	25,000
Profit and loss account (£5,100 – £300 – £267 + £900 – £2,500)	2,933
	27,933

(b)

	Dr	Cr
Worldwide Products Ltd	£1,000	
Purchases		£1,000

Being correction of entry recording goods 'on sale
or return' as purchases

	Dr	Cr
Profit and loss account	£1,000	
Stock account		£1,000

Being reduction of stock as at 31 August 19X7
held 'on sale or return'

0044V

Answers

Workings

(1) Provision for doubtful debts at 31 August 19X7

(£9,200 − £300) @ 3%

$= £8,900 \times \dfrac{3}{100}$

$= £267$

(2) Debtors

	£
Per draft balance sheet	9,200
Less: Bad debt − Cable Products Ltd	(300)
	8,900
Less: Provision for doubtful debts	(267)
	8,633

(3) Trade creditors

	£
Per draft accounts	3,800
Less: Stock purchased on sale or return	(1,000)
	2,800
Less: Payment to trade creditor misposted	(900)
	1,900

3.6 THOMAS SMITH

(a) **Corrected trial balance as at 31 March 19X8**

		£	£
Stock in trade at 1 April 19X7		10,700	
Discounts allowed		310	
Discounts received			450
Provision for doubtful debts			960
Purchases		94,000	
Purchases returns			1,400
Sales			132,100
Sales returns		1,100	
Freehold property	− at cost	70,000	
	− provision for depreciation		3,500
Motor vehicles	− at cost	15,000	
	− provision for depreciation		4,500
Capital − T Smith			84,600
Balance at bank		7,100	
Trade debtors		11,300	
Trade creditors			7,600
Establishment and administrative expenses		16,600	
Drawings		9,000	
		235,100	235,100

(b)   Journal entries

				£	£
(1)	Dr	Opening stock		1,300	
	Cr	Capital account – T Smith			1,300

being undervaluation of opening stock and consequent increase in previous year's profits.

				£	£
(2)	Dr	Trade creditors		210	
	Cr	Purchases returns			210

being return of goods and credit note not previously recorded.

				£	£
(3)	Dr	Sales		1,000	
	Cr	Trade debtors			1,000

being sale credited in error (free samples to J Grey).

				£	£
(4)	Dr	Establishment expenses		150	
	Cr	Purchases			150

being painting costs incorrectly included in purchases.

3.7   HIGHWAY PRODUCTS LTD

(a)

19X8		£	£
30 September	Central Garages Ltd	5,100	
	To retained earnings		5,100

Being the supply of goods to Central Garages Ltd

31 October	Motor vehicles – at cost	5,000	
	To Central Garages Ltd		5,000

Being the purchase of a motor vehicle

Answers

(b)   **Balance sheet as at 31 October 19X8**

	£	£	£
Fixed assets			
Freehold land and buildings	120,000	25,000	95,000
Plant and machinery	60,000	29,000	31,000
Motor vehicles (W1)	48,000	34,400	13,600
	228,000	88,400	139,600
Current assets			
Stock		27,000	
Trade debtors (W2)		17,600	
Balance at bank (W3)		5,710	
		50,310	
Less: Current liabilities			
Trade creditors (W4)	12,500		
Accrued charges (W5)	2,000		
	14,500		
			35,810
			175,410
Less: Long-term loan – J Baker			20,000
			155,410

	£
Capital	
Ordinary shares of £1.00 each fully paid	100,000
Retained earning (W6)	55,410
	155,410

Workings

	£	£
(1) Motor vehicles per trial balance	43,000	
Add: Motor vehicle purchased	5,000	
		48,000
(2) Trade creditors per trial balance	13,000	
Add: J Prince – incorrect posting	4,500	
Central Garages Ltd (£5,100 – £5,000)	100	
		17,600
(3) Balance at bank per trial balance	6,000	
Add: Cheque payment duplicated correction	120	
	6,120	
Less: Bank charges not recorded	410	
		5,710

		£	£
(4)	Trade creditors per trial balance	19,000	
	Less: Payment to John Gray not posted	6,500	
			12,500
(5)	Accrued charges		
	Interest on long-term loan payable 1 Nov 19X8		2,000
(6)	Retained earnings per trial balance	52,600	
	Add: Correction for cheque payment		
	duplicated in the cash book	120	
	Sales of goods to Central Garages Ltd	5,100	
		57,820	
	Less: Bank charges not recorded	(410)	
	Interest accrued on long-term loan	(2,000)	
			55,410
(7)	Suspense account per trial balance	11,000	
	Less: Receipt from J Prince incorrectly posted	(4,500)	
	Payment to John Gray not posted	(6,500)	
			–

3.8 JANE SIMPSON

(a)   Uncorrected trial balance as at 30 April 19X9

	£	£
Fixtures and fittings		
At cost	8,000	
Provision for depreciation		3,000
Motor vehicles		
At cost	9,600	
Provision for depreciation		5,600
Stock in trade	12,000	
Trade debtors	7,000	
Balance at bank	1,700	
Trade creditors		6,900
Sales		132,000
Cost of sales	79,200	
Establishment and administrative expenses	11,800	
Sales and distribution expenses	33,500	
Drawings	9,700	
Capital		30,000
	172,500	
Suspense account	5,000	
	177,500	177,500

Answers

(b)

Trading and profit and loss account
for the year ended 30 April 19X9

		£	£
Sales			132,000
Less:	Cost of sales – per trial balance	79,200	
	Plus error in stock at 30 April 19X8	3,000	
		82,200	
	Less: Goods for own use	600	
			81,600
Gross profit			50,400
Less:	Establishment and administrative expenses	11,800	
	Sales and distribution expenses	33,500	
	Depreciation – fixtures and fittings	913*	
	– motor vehicles	2,400	
	Sales commission	1,008	
			49,621
Net profit			779

Balance sheet as at 30 April 19X9

		Cost £	Depreciation to date £	£
Fixed assets				
	Fixtures and fittings	12,500	3,913	8,587
	Motor vehicles	9,600	8,000	1,600
		22,100	11,913	10,187
Current assets				
	Stock	12,000		
	Trade debtors (£7,000 + £500)	7,500		
	Balance at bank	1,700		
			21,200	
Less:	Current liabilities			
	Trade creditors	6,900		
	Accruals – sales commission	1,008		
			7,908	
				13,292
				23,479

0044V

	£
Represented by: Capital account – At 1 May 19X8	30,000
Add: Adjustment to net profit year ended 30 April 19X8	3,000
	33,000
Add: Net profit year ended 30 April 19X9	779
	33,779
Less: Drawings (9,700 + 600)	10,300
	23,479

* Depreciation

	£
Fixtures and fittings	
10% of £8,000	800
10% of £4,500 for 3 months	113
	913

3.9 AUDREY PRINGLE

(a) **Trading and profit and loss account for the year ended 31 October 19X8**

	£
Sales	126,000
Less: Cost of sales	
(92,000 + (14,000 – 12,600) – 2,000)	91,400
Gross profit	34,600
Less: Overhead expenses	13,000
Net profit	21,600

Trading and profit and loss account for the year ended 31 October 19X9

	£
Sales	136,000
Less: Cost of sales	
(100,000 – (14,000 + 12,600) – 4,000 – 5,000)	89,600
Gross profit	46,400
Less: Overhead expenses	
(24,000 + 3,000 + 5,000)	32,000
	14,400

Balance sheet as at 31 October

	19X8		19X9	
	£	£	£	£
Fixed assets				
Cost	84,000		86,000	
Less: Provision for depreciation	62,000		61,000	
		22,000		25,000
Current assets				
Stock	12,600		12,000	
Debtors	9,000		10,000	
Bank balance	8,000		1,000	
	29,600		23,000	
Creditors: Amounts falling due within one year				
Creditors	(6,000)		(3,000)	
		23,600		20,000
		45,600		45,000
Represented by				
Capital account				
– balance b/f		40,000		45,600
Net profit		21,600		14,400
		61,600		60,000
Less: Drawings (14,000 + 2,000)		16,000		
Drawings (11,000 + 4,000)				15,000
		45,600		45,000

(b) Dr Disposal account   £10,000
　　　　Cr Fixed assets at cost account   £10,000

Being the removal of fixed assets scrapped from accounts.

　　Dr Provision for depreciation   £7,000
　　　　Cr Disposal account   £7,000

Being removal of depreciation on scrapped assets.

　　Dr Profit and loss account   £3,000
　　　　Cr Disposal account   £3,000

Being loss on scrapping of fixed assets.

(c)   Financial ratios

	19X8	19X9	Comment
Gross profit margin ($\frac{\text{Gross profit}}{\text{Sales}}$)	27.5%	34.1%	Improved
Net profit margin ($\frac{\text{Net profit}}{\text{Sales}}$)	17.1%	10.6%	Deteriorated
Fixed asset turnover ($\frac{\text{Sales}}{\text{Fixed assets}}$)	5.73	5.44	Deteriorated
Total asset turnover ($\frac{\text{Sales}}{\text{Total assets}}$)	2.76	3.02	Improved
Return on capital ($\frac{\text{Net profit}}{\text{Capital employed}}$)	47.4%	32 %	Deteriorated
Current ratio ($\frac{\text{Current assets}}{\text{Current liabilities}}$)	4.93	7.67	Improved
Quick ratio ($\frac{\text{Current assets} - \text{stock}}{\text{Current liabilities}}$)	28.3	3.67	Improved

(Tutorial note: Only **three** ratios were required by the question.)

3.10   **ALLSQUARE ENGINEERS LTD**

(a)   Suspense account

19X0	£	19X0	£
31 March: Sales ledger control (K Dodds)	500	31 March: Balance b/f	549
31 March: Discounts allowed	376	31 March: Discounts received	224
31 March: Discounts received	376	31 March: Discounts allowed	224
31 March: Purchase ledger control	495	31 March: Depreciation charge – manufacturing account	750
	1,747		1,747

(b)

	£
Profit on manufacturing	12,760
Depreciation charge	(750)
	12,010

	£
Gross profit	23,410
Credit sales to T Sparkes	1,200
	24,610

	£
Net profit	9,746
Credit sales to T Sparkes	1,200
Discounts received (376 – 224)	152
Discounts allowed (376 – 224	152
Depreciation charge	(750)
	10,500

4 CONTROL ACCOUNTS AND BANK RECONCILIATIONS

4.1 CHARLES POOTER

(a) Journal entries

				Dr £	Cr £
(1)	Dr	Cash		400	
	Cr	Thames Water (memorandum)			400
(2)	Dr	Holloway debtors' ledger control account		1,827	
	Cr	City debtors' ledger control account			1,827
(3)	Dr	Cash		2,100	
	Cr	Creditors' ledger control account			2,100
	Dr	Holloway debtors' ledger control account		235	
	Cr	Creditors' ledger control account			235
(4)	Dr	Cash		12,840	
	Cr	City debtors' ledger control account			2,800
		Holloway debtors' ledger control account			1,020
		Sales			9,020
(5)	Dr	City debtors' ledger control account		4,000	
	Cr	Cash			4,000
(6)	Dr	(already done)		–	
	Cr	Creditors' ledger control account			42

(b) **Bank reconciliation statement at 31 December 19X5**

	£	
Balance per bank statement (bal fig)	2,311	(in hand)
Outstanding lodgements	12,840	
	15,151	
Unpresented cheques (5,884 – 2,100)	3,784	
	11,367	
Bank error	400	
Balance per cash book	11,767	

0044V

Cash book

	£		£
Balance b/f (unadjusted)	427	Overcast	4,000
Bank error	400		
Cheques written back	2,100		
Outstanding lodgements	12,840	Balance c/f	11,767
	15,767		15,767

(c)   **Balance sheet extract at 31 December 19X5**

	£
Creditors (W1)	16,211
Debtors (W2) (12,592 + 8,613)	21,205

Workings

(1)   **Creditors' ledger control account**

	£		£
Balance b/f	42	Balance b/f	13,876
		19X6 cheques	2,100
		Refund – Huttle Ltd	235
Balance c/f	16,211	City debtors' ledger contra	42
	16,253		16,253

(2)   **Holloway debtors' ledger control account**

	£		£
Balance b/f	11,785	Balance b/f	235
City receipts	1,827	Cash	1,020
Refund – Huttle Ltd	235	Balance c/f	12,592
	13,847		13,847

City debtors' ledger control account

	£		£
Balance b/f	9,240	Receipts misanalysed	1,827
Overcast	4,000	Cash	2,800
		Balance c/f	8,613
	13,240		13,240

0044V

4.2   **ARGO LTD**

(a)   Sales ledger control account

		£			£
1 Jan	Balance b/f	8,952	Jan/Dec	Bank	69,471
Jan/Dec	Sundry debtors	74,753	Jan/Dec	Discounts allowed	1,817
			31 Dec	Balance c/f	12,417
		83,705			83,705
31 Dec	Balance b/f	12,417	31 Dec	Credit transfers	198
	Car disposal a/c	1,173		Contras	2,896
				Bad debts	640
				Balance c/f	9,856
		13,590			13,590
1 Jan	Balance b/f	9,856			

		£	£
(b)	Balances at 31 December before adjustment		9,663
	Add: Debit balances not included	191	
	Balances incorrectly picked up	200	
			391
			10,054
	Less: Credit transfers omitted		198
			9,856

(c)   The benefits which accrue from operating controls are:

(i)   Errors are more easily located.

(ii)   Totals of debtors and creditors are available for management use when needed.

(iii)   Risk of error and fraud is reduced.

(iv)   Periodic accounts may be prepared more quickly because the control account totals for debtors and creditors may be used in the trial balance.

4.3   MAINWAY DEALERS LTD

(a)

Debtors' ledger control account May 19X6

	£		£
Balance b/f	16,720	Balance b/f	1,146
Credit sales	19,380	Bank	15,497
Bank	470	Sales returns	1,198
Bank – cheques dishonoured	320	Discounts allowed	430
Bad debts recovered (R Bell)	142	Bad debts written off	131
Balance c/f	670	Creditors' ledger control	
		(Re L Green)	300
		Balance c/f	19,000
	37,702		37,702
Balance b/f	19,000	Balance c/f	670

Creditors' ledger control account May 19X6

	£		£
Balance b/f	280	Balance b/f	7,470
Bank	6,320	Credit purchases	6,700
Purchases returns	240	Bank	130
Discounts received	338	Balance c/f	365
Debtors' ledger control			
(Re L Green)	300		
Balance c/f	7,187		
	14,665		14,665
Balance b/f	365	Balance b/f	7,187

(b)   **Balance sheet as at 31 May 19X6 (extract)**

	£
Current assets	
Trade debtors (£19,000 – £475*) + £365	18,890
(*2½% x £19,000)	
Current liabilities	
Trade creditors (£670 + £7,187)	7,857

4.4   JOHN HENRY LTD (1)

(a)   **Bank reconciliation statement as at 30 September 19X6**

	£	£
Balance as per bank statement		322.98
Add: Lodgements not yet credited 30 September		
S Balk		220.39
		543.37
Deduct: Cheques not yet presented from previous		
reconciliation (W2)	154.18	
23 Sept John Peters Ltd 765423	18.34	
26 Sept J Green Ltd 765426	45.00	
26 Sept G Glinker 765427	174.00	
		391.52
Balance as per cash book and balance sheet		151.85

Workings

	£
(1) Adjustments to cash book	
Balance per question	134.80
Error in lodgement	+10.00
Dividends received	+65.00
Interest – loan account	−41.25
Bank charges	−16.70
Adjusted balance as per above	151.85

	£	£
(2) Bank reconciliation – opening		
Balance as per bank statement	453.26	
Deduct: Cheques not yet presented		
765419 22 Sept	138.35	
765420 25 Sept	160.04	
765418 29 Sept	21.69	
		320.08
		133.18
Balance per cash book		21.00 o/d
Missing figure		154.18

(b)   The major uses of a bank reconciliation statement:

(i)   To provide external evidence of the bank balance at the end of an accounting period.

(ii)   To confirm the accuracy of the accounting records in the cash book.

(iii)   To identify errors in the cash book and allow for their correction.

4.5   JAMES SWIFT LTD

(a)   James Swift Ltd year ended 30 November 19X7
                        Sales ledger control account

	£		£
Balance b/f	10,687	Balance b/f	452
Sales	130,382	Sales returns	1,810
Bad debt recovered		Discounts allowed	
(30.11.X6)	1,200	(£1,306.50 – £127,900)	2,750
		Cash received	127,900
		Cash received	
		(re Bad debt 30.11.X6)	1,200
		Transfer to purchases	
		ledger (J Hancock)	350
		Bad debts written off	
		(T Dick)	560
Balance c/f	1,008	Balance c/f	8,255
	143,277		143,277
Balance b/f	8,255	Balance b/f	1,008

(b)   Purchases ledger control account

	£		£
Balance c/f	1,630	Balance c/f	9,536
Purchases returns		Purchases (£99,000 @ 90%)	89,100
(£600 @ 90%)	540		
Transfer from Sales			
Ledger (J Hancock)	350		
Cash paid	83,500		
Discounts received			
(£85,000 – £83,500)	1,500		
Balance c/f	11,876	Balance c/f	760
	99,396		99,396
Balance c/f	760	Balance c/f	11,876

4.6   CENTRAL MANUFACTURERS

(a)   John Banks' account

	£		£
Balance b/f	3,100	Discounts allowed	8,636
Sales	86,360	Sales returns	160
Disposal of FA (NBV)		Cash received	75,000
5,000 – (18 mths @ 25% depn)	3,125	Discounts allowed	1,100
		Cash received	3,000
		Purchases contra	1,200
		Balance c/f	3,489
	92,585		92,585

Answers

(b)

Provision for doubtful debts

	£		£
Profit and loss a/c	1,390	Balance b/f	2,300
Balance c/f (W1)	910		
	2,300		2,300

Provision for discounts allowed

	£		£
Balance c/f (W1)	594	Profit and loss a/c	594

Workings

(1) **Provision required**

1% x	24,000	=	240
2% x	10,000	=	200
4% x	8,000	=	320
5% x	3,000	=	150
			910

(2) **Provision for discounts**

	£
Debtors (May sales)	24,000
Expected doubtful debts	(240)
	23,760 x 2½% = 594

4.7 JANE BANKS

(a)
Account number 547892 with Central Bank plc, Northtown Branch
Bank reconciliation statement as at 12 November 19X8

		£	£
Balance per cash book			312.20 o/d
Add:	Discount allowed debited in error in cash book		6.00
			318.20 o/d
Less:	Cheque now cancelled – number 162371		47.00
			271.20 o/d
Add:	Bank lodgement not yet recorded in bank statement		29.00
			300.20 o/d
Add:	Car Dealers' Association – standing order not recorded in cash book		25.00
			325.20 o/d
Less:	Unpresented cheques		
	Cheque number 162358	95.10	
	162364	38.90	
	162370	70.00	
	162374	101.00	
	162375	385.70	
	162376	3,500.00	
			4,190.70
Balance per bank statement			3,865.50 in hand

(b) **Reasons why it is necessary to prepare bank reconciliation statements**

(i) Verify cash book balance.

(ii) Identify items 'in transit', eg, unpresented cheques; lodgements not yet credited by bank.

(iii) Identify 'stale' unpresented cheques.

(iv) Identify cash book errors.

Answers

4.8   HIGHGROUND DEALERS LTD

(a)   Purchases ledger control account

19X9		£	19X9		£
1 Jan	Balance b/f	245	1 Jan	Balance b/f	152,498
31 Jan	Bank	157,760	31 Jan	Purchases	
31 Jan	Purchases returns			(142,00–14,200)	127,800
	(4,200–420)	3,780	31 Jan	Balance c/f	180
31 Jan	Discounts received	2,510			
31 Jan	Balance c/f	116,183			
		280,478			280,478
1 Feb	Balance b/f	180	1 Feb	Balance b/f	116,183
28 Feb	Bank	126,150		Purchases	
28 Feb	Purchases returns			(98,000–9,800)	88,200
	(5,700–570)	5,130	28 Feb	Balance c/f	276
28 Feb	Discounts received	1,870			
28 Feb	K Marden (sales				
	ledger control a/c)	3,000			
28 Feb	Balance c/f	68,329			
		204,659			204,659
1 Mar	Balance b/f	276	1 Mar	Balance b/f	68,329
31 Mar	Bank	85,700	31 Mar	Purchases	
31 Mar	Purchases returns			(112,000–11,200)	100,800
	(6,500 – 650)	5,850	31 Mar	Balance c/f	355
31 Mar	Discounts received	1,430			
31 Mar	Balance c/f	76,228			
		169,484			169,484
1 Apr	Balance b/f	355	1 Apr	Balance b/f	76,228

(b)   **Computation of the gross profit for the three months ended 31 March 19X9**

			£	£
Purchases	– January		127,800	
	– February		88,200	
	– March		100,800	
				316,800
Less: Purchases returns	– January		3,780	
	– February		5,130	
	– March		5,850	
				14,760
				302,040
Less: Increase in stock				8,000
Cost of goods sold				294,040

	£	£
Normal gross profit 40% of £284,040 (£294,000 – £10,000)		113,616
Gross profit on goods sold at half price:		
Cost of goods sold sold at half price	10,000	
Less: $\dfrac{£10,000 \times 1.40}{2}$	7,000	
Loss on goods sold at half price		3,000
Gross profit		110,616

4.9 MARY SAUNDERS

(a)

Purchase ledger control account

	£		£
Balance b/f	1,436	Balance b/f	16,892
Bank	264,360	Credit purchases	289,439
Returns outwards	9,400		
Balance c/f	32,072	Balance c/f	937
	307,268		307,268

Sales ledger control account

	£		£
Balance b/f	35,975	Balance b/f	874
Credit sales	417,920	Bank	392,710
Bad debt recovered		Returns inwards	11,556
(Profit and loss)	518	Bad debts written off	1,927
		Bad debt recovered (bank)	518
		Trade discount omitted	200
Balance c/f	572	Balance c/f	47,200
	454,985		454,985

(b) **Trade debtors**

	£
Sales ledger balance	47,200
Less: Provision for doubtful debts (5% x 47,200)	(2,360)
	44,840
Less: Provision for discounts allowable (2½% x 44,840)	(1,121)
	43,719
Add: Purchase ledger debit balances	937
	44,656

0044V

Trade creditors	£
Purchase ledger balance	32,072
Add: Sales ledger credit balances	572
	32,644

4.10 THOMAS P LEE

(a) **Computation of bank balance to be included in balance sheet at 31 October 19X9**

	£
Balance per cash book at 31 October 19X9	894.68
Cheque 176276 incorrectly entered	(9.00)
Bank commission	(169.56)
Bank interest	(109.10)
Dishonoured cheque . T Andrews	(29.31)
Cheque 177145 recorded twice	15.10
Trades credits	210.10
Standing order	(15.00)
Corrected balance at 31 October 19X9	787.91

(b) **Bank reconciliation at 31 October 19X9**

	£
Corrected cash book balance	787.91
Less: outstanding lodgements	(1,895.60)
Add: outstanding cheques	395.80
Balance per bank statement – overdrawn	(711.89)

(c) **Bank reconciliation statements at the year–end** are necessary to:

(i) establish accuracy of cash book entries;
(ii) ensure all items on the bank statement are included in the cash book;
(iii) ensure only correct items on bank statement;
(iv) verify cash book balance.

4.11   JOAN SEAWARD

(a)   Trading account for the three months ended 31 March 19Y0

	£	£	£
Sales: Cash (40% x 609,840)			243,936
Credit (balancing figure)		375,704	
Less: Sales returns		(9,800)	365,904
			————
Total sales			609,840
Less: Cost of sales			
Opening stock		121,000	
Purchases (balancing figure)	454,340		
Less: Purchase returns	(16,500)		
	————		
		437,840	
		————	
(balancing figure)		558,840	
Less: Closing stock (W2)		(73,240)	
		————	
Cost of sales (W1)			485,600
			————
Gross profit			124,240
			————

Purchase ledger control account

19Y0	£	19Y0	£
Returns outwards	16,500	1 Jan Balance b/f	74,000
Discounts received	4,100	Purchases (Trading a/c)	454,340
Bank	410,000		
31 March Balance c/f	97,740		
	————		————
	528,340		528,340
	————		————

Sales ledger control account

19Y0	£	19Y0	£
1 Jan Balance b/f	93,000	Returns inwards	9,800
Credit Sales		Bad debt written off	5,000
(Trading a/c)	375,704	Discounts allowed	2,300
		Bank (575,306 – cash sales	
		from trading a/c 243,936)	331,370
		31 March Balance c/f	120,234
	————		————
	468,704		468,704
	————		————

Answers

Workings

(1)	Gross profit of 40% on cost of sales	£	£
	Gross profit for three months		124,240
	Add: Lost gross profit on goods sold at loss	100,000	
	Gross profit	40,000	
	Normal sales price	140,000	
	Actual sales price	70,000	
	Additional gross profit		70,000
			194,240
	Cost of good sold 194,240 x 100/40		485,600

(2)

$$\text{Stock turnover} = \frac{\text{Cost of sales}}{\text{Average stock}} = 5$$

$$\text{Therefore} = \frac{485,600}{\text{Average stock}}$$

Average stock $= £97,120$

$$97,120 = \frac{121,000 + \text{closing stock}}{2}$$

Closing stock $= 194,240 - 121,000$
$= £73,240$

(b) **Trade debtors at 31 March 19Y0**

	£
Sales ledger control account	120,234
Less: Provision for doubtful debts	(3,800)
Discount allowed (£60,000 x 2½%)	(1,500)
	114,934

5 THE ACCOUNTS OF CLUBS AND SOCIETIES

5.1 SCOTT SOCIAL CLUB

(a)	**Bar trading account for the year to 31 March 19X3**	£	£
	Bar sales		27,000
	Less: Cost of goods sold:		
	Opening stock	2,000	
	Purchases	18,500	
		20,500	
	Less: Closing stock	2,500	
			18,000
	Gross profit		9,000

0044V

(b) **Income and expenditure account for the year to 31 March 19X3**

	£	£
Income		
Bar – gross profit		9,000
Christmas dance	850	
Less: Expenses	150	
	——	
		700
Donations		1,500
Subscriptions (17,000 – 900 + 50 + 600 – 100)		16,650
		——
		27,850
Expenditure		
Depreciation		
Club premises	2,000	
Furniture	1,000	
General expenses	26,200	
Rates (900 – 450 + 500)	950	
	——	
		30,150
		——
Excess of expenditure over income for the year		(2,300)
		——

Balance sheet at 31 March 19X3

	Cost	Dep'n	Net book value
	£	£	£
Fixed assets			
Club premises	50,000	32,000	18,000
Furniture	10,000	8,000	2,000
	——	——	——
	60,000	40,000	20,000
	——	——	
Current assets			
Bar stock		2,500	
Subscriptions due		600	
Cash at bank and in hand		2,200	
		——	
		5,300	
Less: Current liabilities			
Rates	500		
Subscriptions paid in advance	100		
	——		
		600	
		——	
			4,700
			——
			24,700
			——

	£
Financed by:	
Accumulated fund	
Balance at 1.4.X2	27,000
Less: Excess of expenditure over income for the year	2,300
	——
	24,700
	——

0044V

Workings

	£	£
Club premises		20,000
Furniture		3,000
Bar stock		2,000
Subscriptions due		900
Bank and cash in hand		1,600
		27,500
Less: Rates	450	
Subscriptions paid in advance	50	
		500
Balance at 1 April 19X2		27,000

5.2 BUNBURY COUNTRY CLUB

Balance sheet at 30 June 19X6

Fixed assets	Cost £	Dep'n £	£
Fixtures and fittings (W1)	9,840	3,941	5,899
Investments at cost (6,000 – (1,800 – 850))	——	——	5,050
			10,949
Current assets			
Bar stocks (W2)		6,235	
Subscriptions in arrears (W3)		2,800	
Bank – Deposit account (W4)		5,519	
– Current account		9,388	
Cash in hand		2,800	
		26,742	
Current liabilities			
Creditors for bar purchases		4,634	
Subscriptions in advance		200	
		4,834	
			21,908
			32,857
Accumulated fund			
Balance at 1 July 19X5			26,545
Surplus of income over expenditure for the year (bal fig)			6,312
Balance at 30 June 19X6			32,857

Workings

(1)

Fixtures and fittings	Cost £		Depreciation £
Balance at 1.7.X5	10,340		2,840
Disposal 1.7.X5	(1,000)	(100 + 180)	280
	9,340		2,560
Addition	500		
Charge for year:			
20% (9,340 − 2,560)			1,356
20% x 3/12 x £500			25
Balance at 30.6.X6	9,840		3,941

(2) **Bar stocks**

	£
Sales (29,348 + 2,800)	32,148
Cost of sales ($\frac{100}{130}$)	24,729
Less Opening stock	2,180
	22,549
Less: Purchases (27,330 − 3,180 + 4,634)	28,784
Closing stock	6,235

(3)

Subscriptions

	£		£
Bal b/f (in arrears)	2,000	Bal c/f (in advance)	300
Receivable			
(500 x £50)	25,000	Cash	24,100
Bal c/f (in advance)	200	Bal c/f (in arrears – bal fig)	2,800
	27,200		27,200

(4) **Deposit account**

	£
Balance at 1.7.X5	5,000
30.9.X5 Interest 2 1/2%	125
	5,125
31.12.X5 Interest 2 1/2%	128
	5,253
31.3.X6 Interest 2 1/2%	131
	5,384
30.6.X6 Interest 2 1/2%	135
Balance at 30.6.X6	5,519

0044V

5.3 CAWDOR SOCIAL CLUB

(a)
Statement of accumulated fund at 1 January 19X8

	£	£
Assets:		
Billiards equipment		240
Stock		210
Subscriptions due		8
Rates and insurance prepaid		22
Balance at bank (W2)		236
Cash in hand		24
		740
Less: Creditors		
Brewery	230	
Printing and stationery accrued	12	
		242
		498

(b) Income and expenditure account for the year ended 31 December 19X8

	£			£
Rates (W6)	89	Subscriptions (W3)		60
Repairs	64	Bank interest		6
Printing, etc (W7)	88			
Wages	340	Net receipts from bar:		
Commission (10% x 860)	86	Sales (W4)	4,596	
Donations	12	Less: Stock 1.1.X8 210		
Surplus of income over		Purchases 3,752		
expenditure	275	3,962		
		Stock 31.12.X8 226		
			3,736	
				860
		Billiards takings	58	
		Depreciation	30	
				28
	954			954

(c)   **Balance sheet at 31 December 19X8**

	Cost £	Dep'n £	£
Fixed assets			
Billiards equipment	300	30	270
	—	—	
Current assets			
Stock		226	
Debtors and prepaid expenses (6 + 25)		31	
Cash at bank (501 + 160)		661	
Cash in hand		75	
		—	
		993	
Current liabilities			
Creditors and accrued expenses (390 + 14 + 86)		490	
		—	
Net current assets			503
			—
			773
			—
Balance at 1 January 19X8			498
Excess of income over expenditure for the year			275
			—
			773
			—

Workings

(1)   **Cash account**

	£		£
Opening balance	86	Purchases	3,584
Less: o/s cheque	60	Adjustment for o/s cheques	20
	—		—
	26		3,604
Opening cash	24	Billiards equipment	60
Bar takings	4,521	Rates	92
Subscriptions	62	Wages	340
Billiards takings	58	Repairs	64
Transfer deposit account	56	Printing, stationery, etc	86
		Balance c/f	501
	—		—
	4,747		4,747
	—		—

(2)	Opening bank balance	£
	Current account – as above	26
	Deposit account	210
		—
		236

Answers

(3)

Subscriptions

	£		£
Balance b/f	8	Cash	62
Income and expenditure a/c	60	Balance c/f	6
	68		68

(4) Sales

	£
Per question	4,521
Cash not yet banked	75
	4,596

(5)

Creditors' control account

	£		£
Cash	3,604	Balance b/f	230
Balance c/f	390	Transfer donations	12
		Income and expenditure a/c	3,752
	3,994		3,994

(6)

Rates

	£		£
Balance b/f	22	Balance c/f	25
Cash	92	Income and expenditure a/c	89
	114		114

(7)

Printing and stationery

	£		£
Cash	86	Balance b/f	12
Balance c/f	14	Income and expenditure a/c	88
	100		100

0044V

5.4 WOODLANDS HOCKEY CLUB

(a) **Computation of accumulated fund as on 31 May 19X6**

	£	£
Equipment		150
Balance at bank		63
Balance in hand		10
Supporters' subscriptions due		14
Fees due		78
Annual social		6
		321
Rent owing	72	
Secretary's expenses	4	
Refreshments	13	
		89
		232

(b) **Income and expenditure account for the year ended 31 May 19X7**

	£		£	£
Rent	216	Subscription		148
Printing and stationery	21	Game fees		145
Affiliation fees	12	Annual social	128	
Captain's and secretary's		Less: Expenses	102	
expenses	41			
Refreshments	60			26
Depreciation	22	Balance – excess of		
		expenditure over income		53
	372			372

Workings

Subscriptions	£	Game fees	£
Per cash book	150	Per cash book	170
Add: 19X7 debtors	12	Add: 19X7 debtors	53
	162		223
Less: 19X6 debtors	14	Less: 19X6 debtors	78
	148		145

Rent	£	Printing and stationery	£
Per cash book	234	Per cash book	18
Add: 19X7 creditors	54	Add: 19X7 creditors	3
	288		21
Less: 19X6 creditors	72		
	216		

Balance sheet as at 31 May 19X7

			£
Accumulated fund			232
Less: Deficit for current year			53
			179

	£	£	£
Represented by:			
Fixed assets			
Equipment			176
Less: Depreciation			22
			154
Current assets			
Subscriptions in arrears		12	
Game fees		53	
Bank balance		49	
Cash in hand		8	
		122	
Less: Current liabilities			
Rent	54		
Printing	3		
Secretary's expenses	8		
Refreshments	12		
Subscriptions in advance	20		
	97		
			25
			179

5.5   SPRINGTIME GARDENERS CLUB

(a)   Accumulated fund as at 1 January 19X6

	£		£
Membership subscriptions		Bank	876
in advance	240	Debtors: Lawn mower sales	400
Creditors:		Stocks of seeds, at cost	250
Lawn mower supplier	800	Land, at cost	2,000
Seed growers	110		
Balance c/f	2,376		
	3,526		3,526
		Balance b/f	2,376

(b)

Income and expenditure account
for the year ended 31 December 19X6

	£		£
Loss on seeds sales:		Subscriptions	
Sales	1,684	(see W3)	7,040
Less: Cost of sales			
(W1)	1,820		
	136		
National Gardening Show			
(W2)	3,690		
Garden magazines	390		
Secretarial expenses	940		
Rent of club premises	500		
	5,656		
Excess of income over			
expenditure	1,384		
	7,040		7,040

(c)

Balance sheet as at 31 December 19X6

	£	£	£
Fixed assets			
Land at cost		2,000	
Architect fees		1,000	
			3,000
Current assets			
Stocks of seeds, at cost		560	
Debtors – lawn mower sales		1,370	
		1,930	
Less: Current liabilities			
Creditors – Lawn mower supplier	170		
Seed growers	340		
Membership subscriptions in advance	390		
Bank overdraft	270		
		1,170	
			760
			3,760

	£
Represented by	
Accumulated fund: At 1 January 19X6	2,376
Add: Excess of income over expenditure for 19X6	1,384
	3,760

Workings

		£
(1)	Seed purchases: Cash paid	1,900
	Less: Creditors at 1 January 19X6	110
		1,790
	Add: Creditors at 31 December 19X6	340
		2,130
	Less: Stock increase (£560 – £250)	310
		1,820

		£
(2)	National Gardening Show: Purchase of tickets and brochures	3,600
	Coaches	490
		4,090
	Less: Ticket sales to non–members	400
		3,690

		£
(3)	Subscriptions: Cash received	7,190
	Add: Subscriptions paid in advance at 1 January 19X6	240
		7,430
	Less: Subscriptions paid in advance at 31 December 19X6	390
		7,040

5.7 PHOENIX MODEL ENGINEERING SOCIETY

Income and expenditure account for the year ended 31 March 19X9

		£	£
Members' subscriptions (238 @ £50)			11,900
Machinery and tools sales gross profit (W1)			2,900
			14,800
Less:	Rent of temporary office and meeting room (600 – 150)	450	
	Wooden hut – loss on ale (1,300 – 1,100)	200	
	Printing, stationery and postages	860	
	Secretary's honorarium	150	
	Bank charges	14	
	Annual national exhibition – loss (W2)	35	
			1,709
Excess of income over expenditure			13,091

Balance sheet as at 31 March 19X9

	£	£	£
Fixed assets			
Building land, at cost			8,000
Current assets			
Stock – machinery and tools		600	
Subscriptions due		250	
Amount due for annual exhibition tickets		40	
Rent prepaid		150	
Building society investment account		7,500	
Balance at bank (354 – 14)		340	
		8,880	
Less: Current liabilities			
Subscriptions prepaid (W3)	500		
Amount due for annual national exhibition programmes	45		
		545	
			8,335
			16,335

	£
Represented by:	
General fund: At 1 April 19X8 (W4)	3,244
Add excess of income over expenditure for year ended 31 March 19X9	13,091
	16,335

Workings

	£	£
(1) Machinery and tool sales gross profit		
Sales		21,000
Less: Cost of sales		
Opening stock	1,200	
Purchases	17,500	
	18,700	
Less: Closing stock	600	
		18,100
Gross profit		2,900

		£	£
(2)	Annual national exhibition		
	Ticket sales – cash received	300	
	– amount due 31 March 19X9	40	
			340
	Less: Admission charges	220	
	Exhibition programmes	45	
	Coach	110	
			375
	Loss		35

		£	£
(3)	Subscriptions prepaid		
	Total due for year ended 31 March 19X9 – 238 @ £50		11,900
	Due at 1 April 19X8		150
			12,050
	Less: Prepaid at 1 April 19X8	300	
	Due at 31 March 19X9	250	
			550
			11,500
	Less: Cash received 19X8/X9		12,000
	Prepaid 31 March 19X9		500

		£
(4)	General fund at 1 April 19X8	
	Wooden hut at valuation	1,300
	Stocks of machinery and tools	1,200
	Subscriptions due	150
	Balance at bank	894
		3,544
	Less: Subscriptions prepaid by members	300
		3,244

6   INCOMPLETE RECORDS – THE ACCOUNTS OF SOLE TRADERS

6.1   A HIGHTON

Trading and profit and loss account for the year ended 31 March 19X2

	£	£
Sales		
Cash	80,400	
Credit (W1)	9,250	
		89,650
Cost of sales:		
Opening stock	3,500	
Purchases (£17,000 + W4)	64,500	
	68,000	
Less: Closing stock	4,000	
		64,000
Gross profit		25,650
Less: Expenses:		
General shop expenses	100	
Depreciation – motor vehicle (25% x £3,000)	750	
Electricity (W5)	600	
Loan interest (W3)	100	
Motor vehicle expenses (W6)	800	
Property insurance (W2)	100	
Rates	300	
Telephone	400	
Wages	3,000	
		6,150
Net profit		19,500

Balance sheet at 31 March 19X2

	Cost £	Dep'n £	Net book value £
Fixed assets			
Freehold land and buildings	10,000	–	10,000
Motor vehicle	3,000	1,500	1,500
	13,000	1,500	
c/f			11,500

Answers

	Cost £	Dep'n £	Net book value £
b/f			11,500
Current assets			
Stock, at cost	4,000		
Debtors	1,000		
Prepayments	400		
Cash at bank	950		
Cash in hand	450		
		6,800	
Less: Current liabilities			
Creditors	1,800		
Accrual	500		
		2,300	
			4,500
			16,000

Financed by	£	£
Capital as at 1 April 19X1 (W8)		5,250
Net profit for the year	19,500	
Less: Drawings	8,750	
		10,750
		16,000

Workings

(1) Trade debtors account

	£		£
Balance b/f	500	Bank	8,750
Credit sale	9,250	Balance c/f	1,000
	9,750		9,750

(2) Property insurance account

	£		£
Balance b/f	50	Profit & loss account	100
Cash/bank	150	Balance c/f	100
	200		200

(3)
Loan account

	£		£
Bank	10,100	Balance b/f	10,000
		Profit & loss a/c interest	100
	10,100		10,100

(4)
Trade creditors account

	£		£
Bank	47,200	Balance b/f	1,500
Balance c/f	1,800	Credit purchases	47,500
	49,000		49,000

(5)
Electricity account

	£		£
Bank	400	Balance b/f	200
Balance c/f	400	Profit and loss account	600
	800		800

(6)
Motor vehicle expense account

	£		£
Balance b/f	200	Balance b/f	200
Cash/bank	1,000	Profit and loss account	800
Balance c/f	100	Balance c/f	300
	1,300		1,300

Answers

(7)   Cash and bank account

	Cash £	Bank £		Cash £	Bank £
Balance b/f	100	550	Purchases	17,000	47,200
Cash sales	80,400		Drawings	7,000	1,750
Cash banked		52,850	General expenses	100	
Debtors		8,750	Telephone	100	300
			Wages	3,000	
			Cash banked	52,850	
			Loan & interest		10,100
			Electricity		400
			M/V expenses		1,000
			Insurance		150
			Rates		300
			Balance c/f	450	950
	80,500	62,150		80,500	62,150

(8)   Opening capital

	£	£
Freehold land and buildings		10,000
Motor vehicle		2,250
Stock		3,500
Trade debtors		500
Prepayments		250
Cash at bank and in hand		650
		17,150
Less: Loan	10,000	
Trade creditors	1,500	
Accruals	400	
		11,900
Capital as at 1 April 19X1		5,250

6.2   PILTDOWN

(a)   **Statements of adjustments to profit for the year ended 31 December 19X8**

		+ £	– £	Total £
	Profit per draft balance sheet			13,500
(1)	Depreciation: Premises		2,500	
	Motor vehicles		1,800	
(2)	Stock sheet undercast	2,000		
(3)	Drawings from stock (reduces purchases)	225		
(4)	Debt w/o : no adjustment			
	Further provision		125	
(5)	Rates prepayment	500		
(6)	Purchases misclassified: no adjustment			
(7)	Loan interest: £5,000 x 12% x 7/12		350	
		2,725	4,775	
				(2,050)
	Adjusted profit			11,450

Answers

(b)

Balance sheet at 31 December 19X8

	Cost £	Dep'n £	£
Fixed assets			
Leasehold premises	25,000	2,500	22,500
Motor vehicles	7,200	1,800	5,400
	32,200	4,300	27,900
Current assets			
Stock (9,630 + 2,000)		11,630	
Debtors, less provision (5,250 – 125)		5,125	
Prepayments		500	
Cash at bank		3,060	
Cash in hand		375	
		20,690	
Current liabilities			
Creditors	4,920		
Accrued charges	2,295		
Loan interest	350		
		7,565	
			13,125
			41,025
Loan from T Keating			5,000
			36,025
Representing			
Capital introduced			30,000
Profit for the year (part (a))			11,450
			41,450
Drawings (5,200 + 225)			5,425
			36,025

6.3   JEAN SMITH

Trading and profit and loss account
for the year ended 31 March 19X6

	£	£	£
Sales (W4)			50,400
Less: Purchases (W3)		27,400	
Closing stock		1,900	
Cost of sales			25,500
Gross profit (£25,500 – £600)			24,900
Rent (£3,500 – £700)	2,800		
Rates	1,200		
Electricity (£760 + £180)	940		
		4,940	
Postages, stationery and other sundry expenses		355	
Wages		14,700	
Van	890		
Van licence and insurance (£250 – £125)	125		
Van depreciation	750		
		1,765	
Loan interest		125	
			21,885
Net profit			3,015

Balance sheet as at 31 March 19X6

Fixed assets	£	£	£
Motor van: At cost		7,600	
Less provision for depreciation		750	
			6,850
Current assets			
Stock	1,900		
Debtors	2,300		
Prepayments (£700 + £125)	825		
Balance at bank	4,310		
Cash in hand	640		
		9,975	
Less: Current liabilities			
Creditors	880		
Accrued charges (£125 + £180)	305		
		1,185	
			8,790
			15,640
Less: Loan from John Peacock, uncle			10,000
			5,640

		£
Capital at 1 April 19X5		15,000
Add: Net profit for year		3,015
		18,015
Less: Drawings (£3,875 + £8,500)		12,375
		5,640

Workings

(1)

Cash account

	£		£
Total debtors account	48,100	Van running expenses	890
		Postages, stationery and sundry expenses	355
		Banked	42,340
		Drawings (balancing figure)	3,875
		Balance c/f	640
	48,100		48,100
Balance b/f	640		

(2)

Bank account

	£		£
Opening capital	15,000	Total creditors account	
Loan from John Peacock	10,000	(£26,400 + £120)	26,520
Cash banked		Electricity	760
(£42,000 + £340)	42,340	Rent	3,500
		Rates	1,200
		Wages	14,700
		Van	7,600
		Holiday caravan	8,500
		Van licence and insurance	250
		Balance c/f	
		(£4,090 + £340 − £120)	4,310
	67,340		67,340
Balance b/f	4,310		

(3)

Total creditors account

	£		£
Bank (£26,400 + £120)	26,520	Trading account	
Closing creditors c/f	880	(balancing figure)	27,400
	27,400		27,400
		Balance b/f	880

0044V

(4)

Total debtors account

	£		£
Trading account	50,400	Cash account (balancing figure)	48,100
		Balance c/f	2,300
	50,400		50,400

6.4   SKYMASTER

(a)   **Trading and profit and loss account for the year ended 31 March 19X7**

	£	£
Sales		130,000
Less: Cost of sales		
Opening stock of finished goods	7,800	
Market value of goods manufactured	80,000	
	87,800	
Less: Closing stock of finished goods	6,600	
		81,200
Gross profit		48,800
Less: Shop salaries	11,700	
Rent and rates	3,900	
Light and heat	7,600	
Depreciation of shop fixtures and fittings (£49,000 @ 10%)	4,900	
		28,100
Net profit on sales		20,700
Profit on goods manufactured		14,000
Reduction in provision for unrealised profit on goods manufactured (£1,365 – £1,155)		210
Profit for the year		34,910
Retained earnings at 31 March 19X6		10,535
		45,445
Proposed dividend of 10p per share		6,000
Retained earnings at 31 March 19X7		39,445

Answers

(b)

Balance sheet as at 31 March 19X7

	At cost £	Aggregate depreciation £	£
Fixed assets			
Plant and machinery	29,000	16,400	12,600
Shop fixtures and fittings	49,000	14,700	34,300
	78,000	31,100	46,900
Current assets			
Stocks – Raw materials	5,000		
Finished goods (see working 1)	5,445		
Work-in-progress	9,100		
		19,545	
Debtors		12,700	
Balance at bank		4,300	
		36,545	
Less: Current liabilities			
Creditors	8,000		
Proposed dividends	6,000		
		14,000	
			22,545
			69,445

Represented by	£
Share capital	
Ordinary shares of 50p each, fully paid	30,000
Retained earnings	39,445
	69,445

Working

	£
Stock finished goods: at market value	6,600
Less: Provision for unrealised profit	1,155
	5,445

0044V

6.5 JEAN BLACK

(a)

Trading and profit and loss account
for the year ended 31 October 19X7

	£	£	£
Sales (W1)			48,000
Less: Cost of sales:			
Opening stock		1,900	
Purchases (W2)		27,600	
		29,500	
Less: Goods withdrawn for own use		800	
		28,700	
Less: Closing stock		2,500	26,200
Gross profit			21,800
Less: Wages (£7,400 + £810)		8,210	
General expenses (W3)		7,094	
Motor vehicles:			
Depreciation (£9,872 – £7,404)	2,468		
Less: 'Profit' on sale (£500 – £300)	200	2,268	
Bank charges		40	17,612
Net profit for the year			4,188

(b)

Balance sheet as at 31 October 19X7

	£	£	£
Fixed assets			
Motor vehicles valued at			7,404
Current assets			
Stock		2,500	
Trade debtors		3,900	
Cash in hand		250	
		6,650	
Less: Current liabilities:			
Creditors	5,400		
Accruals (£810 + £36)	846		
Bank overdraft (£1,400 + £40)	1,440	7,686	(1,036)
			6,368

	£
Represented by	
Capital account:	
At 1 November 19X6 (W5)	6,480
Add: Capital introduced – legacy	8,000
Net profit for the year	4,188
	18,668
Less: Drawings (W6)	12,300
	6,368

0044V

Answers

Workings

(1) Sales for the year ended 31 October 19X7

			£	£
Cash sales	–	Cash	390	
		Bank	9,200	
				9,590
Credit sales	–	Cash	110	
		Bank	37,500	
			37,610	
Add: Closing debtors			3,900	
Less: Opening debtors			(3,100)	
				38,410
				48,000

(2) Purchases for the year ended 31 October 19X7

	£
Purchases per bank	24,300
Add: Closing creditors	5,400
Less: Opening creditors	(2,100)
	27,600

(3) General expenses for the year ended 31 October 19X7

		£
General expenses paid	– by cash	240
	by bank	6,510
		6,750
Add: Opening debtors		390
Closing creditors		36
		7,176
Less: Opening creditors		(82)
		7,094

(4) Motor vehicle account

	Cost	Depreciation	Net book value £
Balance at 1/11/X6			300
Sale proceeds			500
'Profit' on sale			200
Purchase of new motor vehicle carried forward	£9,872	£2,468	£7,404

192   0044V

(5)   Capital account at 1 November 19X6

	£	£
Motor vehicle – net book value		300
Stock		1,900
Trade debtors		3,100
General expenses prepaid		390
Bank balance		2,830
Cash in hand		142
		8,662
Less: General expenses accrued	82	
Trade Creditors	2,100	
		2,182
		6,480

(6)   Drawings

	£
Cash	900
Bank	10,600
Goods withdrawn for own use	800
	12,300

6.6   MARK BEAN

(a)   **Computation of business bank account balance at 31 May 19X8**

		£	£
Balance at 29 February 19X8			10,000
Receipts	– cash sales	23,000	
	– credit sales	40,000	
	– sale of display cabinet	500	
			63,500
			73,500
Payments	– purchases	33,800	
	– general expenses	11,000	
	– drawings	4,100	
			(48,900)
Balance at 31 May 19X8			24,600

Answers

(b)

**Trading and profit and loss account
for three months ended 31 May 19X8**

	£	£
Sales (W1)		54,000
Cost of sales		
Opening stock	16,000	
Purchases (W2)	31,800	
	47,800	
Closing stock (balancing figure)	10,000	
		37,800
Gross profit (30% of sales)		16,200
Expenses		
General expenses	11,000	
Loss on sale of fixed asset (500 – 1,400)	900	
Depreciation	1,850	
		(13,750)
Net profit		2,450

(c)

Balance sheet as at 31 May 19X8

	£	£
Fixed assets		
Fixtures and fittings (W3)		54,750
Current assets		
Stock	10,000	
Debtors (W1)	4,000	
Cash at bank	24,600	
	38,600	
Current liabilities		
Trade creditors	9,600	
		29,000
		83,750

	£
Capital account	
Balance b/f	86,000
Profit	2,450
	88,450
Drawings (4,100 + 600)	(4,700)
	83,750

0044V

Workings

(1) **Sales**

			£
Cash			23,000
Credit	– March (15,500 – 13,000) x 2		5,000
	– April (11,500 – 2,500) x 2		18,000
	– May (13,000 – 9,000) x 2		8,000 (£4,000 debtor)
			54,000

(2) **Purchases**

	£
March	11,900
April	10,900
May	9,600 (creditor)
	32,400
Less: Goods taken for own use	(600)
	31,800

(3) **Fixtures and fittings**

	£
Cost (76,000 – 2,000)	74,000
Depreciation (18,000 – 600 + 1,850)	19,250
	54,750

0044V

Answers

6.7   MARY GRIMES

(a)

**Trading and profit and loss account
for the year ended 31 August 19X8**

	£	£
Sales (W1)		98,180
Less: Cost of sales – Opening stock	4,900	
Purchases (W2)	70,990	
	75,890	
Less: Closing stock	5,900	
		69,990
Gross profit		28,190
Discount received		1,100
		29,290
Less: Rent and rates (W3)	2,660	
Repairs and renewals	650	
Insurances (W4)	760	
Wages	15,100	
Postages and stationery	1,360	
Motor vehicle expenses	3,350	
Motor vehicle depreciation	2,600	
Motor vehicle profit on sale (W5)	(100)	
Bad debt written off	300	
		26,680
Net profit		2,610

(b)

Balance sheet as at 31 August 19X8

	£	£
Fixed assets		
Motor vehicle		
At cost	13,000	
Less: Provision for depreciation	2,600	
		10,400
Current assets		
Stock in trade	5,900	
Trade debtors (W6)	9,200	
Amounts prepaid	200	
Balance at bank	2,010	
	17,310	
Less: Current liabilities		
Trade creditors	2,590	
Amounts accrued due	260	
	2,850	
		14,460
		24,860

0044V

			£	£
Represented by:				
Capital account:	At 1 September 19X7 (W7)		11,450	
	Add:	Sale of private yacht	20,000	
		Net profit 19X7/X8	2,610	
			34,060	
	Less:	Drawings	9,200	
				24,860

Workings

			£	£
(1)	Sales			
	Trade debtors at 31 August 19X8		9,500	
	Receipts from trade debtors 19X7/X8		96,000	
			105,500	
	Less: Trade debtors at 1 September 19X7		7,320	
				98,180

			£	£
(2)	Purchases			
	Trade creditors at 31 August 19X8		2,590	
	Payments to suppliers 19X7/X8		72,000	
	Discounts received 19X7/X8		1,100	
			75,690	
	Less: Trade creditors at 1 September 19X7		4,700	
				70,990

			£	£
(3)	Rent and rates			
	Accruals at 31 August 19X8		260	
	Payments in 19X7/X8		2,600	
			2,860	
	Less: Accruals at 1 September 19X7		200	
				2,660

			£	£
(4)	Insurances			
	Prepaid at 1 September 19X7		160	
	Payments 19X7/X8		800	
			960	
	Less: Prepaid at 31 August 19X8		200	
				760

(5) Motor vehicle sale	£	£
A123 BWA at cost	10,000
Less: Provision for depreciation at 1 Sept 19X7	8,000
Net book value at 1 September 19X7	2,000
Sale proceeds 19X7/X8	2,100
Profit on sale		100

(6) Trade debtors at 31 August 19X8	£	£
Per list of balances at 31 August 19X8	9,500
Less: Bad debt written off 19X7/X8	300
	9,200

(7) Capital account at 1 September 19X7	£	£
Motor vehicle	
At cost	10,000
Provision for depreciation	8,000
	2,000
Stock in trade	4,900
Trade debtors	7,320
Amounts prepaid	160
Balance at bank	1,970
14,350
Less: Trade creditors	4,700
Amounts accrued due	200
	9,450
	11,450

6.8 HAROLD WEBB

(a)

**Corrected trading and profit and loss account
for the three months ended 30 September 19X8**

	£	£	£
Sales (see note below)			164,000
Less: Cost of sales		
Opening stock		7,680
Purchases		102,720
	110,400
Less: Stock stolen*	4,920	
Closing stock	7,080	
	12,000
		98,400
Gross profit (40% of sales) c/f			65,600

0044V

	£	£	£
Gross profit (40% of sales) b/f			65,600
Less: Establishment and distribution expenditure			
Fixed overheads	25,260		
Variable (10% of sales)	16,400		
		41,660	
Stock stolen		4,920	
Unauthorised payment (J Gale) (£17,220 less £16,400)		820	
Depreciation – Freehold buildings		5,000	
Fixtures and fittings		7,000	
			59,400
Net profit			6,200

* Balancing figure

Note: Computation of sales

	£
Drawings per draft accounts	18,870
Cash drawings (£3,360 per calendar month)	10,080
Excess due to fictitious sales	8,200

	£
Sales per draft account	172,200
Less fictitious sales	8,200
Actual sales	164,000

(b) Claim from James Gale by Harold Webb

	£
Stock stolen – at cost	4,920
Unauthorised holiday expenses (£17,220 – £16,400)	820
Loss of net profit (30% of sales lost, 40% less variable overheads, or 50% of cost of stock stolen)	2,460
Total claimed	8,200

Note: Owing to restrictions in manufacture, it is unlikely that Harold Webb will be able to recover the sales lost.

0044V

6.9   HAROLD WOOD

(a)

Trading and profit and loss account for the three months ended 31 August 19X9

	£	£
Sales – Credit		
(15,522 + 11,973 + 13,494 x 100/97.5)		42,040
– cash (949 + 859 + 1,113)		2,921
		44,961
Less: Cost of sales		
Purchases		
(14,270 + 9,443 + 10,543)	34,256	
Less: Closing stock	2,141	
		32,115
Gross profit		12,846
Less: Expenses		
Wages (500 + 1,100 + 1,100)	2,700	
Rent (12,600 x 3/12)	3,150	
General expenses (1,000 + 970 + 860)	2,830	
Fixtures and fittings depreciation		
(12,000 x 10% x 3/12)	300	
Discounts allowed		
(15,522 x 2.5/97.5)	398	
Provision for discounts allowable		
(11,973 + 13,494 x 2.5/97.5)	653	
		10,031
Net profit		2,815

Balance sheet as at 31 August 19X9

	Cost	Provision for depreciation	NBV
	£	£	£
Fixtures and fittings	12,000	300	11,700
Current assets			
Stock		2,141	
Trade debtors			
(11,973 + 13,494 + 653)	26,120		
Less: Provision for discounts allowable	653		
		25,467	
Prepayment (12,600 x 9/12)		9,450	
		37,058	
Creditors: Amounts falling due within one year			
Bank overdraft	8,140		
Trade creditors	10,543		
		18,683	
			18,375
			30,075
Creditors: Amounts falling due after more than one year			
Loan from T Bunn			(10,000)
			20,075
			£
Capital introduced at 1 June 19X9			20,000
Net profit			2,815
			22,815
Less: Drawings			
(800 + 840 + 1,100)			(2,740)
			20,075

(b) The benefits of accrual accounting in contrast to cashflow accounting include the following:

(i) the amount earned in a period can be measured;
(ii) income and expenditure can be matched;
(iii) a 'profit' figure can be determined;
(iv) assets other than cash are recognised as significant;
(v) a fairer picture of the business can be seen.

Answers

6.10 CURRY AND GRAY

(a) **Net profit expected in year ended 30 April 19Y1**

	£
Maintainable profit as in year ended 30 April 19Y0	30,000
Additional depreciation (W)	(3,200)
Manager's salary	(12,000)
Bad debts written off	(150)
Stolen stock	10,000
Opening stock – write down to cost (15,000 – 9,000)	6,000
Closing stock – write down to cost (24,000 – 16,000)	(8,000)
Adjusted net profit	22,650

(b) If an appropriate rate of return is 10% per annum and the expected profit/return is £22,650 then John Curry may expect to pay £226,500 for the business:

$$\left(\frac{22,650}{226,500} = 10\%\right)$$

Working

Depreciation – currently 20% reducing balance

	£
19Y0 charge 20% x £64,000 =	12,800
19Y1 charge 20% x £80,000 =	16,000
Additional charge	3,200

6.11   J PATEL

Trading and profit and loss account for the year ended 31 October 19Y0

	£	£
Sales		
Credit (W1)		173,770
Cash (balancing figure)		64,370
Total (W3)		238,140
Cost of sales		
Opening stock	16,100	
Purchases (W2)	166,360	
	182,460	
Less: Closing stock	(23,700)	
		158,760
Gross profit		79,380
Expenses		
Depreciation – Fixtures and fittings	1,000	
– Motor vehicles (1,800 + 1,120)	2,920	
Establishment and administrative expenses	33,300	
Sales and distribution expenses	29,100	
Bad debts written off	530	
		66,850
Net profit		12,530

Balance sheet as at 31 October 19Y0

	Cost £	Provision for depreciation £	NBV £
Fixed assets			
Fixtures and fittings	10,000	7,000	3,000
Motor vehicles	20,200	4,720	15,480
	30,200	11,720	18,480
Current assets			
Stock		23,700	
Trade debtor		11,500	
Bank (W4)		6,620	
Cash		200	
		42,020	
Less: Creditors: Amounts falling due within one year			
Trade creditors		(12,700)	
			29,320
			47,800

0044V

Answers

Represented by	£
Capital at 1 November 19X9	30,910
Additional capital – proceeds of private land sale	16,000
Net profit for 19X9/Y0	12,530
	59,440
Less: Drawings (W5)	11,640
	47,800

Workings

(1) Total debtors account

	£		£
Balance b/f	19,630	Bank – Credit sales	181,370
Credit Sales	173,770	Bad debts written off	530
		Balance c/f	11,500
	193,400		193,400

(2) Total creditors account

	£		£
Bank – cash paid	163,100	Balance b/f	9,440
Balance c/f	12,700	Purchases (balancing figure)	166,360
	175,800		175,800

(3) Sales

Cost of sales	£158,760
Sales (£158,760 x 100/66⅔)	£238,140

(4) Bank account

	£		£
Total receipts	258,560	Balance b/f	6,740
		Total payments	245,200
		Balance c/f	6,620
	258,560		258,560

0044V

(5) **Drawings**

	£
Total cash sales (see P & L a/c)	64,370
Cash banked	61,190
	3,180
Less: Increase in float	(40)
Cash drawings	3,140
Bank drawings	8,500
	11,640

7 MANUFACTURING ACCOUNTS

7.1 JENKINS

(a) **Manufacturing, trading and profit and loss accounts for the year ended 31 December 19X9**

	£	£		£
Raw materials consumed:			Finished goods – carried down to trading account	
Stock 1.1.X9	6,800		£(53,750 + 20%)	64,500
Purchases	36,600			
	43,400			
Less: Stock 31.12.X9	8,400			
		35,000		
Factory wages		12,700		
(i) Prime cost		47,700		
Factory overheads				
Salary – manager	1,400			
Rates and insurance £(1,160 – 210)	950			
Sundry expenses	1,100			

Depreciation:	£		
Factory	320		
Plant & machinery	480		
	800		
Interest on capital	1,800		
		6,050	

(ii)	Factory cost of goods produced	53,750		
(iii)	Factory profit c/f	10,750		
		61,500		64,500

Answers

	£		£
Stock 1.1.X9	2,520	Sales	72,000
Manufacturing account – finished goods b/f	64,500		
	67,020		
Less: Stock 31.12.X9	2,400		
	64,620		
Gross profit c/f	7,380		
	72,000		72,000

	£		£
Selling expenses		Gross profit b/f	7,380
Wages & salaries	1,800		
Salary – manager	1,500	Provision for doubtful debts no longer required	60
Rates & insurance £(350 – 50)	300		
Motor expenses	400		
Sundry expenses £(400 + 120)	520		
Bad debts	60		
Depreciation:			
Travellers' cars	650		
Interest on capital	600		
(iii) Sales department profit b/f	1,610		
	7,440		7,440

(iv)

Appropriation of profits

	£	£		£	£
Commission: Owen (20% x £10,750)	2,150		Net profits b/f		
			Factory	10,750	
			Sales dept	1,610	
Commission: Rogers (20% x £1,610)	322				12,360
		2,472	Finished goods stock provision no longer required		20
Jenkins – current a/c		9,908			
		12,380			12,380

0045V

(b)   Balance sheet as on 31 December 19X9

	£	£	Fixed assets	Cost £	Dep'n £	£
Capital a/c		30,000	Freehold land			
			& buildings	20,000	2,240	17,760
Current a/c			Plant &			
Net profit for			machinery	4,800	2,080	2,720
year	9,908		Motor–cars	2,600	1,850	750
Add: Interest on						
capital	2,400			27,400	6,170	21,230
	12,308					
Less: Drawings	2,400		Current assets			
		9,908	Stocks:			
			Raw materials	8,400		
		39,908	Finished goods –			
			£(2,400 – 400)	2,000		
Current liabilities:					10,400	
Trade creditors	4,200					
Expense creditors			Trade debtors			
£(120 + 2,472)	2,592		£(3,540 – 220)		3,320	
		6,792	Prepayments		260	
			Bank balance		11,490	
						25,470
		46,700				46,700

Working

Finished goods stock provision

	£			£
Profit & loss appropriation a/c	20	Balance b/f		
$\frac{20}{120}$ x £2,400	400	$\frac{20}{120}$ x 2,520		420
	420			420

0045V

Answers

7.2   TYBALT

Manufacturing, trading and profit and loss account for the year ended 31 December 19X5

	£	£	£
Sales			79,174
Materials consumed			
Stock – 1 January	5,230		
Purchase of raw materials	33,668		
	38,898		
Less: Stock – 31 December	3,560		
		35,338	
Direct wages		20,700	
Work in progress 1 January	1,670		
Less: Work in progress 31 December	1,740		
		(70)	
Prime cost of goods produced		55,968	
Works indirect expenses			
Factory power	4,176		
Factory rent and rates	1,560		
Factory insurance	610		
Factory light and heat	535		
General expenses	230		
Plant repairs	785		
Plant depreciation	1,600		
		9,496	
Factory cost of goods produced		65,464	
Finished goods at 1 January	7,380		
Less: Finished goods at 31 December	9,650		
		(2,270)	
Cost of goods sold			63,194
Gross profit			15,980
Discounts received			412
			16,392
Administration expenses			
Salaries	3,690		
Rent and rates	312		
Light and heat	107		
Insurance	122		
General expenses	386		
Depreciation of furniture	45		
c/f		4,662	

0045V

	£	£	£
b/f		4,662	
Selling and distribution expenses			
Advertising	830		
Packing and transport	960		
		1,790	
Finance expenses			
Bank charges	120		
Bad debts	605		
Provision for doubtful debts	500		
		1,225	
			7,677
			8,715

Balance sheet at 31 December 19X3

	Cost	Depreciation	
	£	£	£
Fixed assets			
Plant and machinery	17,000	1,600	15,400
Fixtures and fittings	900	45	855
	17,900	1,645	16,255
Current assets			
Stock and work in progress		15,075	
Debtors, less provision (10,560 − 1,500)		9,060	
Prepayments		170	
Cash at bank		3,926	
Cash in hand		175	
		28,406	
Current liabilities			
Creditors		6,150	
Accrued charges		1,173	
		7,323	21,083
			37,338

	£
Representing:	
Capital at 1 January 19X3	36,623
Profit for the year	8,715
	45,338
Less: Drawings	8,000
	37,338

0045V

7.3 MARR

(a) **Manufacturing account for the year ended 31 December 19X0**

	£	£
Raw materials consumed		
Stock 1 January 19X0	3,300	
Purchases	18,500	
	21,800	
Less: Stock		
31 December 19X0	2,800	
		19,000
Factory wages		13,640
Prime cost		32,640
Factory overheads:		
Electricity and power (90%)	6,120	
Depreciation of plant and machinery	2,250	
Rates and insurance (70%)	910	
Loose tools used	400	
Repairs to buildings (80%)	800	
		10,480
Factory cost of goods produced		43,120
Factory profit loading		4,312
Cost of goods transferred to trading account		47,432

Trading and profit and loss account for the year ended 31 December 19X0

	£	£
Sales		66,000
Stock of finished goods, 1 January 19X0	6,600	
Works cost of goods produced	47,432	
	54,032	
Less: Stock of finished goods, 31 December 19X0	(4,290)	
		(49,742)
Gross profit		16,258
Add: Factory profit		4,312
		20,570
Less: Selling and distribution expenses:		
Wages	3,000	
Sales expenses including vehicle running costs	1,400	
Bad and doubtful debts	100	
Depreciation of travellers' cars	800	
	5,300	
Administration expenses:		
Wages	5,500	
Electricity and power (10%)	680	
Rates and insurance (30%)	390	
Repairs to buildings (20%)	200	
Sundry expenses	2,810	
Provision for unrealised profit written back	(210)	
	9,370	
		14,670
Net profit		5,900

0045V

Answers

Balance sheet at 31 December 19X0

Fixed assets	Cost £	Depreciation £	£
Freehold land	15,000	–	15,000
Plant and machinery	15,000	9,250	5,750
Travellers' cars	4,000	3,600	400
	34,000	12,850	21,150

Current assets			
Stocks:			
Raw materials	2,800		
Finished goods, less provision	3,900		
Loose tools	1,600		
		8,300	
Debtors	5,600		
Less: provision	600		
		5,000	
Prepayments		340	
Cash in hand		100	
		13,740	

Current liabilities:			
Creditors	3,580		
Electricity and power	800		
New machinery	500		
Bank overdraft	3,710		
		(8,590)	
			5,150
			26,300

Representing:	£
Capital 1 January 19X0	20,400
Profit for the year	5,900
	26,300

(b) Factory cost per ton produced

	Tons (finished goods)
Sales	210
Add: Closing stock (produced during year)	15
Deduct: Opening stock (not produced during year)	(25)
Tons produced	200
Factory cost (excluding profit loading)	£43,120
Therefore factory cost per ton produced	£215.60

0045V

7.4 MR WORTHING

(a) Manufacturing, trading and profit and loss accounts
for year ended 30 June 19X6

Raw materials consumed	£	£
Opening stock		6,800
Purchases		36,600
		43,400
Less: Closing stock		8,400
		35,000
Direct wages (W1)		12,700
Prime cost		47,700
Factory manager's salary	1,400	
Depreciation: factory	320	
plant and machinery	480	
Rates and insurance (W2)	950	
Sundry expenses	1,100	
		4,250
Factory cost		51,950
Factory profit (20%)		10,390
Transfers to sales department		62,340
Sales		72,000
Less: Cost of finished goods sold:		
Opening stock	2,520	
Transfers from factory	62,340	
	64,860	
Less: Closing stock	2,400	
		62,460
Gross profit		9,540
Less: Expenses:		
Sales manager's salary	1,500	
Wages and salaries	1,800	
Depreciation: cars	650	
Rates and insurance (W2)	300	
Sundry expenses	520	
Motor expenses	400	
		5,170
Net profit		4,370
Add: Factory profit	10,390	
Decrease in finished goods stock provision (W3)	20	10,410
		14,780

Answers

Balance sheet at 30 June 19X6

Fixed assets	Cost £	Dep'n £	NBV £
Freehold factory	20,000	2,240	17,760
Plant and machinery	4,800	2,080	2,720
Travellers' cars	2,600	1,850	750
	27,400	6,170	21,230

Current assets

Stock (W4)		10,400	
Debtors	3,540		
Less: Provision for doubtful debts	220		
		3,320	
Prepayments		260	
Cash at bank		11,490	
		25,470	

Current liabilities

Creditors	4,200		
Accruals	120		
		4,320	
			21,150
			42,380

	£
Capital at 1 July 19X5	30,000
Add: Profit for year	14,780
	44,780
Less: Drawings	2,400
	42,380

(b) **Purpose and implications of mark–up**

Outline answer

(i) **Purpose**

- To allocate profits fairly between factory and sales department.

- To give factory manager and staff incentives.

- To avoid complacency in sales department.

- To give a truer and fairer picture of the respective performances of the departments: if the sales department had bought the goods from outside, it would have paid a higher price than by having them manufactured internally.

(ii) **Implications**

    – Results in the trading account showing cost of sales at a higher figure than if there were no mark-up.

    – This does not matter if all goods are sold during the period; but any goods still in stock at the end of the period must not be shown at more than the lower of cost and net realisable value (SSAP 9).

    – Therefore a provision for unrealised profit must be deducted from closing stock in the balance sheet (20/120 x £2,400 in this example), and the movement between opening and closing provisions shown in the profit and loss account.

Workings

(1) **Direct wages**

	£	£
Wages and salaries, as per TB		19,800
Less: Salary: Factory manager	1,400	
Sales manager	1,500	
Drawings: Worthing	2,400	
Sales department's salaries and wages	1,800	
		7,100
		12,700

(2) **Rates and insurance**

Rates and insurance (factory)

	£		£
Cash	1,160	Profit and loss account	950
		Balance c/f (260 – 50)	210
	1,160		1,160

Rates and insurance (sales department)

	£		£
Cash (1,510 – 1,160)	350	Profit and loss account	300
		Balance c/f	50
	350		350

(3) Provision for unrealised profit

	£		£
Profit and loss account	20	Balance b/f	420
Balance c/f (1/6 x 2,400)	400		
	420		420

(4) **Stock in balance sheet**

	£	£
Raw materials		8,400
Finished goods	2,400	
Less: Provision for unrealised profit	400	
		2,000
		10,400

7.5 **WILLIAM SPEED**

**Manufacturing, trading and profit and loss account
for the year ended 31 December 19X5**

	£	£
Materials consumed:		
Opening stock	7,000	
Purchases	38,000	
	45,000	
Less: Closing stock	9,000	
		36,000
Direct labour (£28,000 + £3,000)		31,000
Prime cost		67,000
Factory overheads		
Variable	16,000	
Fixed	9,000	
Depreciation – plant and machinery	3,000	
		28,000
		95,000
Work in progress		
Add: Opening	5,000	
Less: Closing	8,000	
		(3,000)
Total factory cost		92,000
Factory profit (25% of factory cost)		23,000
Transfer to trading account		115,000

	£	£	£
Sales			192,000
Less: Cost of sales			
Opening stock		6,900	
Transferred from the			
manufacturing account		115,000	
		121,900	
Less: Closing stock		10,350	
			111,550
Gross profit			80,450
Factory profit			23,000
			103,450
Administrative expenses:			
Rent and rates (£19,000 – £2,000)		17,000	
Heat and light		6,000	
Stationery and postages		2,000	
Staff salaries		19,380	
		44,380	
Motor vehicle expenses:			
Running costs	4,500		
Depreciation	4,000		
		8,500	
Increase in provision for unrealised profit (W1)		690	
			53,570
Net profit			49,880

Answers

Balance sheet as at 31 December 19X5

	Cost £	Depreciation £	£
Fixed assets			
Plant and machinery	30,000	15,000	15,000
Motor vehicles	16,000	8,000	8,000
	46,000	23,000	23,000
Current assets			
Stocks: Raw materials		9,000	
Work in progress		8,000	
Finished goods	10,350		
Less: Provision for unrealised profit (W1)	2,070		
		8,280	
		25,280	
Debtors		28,000	
Prepayments – rent and rates		2,000	
Balance at bank		16,600	
		71,880	
Less: Current liabilities			
Creditors	5,500		
Accrual – wages	3,000		
		8,500	
			63,380
			86,380

	£
Capital account	
At 1 January 19X5	48,000
Add: Net profit for year	49,880
	97,880
Less: Drawings	11,500
	86,380

Workings

(1)

Unrealised profit account

	£		£
		Balance b/f	
Balance c/f		$6,900 \times \frac{25}{125}$	1,380
$10,350 \times \frac{25}{125}$	2,070	Profit and loss account	690
	2,070		2,070

7.6 JANE SEYMOUR

(a)

Manufacturing, trading and profit and loss account for the year ended 31 July 19X6

	£	£
Direct factory wages		39,000
Direct materials purchased	43,000	
Less: Stock 31 July 19X6	7,000	
		36,000
Prime cost		75,000
Indirect factory wages	8,000	
Machinery repairs	1,600	
Light and power [⅔ x (£5,000 + £1,000)]	4,000	
Rent and insurance [⅔ x (£11,600 – £800)]	7,200	
Loose tools (£9,000 – £5,000)	4,000	
Motor vehicle running expenses (½ x £12,000)	6,000	
Depreciation: Motor vehicles (½ x £7,500)	3,750	
Plant and machinery	6,000	
		40,550
		115,550
Less: Work in progress at 31 July 19X6		12,300
		103,250
Transfer to trading account for goods manufactured		95,000
Loss on manufacture		8,250
Sales		170,000
Less: Cost of goods sold		
Goods manufactured	95,000	
Less: Stock at 31 July 19X6	10,000	
		85,000
Gross profit		85,000
Less: Administrative staff salaries	31,000	
Administrative expenses	9,000	
Sales and distribution staff salaries	13,000	
Light and power [⅓ x (£5,000 + £1,000)]	2,000	
Rent and insurances [⅓ x (£11,600 – £800)]	3,600	
Motor vehicle running expenses (½ x £12,000)	6,000	
Motor vehicles depreciation (½ x £7,500)	3,750	
		68,350
Net profit		16,650
Loss on manufacture		8,250
Transferred to capital account		8,400

(b) (i) **Conservatism** – This concept is better known as prudence and requires that losses should be accounted for immediately we become aware of them but profits should only be recognised when realised. In general terms this has been applied in this question by writing off all expenses arising in the period other than those which have increased the value of the assets remaining at the end of the period. This last situation can clearly be seen in the valuation of work–in–progress. Assets are not increased in value in the accounting records even where it is reasonable to assume that they will eventually realise higher values, eg, raw materials will be valued at cost and finished goods at cost plus overheads even though selling price may be materially higher.

(ii) **Matching** – This concept has been applied by carrying forward unsold stocks at the end of the period and charging against the revenues from sales only the cost of those items sold. Expenses throughout have been adjusted for accruals and prepayments so that the amount charged in the profit and loss account reflects the costs related to the period under review. Depreciation has been included so as to match the cost of the capital equipment used during the period with the revenues of the period.

(iii) **Going concern** – This concept has been applied particularly in relation to the fixed assets which are carried to the accounts at cost less depreciation, this residual value or carrying amount reflects the expected future use of the asset in the business. Without the application of this concept such assets would be carried forward only at the amount they could be expected to realise.

7.7 LONG MEASURES LTD

Manufacturing, trading and profit and loss accounts for the year ended 31 March 19X8

Manufacturing account

	£	£
Raw materials		
Opening stock	4,100	
Purchases and carriage inwards	41,000	
	45,100	
Closing stock	(3,600)	
		41,500
Direct labour (33,000 + 200)		33,200
Prime cost		74,700
Variable overheads	23,000	
Fixed overheads	34,000	
Depreciation: Freehold (2½% x 80,000 x ½)	1,000	
Plant and machinery (10% x 44,000)	4,400	
		62,400
c/f		137,100

	£	£
c/f		137,100
Opening work in progress	12,600	
Closing work in progress	9,500	
		3,100
Factory cost (unit cost £70.10)		140,200
Factory profit		9,800
Value of goods transferred		150,000

Trading and profit and loss account

	£	£
Sales		320,000
Cost of sales		
Opening stock of finished goods	35,000	
Value of goods transferred	150,000	
Purchases of finished goods	67,500	
	252,500	
Closing stock of finished goods	28,000	
		224,500
Gross profit		95,500
Expenses		
Establishment (29,400 – 600)	28,800	
Administrative	17,100	
Sales and distribution	23,500	
Depreciation of freehold	1,000	
		70,400
Net profit		25,100
Factory profit		9,800
Total profit		34,900

Note: It is not possible to adjust for the unrealised profit element of finished goods stock since we do not know the breakdown of stock between manufactured and purchased goods.

7.8 JOHN KING

Manufacturing, trading and profit and loss account
for the three months ended 31 October 19X8

	£	£
Raw materials		
Opening stock	21,300	
Purchases	256,000	
	277,300	
Less: Closing stock	16,400	
		260,900
Direct labour		230,000
Prime cost		490,900
Overheads		
Variable	170,000	
Fixed	71,000	
Depreciation fixed assets	24,000	
		265,000
Cost of manufacture		755,900
Manufacturing profit		54,100
Transferred to finished goods stock 810 units at £1,000 each		810,000

	£	£	£
Sales			950,000
Cost of sales			
Goods manufactured by John King			
Opening stock	25,000		
Manufactured 19X7/X8	810,000		
	835,000		
Less: Closing stock	33,000		
		802,000	
Goods bought by John King			
Opening stock	11,000		
Purchases 19X7/X8	45,000		
Carriage inwards	6,000		
	62,000		
Less: Closing stock	7,000		
		55,000	
			857,000
Gross profit c/f			93,000

		£	£
Gross profit	b/f		93,000
Less: Establishment expenditure		45,000	
Administrative expenditure		28,000	
Showroom and administrative offices depreciation		8,000	
			81,000
Net profit			12,000
Manufacturing profit			54,100
Total profit for the year			66,100

7.9 FAIRDEAL MANUFACTURERS LTD

Manufacturing, trading and profit and loss account for year ended 30 April 19Y0

	£	£
Raw materials purchased	41,000	
Less: Closing stock	(3,000)	
		38,000
Factory labour – machine operatives		36,000
Prime cost		74,000
Factory expenses		
Factory labour – supervisory	7,000	
Factory plant and machinery repair	8,710	
Heat, light and power (24,750 + 2,300 x ¾)	20,287	
Rates and insurance (2,550 – 600 x ¾)	1,463	
Factory plant and machinery depreciation (120,000 x 10%)	12,000	
		49,460
		123,460
Less: Closing work in progress		(24,000)
		99,460
Factory profit		540
Wholesale price of goods manufactured		100,000

	£	£
Sales		136,500
Less: Cost of sales goods manufactured	100,000	
Less: Closing stock	(10,000)	
		90,000
Gross profit		46,500
Profit on manufacture		540
		47,040
Less: Expenses		
Motor delivery vehicles depreciation (25,000 x 25%)	6,250	
Heat, light and power ((24,750 + 2,300) x ¼)	6,763	
Rates and insurance ((2,550 – 600) x ¼)	487	
General administrative expenses	9,400	
Administrative salaries	12,090	
		34,990
		12,050
Increase in provision for unrealised profit on closing stock (540 x 1/10)		(54)
Net profit		11,996

(b)

Balance sheet as at 30 April 1990

	Cost	Provision for depreciation	NBV
	£	£	£
Factory plant and machinery	120,000	12,000	108,000
Motor delivery vehicles	25,000	6,250	18,750
	145,000	18,250	126,750
Current assets			
Stock – Raw materials		3,000	
– Work in progress		24,000	
– Finished goods	10,000		
Less: Provision for unrealised profit	(54)		
		9,946	
Trade debtors		12,000	
Prepayments		600	
		49,546	
Creditors: Amounts falling due within one year			
Bank overdraft	4,900		
Trade creditors	7,100		
Accruals	2,300		
		(14,300)	
			35,246
			161,996

0045V

Share capital and reserves	£
Ordinary £1 shares, fully paid	120,000
Share premium	30,000
Retained profits	11,996
	161,996

8 THE ACCOUNTS OF PARTNERSHIPS

8.1 RAY AND MOND

(a) **Profit and loss appropriation accounts for the year to 31 May 19X3**

	£	£	£
Gross profit			35,000
Less: Expenses:			
Bad debt		500	
Depreciation – furniture		400	
Increase in provision for doubtful debts		200	
Office expenses		10,000	
Rates		5,000	
			16,100
Net profit			18,900
Less: Appropriations:			
Mond – salary		6,000	
Balance – Ray (2/3)	8,600		
Mond (1/3)	4,300		
		12,900	
			18,900
			–

(b) **Partners' current accounts**

		Ray £	Mond £			Ray £	Mond £
31.5.X3	Drawings	10,000	9,000	1.6.X2	Balances b/f	5,000	2,000
	Balances c/f	3,600	3,300	31.5.83	Salary	–	6000
					Profit	8,600	4,300
		13,600	12,300			13,600	12,300
				1.6.X3	Balances b/f	3,600	3,300

Answers

(c)

Balance sheet at 31 May 19X3

	Cost	Dep'n	Net book value
	£	£	£
Fixed assets			
Premises	28,000	–	28,000
Furniture	4,000	2,400	1,600
	32,000	2,400	29,600
Current assets			
Stocks		1,500	
Trade debtors (£12,500 – £500)	12,000		
Less: Provisions for doubtful debts	600		
		11,400	
Cash at bank		400	
		13,300	
Less: Current liability			
Trade creditors		6,000	
			7,300
			36,900
Financed by:		£	£
Capital accounts			
Ray		20,000	
Mond		10,000	
			30,000
Current accounts			
Ray		3,600	
Mond		3,300	
			6,900
			36,900

8.2 JACK AND FRED

(a)

Profit for the year before adjustment	£	£	£
Shares of profits			4,500
Salary			1,500
Interest on capital			900
			6,900

Adjustments	+	–	
Overvaluation of stock		140	
Bank charges		70	
Depreciation		450	
Purchases		370	
Interest on loan – Jack		150	
Prepayments of rates	80		
	80	1,180	
			1,100
Adjusted net profit			5,800

(b)

Current assets

	Jack £	Fred £		Jack £	Fred £
Drawings	3,160	3,960	Opening balance	1,140	780
			Salary	–	1,400
			Interest on loan	150	–
			Interest on capital	500	300
Closing balance	630	120	Share on profit	2,000	1,600
	3,790	4,080		3,790	4,080

(c)

Balance sheet as at 31 March 19X6

	£	£		£	£
Capital accounts			Fixed assets		
Jack	5,000		Land & buildings		
Fred	4,000		(cost)	8,000	
		9,000	Depreciation	1,560	
					6,440
Current accounts					
Jack	630		Machinery (cost)	9,000	
Fred	120		Depreciation	4,750	
		750			4,250
					10,690
Loan		2,000			
Trade creditors	1,200		Current assets		
Accruals	90		Stock	1,040	
Overdraft	340		Debtors	1,350	
		1,630	Prepayments	220	
			Cash in hand	80	
					2,690
		13,380			13,380

0045V

(d) (i) Interest on a bank loan is a charge against profits while interest on a partner's capital account is regarded by accountants as a part of the partner's profit–sharing package which adjusts for differences in capital contribution.

(ii) Salary to an employee is also a charge against profits while a salary to a partner is an element in the profit–sharing agreement which compensates for differing working contributions by the partners.

8.3 STRONGCOLOUR FABRICS

(a)

Trading and profit and loss account
for the nine months ended 31 December 19X5

	£
Sales	210,000
Cost of sales	147,000
	———
Gross profit	63,000
Establishment and distribution expenses	(22,500)
Salary	(9,000)
Depreciation:	
Fixtures and fittings	(2,700)
Motor vehicles	(2,250)
	———
Net profit	26,550
	———

(b) **Allcolour Cloths**

Trading and profit and loss account
for the three months ended 31 March 19X6

		£
Sales		30,000
Cost of sales		21,000
		———
Gross profit		9,000
Establishment and distribution expenses		(7,500)
Depreciation		
Fixtures and fittings		(900)
Motor vehicles		(750)
Interest on loan		(250)
		———
Loss		(400)
Appropriation		
John Brown	(200)	
Peter Grey	(200)	
	———	
		(400)
		———

(c)   Allcolour Cloths

Balance sheet as at 31 March 19X6

	Cost or valuation	Deprec- iation	
Fixed assets	£	£	£
Freehold property at valuation	50,000	–	50,000
Fixtures and fittings at cost	30,000	9,000	21,000
Motor vehicles at cost	12,000	8,000	4,000
	92,000	17,000	75,000
Current assets	£	£	
Stock		5,100	
Debtors		14,000	
Bank		5,700	
		24,800	
Creditors: amounts falling due within one year			
Creditors	9,000		
Accruals	1,000		
		10,000	
			14,800
			89,800
Loan – John Brown			20,000
			69,800
		£	£
Capital accounts (W1)			
John Brown		63,000	
Peter Grey		3,000	
			66,000
Current accounts (W2)			
John Brown		4,000	
Peter Grey		(200)	
			3,800
			69,800

Answers

Workings

(1)

Capital accounts

	Peter Grey £	John Brown £		Peter Grey £	John Brown £
Loan account		20,000	Balance		61,000
Balance c/f		69,000	Goodwill		12,000
			Freehold property		16,000
		89,000			89,000
Goodwill	6,000	6,000	Balance b/f		69,000
Balance c/f	3,000	63,000	Salary due	9,000	
	9,000	69,000		9,000	69,000

(2)

Current accounts

	Peter Grey £	John Brown £		Peter Grey £	John Brown £
Drawings		22,600	Net profit 9 mths to 31 December		26,550
Balance c/f		3,950			
		26,550			26,550
Loss	200	200	Balance b/f		3,950
Balance c/f		4,000	Interest		250
			Balance c/f	200	
	200	4,200		200	4,200

8.4 PETER JAMES AND ANGUS VICTOR

(a)

Profit and loss account for the year ended 30 September 19X6

		£	£
Gross profit:	October 19X5 to March 19X5	13,000	
	April to September 19X6	26,000	
			39,000
Less:	Establishment and administrative expenses (£9,100 + £360)	9,460	
	Sales and distribution expenses	13,000	
	Depreciation: Freehold property	1,500	
	Fixtures and fittings	1,800	
	Loan interest	500	
	Sales commission (2% of £26,000)	520	
			26,780
Net profit c/f			12,220

0045V

		£	£
Net profit b/f			12,220
Partner's salary – Angus Victor		5,000	
Interest on capital accounts –	Peter James	1,250	
	Angus Victor	750	
Balance of net profit divisible –	Peter James	2,610	
	Angus Victor	2,610	
			12,220

(b) **Balance sheet as at 30 September 19X6**

Fixed assets	Cost	Aggregate depreciation	
	£	£	£
Freehold property	30,000	7,500	22,500
Fixtures and fittings	18,000	11,400	6,600
	48,000	18,900	29,100
Current assets			
Stocks		11,000	
Debtors		4,600	
Balance at bank		2,700	
		18,300	
Less: Current liabilities			
Creditors	5,800		
Accrued charges (£500 + £360 + £520)	1,380	7,180	
			11,120
			40,220

		£	£
Capital accounts			
Peter James			25,000
Angus Victor			15,000
			40,000
Current accounts			
Peter James		(5,840)	
Angus Victor		(3,940)	
			(9,780)
			30,220
Loan account: Peter James			10,000
			40,220

(c) Reference should be made to the level of partners' drawings or the debit balances as at 30 September 19X6 of the partners' current accounts.

Notes

(1)   Partners' capital accounts: as at 30 September

		£
19X5 –	Peter James	25,000
	Angus Victor	15,000
		40,000

(2)   Partners' current accounts

	£	£
As at 30 September 19X5	6,000	2,300 debit
Add: Partner's salary		5,000
Interest on capital accounts	1,250	750
Balance of net profit	2,610	2,610
	9,860	6,060
Less: Drawings	15,700	10,000
	5,840 debit	3,940 debit

As at 30 September 19X6   Total   £9,780 debit

8.5   TWIGG AND BRANCH

(a)

Capital accounts

John Twigg

19X6		£	19X6		£
Jul 1	J Twigg loan	1,800	Jan 1	Balance c/f	25,000
Jul 1	Balance c/f	35,000	Jul 1	R Branch (goodwill) (W1)	6,800
			Jul 1	Land (revaluation)	5,000
		36,800			36,800
			Jul 1	Balance b/f	35,000

Raymond Branch

19X6		£	19X6		£
Jul 1	J Twigg capital (goodwill) (W1)	6,800	Jul 1	Balance b/f	10,000
Jul 1	Balance c/f	13,200	Jul 1	Sales	10,000
		20,000			20,000
			Jul 1	Balance b/f	13,200

Working 1: Goodwill adjustment = 2/5ths x £17,000 = £6,800.

(b)
**Partnership profit and loss appropriation account
for the period from 1 July to 31 December 19X6**

	£	£		£
Partner's salary			Net profit b/f	
Raymond Branch		4,500	(W2)	15,910
Interest on partners' capital				
John Twigg	875			
Raymond Branch	330			
		1,205		
		5,705		
Balance divisible				
John Twigg (3/5ths)	6,123			
Raymond Branch (2/5ths)	4,082			
		10,205		
		15,910		15,910

Working 2: Net profit 1 July to 31 December 19X6

	£
Net profit for 19X6 per trial balance at 31 December 19X6	42,000
Less: Transferred to Raymond Branch capital account	10,000
	32,000

	£
Adjusted net profit for six months ended 31 December 19X6 before interest on partner's loan account	16,000
Less: Interest on John Twigg's loan account	90
	15,910

8.6 RIVER, STREAM AND POOL

(a)
**Profit and loss appropriation account
for the year ended 30 September 19X7**

	£	£		£
Partner's salary – Pool		11,000	Net profit b/f	47,300
Interest on partners'			(see W1)	
capital @ 5%				
River (£19,000 @ 5%)	950			
Stream (£24,600 @ 5%)	1,230			
Pool (£9,400 @ 5%)	470			
		2,650		
Balance – (Divisible (5:3:2)				
River	16,825			
Stream	10,095			
Pool	6,730			
		33,650		
		47,300		47,300

0045V

Answers

(b)

Partners' capital accounts year ended 30 September 19X7

	R £	S £	P £		R £	S £	P £
Adjustment Stock Valuation Goodwill (see W2)	1,000	1,000		Balance b/f per draft accounts	30,000	20,000	15,000
Goodwill (see W2)			5,600	Goodwill (see W2)		5,600	
Transfer to Loan a/c	10,000						
Balances c/f	19,000	24,600	9,400				
	30,000	25,600	15,000		30,000	25,600	15,000
				Balances b/f	19,000	24,600	9,400

Partners' current accounts year ended 30 September 19X7

	R £	S £	P £		R £	S £	P £
Drawings	21,000	13,000	11,000	Bal b/f	1,000	700	–
				Loan interest	1,000		
				Interest on capital	950	1,230	470
				Salary			11,000
				Balance of profit	16,825	10,095	6,730
Bal c/f	–	–	7,200	Bal c/f	1,225	975	–
	21,000	13,000	18,200		21,000	13,000	78,200
Bal b/f	1,225	975		Bal b/f			7,200

Workings

(1)

Adjusted net profit for the year ended 30 September 19X7	£
Net profit per draft accounts	46,300
Add: Reduction in valuation of stock as at 1 October 19X6 (£9,000 – £7,000)	2,000
	48,300
Less: Interest to be credit to River £10,000 @ 10%	1,000
Adjusted net profit	47,300

(2)   Goodwill

	Total £	River £	Stream £	Pool £
Goodwill of old partnership (No formal partnership agreement)	28,000	14,000	14,000	
Goodwill of new partnership (Ratio 5:3:2)	28,000	14,000	8,400	5,600
Difference	Nil	Nil	(5,600)	5,600

8.7 BELL, RING AND GONG

(a)

**Profit and loss appropriation account
for the year ended 31 March 19X9**

	£	£
Net profit per trial balance at 31 March 19X9		44,000
Add: Depreciation deleted on motor vehicle acquired by Ring on 1 October 19X8 (for six months from 1 October 19X8)	300	
Less: Loss on 'sale' of motor vehicle (£2,400 – £300 – £2,000)	(100)	
		200
		44,200
Partners' salaries		
Ring	(10,000)	
Gong	(13,000)	
		(23,000)
Interest on partners' capital accounts (10% pa)		
Bell	(3,000)	
Ring	(2,120)	
Gong	(2,280)	
		(7,400)
Balance divisible		
Bell	(6,900)	
Ring	(4,140)	
Gong	(2,760)	
		(13,800)

0045V

Answers

(b) Balance sheet as at 31 March 19X9

	At valuation £	Aggregate depreciation £	£
Fixed assets			
Freehold land and buildings	50,000	1,250	48,750
Plant and machinery	21,000	2,100	18,900
Motor vehicles	9,600	2,400	7,200
	80,600	5,750	74,850
Current assets			
Stock		9,000	
Debtors		4,000	
Balances at bank		600	
		13,600	
Less: Current liabilities			
Creditors		5,250	
			8,350
			83,200

Represented by (see note below)

	Capital accounts £	Current accounts £	Total accounts £
Bell	30,000	(3,100)	26,900
Ring	21,200	3,260	24,460
Gong	22,800	9,040	31,840
	74,000	9,200	83,200

Note: Capital accounts movements year ended 31 March 19X9

	Per trial balance 31.3.X9 £	Goodwill 'introduced' £	Goodwill 'deleted' £	Adjusted balances 31.3.X9 £
Bell	40,000	8,000 Cr	18,000 Dr	30,000
Ring	20,000	12,000 Cr	10,800 Dr	21,200
Gong	14,000	16,000 Cr	7,200 Dr	22,800
	74,000	36,000 Cr	36,000 Dr	74,000

Current account movements year ended 31 March 19X9

	Partners' salaries £	Interest on partners' capital £	Balance of profits £	Drawings £	Balance at 31.3.X9 £
Bell	–	3,000	6,900	(13,000)	(3,100)
Ring	10,000	2,120	4,140	(13,000)	3,260
Gong	13,000	2,280	2,760	(9,000)	9,040
	23,000	7,400	13,800	(35,000)	9,200

8.8 A ABLE AND B BAKER

(a)   Profit and loss account for the year ended 30 September 19X8

	Oct to March £	April to Sept £		Oct to March £	April to Sept £
Establishment expenses	10,000	5,000	Gross profit b/f	45,000	45,000
Sales & distribution exps	16,000	8,000			
Loan interest	3,125	3,125			
	29,125	16,125			
Net profit	15,875	28,875			
	45,000	45,000		45,000	45,000

Profit and loss appropriation account for the year ended 30 September 19X8

	Oct to March £	April to Sept £		Oct to March £	April to Sept £
Partners' salaries					
A Able	6,000	4,500	Net profit	15,875	28,875
B Baker	5,250	5,250			
Interest on capital (10% pa)					
A Able	7,300	7,300			
B Baker	2,700	2,700			
	21,250	19,750			
Balance divisible					
A Able (3/5ths)	(3,225)	5,475			
B Baker (2/5ths)	(2,150)	3,650			
	15,875	28,875		15,875	28,875

(b)

Partners' capital accounts per year ended 30 September 19X8

	A Able £	B Baker £			A Able £	B Baker £
19X7				**19X7**		
1 Oct A Able (goodwill)*		16,000		1 Oct Balance b/f	180,000	70,000
1 Oct A Able loan	50,000			1 Oct Bank		
19X8				1 Oct B Baker (goodwill)*	16,000	
30 Sept Balances c/f	146,000	54,000				
	196,000	70,000			196,000	70,000
				19X8		
				1 Oct Balances b/f	146,000	54,000

*Goodwill

	Credit £	Debit £	Net £
A Able Goodwill 'creation'	40,000		
A Able Goodwill 'deletion'		24,000)	16,000 credit
B Baker Goodwill 'deletion'		16,000)	16,000 debit
	40,000	40,000	–

(c)

Partners' current accounts per year ended 30 September 19X8

	A Able £	B Baker £			A Able £	B Baker £
19X8				**19X8**		
30 Sept Drawing	21,000	16,000		30 Sept Loan interest	6,250	
30 Sept Balances c/f	12,600	1,400		30 Sept Partners' salaries	10,500	10,500
				30 Sept Interest on partners' capital	14,600	5,400
				30 Sept Balance of profits/losses	2,250	1,500
	33,600	17,400			33,600	17,400
				1 Oct Balances b/f	12,600	1,400

238

8.9   CLIVE ABEL

(a)   **Clive Abel: Trading and profit and loss account for
six months ended 31 March 19X9**

	£	£
Sales (396,090 x ⅔)		264,060
Less: Cost of sales		
Opening Stock	32,000	
Purchases (286,500 x ⅔)	191,000	
(Purchases assumed to accrue in		
same manner as sales)	223,000	
Less: Closing stock (bal. figure)	(27,400)	
Cost of sales (293,400 (W1) x ⅔)		195,600
		68,460
Less: Expenses		
Fixtures and fittings depreciation		
(£94,000 x 10% x 6/12)	4,700	
Establishment expenses		
(16,450 + 1,020 x 6/12)	8,735	
Administrative expenses		
(9,310 x 6/12)	4,655	
Sales and distribution expenses		
(13,219 – 364 x ⅔)	8,570	
		26,660
Net profit		41,800

(b)   **Clive Abel and John McBain: Trading and profit and loss appropriation
account for the six months ended 30 September 19X9**

	£	£
Sales (396,090 x ⅓)		132,030
Less: Cost of sales		
Opening Stock (part a)	27,400	
Purchases (286,500 x ⅓)	95,500	
	122,900	
Less: Closing stock	25,100	
		97,800
		34,230
Less: Expenses		
Freehold building depreciation		
(50,000 x 2% x 6/12)	500	
Fixtures and fittings depreciation		
(94,000 x 10% x 6/12)	4,700	
Establishment expenses (16,450 + 1,020 x 6/12)	8,735	
Administrative expenses (9,310 x 6/12)	4,655	
Sales and distribution expenses		
(13,219 – 364 x ⅓)	4,285	
Loan interest (12,000 x 10% x 6/12)	600	
		23,475
Net profit		10,755

Answers

Appropriation

	£
Clive Abel – salary (8,000 x 6/12)	4,000
Interest on partners capital accounts	
Clive Abel (113,200 (W2) x 5% x 6/12)	2,830
John McBain (43,600 (W2) x 5% x 6/12)	1,090
Remaining profit shared 3:2	
Clive Abel	1,701
John McBain	1,134
	10,755

(c) **Balance sheet as at 30 September 19X9**

	Cost £	Provision for depreciation £	NBV £
Fixed assets			
Freehold building	50,000	500	49,500
Fixtures and fittings	94,000	37,600	56,400
	144,000	38,100	105,900
Current assets			
Stock		25,100	
Trade Debtors		34,410	
Prepayments		364	
Balance at bank		15,171	
		75,045	
Creditors: Amounts falling due within one year			
Trade creditors	19,380		
Accruals (1,020 + 600)	1,620		
		(21,000)	
			54,045
			159,945
Creditors: Amounts falling due after more than one year			
Loan – John McBain			(12,000)
			147,945

	£
Capital accounts (W2)	
Clive Abel	113,200
John McBain	43,600
Current accounts (W3)	
Clive Abel	(2,079)
John McBain	(6,776)
	147,945

0045V

Workings

(1) **Cost of sales**

	£
Opening Stock	32,000
Purchases	286,500
	318,500
Less: Closing Stock	(25,100)
	293,400

(2) **Partners' capital account**

	Clive Abel £	John McBain £
Opening balance 1 Oct 19X8	65,000	–
Capital introduced	–	50,000
Goodwill introduced	16,000	–
Goodwill eliminated (3:2)	(9,600)	(6,400)
Net profit for six months ended 31 March 19X9	41,800	–
	113,200	43,600

(3) **Current accounts**

	Clive Abel £	John McBain £
Partners' salary	4,000	–
Interest on capital accounts	2,830	1,090
Profit for six months ended 30 September 1989	1,701	1,134
Less: Drawings	(10,610)	(9,000)
	(2,079)	(6,776)

8.10 STONE, PEBBLE AND BRICK

(a) **Profit and loss appropriation account for the year ended 31 March 19Y0**

	April to December 19X9 £	January to March 19Y0 £
Net profit per draft accounts (£36,300)	27,225	9,075
Loan interest – Stone (W1) (£14,000 x 11% x 3/12)	–	385
	27,225	8,690

Answers

Appropriation

				£
Interest on capital accounts				
Stone (5% x 3/12 x 20,000) (W1)				250
Pebble (5% x 3/12 x 16,000) (W1)				200
Brick (5% x 3/12 x 10,000) (W1)				125
Partner's salary				
Brick (£8,500 x 3/12)				2,125
Profit share				
Stone	(⅓)	9,075	(5/10)	2,995
Pebble	(⅓)	9,075	(3/10)	1,797
Brick	(⅓)	9,075	(2/10)	1,198
		27,225		8,690

(b) Capital accounts

	Stone £	Pebble £	Brick £
Balance at 1 April 19X9	26,000	18,000	16,000
Net goodwill adjustment (W1)	8,000	(2,000)	(6,000)
Transfer to loan account	(14,000)	–	–
	20,000	16,000	10,000

Current accounts

	Stone £	Pebble £	Brick £
Interest on capital accounts	250	200	125
Salary	–	–	2,125
Profit share			
April to December 19X9	9,075	9,075	9,075
Jan to March 19Y0	2,995	1,797	1,198
Drawings	(8,200)	(9,600)	(7,200)
	4,120	1,472	5,323

Workings

(1) Partnership capital

	Stone £	Pebble £	Brick £
Balance at 1 April 19X9	26,000	18,000	16,000
Goodwill introduced	30,000	20,000	16,000
Goodwill eliminated	(22,000)	(22,000)	(22,000)
	34,000	16,000	10,000
Transfer to loan account	(14,000)	–	–
	20,000	16,000	10,000

0045V

8.11 BRICK AND STONE

Trading and profit and loss account for the year ended 30 September 19Y0

	£	£	£
Sales			322,100
Less: Sales return			(2,100)
			320,000
Cost of sales			
Opening stock		23,000	
Purchases	208,200		
Add: Carriage inwards	1,700		
	209,900		
Less: Purchases returns	(6,100)		
	203,800		
Less: Drawings – Stone	(1,000)		
		202,800	
		225,800	
Less: Closing stock		(32,000)	
			193,800
Gross profit			126,200
Discounts receivable			370
			126,570
Less: Establishment expenses			
Rent and rates (10,300 – 600)	9,700		
Heat and light	8,700		
Depreciation: Fixtures and fittings	2,600		
		21,000	
Administrative expenses			
Printing, stationery and postage	3,500		
Staff salaries	36,100		
Telephone charges (2,900 + 400)	3,300		
		42,900	
Sales and distribution expenses			
Motor vehicle running costs	5,620		
Depreciation and motor vehicles	9,200		
Carriage outwards	2,400		
		17,220	
Finance expenses			
Discounts allowable	950		
Loan interest (10,000 x 10% x 3/12)	250		
		1,200	
			82,320
Net profit			44,250

Balance sheet as at 30 September 19Y0

	Cost £	Provision for depreciation £	NBV £
Fixed assets			
Fixtures and fittings	26,000	13,800	12,200
Motor vehicles	46,000	34,200	11,800
	72,000	48,000	24,000
Current assets			
Stock		32,000	
Trade debtors (9,300 – 300)		9,000	
Prepayments		600	
Bank balance		7,700	
		49,300	
Creditors: Amounts falling due within one year			
Trade creditors	8,400		
Accruals	400		
		(8,800)	
			40,500
			64,500
Creditors: Amounts falling due after more than one year			
Loan – Brick			(10,000)
			54,500

Represented by:

Partners' capital accounts	Brick £	Stone £	£
Balance at 1 October 19X9	33,000	17,000	
Less: Transfer to Brick Loan Account 1 July 19Y0	(10,000)		
	23,000	17,000	40,000

Partners' current accounts	Brick £	Stone £	£
Balance at 1 October 19X9	3,600	2,400	
Loan interest (10,000 x 10% x 3/12)	250		
Salary		6,000	
Profit share (W1)	22,950	15,300	
	26,800	23,700	
Less: Drawings – goods	–	(1,000)	
– cash	(24,000)	(11,000)	
	2,800	11,700	
			14,500
			54,500

0045V

Working: Profit share

	£
Net profit	44,250
Less: Stone's salary	6,000
	38,250

Profit share	
Brick 3/5	22,950
Stone 2/5	15,300
	38,250

9   <u>THE ACCOUNTS OF LIMITED COMPANIES</u>

9.1   IMP PLC

Balance sheet as at 30 June 19X4

	Cost £	Depreciation £	£
Intangible asset: goodwill	50,000	–	50,000
Tangible assets:			
Freehold property	100,000	–	100,000
Motor vehicles	54,000	37,750	16,250
	204,000	37,750	166,250
Investments:			
Unquoted		27,500	
Quoted (market value £13,492)		12,400	
			39,900
			206,150
Current assets			
Stocks		176,480	
Debtors and prepayments		68,647	
Bank balance		130,670	
		375,797	
Creditors	60,992		
Taxation	70,000		
Proposed dividend	50,000		
		180,992	
			194,805
			400,955

Answers

Capital and reserves £
Called up share capital 250,000
General reserve 40,000
Profit and loss account 110,995
_____
400,955
_____

Profit and loss account for the year ended 30 June 19X4

	£	£
Turnover		1,086,000
Cost of sales		825,360
		_____
Gross profit		260,640
Net operating expenses:		
Distribution	50,654	
Administration	75,981	
	_____	
		126,635
		_____
Operating profit		134,005
Investment income		
Unquoted	2,750	
Quoted	1,200	
	_____	
		3,950
		_____
Profit before taxation		137,955
Corporation tax		70,000
		_____
Profit after tax		67,955
Dividend proposed		50,000
Retained profit for the year		17,955
Add: Retained profit brought forward		93,000
		_____
Retained profit carried forward		110,955
		_____

Workings £

Profit per question		153,278
Less: Additional provision for		
Doubtful Debts (£3,613 – 2,340)	1,273	
Depreciation	13,500	
Director's Fees	4,500	
	_____	
		19,273
		_____
		134,005
		_____

Note: All of the above are taken as adjustments to administration expenses.

0045V

9.2 MARMADUKE LTD

(a) **Profit and loss account for year ended 31 December 19X5**

	£	£
Turnover		103,250
Less: Cost of sales (W1)		67,025
Gross profit		36,225
Less: Distribution costs (W2)	11,025	
Administrative expenses (W3)	10,450	
		21,475
Trading profit		14,750
Investment income		170
Rental income		1,800
		16,720
Interest payable:		
Bank	291	
Debenture	525	
		816
Profit before taxation		15,904
Less: Corporation Tax		6,350
		9,554
Less: Dividends:		
Interim (paid)	630	
Final (proposed)	2,100	
		2,730
Retained profit for the year		6,824
Profit brought forward from previous years		8,926
Retained profit at 31 December 19X5		15,750

Answers

(b)

Balance sheet at 31 December 19X5

Fixed assets	Cost	Depreciation	
	£	£	£
Freehold properties	37,500		37,500
Motor vans	1,200	475	725
	38,700	475	38,225
Current assets			
Stock		8,350	
Investments		3,375	
Debtors		15,500	
		27,225	
Creditors: amounts falling due within one year			
Creditors		12,175	
Corporation tax		6,350	
Proposed dividend		2,100	
Bank overdraft		575	
		21,200	
Net current assets			6,025
Total assets less current liabilities			44,250
Creditors: amounts falling due after more than one year: 7% debentures			7,500
			36,750

Representing		£
Share capital		
Ordinary shares of £1 each, fully paid		21,000
Reserves		
Profit and loss account		15,750
		36,750

Workings

(1) **Cost of sales**	£
Opening stock	6,000
Purchases	69,375
	75,375
Less: Closing stock	8,350
	67,025

0045V

(2) **Distribution costs**

		£
Selling expenses		4,625
Directors' remuneration		6,250
Depreciation (W6)		313
		11,188
Profit on disposal of van (W7)		163
		11,025

(3) **Administrative expenses**

		£
Administration expenses		4,200
Directors' remuneration		6,250
		10,450

(4)

Motor vehicles account

	£		£
Balance b/f	1,250	Disposal account	450
New van – garage	400	Balance c/f	1,200
	1,650		1,650

(5)

Provision for depreciation account

	£		£
Disposals	338	Balance b/f	500
Balance c/f	475	Depreciation account	313
		(25% x £1,250)	
	813		813

(6)

Depreciation expense account

	£		£
Provision for depreciation	313	Profit and loss account	313

(7)

Disposals account

	£		£
Motor vehicles account	450	Provision for depreciation	338
Profit and loss account		Proceeds – garage	275
Profit on disposal	163		
	613		613

(8)

Garage account

	£		£
Proceeds old van	275	New van cost	400
Balance carried down	125		
	400		400

Note: At 31 December 19X5 £125 is owed by Marmaduke Ltd to the garage.

0045V

Answers

9.3 ALPHA CO LTD

(a) Appropriation accounts for the year ended 31 December 19X5

			£	£
Profit on ordinary activities after taxation				72,000
Dividends:				
Ordinary:	Interim paid		5,000	
	Final proposed		5,000	
Preference:	Interim paid		10,000	
	Final proposed		10,000	
				30,000
				42,000
Goodwill written off				20,000
Retained profit for the financial year				22,000

Note

Authorised share capital		£
200,000	£1 ordinary shares	200,000
250,000	8% £1 redeemable preference shares	250,000
		450,000

Notes

Reserves

General reserve	£
At 1 January	55,000
Added in the year	25,000
	80,000

Profit and loss account	£
At 1 January	73,000
Added in the year	22,000
	95,000
Transfer to general reserve	25,000
	70,000

Balance sheet as at 31 December 19X5

	Cost £	Dep'n £	£
Fixed assets			
Intangible assets			
Goodwill at cost less written off			40,000
Tangible assets			
Land and buildings (at valuation)			270,000
Fittings	175,000	75,000	100,000
Vehicles	397,000	187,000	210,000
			620,000
Current assets			
Stock		148,000	
Debtors and prepayments less provision		83,000	
Short term investments			
(market value £43,000)		39,000	
		270,000	
Current liabilities			
Creditors and accruals	48,000		
Bank overdraft	27,000		
Proposed dividends	15,000		
		90,000	
Net current assets			180,000
Total assets less current liabilities			800,000
Creditors			
Amount falling due after more than one year			
10% Debentures			80,000
Net assets			720,000

	£
Capital and reserves	
Called up share capital	
100,000 £1 ordinary shares	100,000
250,000 8% £1 redeemable	
preference shares	250,000
	350,000
Share premium account	20,000
Capital redemption reserve fund	150,000
Revaluation reserve	50,000
General reserve	80,000
Profit and loss accounts	70,000
	720,000

(b) (i) The unissued ordinary shares may be issued to the public at any time at the company's option.

(ii) $\frac{80,000}{800,000}$ = 10%. This is a measure of the overall profitability of the company's operations.

(iii) £180,000. The company has adequate resources to meet its debts as they fall due. The ratio of current assets to current liabilities is 3 : 1, which is high for the type of trade carried on (retailing).

(iv) The 'goodwill' could have arisen when the company took over another business at a price in excess of the book value of its assets.

(v) £150,000 (less preference dividend £20,00 = £130,000 for the ordinary shareholders). The share premium account, the capital redemption reserve fund and the revaluation reserve are not distributable.

(vi) The market value of the shares is the result of the balancing of the forces of supply and demand for the shares, allowing for the value of the underlying assets and the profitability of the company: the book value is simply the nominal value of the shares issued on formation or later.

(vii) Share premium account represents the fact that shares have been issued by the company at a figure in excess of their nominal value.

9.4 ARAD LTD

Trading and profit and loss account for the year ended 31 March 19X4

	£	£
Sales		102,240
Less: Stock at 31 March 19X3	6,900	
Add: Purchases	85,640	
	92,540	
Less: Stock at 31 March 19X4	8,870	
Cost of sales		83,670
		18,570
Less: Expenses		
Wages and salaries	6,950	
Staff bonus	224	
Rent and rates	885	
Lighting and heating	610	
Trade expenses	1,722	
Motor expenses	2,510	
Repairs and renewals	480	
Audit fee	180	
Bank charges and interest	143	
Provision for doubtful debts	637	
Depreciation		
Office furniture and fittings	120	
Motor vehicles	1,068	
		15,479
Profit for the year before taxation		3,091
Less: Taxation – corporation tax		1,200
Profit for the year after taxation		1,891
Add: Balance brought forward from previous year		5,800
Balance carried forward		7,691

0045V

Balance sheet as at 31 March 19X4

	Cost £	Dep'n £	£
Authorised share capital			
20,000 ordinary shares of £1 each			20,000
			£
Issued share capital			
8,500 ordinary shares of £1 each, fully paid			8,500
Reserves			
Profit and loss account			7,691
Shareholders' funds			16,191
Represented by:			
Fixed assets			
Office equipment	1,570	490	1,080
Motor vehicles	8,890	4,618	4,272
	10,460	5,108	5,352
Current assets			
Stock at the lower of cost or net realisable value		8,870	
Trade debtors	14,340		
Less: Provision for doubtful debts	717		
		13,623	
Prepayment – motor licences		120	
Cash in hand		85	
		22,698	
Current liabilities			
Creditors	8,059		
Corporation tax	1,200		
Bank overdraft	2,600		
		11,859	
Net current assets			10,839
			16,191

Workings

	£
(1) Sales	
Per trial balance	102,480
Less: Goods on sale or return	480
	102,000
Add: Debtors re goods sold	240
	102,240
(2) Staff bonus – 10% x 2,240	£224

0045V

Answers

(3)   Creditors £

Trade, per trial balance	7,460
Accrued repairs and renewals	100
Trade expenses	95
Audit fee	180
Staff bonus	224
	8,059

(4)   Trade debtors £

Per trial balance	14,980
Less: Goods on sale or return	240
	14,740
Less: Bad debts written off	400
	14,340

(5)   Provision for doubtful debts £

Per trial balance	480
Less: Debt written off	400
	80
Profit and loss account – charge	637
Adjusted provision – 5% 14,340	717

(6)   Stock £

Per question	8,670
Add: Goods on sale or return	200
Total stock at 31 March 19X4	8,870

9.5 PRIME PRODUCTS LTD

Corrected balance sheet as at 30 September 19X6

	Cost	Aggregate depreciation	Net book value
	£	£	£
Fixed assets			
Plant and machinery	31,000	19,375	11,625
Motor vehicles	17,000	10,200	6,800
	48,000	29,575	18,425
Current assets			
Stock (£12,400 + £1,200)		13,600	
Trade debtors and prepayments (note 1)		8,110	
Balance at bank (£3,900 – £150)		3,750	
		25,460	
Less: Current liabilities			
Creditors and accrued charges			
(£5,100 – £64) (note 2)		5,036	
			20,424
			38,849
Financed by:			
Share capital – ordinary shares of £1 each, fully paid			
(£20,000 + £5,000)			25,000
Reserves – General			10,000
Retained earnings (£4,225 + £300 + £64 –			
£150 – £400 – £190)			3,849
			38,849

Notes

		£
(1)	Trade debtors per draft balance sheet as at	
	30 September 19X6 – (£9,600 – £400)	9,200
	Less: Goods not sold but on sale or return basis	
	(at selling price)	1,600
		7,600
	Less: Provision for doubtful debts (2½% of trade debtors)	190
		7,410
	Prepayments (£400 + £300)	700
		8,110

		£
(2)	Correction of sales manager's bonus	
	Reductions in gross profit for the year ended	
	30 September 19X6	
	Re Goods not sold but on sale or return basis	400
	Re Stock valuation error at 30 September 19X5	6,000
		6,400
	Reduction in sales manager's commission 1% of £6,400	£64

0045V

9.6   BROADBENT LTD

(a)   **Balance sheet as at 31 October 19X6**

	£
Net assets (balancing figure)	154,000
Capital – Ordinary shares of 50p each	100,000
Retained profits (W)	54,000
	154,000

(b)   **Benefits year ended 31 October 19X7**

	£
Alan Smith	
Director's salary	15,000
Dividends (Proposed 100,000 @ 10p)	10,000
	25,000

	£
Norman Smith	
Partner's salary	15,000
Half share balance of profits (£36,000 – £15,000) x ½	10,500
	25,500

(c)   **Assuming partnership had been a limited company during year ended 31 October 19X7**

	£
Net profit per partnership accounts	36,000
Less: Salary of Norman Smith at market rate	16,000
Net profit for company	20,000

(d)   Advantages and disadvantages of converting Alan Smith's shareholding to loan stock are outlined below.

Advantages

(i)   The loan stock would provide interest of £5,000 pa (£50,000 x 10%) regardless of the profits earned or dividend policy of the company.

(ii)   The loan stock interest is a liability which the company has to honour. Alan Smith may wish to devote part of his working time elsewhere which may affect the Company profits.

Disadvantages

Should the company continue to enjoy increasing profits, Alan Smith's return would be limited to the £5,000 loan stock interest since he would not receive any improved dividends or any increased capital value of the ordinary shares.

Working

Retained profit as at 31 October 19X6

	£
Net profit, after tax, for year ended 31 October 19X7	26,000
Less: Dividend proposed for year ended 31 October 19X7	
$\dfrac{£100,000}{50p}$ x 10p	20,000
Retained profits for year excluding dividend	6,000

	£
Retained profits at 31 October 19X7	60,000
Less: profits for year	(6,000)
Retained profits as at 31 October 19X6	54,000

9.7 LOWDALE LTD

(a) **Journal entries**

	£	£

30 November 19Y0

	£	£
Profit and loss account	3,088	
Stock – finished goods		3,088
(10,808 x 40/140)		

Being reduction of finished goods stock at 30 November 19Y0 from selling price to cost price.

30 November 19Y0

	£	£
Suspense account (W1)	2,200	
Prepayments and accrued income		1,100
Accrued expenditure		1,100

Being transfer of accrued establishment expenses from 'prepayments and accrued income' to 'accrued expenditure' and clearing of suspense account.

30 November 19Y0

	£	£
Profit and loss account	16,000	
Proposed final dividend (160,000 shares x 10p)		16,000

Being proposed final dividend of 10p for the year ended 30 November 1990.

Answers

(b)   **Balance sheet as at 30 November 19Y0**

	Cost £	Provision for depreciation £	NBV £
Fixed assets			
Land and buildings			
(100,000 – 10,000)	90,000		
(32,000 – 10,000 x 2%)		31,800	58,200
Plant and machinery			
(74,000 + 10,000)	84,000		
(26,000 + 10,000 x 12½%)		27,250	56,750
Motor vehicles	28,000	15,000	13,000
	202,000	74,050	127,950
Current assets			
Stocks: Raw materials	19,400		
Finished goods			
(10,808 – 3,088)	7,720		
		27,120	
Trade debtors (43,800 – 1,500)		42,300	
Prepayments and accrued income (3,092 – 1,100)		1,192	
Cash in hand		7,900	
		79.312	
Less: Creditors: Amounts falling due within one year			
Bank overdraft	7,300		
Trade creditors (18,900 – 1,300)	17,600		
Accrued expenditure (1,800 + 1,100)	2,900		
Proposed dividend	16,000		
		(43,800)	
			35,512
			163,462
Less: Creditors: Amounts falling due in more than one year			
10% Loan stock 2000/05			40,000
			123,462
Called–up share capital			80,000
Share premium account			20,000
General reserve			22,000
Profit and loss account (W2)			1,462
			123,462

Workings

(1)

Suspense account

	£		£
Cash to creditor not recorded	1,300	Accrued establishment expenses	2,200
Balance c/f	900		
	2,200		2,200

(2)   Amended profit and loss account

	£
Profit and loss account per trial balance	23,100
Provision for doubtful debts	(1,500)
Land and buildings depreciation	200
Plant and machinery depreciation	(1,250)
Correction of finished goods stock	(3,088)
Proposed final dividend	(16,000)
	1,462

10   ACCOUNTING RATIOS AND INTERPRETATION

10.1   K GEORGE

(a)   **Gross profit ratio**

$$\frac{\text{Gross profit} \times 100}{\text{sales}} = \frac{50,000 \times 100}{100,000} = 50\%$$

(b)   **Mark–up on cost of goods sold ratio**

$$\frac{\text{Gross profit} \times 100}{\text{Cost of goods sold}} = \frac{50,000 \times 100}{50,000} = 100\%$$

(c)   **Net profit on sales ratio**

$$\frac{\text{Net profit} \times 100}{\text{Sales}} = \frac{25,000 \times 100}{100,000} = 25\%$$

(d)   **Return on capital employed**

$$\frac{\text{Net profit} \times 100}{\text{Capital}} = \frac{25,000 \times 100}{33,000} = 75.8\%$$

(e)   **Stock turnover**

$$\frac{\text{Cost of goods sold}}{\text{Closing stock}} = \frac{50,000}{12,000} = 4.2$$

or

$$\frac{\text{Cost of goods sold}}{\text{Average stock}} = \frac{50,000}{(10,000 + 12,000)/2} = 4.5$$

Answers

(f) Debtor collection period

$$\frac{\text{Trade debtors} \times 365}{\text{Credit sales}} = \frac{7,000 \times 365}{100,000} = 26 \text{ days}$$

(g) Current ratio

$$\frac{\text{Current assets}}{\text{Current liabilities}} = \frac{20,000}{5,000} = 4$$

(h) Quick (or acid test) ratio

$$\frac{\text{Current assets} - \text{stocks}}{\text{Current liabilities}} = \frac{20,000 - 12,000}{5,000} = 1.6$$

10.2 WHITE AND BLACK

Generally the two businesses are producing the same net profit, bearing in mind that Black is depreciating his buildings whereas White is not, but by different managment policies.

Black seems to be much more effective in controlling his working capital than White as is illustrated by the following:

	Black	White
Credit period allowed (weeks)	4 1/2	6 1/2
Credit period taken (weeks)	6 1/2	4 1/2
Stock turnover (times per annum)	12	8
Capital turnover (times per annum)	5	3

It can be seen from these figures that Black is obtaining two weeks' credit on balance between his debtors and creditors whereas White is giving two weeks' credit.

This does not seem to have had an adverse effect on Black's sales as he has produced a substantially higher sales figure than White. In doing so he has a lower gross profit margin than White (22% against 25%) and, owing to additional selling and distribution expenses and differing depreciation policies, a lower net profit margin (6% to 8%). Because this was done with less equity, Black has a higher gross profit on sales (25% against 22%) at the expense of a significantly lower liquidity ratio (0.8 against 2.2) thus rendering him somewhat vunerable to adverse conditions.

Any comparison on the basis of such evidence may only be general in its conclusions.

Information required before reaching firmer conclusions might include:

(a) a valuation of the properties;

(b) full details of accounting policies, particularly in respect of:

    (i) depreciation of fixed assets;
    (ii) stock valuation;
    (iii) provisions for bad debts;

(c) an indication of work done by Black and White and salaries charged, if any.

10.3 HARCOURT LTD

(a) (i) Computation of net working capital

	19X7 £	19X6 £	19X5 £
Current assets	500	600	750
Current liabilities	400	300	250
Net working capital	100	300	500

(ii) Computation of the current ratio:

	19X7	19X6	19X5
19X7 £500: £400	1.25 to 1		
19X6 £600: £300		2 to 1	
19X5 £750: £250			3 to 1

(iii) Computation of the debt/equity ratio

	£	£	£
Current liabilities	400	300	250
Long-term liabilities	1,900	1,000	500
	2,300	1,300	750 (a)

	£	£	£
Capital	2,500	2,000	2,000
Undistributed profits	1,300	1,000	750
Total shareholders' equity	3,800	3,000	2,750 (b)
Debt/equity ratio (a) – (b)	0.61 to 1.0	0.43 to 1	0.27 to 1

(b) **The profit and loss accounts as % of sales**

Comparative profit and loss accounts in percentage of sales for the years ended 31 December 19X5, 19X6, 19X7

	19X7 %	19X6 %	19X5 %
Sales	100.0	100.0	100.0
Cost of goods sold	65.0	62.0	60.0
Gross profit	35.0	38.0	40.0
Selling expenses	5.0	5.0	5.0
Administration expenses	14.0	9.6	9.0
Total expenses	19.0	14.6	14.0
Net profit before taxes	16.0	23.4	26.0
Taxation	9.6	14.1	15.6
Profit after tax	6.4%	9.3%	10.4%

Answers

(c) The balance sheet in trend percentages:

	19X7 %	19X6 %	19X5 %
Assets			
Current assets	67	80	100
Long term investments	40	80	100
Plant and equipment (net)	220	140	100
	174%	123%	100%

	%	%	%
Liabilities and capital			
Current liabilities	160	120	100
Long-term liabilities	380	200	100
Capital (ordinary £1 shares fully paid)	125	100	100
Undistributed profits	173	133	100
	174%	123%	100%

(d) Harcourt Company's current position has deteriorated significantly over the three-year period. In 19X7 net working capital is only one-fifth of what it was in 19X5, and the current ratio has dropped by nearly two thirds. At the same time, the debt/equity ratio has risen significantly with creditors providing 61p for every pound of assets provided by shareholder in 19X7 as compared to creditors providing only 27p for each pound two years earlier in 19X5.

Looking at the trend percentages on the balance sheet, it appears that the company's rapid expansion of plant and equipment has been largely responsible for the deteriorating financial position. This expansion has severely strained the resources of the company, requiring the sale of additional shares in 19X7 as well as requiring the taking on of large amounts of additional debts. The expansion in plant and equipment was initiated at the same time that the company's earning ability was shrinking. Notice from the percentages on the income statement that in the most recent year, 19X7, the company realised only 6.4p in net profit for every pound of sales as compared to 10.4p for every pound of sales two years earlier, in 19X5. This reduction in net profit per pound of sales is traceable to an increased cost of goods sold and to increased administrative expenses. The increased cost of goods old indicates that selling prices are not rising as rapidly as costs which Harcourt Company is being required to pay its suppliers for stock items. The increase in administrative expenses is probably traceable for the most part to increased depreciation from the new plant and equipment, and to interest on the greatly expanded long-term debt.

It may be, of course, that the profitability of 19X5 and 19X6 was due to the use of written of plant nearing the end of its life span and that the company is now in a far better position for the future but careful financial management will be required to ensure the working capital reduction does not become critical.

10.4   GORDON RAY

(a)   (i)   **Return on capital employed**

Gordon Ray

$$\frac{\text{net profit} - \text{notional salary}}{\text{net capital employed}}$$

$$= \frac{15,000 - 12,000}{100,000} \times 100 = 3\%$$

Smooth Dealers Ltd

$$\frac{\text{net profit} + \text{interest}}{\text{net capital employed}}$$

$$= \frac{5,000 + 3,000}{160,000} \times 100 = 5\%$$

Smooth Dealers Ltd obviously has the better return. The adjustment for a notional salary for Gordon Ray is necessary to bring his cost in running the business in line with that of the chairman of Smooth Dealers Ltd. Profits before interest must be compared to net capital employed as this includes the 10% debenture stock in Smooth Dealers Ltd.

(ii)   **Net profit percentage**

Gordon Ray

$$\frac{\text{net profit (as above)}}{\text{sales}} \times 100 = \frac{3,000}{90,000} \times 100 = 3.33\%$$

Smooth Dealers Ltd

$$\frac{\text{net profit (as above)}}{\text{sales}} \times 100 = \frac{8,000}{150,000} \times 100 = 5.33\%$$

Again the net profit % of Smooth Dealers Ltd is superior to that of Gordon Ray. This may arise from different selling prices, perhaps because of the quality of goods, or from better control of costs.

(iii)   **Gross profit percentage**

$$\frac{\text{gross profit}}{\text{sales}} \times 100$$

Gordon Ray $\dfrac{42,000}{90,000} \times 100 = 46.67\%$

Smooth Dealers Ltd $\dfrac{70,000}{150,000} \times 100 = 46.67\%$

These are identical indicating that probably selling prices and buying prices are the same. Any difference in net profit percentage is therefore due to control of the remaining costs.

(iv)   Asset turnover

$$\frac{\text{sales}}{\text{net capital employed}}$$

Gordon Ray $\frac{90,000}{100,000}$ = .9

Smooth Dealers Ltd $\frac{150,000}{160,000}$ = .9375

The difference here is not substantial, both businesses appear to generate approximately the same level of sales per £ of capital employed.

(v)   **Current ratio**

Current assets : Current liabilities

Gordon Ray   56:16 = 3.5:1

Smooth Dealers Ltd   135:25 = 5.4:1

Both businesses have high levels of liquidity and should not experience any difficulty in meeting their liabilities as they fall due.

Note: A considerable number of other ratios could be compiled. Those above are perhaps the more obvious calculations.

Interesting ratios to calculate include:

Fixed asset utilisation = $\frac{\text{sales}}{\text{fixed assets}}$

1.5   and   3.0

Administration expenses to sales

26.67%   and   24.67%

(The difference in net profit 2%.)

(b)   Three reasons why the comparison of profit earned by different businesses should be approached with great care are:

(i)   Different status of owners and managers of the business (as above).

(ii)   Different cost structures arising from owning different assets, eg, one business may own its premises whilst another may rent.

(iii) Different capital structures where a business financed by loans will incur a charge against profit for the interest.

Note: A number of other factors could be covered. Of particular interest would be: accounting policies, age of fixed assets, accounting convention followed, eg, historic cost or replacement cost.

10.5   **JAMES SIMPSON**

(a)   **Years ended 31 December**

	19X3	19X4	19X5
Return on capital employed	£20,000	£18,000	£19,000
	£95,000	£167,000	£187,000
	= 21.05%	= 10.78%	= 10.16%
Acid or quick	£31,000	£79,000	£68,000
	£8,000	£12,000	£18,000
	= 387.5%	= 658.3%	= 377.8%
Stock turnover	£60,000	£72,000	£98,000
	£15,000	£18,000	£24,500
	= 4 times	= 4 times	= 4 times
Net profit* to sales	£20,000	£18,000	£19,000
	£100,000	£120,000	£140,000
* After adding back loan interest	= 20%	= 15%	= 13.6%

(b)   **Sales**

Capital employed

19X3 $\dfrac{100}{95}$ =   1.05

19X4 $\dfrac{120}{167}$ =   0.72

19X5 $\dfrac{140}{187}$ =   0.75

This shows that very little use has been made of the loan to increase the level of activity in the business. 19X4 is misleading as the loan was only received on 31 December and if we exclude the loan the ratio becomes $\dfrac{120}{117}$ = 1.03.

Expenses excluding loan interest to sales.

19X3 $\dfrac{20}{100}$ x   100   =   20%

19X4 $\dfrac{30}{120}$ x   100   =   25%

19X5 $\dfrac{23}{140}$ x   100   =   16.4%

This shows that the level of expenses is falling relative to sales, possibly because of the new fixed assets financed by the loan.

Answers

Note: Other ratios which could be used here are:

Current ratio – current assets to current liabilities.

Debtors to turnover – expressed as a number of days.

Stock to cost of sales – expressed as a number of days.

Fixed assets to sales – expressed as £ of sales per £ of fixed assets.

Gross profit to sales.

(c)

Years ended 31 December	19X3	19X4	19X5
	£	£	£
Net profit	20,000	18,000	14,000
Less: Estimated value of James Simpson's services	12,000	12,000	12,000
Return on James Simpson's investment	8,000	6,000	2,000
	= 9.2%	= 5.7%	= 1.7%

The continuance of the business on financial grounds is not justified bearing in mind that James Simpson can invest in a bank deposit account producing interest at the rate of 8% per annum.

(d) In section (a) of this answer the return on capital employed for 19X5 is shown at 10.16%, a modest margin above the rate of interest being paid on the loan of £50,000. However, as noted in (c) the real return overall after taking into account James Simpson's services is well below 10%. Again, even on the incremental basis the loan does not appear to be producing any significant return.

In conclusion, it does not appear to have been a sound decision to borrow the £50,000, although further growth in turnover in 19X6 could change this position.

10.6 JOHN BRIGHT

(a) Any four ratios from the following.

Thomas Bright

Year ended	31 March 19X6		31 March 19X7	
$\dfrac{\text{Net profit}}{\text{Net capital employed}}$	$\dfrac{£8,000}{£85,000}$	= 9.4%	$\dfrac{(£1,000)}{£100,000}$	= Loss 1%
$\dfrac{\text{Net profit}}{\text{Sales}}$	$\dfrac{£8,000}{£100,000}$	= 8.0%	$\dfrac{(£1,000)}{£140,000}$	= Loss 0.7%
$\dfrac{\text{Gross profit}}{\text{Sales}}$	$\dfrac{£40,000}{£100,000}$	= 40.0%	$\dfrac{£50,000}{£140,000}$	= 35.7%

Working capital =

$\dfrac{\text{Current assets}}{\text{Current liabilities}}$	$\dfrac{£20,000}{£5,000}$ = 400.0%	$\dfrac{£32,000}{£12,000}$ = 266.7%
$\dfrac{\text{Debtors}}{\text{Sales}}$	$\dfrac{£11,000}{£100,000}$ = 11%	$\dfrac{£24,000}{£140,000}$ = 17.1%

(b) **Reasons for closing the business**

(i)   If Thomas Bright obtains employment offering a salary of £10,000 per annum, his earnings would be higher than if he continues the business.

(ii)   The business seems to have deteriorated in the second year.

(iii) John Bright could achieve a higher return (at 10%) by simply placing an investment in a bank deposit account.

Reasons in favour of continuance

(i)   The business has only just started. Further examination of the variable overheads might reveal concealed growth.

(c) **Distinguishing between fixed and variable overheads**

Important to determine breakeven point, since variable costs are directly related to the units produced and sold whereas fixed overheads are independent and will occur in any event.

10.7   JOHN TIMPSON

(a)   John Timpson's optimistic view of the progress of his business:

Financial Ratios which all show profit growth:

	19X5/X6		**19X6/X7**	
(i) Gross profit percentage				
	$\dfrac{60,000}{200,000}$ x 100%	30%	$\dfrac{108,000}{300,000}$ x 100%	36%

An increase in gross profit to sales

(ii) Current ratio				
	$\dfrac{120,000}{50,000}$	2.4	$\dfrac{210,000}{84,000}$	2.5

Improved current ratio (current assets:current liabilities)

(iii) Debtors turnover ratio				
	$\dfrac{200,000}{45,000}$	4.4	$\dfrac{300,000}{58,000}$	5.2

Answers

    (iv)   Debtors collection period

$$\frac{360}{4.4} \qquad \text{81 days} \qquad \frac{360}{5.2} \qquad \text{69.6 days}$$

    Reduction of debtors' collection period.

    (v)   Sales, gross profit and net profit have all increased

(b)   Accountant's warning concerning developments in John Timpson's business

The accountant will draw attention to the following ratios

		19X5/X6	19X6/X7
(i)	Return on net capital employed		
	$\dfrac{\text{Net profit}}{\text{Net capital employed}}$	12½%	10%
(ii)	Liquidity (quick ratio)		
	$\dfrac{\text{Balance at bank + debtors}}{\text{Creditors}}$	160%	75%
(iii)	$\dfrac{\text{Net profit}}{\text{Sales}}$	15%	12.5%
(iv)	$\dfrac{\text{Sales}}{\text{Net capital employed}}$	83.3%	79.8%
(v)	Stock turnover (using closed stock)	3.5 times	1.3 times

(vi)   Great increase in creditors, evidence of possible extended credit being taken

The accountant can point to:

    (i)   Falling return on net capital employed.

    (ii)   Substantial decline in liquidity (illustrated by excluding stock from the current ratio).

    (iii) Fall in net profit/sales percentage (as opposed to increase in gross profit percentage).

    (iv) Poorer utilisation of capital employed in trading activities.

    (v)   Effect of capital expenditure incurred in 19X6/X7 on liquidity position.

    (vi) Doubtful jurisdiction for increased loan at 10% pa.

    (vii) Doubtful justification for capital expenditure in 19X6/X7. (Note capital expenditure **more** than £70,000).

10.8 JOAN STREET

(a)

**Trading and profit and loss account
for the year ended 31 March 19X8**

	£	£
Sales (180,000 ÷ 0.75)		240,000
Cost of sales (10% x average stock = 180,000)		
Opening stock (given)	21,000	
Purchases (balancing figure)	174,000	
	195,000	
Closing stock (21,000 – 6,000)	15,000	
		180,000
Gross profit (25% of sales)		60,000
Expenses (balancing figure)		38,400
Net profit (9% of sales)		21,600

Balance sheet as at 31 March 19X8

		£	£
Fixed assets (45% x sales)			108,000
Current assets			
Stock (21,000 – 6,000)		15,000	
Debtors (sales x 36½ ÷ 365)		24,000	
Bank (balancing figure)		9,000	
	(36,000 x 4/3)	48,000	
Current liabilities (36,000 ÷ 3)		12,000	
			36,000
			144,000

	£
Capital	
Balance at 1 April 19X7 (balancing figure)	122,400
Profit for the year (from above)	21,600
Balance at 31 March 19X8 (21,600 ÷ 0.15)	144,000

(b) **Favourable comparisons**

Any two from:

(i)   liquidity (acid test rato);
(ii)   working capital;
(iii) net profit to sales;
(iv) stock turnover.

Unfavourable comparisons

Any two from:

(i) net profit to capital employed;
(ii) sales to capital employed;
(iii) gross profit to sales;
(iv) debtors collection period.

(c) **Drawbacks of this type of comparison**

Any two from the following.

(i) The size of Joan's business relative to the industry average is not known.

(ii) There is no data on previous years' results to ascertain trends.

(iii) The statistics given do not give a **complete** picture of Joan's business.

(iv) It is not known whether the accounting policies employed by Joan in arriving at these figures are typical of her industry.

10.9 GRAY PRODUCTS

The report to John Street should include a consideration of the following.

(1) Presentation of information on the two businesses on a comparable basis:

	Mary Penney's business £	Gray Products Ltd's business £
Net profit per accounts per annum	28,000	22,000
Less: Manager's salary per annum	(14,000)	–
Directors' fees per annum	(4,000)	–
Premises rent per annum	–	(6,000)
Adjusted profit on a comparable basis	10,000	16,000
Sale price of business	100,000	125,000
Less: Sale price of premises	–	35,000
Net investment in business	100,000	90,000
Annual return on net investment	10.0%	17.8%
Annual return on sale price of business	10.0%	17.6%

(2) It is assumed that John Street will not wish to terminate his employment as a sales representative and be engaged in the operation of any business purchased.

(3) John Street's present capital would enable him to purchase the business of Mary Penney, but the present return of 10.0% per annum is not attractive particularly in view of the obvious risk involved when a similar return is currently obtainable from a bank deposit account.

However, if the future prospects of Mary Penney's business are promising the view expressed in the previous paragraph may be reviewed.

(4)   If John Street is able to borrow £25,000 on a short–term basis, the purchase of Gray's Products Ltd's business is an attractive proposition. Immediately the purchase is completed, John Street could sell the premises for £35,000 and repay his loan.

In the event of John Street being able to borrow £25,000 on a long–term basis at a rate of interest of less than 17% per annum, it is recommended that John Street should not sell the premises.

10.10   JOYCE WALTERS

(a)   **Balance sheets as at 31 March**

	19X8 £	19X8 £	19X9 £	19X9 £	19Y0 £	19Y0 £
Fixed assets						
Freehold land						
– cost		30,000		30,000		30,000
Freehold buildings						
– cost	60,000		60,000		60,000	
– depreciation	–		1,500		3,000	
		60,000		58,500		57,000
Motor vehicles						
– cost	12,000		12,000		12,000	
– depreciation	–		2,400		4,800	
		12,000		9,600		7,200
		102,000		98,100		94,200
Current assets						
Stock (W1)	14,000		23,500		18,500	
Trade debtors	–		8,600		9,800	
Bank balance	4,800		2,300		2,800	
	18,800		34,400		31,100	
Creditors: Amount falling due within one year						
Trade creditors	–		(13,800)		(3,900)	
		18,800		20,600		27,200
Total capital		120,800		118,700		121,400

Workings

$$\text{Stock turnover} = \frac{\text{Cost of sales}}{\text{Average stock}}$$

Answers

31 March 19X9

Cost of sales	$= £210,000 \times 100/140$
	$= £150,000$
Stock turnover	$= 8$

$$\text{Therefore } 8 = \frac{150,000}{\text{Average stock}}$$

Average stock $= £18,750$

$$\text{Average stock} = \frac{\text{Opening stock} + \text{closing stock}}{2}$$

$$18,750 = \frac{14,000 + \text{closing stock}}{2}$$

Closing stock $= £23,500$

31 March 19Y0

Cost of sales	$= £294,000 \times 100/140$
	$= £210,000$
Stock turnover	$= 10$

$$10 = \frac{210,000}{\text{Average stock}}$$

Average stock $= £21,000$

$$21,000 = \frac{23,500 + \text{closing stock}}{2}$$

Closing stock $= £18,500$

(b) **Statement of net profit or loss for the year ended 31 March 19X9 and 19Y0**

	31 March 19X9 £	31 March 19Y0 £
Increase/(decrease) in total capital during year		
(120,800 = 118,700)	(2,100)	
(118,700 – 121,400)		2,700
Add: Drawings – cash	9,000	9,400
– goods	8,500	13,000
Net profit	15,400	25,100

10.11   T CARR LTD

(a)   **Accounting ratios**

		Year ended 30 September		
		19X8	19X9	19Y0
Gross margin	$\left(\dfrac{\text{Gross profit}}{\text{Salary}}\right)$	33%	25%	20%
Asset turnover	$\left(\dfrac{\text{Sales}}{\text{Capital employed}}\right)$	1.5	1.8	2.25
Gross return on capital employed	$\left(\dfrac{\text{Gross profit}}{\text{Capital employed}}\right)$	50%	45%	45%
Net return on capital employed	$\left(\dfrac{\text{Net profit}}{\text{Capital employed}}\right)$	15%	8%	5.8%
Fixed asset turnover	$\left(\dfrac{\text{Sales}}{\text{Fixed assets}}\right)$	4.0	3.0	3.375
Current ratio	$\left(\dfrac{\text{Current assets}}{\text{Current liabilities}}\right)$	3.5	2.14	1.73
Acid test	$\left(\dfrac{\text{Current assets less stock}}{\text{Current liabilities}}\right)$	2.3	1.43	1.0
Variable overheads / Sales		15%	15%	10%
Fixed overheads / Sales		8.3%	5.6%	7.4%
Total overhead / Sales		23.3%	20.6%	17.4%

Note: only **four** ratios are required in the answer.

(b)   **Report to James and Henry Carr on T Carr Ltd**

Dear Sir

Examination of the summarised trading and profit and loss account and balance sheet for T Carr Ltd has highlighted the following points.

(1)   The company has achieved its stated objective of a 50% increase in turnover in each of the two immediately preceding years. However, it is unlikely, depending upon T Carr Ltd's market, that this increase can be continued indefinitely.

(2)   Whilst sales have increased each year, profitability (in terms of both gross and net profit) has declined. This is particularly true in the return on capital employed.

(3)   The decrease in profit margin comes largely from cost of sales, as neither variable nor fixed overheads have increased in line with turnover. Attention should be paid to these increasing cost of sales proportions.

(4)   The decrease in profitability is not due to inefficient use of assets, indeed total asset turnover has improved. However there is some deterioration in fixed asset turnover (ie, usage of fixed assets) which may merit further investigation.

(5)   Turning to the company's liquidity, this has declined over the three years. Without information regarding the type of business of T Carr Ltd it is not possible to tell whether this is a problem or a sign of better asset management.

(6)   In 1990 the company's net return on capital employed was only 5.8%. Again, depending upon the type of business, this is very low. This could be improved if the cost of sales situation could be improved.

It would appear that despite T Carr's increasing turnover, its profitability or return is declining. There would seem to be no apparent reason for increased investment in T Carr Ltd and management would be well advised to consider cost of sales, return on capital employed and liquidity rather than simply turnover.

Tutorial note: Any of the above comments relevant to the ratios you have used should be made.

11   VAT

11.1   AK LTD

(a)   (i)   Bank cash book (receipts side)

Date	Details	Memo discount £	Total £	Debtors ledger £
Feb 19	B Limited	682	29,318	29,318
Feb 20	C & Co Limited	500	21,500	21,500
		1,182	50,818	50,818
Feb 1	Balance	b/f	21,831	
			72,649	

Date		Details	Memo discount £	Total £	Creditors ledger £	Input VAT £	Other £
Feb	21	K & Sons	340	14,660	14,660		
	21	J Ltd	640	27,860	27,860		
	21	VAT paid		2,845			2,845
		PAYE		1,900			1,900
		National insurance		1,240			1,240
		Telephone		44		4	40
		Plant & machinery		6,600		600	6,000
		Dividends		14,000			14,000
		ACT		6,000			6,000
		Net salaries		7,500			7,500
			980	82,649	42,520	604	39,525
		Balance overdraft c/f		(10,000)			
				72,649			

(ii) Sales day book

Date		Details	Total £	Net sales Y £	Net sales Z £	VAT £
Feb	1	B Ltd	22,000	9,000	11,000	2,000
	12	C & Co Ltd	44,000	14,000	26,000	4,000
	22	B Ltd	22,000	7,000	13,000	2,000
			88,000	30,000	50,000	8,000

(iii) Purchases day book

Date		Details	Total £	Net purchases W £	Net purchases X £	VAT £
Feb	8	K & Sons	17,600	7,000	9,000	1,600
	16	J Ltd	35,200	14,000	18,000	3,200
			52,800	21,000	27,000	4,800
	25	J Ltd – credit	3,300	1,000	2,000	300
			49,500	20,000	25,000	4,500

(b), (c) and (d) Sales account

			Product Y £	Product Z £
Jan		Sundries	20,000	30,000
Feb		Do	30,000	50,000
			50,000	80,000

Purchases account

		Material W £	Material X £
Jan	Sundries	10,000	15,000
Feb	Do	20,000	25,000
		30,000	40,000

VAT account

		£			£
Feb	Cash book	2,845	Jan	Balance	2,849
Feb	Purchases day book	4,500	Feb	Sales day book	8,000
Feb	Cash book	604			
	Balance c/f	2,900			
		10,849			10,849

Debtors ledger control

		£			£
Jan	Balance b/f	64,000	Feb	Cash book	50,818
Feb	Sales day book	88,000	Feb	Discounts allowed	1,182
				Balance b/f	100,000
		152,000			152,000

Creditors ledger control

		£			£
Feb	Cash book	42,520	Jan	Balance c/f	44,000
Feb	Discounts received	980	Feb	Purchases day book	49,500
	Balance c/f	50,000			
		93,500			93,500

Salaries payroll control

		£			£
Feb	Cash book	7,500	Feb	Transfer to office	
	PAYE	2,000		Salaries	10,000
	National insurance	500			
		10,000			10,000

Creditor – PAYE

		£			£
Feb	Cash book	1,900	Feb	Balance b/f	1,900
	Balance c/f	2,000		Salaries control	2,000
		3,900			3,900

Creditor – National insurance

		£			£
Feb	Cash book	1,240	Feb	Balance b/f	1,240
	Balance c/f	1,300		Salaries control	500
				N I employer's	
				contribution	800
		2,540			3,900

Discount received

		£			£
			Jan	Balance b/f	1,020
			Feb	Creditors	980
					2,000

Discount allowed

		£
Jan	Balance b/f	1,118
Feb	Debtors	1,182
		2,300

Office salaries

		£
Jan	Balance b/f	10,000
Feb	Salaries control	10,000
		20,000

National insurance – Company's contribution

		£
Jan	Balance b/f	700
Feb	National insurance creditors	800
		1,500

Plant & machinery – at cost

		£
Jan	Balance b/f	294,000
Feb	Cash book	6,000
		300,000

Telephone

		£
Jan	Balance b/f	60
Feb	Cash book	40
		100

Dividends paid

		£
Feb	Cash book	14,000

ACT

		£
Feb	Cash book	6,000

Debtors ledger (memo)

B Ltd

		£			£
Jan	Balance b/f	36,000	Feb	Cash and discount	30,000
Feb	Sales day book	22,000		Balance c/f	50,000
Feb	Do	22,000			
		80,000			80,000

C and Co Ltd

		£			£
Jan	Balance b/f	28,000	Feb	Cash and discount	22,000
Feb	Sales day book	44,000		Balance c/f	50,000
		72,000			72,000

Creditors ledger (memo)

K & Sons

		£			£
Feb	Cash and discount	15,000	Jan	Balance c/f	15,000
	Balance c/f	17,600	Feb	Purchases day book	17,600
		32,600			32,600

J Ltd

		£			£
Feb	Purchases day book	3,300	Jan	Balance b/f	29,000
Feb	Cash & discount	28,500	Feb	Purchases day book	35,200
	Balance c/f	32,400			
		64,200			64,200

(e) **Balances at 28 February 19X2**

	Dr £	Cr £
Bank cash		10,000
Sales – Y		50,000
– Z		80,000
Purchases – W	30,000	
– X	40,000	
Creditors – VAT		2,900
Debtors ledger control	100,000	
Creditors ledger control		50,000
Creditors – PAYE		2,000
Creditors – National insurance		1,300
Discounts received		2,000
Discounts allowed	2,300	
Office salaries	20,000	
National insurance – expense	1,500	
Plant and machinery at cost	300,000	
Telephone	100	
Dividends paid	14,000	
ACT	6,000	

11.2 JOHN HENRY LTD (2)

(a) Purchases day book

		Total £	VAT £	Purchases £	Fixed assets motor vehicles £	Vehicle expenses £	Fixed assets machinery £
March 12	Highway Garage Ltd	11,025.00	1,425.00		9,500.00	100.00	
March 19	Smith Motors Ltd	9,300.00	1,230.00		9,200.00	100.00	
April 23	Super Machines Ltd	9,430.00					8,200.00
May 7	Highway Garage Ltd	241.50	31.50			210.00	
May 20	Machine Repairs Ltd	575.00	75.00				500.00
May 31	Raw materials	208,828.50	27,238.50	181,590.00			
		239,400.00	30,000.00	181,590.00	18,700.00	410.00	8,700.00

280

(b)

HM Customs and Excise – VAT

19X6		£	19X6			£
March 20	Bank	84,000	March 1		Balance b/f	84,000
May 31	Input tax (note 2)	30,000	May 31		Sales (output tax) (note 1)	93,000
31	Balance c/f	65,250		31	Cost of sales (note 2)	2,250
		179,250				179,250
			June 1		Balance b/d	65,250

Notes

(i)   Sales – output tax 15% of £620,000 = £93,000.

(ii)   Input tax not reclaimable:

$$\frac{£60,000}{£800,000} \times £30,000 = £2,250$$

For convenience this will normally be added to cost of sales but may be apportioned back over the items giving rise to the input tax of £30,000.

Alternatively, input tax debited of £27,750 would be accepted instead of the entries above (eg, debit 'input tax £30,000' and credit 'cost of sales £2,250').

11.3   HAROLD PEACOCK

(a)   **T King and Sons Ltd**

			19X6		£
			Sept 18	Purchases	660.24

XL Garages Ltd

			19X6		£
			Sept 22	Motor car, at cost	9,200.00

G Siddle Ltd

19X6		£
Sept 25	Sales	1,169.94

Purchases

19X6		£
Sept 18	T King and Sons Ltd	576.00

Sales

	19X6		£
	Sept 25	G Siddle Ltd	1,020.00

HM Customs and Excise

19X6		£	19X6		£
Sept 18	Purchases (T King and Sons Ltd)	84.24	Sept 21	Sales (G Siddle Ltd)	149.94

Motor car, at cost

19X6		£
Sept 22	XL Garages Ltd	9,200.00

Notes

(1)   Purchases from T King and Sons Ltd

	£
List price	640.00
Less trade discount 10%	64.00
	576.00
Less cash discount 2½%	14.40
	561.40
VAT 15% of £561.40	£84.24

(2)   Sale to G Siddle Ltd

	£
List price	1,200.00
Less trade discount 15%	180.00
	1,020.00
Less cash discount 2%	20.40
	999.60
VAT 15% of £999.60	£149.94

(3)   Car purchase 22 September 19X6 – non–deductible item for VAT purposes.

Cost to business £8,000 + 15% = £9,200.

(b) **Timber Products Ltd**

(i) Sales ledger account balances at 31 October 19X6

	£	Debit £	Credit £
Per draft final accounts		21,700.00	700.00
Less: Accounts written off as bad:			
K Milson	250.00		
T Longdon	150.00		
	400.00		
		21,300.00	
Less: Receipt from T Bean Sept 19X6 transferred to profit and loss account – bad debt recovered			400.00
Corrected balances		21,300.00	300.00

(ii) Provision for doubtful debts account

19X6		£	19X6		£
Oct 31	Profit & loss	251.00	Nov 1	Balance b/f	890.00
Oct 31	Balance c/f	639.00*			
		890.00			890.00
			19X6		
			Nov 1	Balance b/f	639.00

* 3% of £21,300.00

11.4 GRANDBAY MACHINISTS LTD

Journal

19X9		£	£
10 April	Motor cars, at cost (including VAT)	9,200	
	Circle Garages Ltd		9,200
13 April	Motor lorries, at cost	42,000	
	Customs and Excise – VAT	6,300	
	Heavy Goods Trucks Ltd		48,300
17 April	Motor car repairs	300	
	Customs and Excise – VAT	45	
	Quickservices Ltd		345
19 April	Motor car repairs	80	
	Customs and Excise – VAT	12	
	Car Supplies Ltd		92

Answers

(b)   Tip Top Dealers Ltd

(i)   Provision for doubtful debts account

19X9		£	19X8		£
31 May	Profit and loss	168	1 June	Balance b/f	410
31 May	Balance c/f (note 1)	242			
		410			410
			19X9		
			1 June	Balance b/f	242

Note 1

Sales ledger debit balances at 31 May 19X9

	£	£
Per trial balance at 31 May 19X9		12,360
Less: Bad debts written off:		
L Pink	210	
G Slack	50	
		260
		12,100

Provision for doubtful debts at 31 May 19X9 = 2% of £12,100 = £242.

(ii)   Balance sheet as at 31 May 19X9 (extract)

Debtors (see note 2)	£12,512
Creditors (see note 3)	£8,064

Note 2

Debtors

	£
Sales ledger control account – debit balance	12,360
Less: Bad debts written off	260
	12,100
Less: Provision for doubtful debts	242
	11,858
Purchases ledger control account – debit balance	654
	12,512

Note 3

Creditors

	£
Purchases ledger control account – credit balance	7,348
Sales ledger control account – credit balance	716
	8,064

0045V

Time allowed – 3 hours

Number of questions on paper – 7

Answer **five** questions only –
two questions (**compulsory**) from Section A, and
two questions from Section B.

All questions carry equal marks

All workings must be shown

SECTION A: Answer both questions

1   **J GREGG**

J Gregg operates an incomplete system of bookkeeping, from which the following information has been extracted for the year to 31 March 19X4.

Bank account summary

	£		£
Bank balance at 1 April 19X3	3,000	Cash paid to trade creditors	78,000
Cash received from trade debtors	76,000	Electricity	900
		Office expenses	1,500
Cash sales	4,900	Rates	2,500
Bank balance at 31 March 19X4	5,700	Telephone	400
		Wages	5,000
		Van expenses	1,300
	89,600		89,600

Additional information obtained was as follows.

Assets and liabilities at:

	1 April 19X3	31 March 19X4
Furniture and fittings, at cost	2,000	2,000
Van, at cost	5,000	5,000
Stocks	10,000	12,000
Trade debtors	15,000	20,000
Prepayments – Rates	1,000	1,500
– Van insurance	200	300
Cash in hand	100	200
Depreciation – Furniture and fittings	600	600
– Van	2,000	2,000
Provision for doubtful debts	400	400
Trade creditors	14,000	12,000
Accruals – Electricity	300	400
– Telephone	200	100

Notes

(1)   Gregg allowed his trade customers discounts of £9,000 and he also benefited from discounts received of £4,000.

(2)   Cash drawings from the till to pay for personal expenses amounted to £5,000, and goods withdrawn during the year for personal use were valued at £3,000.

(3)   Depreciation is to be charged at the rate of 10% straight line on furniture and fittings and 25% straight line on the van.

(4)   The provision for doubtful debts is to be adjusted to 3% of total debtors.

Required

(a)   prepare J Gregg's trading, profit and loss account for the year to 31 March 19X4;   (17 marks)

(b)   prepare a balance sheet at 31 March 19X4.   (8 marks)
                                                        (Total 25 marks)

2   BROWN, ALLEN AND CAMPBELL

On 30 June 19X6, Campbell was admitted as a partner to the firm of Brown and Allen. He introduced £4,000 by way of capital, and as he could not immediately find additional monies to pay for his share of goodwill, it was agreed to create a goodwill account for £12,000. Prior to his admission, Brown and Allen shared profits and losses in the ratio of 3 : 1, but the new partnership profit sharing ratio was agreed at 3 : 2 : 1. Interest was allowed on capital at 8% per year.

At the year ended 31 December 19X6, the trial balance was:

	£	£
Capital		
Brown		15,000
Allen		12,000
Current accounts		
Brown		900
Allen	259	
Campbell		700
Suspense account – Campbell		4,000
5% loan – Brown		4,000
Interest on loan	200	
Sales		50,630
Purchases	47,300	
Stock at 1.1.X6	9,250	
Discounts allowed and received	650	950
Wages	2,120	
Lighting and heating	860	
Rates	870	
Depreciation – buildings		3,100
– vehicles		4,000
Buildings (cost)	23,000	
Vehicles (cost)	9,000	
Debtors and creditors	5,300	5,300
Provision for doubtful debts		130
Bad debts	150	
Vehicle running expenses	680	
Miscellaneous expenses	471	
Bank	600	
	100,710	100,710

The following data is to be taken into account:

(1)   Stock at 31 December 19X6 was valued at £14,200.

(2)   Wages owing at 31 December 19X6 amounted to £80.

(3)   Rates include £80 in respect of the period 1 January 19X7 – 31 January 19X7.

(4)   Depreciation is to be provided on buildings at 2% on cost, and on vehicles at 10% on cost. No new vehicles have been acquired during the year.

(5)   The provision for doubtful debts is to be increased to 3% of debtors.

(6)   All revenues and expenses can be deemed to accrue evenly through the year.

Required

(a)   Prepare journal entries to record Campbell's admission as a partner.

(b)   Prepare a trading and profit and loss account and appropriation account for the period ended 31 December 19X6, and a balance sheet as at that date.

SECTION B: Answer any two questions

3   ALEX AUTOS

The following information has been extracted from the incomplete records of Alex Autos for the year to 31 October 19X4:

	£
Doubtful debts general provision (at 1 November 19X3)	6,300
Cash paid to trade creditors	274,000
Cash received from trade debtors	663,000
Credit purchases	310,000
Credit sales	690,000
Discounts allowed	14,000
Discounts received	15,000
Purchases returned (all credit)	10,000
Sales returned (all credit)	8,000
Trade creditors (at 1 November 19X3)	43,000
Trade debtors (at 1 November 19X3)	63,000

The following additional information for the year to 31 October 19X4 is to be taken into account:

(1)   The doubtful debts provision should be made equal to 10% of the outstanding trade debtors as at 31 October 19X4 after providing for specific debtors.

(2)   One of Alex Autos' customers went into liquidation on 1 August 19X4 owing the company £7,000. It is most unlikely that this debt will ever be recovered.

(3)   A cheque for £3,000 received from a trade debtor was returned by the bank marked 'refer to drawer'. A full provision is to be made for this amount.

(4)   Alex Autos owed a customer £4,000 and it was agreed that this amount should be offset against an amount owing to Alex Autos by the same customer.

(5)   A return of goods totalling £2,000 by a customer had been accounted for as a purchase by Alex Autos.

Required

Write up the following accounts for the year to 31 October 19X4:

(a)	doubtful debts provision;	(6 marks)
(b)	trade creditors control (or total) account; and	(8 marks)
(c)	trade debtors control (or total) account;	(11 marks)
		(Total 25 marks)

4   **INEPT LTD**

When Inept Ltd received a bank statement for the period ended 30 June 19X0, this did not agree with the balance shown in the cash book of £2,972 in the company's favour.

An examination of the cash book and bank statement disclosed the following.

(1)   A deposit of £492 paid in on 29 June 19X0 had not been credited by the bank until 1 July 19X0.

(2)   Bank charges amounting to £17 had not been entered in the cash book.

(3)   A debit of £42 appeared on the bank statement for an unpaid cheque, which had been returned marked 'out of date'. The cheque had been redated by the customer of Inept Ltd and paid into the bank again on 3 July 19X0.

(4)   A standing order for payment of an annual subscription amounting to £10 had not been entered in the cash book.

(5)   On 25 June the managing director had given the cashier a cheque for £100 to pay into his personal account at the bank. The cashier had paid it into the company's account by mistake.

(6)   On 27 June two customers of Inept Ltd had paid direct to the company's bank account £499 and £157 respectively in payment for goods supplied. The advices were not received by the company until 1 July and were entered in the cash book under that date.

(7)   On 30 March 19X0 the company had entered into a hire purchase agreement to pay by banker's order a sum of £26 on the 10th day of each month, commencing April. No entries had been made in the cash book.

(8)   £364 paid into the bank had been entered twice in the cash book.

(9)   Cheques issued amounting to £4,672 had not been presented to the bank payment until after 30 June 19X0.

(10)   A customer of the company, who received a cash discount of 2.5% on his account of £200, paid the company a cheque on 10 June. The cashier, in error, entered the gross amount in the bank column of the cash book.

After making the adjustments required by the foregoing the bank statement reconciled with the balance in the cash book.

Required

(a)   Show the necessary adjustments in the cash book of Inept Ltd, bringing down the correct balance on 30 June 19X0.   (16 marks)

(b)   Prepare a bank reconciliation statement as at that date.   (9 marks)
    (Total 25 marks)

5   SPEED

You are provided with the following information relating to Speed, a firm of delivery merchants, for the year to 31 October 19X3.

(1)   Balance sheet (extract) at 31 October 19X2

	£
Vans, at cost	14,000
Less: depreciation to date	6,000
Net book value	8,000

(2)   Purchases of vans

Date	Registration number	Cost
		£
1.1.W9	AAT 10	2,000
1.5.X0	BAT 20	3,000
1.12.X1	CAT 30	4,000
1.8.X2	DAT 40	5,000
1.12.X2	EAT 50	6,000
1.8.X3	FAT 60	9,000

(3)   Sales of vans

Date	Registration number	Sale proceeds
		£
30.11.X2	AAT 10	500
1.8.X3	CAT 30	2,000
30.9.X3	DAT 40	4,000

(4)   On 1.8.X3 CAT 30 was traded in part exchange against the cost of FAT 60. The amount shown above is the net cost of FAT 60.

(5)   Vans are depreciated at a rate of 20% per annum on cost. A full year's depreciation is charged in the year of purchase, but no depreciation is charged in the year of disposal.

Required

(a)   enter the above transactions in the following accounts for the year to 31 October 19X3, being careful to bring down the balances as at 1 November 19X3: (i) vans account; (ii) vans depreciation provision account; and (iii) vans disposal account; and

(18 marks)

(b)   state briefly whether you think that the reducing balance method of depreciation would be a more appropriate method of depreciating delivery vans.

(7 marks)

(Total 25 marks)

6   SUSPENSE ADJUSTER

Show journal entries to correct the following entries and the adjusted trial balance after all corrections.

(a)   Bank charges of £1,000 have been completely omitted from the books. The bank account balance has not been reconciled.

(b)   Fixed assets costing £11,879 and accumulated depreciation of £10,943 have been sold for £2,000. This amount is shown as a separate item in the final balance and no entries have been made in the nominal ledger accounts. Any surplus or deficit should be taken to capital surplus.

(c)   Deductions of £6,088 for PAYE income tax and £1,766 for national insurance, graduated pension, etc, were made from employees' wages and salaries during the year. The company's contribution for national insurance, graduated pensions etc, amounted to £3,000. No entries have been made for these items.

(d)   In addition to allowing discounts of £240 and receiving discount of £260, various debtors and creditors amounting to £10,000 were set off by contra. No entries whatever have been made in respect of these items.

(e)   Debtors amounting to £2,000 are bad and need to be written off.

(f)   Goods returned from a debtor of £630 have been correctly entered in the debtor's account, but by mistake were entered in the returns outward book.

(g)   A payment for stationery of £234 was correctly entered in the cash book but debited in the ledger as £243.

(h)   A payment of £76 for packing materials has been correctly entered in the cash book but no other entry has been made.

(i)   A cheque payment of £26 for insurance has been recorded in all accounts as £62.

(j)   A page in the purchase day book correctly totalled as £125,124 was carried forward to the top of the next page as £125,421, and due to this the purchases were overstated only.

	Dr £	Cr £
Ordinary share capital		100,000
Retained profit at 1 January 19X6		50,000
10% Debentures		30,000
Debtors	77,240	
Creditors		60,260
Cash in hand	1,000	
Bank overdraft		5,036
Stock and work in progress 1 January 19X6	108,000	
Fixed assets	161,879	
Provision for depreciation 31 Dec 19X6		60,943
Depreciation for the year		
Sales		400,000
Purchases	300,297	
Returns inwards	4,370	
Returns outwards		4,630
Discount allowed	9,760	
Discount received		6,740
Wages and salaries (net)	12,146	
Payment of PAYE	5,988	
National insurance	4,766	
Creditors for PAYE at 1 Jan 19X5		900
Proceeds of sale of fixed assets		2,000
Rent, rate and insurance	18,036	
Postage, telephone and stationery	3,009	
Repairs and maintenance	2,124	
Advertising	4,876	
Packing materials	924	
Motor expenses	2,000	
Sundry expenses	1,000	
Debenture interest	4,000	
Capital surplus account		16,936
Suspense account	1,030	
	737,445	737,445

7 HILLTOWN TRADERS LTD

Stephen House, the principal shareholder of Hilltown Traders Ltd, is very concerned that although the company's net profit has increased in the past year the bank is reluctant to continue the company's overdraft facility.

The summarised results of Hilltown Traders Ltd for the last three financial years are as follows.

Trading and profit and loss accounts years ended 31 December

	19X2 £'000	19X3 £'000	19X4 £'000
Turnover	100	130	150
Less: Cost of sales	80	110	125
Gross profit	20	20	25
Less: Administrative expenditure	4	6	7
Distribution expenditure	6	5	5
	10	11	12
Net profit	10	9	13

Balance sheets as at 31 December

	19X2 £'000	£'000	19X3 £'000	£'000	19X4 £'000	£'000
Fixed assets		60		60		60
Current assets						
Stock	10		24		40	
Debtors	6		7		9	
Balance at bank	2		–		–	
	18		31		49	
Current liabilities						
Creditors	8		9		13	
Bank overdraft	–		3		4	
	8		12		17	
Net current assets		10		19		32
Net capital employed		70		79		92
Capital						
Ordinary share capital		50		50		50
Reserves		20		29		42
		70		79		92

Required

(a) Calculate five financial ratios of Hilltown Traders Ltd which will indicate to the company those aspects which have improved and those which have weakened in the past three years. (18 marks)

(b) Outline three significant and distinct limitations of financial ratios. (7 marks)

(Total 25 marks)

0047V

1   **J GREGG**

(a)

**Trading, profit and loss account
for the year to 31 March 19X4**

	£	£	£
Sales (W1 & W2)			100,000
Less: Cost of goods sold –			
Opening stock		10,000	
Purchases (W3)	80,000		
Less: Goods withdrawn for personal consumption	3,000		
		77,000	
		87,000	
Less: Closing stock		12,000	
			75,000
Gross profit			25,000
Add: Income –			
Discounts received			4,000
			29,000
Less: Expenses –			
Doubtful debts provision – increase (W4)		200	
Depreciation: Furniture and fittings (10% x 2,000)		200	
Van (25% x 5,000)		1,200	
Discounts allowed		9,000	
Electricity (£900 – £300 + £400)		1,000	
Office expenses		1,500	
Rates (£2,500 + £1,000 – £1,500)		2,000	
Telephone (£400 – £200 + £100)		300	
Wages		5,000	
Van expenses (£1,300 + £200 – £300)		1,200	
			21,650
Net profit for the year			7,350

(b)   Balance sheet at 31 March 19X4

	Cost £	Depreciation £	Net book value £
Fixed assets			
Furniture and fittings	2,000	800	1,200
Van	5,000	3,250	1,750
	7,000	4,050	2,950
Current assets			
Stocks		12,000	
Trade debtors	20,000		
Less: Provision for doubtful debts	600		
		19,400	
Prepayments (£1,500 + £300)		1,800	
Cash in hand		200	
		33,400	
Less: Current liabilities			
Trade creditors	12,000		
Accruals (£400 + £100)	500		
Bank overdraft	5,700		
		18,200	
			15,200
			18,150

	£	£
Financed by:		
Capital		
Balance at 1 April 19X3		18,800
Add: Net profit for the year	7,350	
Less: Drawings (£5,000 + £3,000)	8,000	
		(650)
		18,150

Workings

(1)   Credit sales

Debtors account

	£		£
Balance b/f	15,000	Bank	76,000
		Discount allowed	9,000
Sales account	90,000	Balance c/f	20,000
	105,000		105,000

(2)   Cash sales

Cash account

	£		£
Balance b/f	100	Drawings	5,000
Sales account	10,000	Banked	4,900
		Balance c/f	200
	10,100		10,100

(3)   Purchases

Creditors account

	£		£
Bank	78,000	Balance b/f	14,000
Discount received	4,000	Purchases account	80,000
Balance c/f	12,000		
	94,000		94,000

(4)

Provision for doubtful debts

	£		£
		Balance b/f	400
Balance c/f (20,000 x 3%)	600	Profit and loss account	200
	600		600

2   BROWN, ALLEN AND CAMPBELL

(a)

			Dr £	Cr £
30 June	Suspense account – Campbell		4,000	
	Campbell – capital account			4,000

Being introduction by Campbell of capital
of £4,000.

30 June	Goodwill		12,000	
	Capital account			
		Brown		9,000
		Allen		3,000

Being goodwill attributed to Brown and Allen in
the old profit sharing ratios in respect of the
admission of Campbell.

(b)

Trading and profit and loss and appropriation account for the year ended 31 December 19X6

	£	£	£
Sales			50,630
Stock at 1 January	9,250		
Purchases	47,300		
		56,550	
Less: Stock at 31 December		14,200	
			42,350
Gross profit			8,280
Discounts received			950
			9,230
Less: Discounts allowed		650	
Wages		2,200	
Lighting and heating		860	
Rates		790	
Depreciation			
Buildings	460		
Vehicles	900		
		1,360	
Bad and doubtful debts		179	
Vehicle running expenses		680	
Miscellaneous		471	
			7,190
Net profit for year			2,040

Workings

	£	£
Net profit for first half year		1,020
Interest on loan – Brown	100	
Interest on capital to 30 June		
Brown	600	
Allen	480	
		1,180
Loss after charging interest on capital		160

	£	£
Share of loss:		
Brown 3/4	120	
Allen 1/4	40	
		160

	£	£
Net profit for second half year		1,020
Interest on loan – Brown	100	
Interest on capital:		
30 June to 31 December		
Brown	960	
Allen	600	
Campbell	160	
		1,820
Loss after charging interest on capital		800

	£
Share of loss:	
Brown (1/2)	400
Allen (1/3)	267
Campbell (1/6)	133
	£800

Current accounts

	Brown £	Allen £	Campbell £		Brown £	Allen £	Campbell £
Allen	–	259	–	Balance	900	–	700
Share of loss	520	307	133	Interest on			
Closing balance	1,940	514	727	capital	1,560	1,080	160
	2,460	1,080	860		2,460	1,080	860

Balance sheet as at 31 December 19X6

	£	£
Capital accounts		
Brown	24,000	
Allen	15,000	
Campbell	4,000	
	———	
		43,000
Current accounts		
Brown	1,940	
Allen	514	
Campbell	727	
	———	
		3,181
Loan		4,000
		———
Capital employed		50,181
		———

Represented by:	£	£	£	£
Fixed assets:				
Buildings (cost)			23,000	
Less: Depreciation			3,560	
			———	
				19,440
Vehicles (cost)			9,000	
Less: Depreciation			4,900	
			———	
				4,100
Goodwill				12,000
				———
				35,540
Current assets:				
Stock		14,200		
Debtors	5,300			
Less: Provision	159			
	———			
		5,141		
Prepayments		80		
Cash at bank		600		
		———		
		20,021		
Less: Current liabilities				
Creditors		5,300		
Accruals		80		
		———		
		5,380		
		———		
				14,641
				———
				50,181
				———

0047V

3   ALEX AUTOS

(a)

Doubtful debts provision account

		£			£
31.10.X4	Balance c/f		1.11.X3	Balance b/f	6,300
	– Specific	3,000		Profit & loss	2,200
	– General				
	(10% x 55,000)	5,500			
		8,500			
		8,500			8,500
			1.11.X4	Balance b/f	8,500

(b)

Trade creditors account

		£			£
31.10.X4	Discounts received	15,000	1.11.X3	Balance b/f	43,000
	Purchases returned	10,000	31.10.X4	Purchases	310,000
	Trade debtors –				
	contra	4,000			
	Cash paid	274,000			
	Sales return	2,000			
	Balance c/d	48,000			
		353,000			353,000
			1.11.X4	Balance b/f	48,000

(c)

Trade debtors account

		£			£
1.11.X4	Balance b/f	63,000	31.10.X4	Discounts allowed	14,000
31.10.X4	Sales	690,000		Sales returned	8,000
	Cheque returned	3,000		Bad debt (P/L acc)	7,000
				Trade creditors –	
				contra	4,000
				Cash received	663,000
				Sales return	2,000
				Balance c/f	58,000
		756,000			756,000
1.11.X4	Balance b/f	58,000			

4   INEPT LTD

(a)   Cash book

		£			£
30.6.X0	Balance b/f unadjusted	2,972	30.6.X0	Bank charges (2)	17
27.6.X0	Debtors – cash received (6)	656		Debtors – returned cheque (3)	42
				Subscription (4)	10
			10.4.X0	HP creditor – cash (7)	26
			10.5.X0	HP creditor – cash (7)	26
			10.6.X0	HP creditor – cash (7)	26
			30.6.X0	Adjustment – cheque entered twice (8)	364
			10.6.X0	Discount allowed (10)	5
			30.6.X0	Balance c/f	3,112
		3,628			3,628

Notes

(1)   It is assumed that no entries had been made in the cash book in respect of the managing director's cheque.

(2)   A further adjustment will have to be made on 1 July to cancel the entry made on that date in respect of item (6).

(b)   **Bank reconciliation statement on 30 June 19X0**

	£	£
Balance per bank statement on 30 June 19X0		7,392
Add: Deposit not yet credited (1)		492
		7,884
Less: Cheques issued but not yet presented (9)	4,672	
Cheque for managing director's refund not yet presented (5)	100	
		4,772
Balance per cash book on 30 June 19X0		3,112

Tutor's note: Bank reconciliations will, in practice, start with the balance per bank statement and conclude with the balance per cash book. It is, therefore, recommended that this layout be used although in this question the bank balance is deduced from the amended cash book balance.

5   **SPEED**

(a)

Van account

		£			£
1.11.X2	Balance b/f	14,000	30.11.X2	Van disposal	
1.12.X2	Bank (EAT 50)	6,000		(AAT 10)	2,000
1.8.X3	Bank (FAT 60) 9,000		31. 7.X3	Van disposal	
	Disposal (CAT 30) 2,000			(CAT 30)	4,000
		11,000	30. 9.X3	Van disposal	
				(DAT 40)	5,000
			31.10.X3	Balance c/d	20,000
		31,000			31,000
1.11.X3	Balance b/f	20,000			

Van depreciation account

		£			£
30.11.X2	Van disposal		1.11.X2	Balance b/f	6,000
	(AAT 10) – 4 yrs	1,600	31.10.X3	Profit & loss a/c –	
31. 7.X3	Van disposal			depreciation for	
	(CAT 30) – 2 yrs	1,600		the year (20% x	
30. 9.X3	Van disposal			£20,000)	4,000
	(DAT 40) – 1 yr	1,000			
31.10.X3	Balance c/f	5,800			
		10,000			10,000
			1.11.X3	Balance b/f	5,800

Van disposal account

		£			£
30.11.X2	Van a/c (AAT 10)	2,000	30.11.X2	Van dep (AAT 10)	1,600
31. 7.X3	Van a/c (CAT 30)	4,000	30.11.X2	Bank (AAT 10)	500
30. 9.X3	Van a/c (DAT 40)	5,000	31. 7.X3	Van dep (CAT 30)	1,600
			31. 7.X3	Van a/c (FAT 60)	2,000
			30. 9.X3	Van dep (DAT 40)	1,000
			30. 9.X3	Bank (DAT 40)	4,000
			31.10.X3	Profit & loss a/c:	
				loss on disposal	
				of vehicles	300
		11,000			11,000

(b)   The reducing-balance method charges a higher depreciation rate in the first few years of asset life. This reflects the higher flow of benefits derived from an asset in its 'new' condition. As the asset ages its depreciation charge is reduced reflecting a lower flow of benefits.

The method requires the application of a set percentage to the written down book value to calculate the depreciation to be charged each year.

Speed uses the straight–line method of depreciating its vans. However this method is not appropriate for motor vehicles as they tend to depreciate rapidly during their early life and less rapidly as they become older, whilst maintenance and repair costs tend to be smaller in earlier years and heavier as the vehicles get older.

To reflect the pattern of depreciation and repairs and maintenance expenditure the reducing balance method is to be preferable than the straight–line method as this reflects more closely the declining value of assets such as motor vehicles.

6   SUSPENSE ADJUSTER

		Dr £	Cr £
(a)	Bank charges account	1,000	
	Cash book		1,000

Error due to omission of bank charges.

		Dr £	Cr £
(b)	Provision for depreciation account	10,943	
	Proceeds of sale of fixed assets	2,000	
	Fixed asset account		11,879
	Capital surplus account		1,064

Profit of £1,064 on sale of fixed assets.

		Dr £	Cr £
(c)	Wages and salaries	6,088	
	Wages and salaries	1,766	
	Payment of PAYE income tax		6,088
	Payment of national insurance		4,766
	National Insurance (company's contribution)	3,000	

PAYE deduction and National Insurance expenses on wages and salaries.

		Dr £	Cr £
(d)	Creditors	10,000	
	Creditors	260	
	Discount received		260
	Debtors		10,000
	Debtors		240
	Discount allowed	240	

£10,000 contra set off and £260 and £240 discount received and discount allowed.

		Dr £	Cr £
(e)	Bad debts account	2,000	
	Debtors		2,000

Writing off bad debts.

		Dr £	Cr £
(f)	Sales returns	630	
	Purchase returns	630	
	Suspense account		1,260

Error in recording of sales returns.

		Dr £	Cr £
(g)	Suspense account	9	
	Postage, telephone and stationery		9
	Transposition error between £234 and £243.		
(h)	Packing material	76	
	Suspense account		76
	Omission of charge to packing materials account		
(i)	Bank overdraft	36	
	Insurance		36
	Transposition error between £62 and £26.		
(j)	Suspense account	297	
	Purchase account		297
	Transposition error in purchase day book.		

Trial balance

	Dr £	Cr £
Ordinary share capital		100,000
Retained profit 1 January 19X6		50,000
10% debentures		30,000
Debtors	65,000	
Creditors		50,000
Cash in hand	1,000	
Bank overdraft		6,000
Stock and work in progress since 1 January 19X6	108,000	
Fixed assets at cost	150,000	
Provision for depreciation 31 December 19X6		50,000
Depreciation for year	15,000	
Purchases	300,000	
Sales		400,000
Returns inwards	5,000	
Returns outwards		4,000
Discount allowed	10,000	
Discount received		7,000
Wages, salaries and NHI	23,000	
PAYE creditors		1,000
Rent, rates and insurance	18,000	
Postage, telephone and stationery	3,000	
Advertising	4,876	
Repair and maintenance	2,124	
Packing material	1,000	
Motor expenses	2,000	
Sundry expenses	1,000	
Debenture interest	4,000	
Bank charges	1,000	
Bad debts	2,000	
Capital surplus account		18,000
	716,000	716,000

7   HILLTOWN TRADERS LTD

(a)   Ratios

	19X2	19X3	19X4
Gross profit to sales	20.0%	15.4%	16.7%
Net profit to sales	10.0%	6.9%	8.7%
Net profit to capital employed	14.3%	11.4%	14.1%
Acid test			
(Liquid assets : Current liabilities)	100.0%	58.3%	52.9%
Debtors collection period	21.9 days	19.6 days	21.9 days

(b)   (i)   In practice there are no perfect ratios at which a business should aim and ratios may only be assessed on a broad basis. The trend revealed is more interesting than the absolute figures produced.

(ii)   Where accounting policies differ then ratios cannot be used to compare different entities or even divisions without qualification.

(iii)   The use of historic cost in accounts rather than 'values' may lead to peculiar results where, for example, machinery is used which although completely written off in the accounts, is still operating efficiently.

1   This question follows the normal format of incomplete records questions. The accounts when prepared have a number of missing figures which can be found by balancing each account in turn.

In this question the sales and purchases figures need to be derived from balancing the appropriate accounts. The expense accounts need to account for any prepayments and accruals.

The balance on capital account at 1 April 19X3 can be constructed by preparing the opening balance as follows:

Balance sheet as at 31 March 19X3

	£	£	£
Fixed assets			
Furniture and fittings (2,000 – 600)			1,400
Van (5,000 – 2,000)			3,000
			4,400
Current assets			
Stocks		10,000	
Debtors (15,000 – 400)		14,600	
Prepayments		1,200	
Cash at bank		3,000	
Cash in hand		100	
		28,900	
Less: Current liabilities			
Creditors	14,000		
Accruals	500		
		14,500	
			14,400
			18,800
Represented by:			
Capital			£18,800

2   In answering this question, you should think of the suspense account as a capital account: the goodwill account represents the excess of 'real asset value' to the business over book value. This surplus should be allocated to the former partners, since this has resulted from their capital and efforts.

Profit allocation is quite complicated in this case. The new partner's admission half-way through the year results in two half-yearly profit allocations. Interest must be allocated first, leading on to losses which must be shared in the same way as profits.

0047V

3   A fairly straightforward question requiring you to write up the accounts. From the information given you need to bring down the opening balances and write up the accounts from the transactions. There should not be any difficulty in dealing with these so long as you bear in mind the corresponding entries. The balance to be carried down on the provision for doubtful debt account can only be ascertained once the debtors account is completed and balanced.

4   An unusual question on bank reconciliation in that no bank statement balance is given but has to be derived.

The first step is to identify and make the adjustments for those items which affect the cash book.

The items that are not of adjusting nature but appear on the reconciliation statement are 1, 5 and 9, which you should have recognised from your studies.

5   A typical question on depreciation and if you know the entries, then the question itself is pretty straightforward.

You could have had a separate disposal account for each of the vans sold in which case the profit or loss on disposal will be:

			£
1	Van AAT 10	profit	100
2	Van CAT 30	loss	400
3	Van DAT 40		Nil
	Net loss		300

6   This type of question is fairly common at this level. The key technique is to ask yourself what has actually happened, what should have happened and correct any errors.

7   An area in which we must expect regular questions to appear.

Other areas where ratios could have been calculated and would have shown significant charges include:

(a)   stock to cost of sales (or turnover);
(b)   creditors to cost of sales;
(c)   fixed assets to turnover;
(d)   current ratio (current assets : current laibilities);
(e)   distribution costs to sales.

All of the above would have been as acceptable to the examiner as the perhaps more obvious ratios given in the answer.

The second part of the question gives you the opportunity to show your understanding of this topic but your answer must be short as only seven marks are allocated to this part – say, two marks for each limitation.

Enthusiasts' books from Veloce -

• Colour Family Album titles •
Citroën 2CV: The Colour Family Album by Andrea & David Sparrow
Citroën DS: The Colour Family Album by Andrea & David Sparrow
Bubblecars & Microcars: The Colour Family Album by Andrea & David Sparrow
VW Beetle: The Colour Family Album by Andrea & David Sparrow
Vespa: The Colour Family Album by Andrea & David Sparrow

• Other titles •
Alfa Romeo Giulia Coupé GT & GTA by John Tipler
Alfa Romeo. How to Power Tune Alfa Romeo Twin Cam Engines by Jim Kartalamakis
Alfa Romeo Modello 8C 2300 by Angela Cherrett
Alfa Romeo Owner's Bible by Pat Braden
Bugatti 46 & 50 - The Big Bugattis by Barrie Price
Bugatti 57 - The Last French Bugatti by Barrie Price
Chrysler 300 - America's Most Powerful Car by Robert Ackerson
Cobra - The Real Thing! by Trevor Legate
Daimler SP250 (Dart) V-8 by Brian Long
Fiat & Abarth 124 Spider & Coupé by John Tipler
Fiat & Abarth 500 & 600 by Malcolm Bobbitt
Lola T70 by John Starkey
Mazda MX5/Miata Enthusiast's Workshop Manual by Rod Grainger & Pete Shoemark
MG Midget & A-H Sprite, How To Power Tune by Daniel Stapleton
MGB (4cyl), How To Power Tune by Peter Burgess
MGB. How To Give Your MGB V-8 Power by Roger Williams
MGs, Making by John Price Williams
Mini Cooper - The Real Thing! by John Tipler
Morgan, Completely - Three Wheelers 1910-52 by Ken Hill
Morgan, Completely - Four Wheelers 1936-68 by Ken Hill
Morgan, Completely - Four Wheelers from 1968 by Ken Hill
Morris Minor, The Secret Life of by Karen Pender
Motorcycling in the '50s by Jeff Clew
Nuvolari: When Nuvolari Raced ... by Valerio Moretti
Porsche 356 by Brian Long
Porsche 911R, RS & RSR by John Starkey
Rolls-Royce Silver Shadow & Bentley T-Series by Malcolm Bobbitt
Rover P4 by Malcolm Bobbitt
Triumph Motorcycles & The Meriden Factory by Hughie Hancox
Triumph TR6 by William Kimberley
V8 Short Block, How To Build For High Performance by Des Hammill
VW Beetle - the Rise from the Ashes of War by Simon Parkinson
VW Karmann Ghia by Malcolm Bobbitt
Weber & Dellorto Carburetors, How To Build & Power Tune by Des Hammill

First published in 1994 by Veloce Publishing Plc., 33 Trinity Street, Dorchester, Dorset DT1 1TT, England. Fax 01305 268864. Reprinted 1996.

ISBN 1 874105 05 7.

Readers with ideas for automotive books, or books on other transport or related hobby subjects, are invited to write to the editorial director of Veloce Publishing at the above address.

British Library Cataloguing in Publication Data -
A catalogue record for this book is available from the British Library.

Typesetting (Bookman), design and page make-up all by Veloce on Apple Mac.

Printed by Studio Europa - Trento - Italy

Cobra
The Real Thing!

TREVOR LEGATE

VELOCE PUBLISHING PLC
PUBLISHERS OF FINE AUTOMOTIVE BOOKS

CONTENTS

**FOREWORD
BY
W.D.HURLOCK**
CHAIRMAN,
AC CARS LTD
(1920 - 1992)

In 1961 a phone call had been made from the USA to our works director, Mr E.H. Sidney, to the effect that Carroll Shelby had an ambition to install a new engine in our AC Ace with the intention of selling the car in America.

Very shortly afterwards one of our work force reported that an engine had arrived from Japan. It had the word 'FoMoCo' written on the label, which somebody had associated with a Japanese word! It turned out, of course, to be one of the new 221 cu in thinwall cast-iron Ford V8 engines.

A few weeks later I was standing outside the Thames Ditton factory talking to Reg Parnell of Aston Martin, when a taxi stopped and out stepped Carroll Shelby. Reg could hardly believe his eyes and, after an exchange of pleasantries, inquired whether Carroll had come all the way by taxi. "No" replied Carroll, "I came down on the trolley" (referring to British Rail's main line from London to Portsmouth).

That was the beginning, and with the eventual assurance from Ford USA regarding finance, plus the approval of the board, we began work on the prototype, hoping our new model would continue the success of the Ace. The AC board at that time consisted of my father, William A.E. Hurlock (Chairman), his brother Charles F. Hurlock (Managing Director), E.H. Sidney (Works Director) and myself, the headstrong junior.

With the project underway, Mr A.D. Turner, the Chief Engineering Designer, started work stressing and strengthening the chassis to take the strain.

Amongst the requests from the USA came the instructions to fit inboard rear brakes. I thought this somewhat strange as I recalled a previous occasion when sharing the Goodwood circuit with Aston Martin during a test day. Carroll and Reg Parnell bemoaned the fact that the inboard rear brakes of the Aston could never be successfully cooled without huge vent pipes coming from the front of the car through the cockpit. However, the first Cobra was produced with rear inboard disc brakes, but was the only example with this layout.

We had a marvellous team at the time, without whom the Cobra would never have achieved the success it did. Naturally, the car went through several phases of redesign, the most important of which was the change from transverse leaf suspension to coil springs. At that point we received help from the technicians at Ford USA who, along with their computer read-outs, came to the factory to redesign the suspension geometry. They were all very competent people and with Alan Turner presiding over the operation it turned out to be a very efficient independent suspension design.

One gentleman from Shelby American will always be remembered above all others and that was Phil Remington. I shall certainly never forget him and will not attempt to describe him, for he was so capable in every way. He called himself simply a mechanic but as one of the chiefs in the Ford hierarchy is reported to have said ... "If Phil Remington is a mechanic then at least 99 per cent of the others who carry that title are imposters" ...

He worked along with our team in the Experimental Shop, including Vin Davidson who had helped construct the original Tojeiros and had joined us at the outset of the Ace. The good natured slanging matches which went on regarding the varying American descriptions of the anatomy of an automobile and those of our own mechanics was humour indeed.

One abiding memory will be of our special Le Mans car which caused a sensation when we innocently descended on the M1 motorway very early one morning in June 1964, to test it at over 180mph. It really was a super car and differed from the Cobra in that the seats were down level with, and outside, the main 4 inch chassis tubes. It had a very fundamental coupé body designed by Alan Turner and I was very proud of it. This car was entirely an AC effort and unfortunately totally wrecked at Le Mans after a tyre burst. For me, that car marked the end of the era for front-engined sports cars.

Philip Lewis 1981

I

THE AC STORY

Phillip Lewis 1981.

The Cobra is a very emotive sports car - loved by so many enthusiasts for its shattering performance against the clock, while others decry its spartan comforts and its handling which can catch out the unwary. Equally, its very appearance arouses passions both for and against. Admittedly the basic concept of the car was ten years out of date when it was launched, but the injection of an almost embarrassing amount of horsepower found a niche among a brave, hardy band of motorists, and resulted in the car becoming infamous as the fastest sports car of the sixties (among the fastest of all time) while the low level of production ensured that both its legend and its value grew with the passing years.

It is ironic that such a car should originate not from Modena or Stuttgart or indeed from any major manufacturer, but from one of the oldest and smallest car producers in Great Britain, situated in the quiet Surrey village of Thames Ditton.

The Early Days of AC

AC Cars Limited can trace its ancestry back to the beginning of the twentieth century, when a talented and highly innovative engineer, John Weller, began to construct a series of three- and four-wheeled vehicles which served to demonstrate his unquestioned mechanical talent. He was supported in his efforts by a successful businessman, John Portwine, who, like Weller, saw a promising future for the 'horseless carriage'. The first vehicle to be seen in public, at the 1903 Crystal Palace Motor Show, was a 20hp four-seater car built to rival the finest vehicles that the Continental manufacturers could offer. Sadly, this impressive design failed to reach production and instead, in 1904, Weller and Portwine formed a company called Autocars and Accessories with the intention of building a cheap and relatively simple three-wheeled, single-cylinder vehicle for the tradesman, which made a viable alternative to the pony and trap. The Auto-Carrier, with its large box in the front, was soon in demand and business grew to a point where a passenger version could be produced with two seats replacing the box. Called the Sociable, this small vehicle remained in production until the First World War. In 1907 the company changed its name to Auto-Carriers Limited and, in 1911, production was transferred from West Norwood to Thames Ditton.

A range of excellent light cars and engines followed after the First World War, including the famous six-cylinder engine which broke new ground with its efficient design (the camshaft drive design can still be found in many cars today) and began a production run so far unequalled, culminating in the Cobra's progenitor, the AC Ace.

The first notable change during the company's eighty-year history occurred in 1921 with the arrival of an Australian, Selwyn Francis Edge, who took an interest in the company and became its chairman during that year. He became its governing director the following year, when both Weller and Portwine departed. S.F. Edge was a well-

The Individual Car

"There is hardly anything in the world that some man cannot make a little worse, and so sell a little cheaper, and the people who consider price only, are this man's lawful prey."
John Ruskin.

SINCE constructing the first Light Six in 1926, the A.C. Car Company have maintained a consistent policy of fine craftsmanship. A.C. Cars are built to last. They are designed for fast easy driving, easy maintenance and extreme reliability. Our name has always been associated with quality and outstanding dependability. This reputation is closely guarded and well maintained.

For the purchaser requiring immediate delivery, there is an ample selection of models at our Park Lane Showrooms, but the A.C. is essentially an individual car. Customers come to our showrooms, as they would go to the tailors, choose their upholstery, select colour schemes to their wishes, modify the design with regard to the comfort of seating position to meet their individual requirements, height of steering wheel, etc., etc., for all of which service there is no extra charge.

Showrooms
107 PARK LANE, LONDON W.1
Telephone : MAYFAIR 3638

The A.C. Showrooms are one minute from Marble Arch. A full range of cars is always available for inspection and demonstration. Arrangements can be made for customers who wish to visit the works at Thames Ditton. These works are always open for inspection at any time during working hours. Should you wish to purchase through your local agent, the above facilities are still available, and every courtesy and attention will be shown to you on behalf of your agent.

Trial Runs

Trial Runs may be arranged without any obligation at almost any time and place to suit your convenience. Please advise either Park Lane or Thames Ditton, or your own local agent will be pleased to make the arrangements for you.

A.C. (ACEDES) CARS LIMITED

Registered Offices and Works — THAMES DITTON · SURREY · ENGLAND
Sales, Service and Repairs Department — HIGH STREET · THAMES DITTON

Telephone
Emberbrook 2340-1

Codes
A.B.C. 5th Edition, Marconi and privals

Telegrams
"Autocarrier, Thames Ditton"

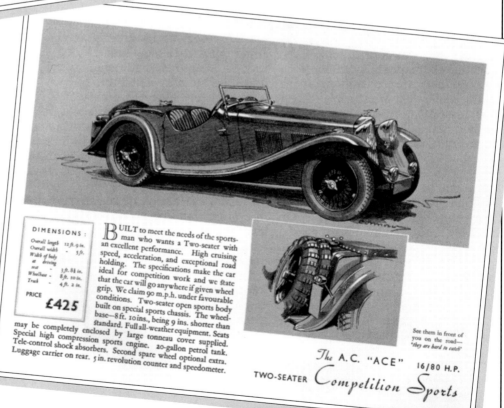

DIMENSIONS :

Overall length 12 ft. 9 in.
Overall width · 5 ft.
Width of body
at driving
seat · 3 ft. 8½ in.
Wheelbase · 8 ft. 10 in.
Track · 4 ft. 2 in.

PRICE
£425

BUILT to meet the needs of the sportsman who wants a Two-seater an excellent performance. High cruising speed, acceleration, and exceptional road holding. The specifications make the car ideal for competition work and we state that the car will go anywhere if given wheel grip. We claim 90 m.p.h. under favourable conditions. Two-seater open sports body built on special sports chassis. The wheelbase—8 ft. 10 ins., being 9 ins. shorter than standard. Full all-weather equipment. Seats may be completely enclosed by large tonneau cover supplied. Special high compression sports engine. 20-gallon petrol tank. Tele-control shock absorbers. Second spare wheel optional extra. Luggage carrier on rear. 5 in. revolution counter and speedometer.

See them in front of you on the road—
'they are hard to catch'

The A.C. "ACE" 16/80 H.P.
TWO-SEATER *Competition Sports*

The 1936 AC sales brochure shows a degree of style and elegance sadly lacking today.

known figure in the motoring world, having won the famous Gordon Bennett Trophy race of 1902, and having been closely connected with promoting Napier motor cars. Unfortunately he was equally fond of promoting S.F.Edge, and his egocentric approach to the business won him few friends. He was responsible for transferring the company to new premises in Thames Ditton (where it remained until 1982), but with the loss of John Weller development virtually came to a standstill.

Despite healthy sales in 1921, the same models were being left behind by 1926. In 1927 the existing company was liquidated and a new one, AC (Acedes) Ltd, was formed with Edge providing the capital. By 1929, however, the banks were cautious about lending money following the Wall Street Crash and AC were once again forced into liquidation. Edge had lost both his money and his health.

Enter The Hurlocks

The remains of the company were acquired in 1930 by two brothers, Charles and William Hurlock, who were primarily interested in using the large premises for their commercial-vehicle operations. Since AC were still servicing customers' cars they decided to allow this to continue, and when William Hurlock mentioned to the service manager that he needed a new car, the remaining staff constructed one from available parts. Suitably impressed, he allowed further examples to be built to special order and, before he knew it, AC were building cars once more. There followed an impressive range of modern

sports and Grand Touring models which the Hurlocks actively promoted in competition. With many outside engineering contracts helping to keep the company profitable, a steady flow of cars left Thames Ditton before and after the Second World War. During hostilities production was halted to meet military and Home Office requirements, and afterwards AC were given contracts to design and build invalid tricycles with fully enclosed fibreglass bodies for the Ministry of Pensions. They also built four electric trains for the Southend Pier Railway as well as rail buses for British Railways.

However, in 1947 AC Cars Ltd announced their new model, a large saloon using their traditional six-cylinder engine and called the AC Two-Litre. Despite its relative lack of sophistication, British motorists were happy to buy a good quality car which offered some degree of comfort and it sold steadily for a number of years until other manufacturers' products left it behind.

Charles Hurlock appreciated from the start that the saloon could not expect a long production run, but the problem lay in what to replace it with. Ideas were put on paper, a new flat-six engine was designed and expensive prototypes were constructed, but the saviour was to be found outside the company and at the end of the troubled decade; the forerunner of the Cobra was about to be built.

During 1950, John Tojeiro, a club-racing driver competing with a modified MG TA, decided to build his own chassis using a non-independent leaf-

Right & below: The 2-litre Bristol-engined Tojiero which began it all ...

The ACE Two-seater Sports

The ACE Two-seater Sports

BEAUTIFUL body styling has been achieved by skilful design. The lightweight aluminium panelled body on steel tube framing provides great strength and durability, and reduces body weight to a minimum. Adequate all-weather protection is provided by hood and rigid Perspex sidescreens. Body trimming is in leather throughout.

THIS exciting car of character has the essential features required by the Sportsman. The ultra lightweight chassis provides a power weight ratio to allow exceptional acceleration and road speeds in excess of 100 miles per hour.

spring suspension which proved unsatisfactory and was subsequently scrapped. However, he tried again during the winter of 1952-1953 with a new design consisting of an H-shaped frame built from three large diameter steel tubes with a different all-independent suspension system comprising transverse leaf-springs with fabricated wishbones; this particular design proved much more successful. The inspiration for the bodywork to clothe the Tojeiro chassis came from one of the most beautiful sports-racing cars of the time, the Superleggera Touring Barchetta body style which appeared on the Ferrari Tipo 166 Mille Miglia. Despite its flowing and comparatively simple lines, its construction proved quite a challenge for master panel-beater Eric Gray, since the curved and fluted feature was produced symmetrically at each corner of the body and involved panel-rolling and seam-welding. The finished car appeared with great success at circuits around the country; its body was left as polished aluminium, and it carried the registration number LOY 500. The steering utilised a Morris rack-and-pinion unit, brakes and shock-absorbers were provided by Girling and, with an ENV/ Jaguar back axle transmitting the power to the road, its owner/driver Cliff Davies caused a great deal of consternation among the established

teams of the time, despite at first having to install a down-on-power 2-litre Bristol engine. The Bristol Motor Company soon saw the car's potential and were eventually persuaded to part with a more competitive engine. Outright wins against strong opposition were obtained at Goodwood, Silverstone and Crystal Palace in 1953.

The AC company were at this time turning their thoughts to reviving their pre-war sporting image which had been dormant for quite a while. The lightness and general simplicity of the Tojeiro design appealed to AC, and an arrangement was quickly forged between them and John Tojeiro to put the car into production with the necessary refinements for road use.

Ace at Earls Court
One of the highlights of the 1953 Earls Court Motor Show was the unexpected (and greatly welcomed) eve-of-show appearance of this new sports car, which revived the pre-war name 'Ace'. The bodywork was little changed from the Tojeiro design as was the suspension layout, but naturally a civilised interior, hood and side-screens were added and the whole car was made more robust than the original lightweight racer.

Originally the car appeared with the long-serving 1991cc cylinder engine with light alloy cylinder block and

*1953 AC Ace sales brochure shows
the car in its original 'Tojiero' guise.*

*Below: AC Ace Bristol on display at
the 1956 Earls Court Motor Show.*

wet liners, five-bearing crankshaft and chain-driven overhead camshaft with carburation by three horizontal SU carburettors; the unit producing 85bhp at 4500rpm. As is so often the case with a small manufacturer, there were a few subtle changes made to the body styling by the time the first customers' cars were built in 1954, the most notable being a change around the car's front grill treatment, giving the body a less heavy, more streamlined look. In December 1954 the list price of the Ace was £1015 exclusive of purchase tax, making it an expensive car at the time

Right and below: The elegant and well-balanced lines of the Aceca - one-time plans for a V8 version came to nought.

but certainly a very popular one among sporting motorists since, apart from the Lagonda, this was the only car available with independent front and rear suspension, giving the car a notable handling advantage over its more powerful competitors.

The Aceca

AC quickly evolved a new body style to complement and increase their model range and this was a fixed-head fastback coupé called the Aceca. Both this and the Ace were sold with the AC engine, this until being persuaded to give 110bhp at 4800rpm before its retirement after 44 years of reliable service. The more powerful Bristol engine was offered as an option in 1956, this 1971cc unit giving 125bhp and being supplied with a Bristol gearbox as opposed to the Moss version matched to the AC engine, turning the Ace into a very nimble road car capable of reaching 60mph in under eight seconds.

With competition versions producing 130 to 15bhp, the Ace-Bristol was naturally very successful in club racing, running away with the National E Class title for three successive years in America where the car gained a strong following and excellent reputation. In fact, it was so successful in Class E it was upgraded to Class C, via Class D, to compete against Mercedes and Jaguars. It won both those classes as well. Much the same thing happened in England where, after Ken Rudd had finished runner-up in the 1956 and 1957 Production Sports Car Championship, the Bristol-engined Aces were

forced to race in a Super-Sports category against D-type Jaguars, Lotuses, Aston Martin DB3s and Maseratis.

From Bristol to Ford

In 1959, however, the Bristol company decided on a change of policy which was to have an important effect on the future of the AC company. They decided to end production of their old, although still effective, 2-litre engine which left AC with a serious supply problem. Fortunately, Ken Rudd, a Worthing-based car dealer and long-time AC enthusiast, came up with the idea of installing the cheaper mass-produced Ford Zephyr 2.6-litre engine which helped keep down spiralling costs without sacrificing performance. The car could be supplied in three stages of

Illustration shows 3 Weber double choke carburetters

Illustration shows 3 1½ S. U. carburetters on six port head

Open Motoring at its Best

The ACE fitted with A.C. and Bristol engines has earned many tributes from the Motoring Press in the past, and the success of this model in competition requires no enlargement here.

There is no doubt that the 2.6 ACE now lowered with restyled bodywork is the fastest production model ever produced by the A.C. Company, and maximum speeds in the 125 m.p.h. range may be expected, with acceleration to match.

John Bolster Autosport states it is possible to employ the full power in acceleration thanks to the independent rear end which results in performance figures that are simply breathtaking. To accelerate from a standstill to 80 m.p.h. in 12.1 seconds is something that the average sports car driver can barely imagine.

We have never claimed the ACE as a racing car and it has always been the policy of the company to provide a true sports car which can be driven on the public highway and used for normal motoring day by day. The fact that each year the ACE excels in competition is a tribute to the soundness of the design.

Technical Excellence

Designed by enthusiasts for enthusiasts. Independent suspension on all four wheels by transverse leaf springs and wishbones. Hand-built to a tight specification. Correct weight distribution. Ideal sought and attained.

Tubular construction of the chassis and body framing provides tremendous strength, from the robust 3″ tubing of the main chassis frame to the 1½″ scuttle   roll bar and the ¾″ body assembly tube, the whole welded to provide a simple yet robust structure.

The weight distribution is such that there is 18% more on the rear wheels than on the front. This is another feature which has assisted in providing the stability for which this Ace chassis is now well renowned. Centre lock wire wheels, Girling disc brakes and Al-Fin brakedrums are included in the standard specification.

The all weather equipment is extremely comprehensive and use is made of plastic hooding which has the advantage of remaining impervious to the sun, and is also easily cleaned, the whole being stretched over two steel detachable uprights. Rigid perspex sidescreens 3/16″ thick provide their own support, and the rear portion swivels forward from a fulcrum in the centre middle corner. This produces an easy means of entry, and also allows simple and unobstructed hand signalling.

The ACE 2·6

A.C. Cars Ltd. are pleased to announce that with the co-operation of the Ford Motor Company, they are able to offer the 2.6 unit produced by this Company, as an alternative to the A.C. and Bristol engines which will still be offered in all models. The tuned Ford 2.6 litre engine produces exceptionally high power from 2,000 r.p.m. onwards with the added virtues of silence and excellent torque characteristics. The ACE 2.6 may, therefore, be driven as a town carriage or full use may be made of the considerable power available when 100 m.p.h. may be achieved in 18 seconds or 110 m.p.h. in 24 seconds.

The road holding of the ACE coupled with the considerable power produced by the larger engine makes the 2.6 litre ACE one of the fastest production sports cars available to-day.

The Designers have been successful in providing a roomy luggage locker without detracting in any way from the pleasant external appearance of the car, and although the spare wheel and the envelope containing sidescreens and hood cover must also be accommodated, room is still left to meet reasonable luggage requirements.

The petrol tank is situated immediately below the luggage locker. Clear plastic enables a large rear view light to be incorporated in the hood or top and an unrestricted view is provided in any direction. Double dual rear lamps incorporate stop reflectors and flashing indicator lighting.

Fibreglass Hardtop

Ford-engined AC Ace sales brochure.

tune: 125bhp or 150bhp with triple SU carburettors for road use or a maximum of 170bhp with triple Weber carburettors for competition purposes, albeit to the eventual detriment of the bottom end. Although the Ford lacked the mechanical finesse of the Bristol engine, it could deliver an impressive amount of mid-range torque, reducing the 0-100mph time by around eight seconds. The lower Ford engine also allowed AC the opportunity to restyle the bonnet line with a longer nose and smaller grille treatment.

Despite the introduction of the Ruddspeed Ace, sales faltered. A new engine was needed to fill the gap left by Bristol, and Ken Rudd and AC looked around for any likely alternative. Both parties thought that one of the most potentially suitable engines would be the lightweight Buick V8, but a problem arose in that Rover were already negotiating with General Motors to use this same unit, so AC were therefore obliged to withdraw. The intention of AC was to use this engine in their four-seater, the Greyhound, which looked like a longer version of the Aceca, although it was a very different car under the skin.

Other candidates were, almost inevitably, the six-cylinder Jaguar engine and the V8 from the Daimler Dart sports car. The Jaguar proved to be a problem as its length and weight created installation difficulties, although individual Ace owners did carry out the transplant for themselves, risking the problems of tricky handling. The Dart V8 was much preferred as it was more compact, but company politics intervened to put an end to AC offering a threat in the same market as the Daimler. Even the assistance of 'Lofty' England failed to forge an agreement between Coventry and Thames Ditton.

With engines being tried and rejected, and companies unwilling to co-operate, the future for AC seemed unpromising to say the least. But, as luck would have it, an American ex-Le Mans winner was looking for a suitable lightweight chassis with which to mate an American V8 in order to fulfil a dream of his own - to build and manage his own team of racing cars to challenge the best Europe could offer. On hearing of the problem caused by the demise of the Bristol engine, Carroll Shelby wrote a letter to Charles Hurlock in September 1961: another new chapter in the history of AC (and of motor racing) was about to begin ...

Overleaf: The classic lines of the AC Ace are timeless.

17

II

THE SHELBY STORY

Carroll Shelby was the catalyst responsible for transforming a successful 1950s sports car into the phenomenally powerful machine known as the Cobra, which in the 1960s went on to beat Ferrari in the World Championship for Makes, which Ferrari considered almost his own. When Shelby wrote his letter in 1961 even he did not know about the most important factor in the equation - the new lightweight Ford V8 engine. His own line of thinking virtually paralleled that of AC and Ken Rudd in that the Buick engine was the most likely candidate, although he also considered Oldsmobile or Chevrolet engines as other possibilities, despite their greater weight. The chance to utilise the then brand new 221 cu in Ford engine came about from a chance meeting earlier in the year which forged a vital connection, although neither party realised it at the time. It was also another stroke of good fortune that, during 1961 and 1962, the mighty Ford company was beginning to turn its attention to the younger segment of the market which led to the promotion of the performance aspect of Ford cars - 'Total Performance' as they called it. Naturally, success on the racing circuit was called for to back up their advertising campaign, and when a golden opportunity like that occurs a man like Carroll Shelby is hardly likely to be found looking the other way; for which let all sports car fans be truly grateful.

The Young Shelby
Carroll Shelby was born in Leesburg, East Texas on 11 January 1923. His father delivered mail for a living, so Carroll's background was not one which prepared him for his eventual profession as a successful racing driver, nor did it provide him with the necessary finances. As so many young boys do, he soon developed a fascinating for automobiles, and in his early teens would watch the local stock-car racers driving around dirt track ovals. All he could think of was driving race cars when he left high school and, although his father could understand Carroll's motivation, there appeared little future for him because of the lack of money. The only other possibility, since his family were unable to put him through college, was to join the Air Corps on leaving high school. This he eventually did and, like all recruits, he began at the bottom; in September 1942 he graduated as a pilot. He spent the war years as an instructor so fortunately never left the USA. He married his wife, Jeanne, in December 1943 and left the Air Force as soon as war ended in 1945.

Various occupations followed: running a small fleet of trucks carrying ready-mix concrete; hauling timber and later working for his father-in-law in the Texas oil fields. These jobs were followed by his idea to make a great deal of money very quickly by raising chickens, since credit for such a project was easily obtained. However, when his second batch of chickens was wiped out by disease the lack of capital forced him into bankruptcy.

Shelby Goes Motor Racing
While Carroll was wondering what he

Carroll Shelby. (Courtesy AC Cars).

could turn his hand to next he happened to meet an old friend who had built his own backyard special and who, to Shelby's surprise, invited him to drive it at a local drag meeting. As it turned out, this special was quite well engineered and his friend was so delighted to see his own car win the meeting that he suggested entering a real race at a circuit in Oklahoma. Shelby didn't need to be asked twice. Driving his friend's standard MG TC he won the first event against similar opposition by virtue of sitting behind them and waiting for them to make a mistake. When invited by the organizers

to take part in the next race against considerably stronger opposition in the form of Jaguar XK120s, he decided that although another win was not on the cards it was worth trying just for experience. It goes almost without saying that he won this race as well. Despite the Jaguars' much greater straight-line speed, the little MG could drift through the wide airport runway turns without resorting to the heavy braking of the opposition. Nobody was more surprised or delighted than Carroll Shelby.

The seeds of his racing career were sown and offers of other drives began

to come in. Although trophies followed, the money stayed away since, in 1952, one did not accept payment for the honour of racing; hence none was offered. Shelby at this time barely scraped a living, selling whatever he could and raising Irish setters and pheasants on what little remained of his chicken farm, although these could not meet all his expenses.

During 1953 he was offered drives almost exclusively in Cadillac-engined Allards and showed great skill in handling these brutal, over-engined cars. It was during this time that he entered a race one hot August day wearing his

striped farm overalls, having decided that his usual racing outfit was too uncomfortable. Since he received far more press coverage from wearing these than for winning the race, he decided the overalls should stay and his 'trade mark' was born.

In 1954 he had the opportunity to drive in Buenos Aires, again in an Allard, in a 1000-kilometer event. Although not very successful, with bits falling off the car, his driving caught the eye of the Aston Martin team manager, John Wyer, who shortly afterwards enquired whether he was interested in driving their new DB3 at Sebring. Although the car retired the connection was made. Shelby then went to England and raced a DB3 at Aintree, finishing second to Duncan Hamilton's C-type Jaguar, which was enough to earn him a race at Le Mans with the factory team, co-driving with the Belgian journalist, Paul Frere. Unfortunately, Shelby went off early in the race at the end of the Mulsanne straight and was trapped in the sandbank for 45 minutes. The team made up lost time until 1.50am when Shelby detected a vibration in the front of the car. When the car pulled into the pits for an inspection, a front wheel dropped off as soon as it was jacked clear of the ground. Another lap in that car could have been Shelby's last.

Various offers continued to come his way, such as a record-breaking run with Donald Healey on the Bonneville salt flats which, in turn, led to a drive in a Healey in the last Carrera Pan Americana Mexico race, which ended with Shelby suffering a badly broken

arm following a spectacular crash. He was prevented from receiving specialist treatment for the injury, since the Mexicans detained him in their country for a week because he had signed to enter the country with a car and had to leave with it. (When the wreck arrived it had only two wheels. The officials insisted that since it arrived with four wheels, it had to have four when it left! So the problem dragged on ...).

1955 saw Carroll Shelby have his share of success and some disappointment with cars as diverse as 4.9-litre Ferraris and 1500cc Porsche RS

Spyders, while 1956 saw him open his sportscar dealership in Dallas along with his now full schedule of races around the country. Early in 1957 he was approached by Ferrari regarding the possibility of a works drive that year, but on arrival at the factory he found he was expected to drive for the honour as opposed to driving for money.

A short trip to the Maserati factory proved more rewarding and Carroll Shelby and his sponsor, John Edgar, found themselves with a works-supported Maserati which claimed victory in the majority of the major SCCA races that season. He even had a contract to become the first American to race Maserati Grand Prix cars and had planned to make his debut in the Monaco Grand Prix of that year as teammate to Stirling Moss and Fangio, no less. Regrettably, the deal fell through.

Shelby Races in Europe

The 1958 and 1959 seasons found Carroll Shelby racing in Europe, first taking part in all the classic sports car events with an Aston Martin and then, after the 1958 Le Mans, taking up an offer to race in Formula 1 with a Maserati 250F which, by now, was becoming outdated with the advent of rear-engined Cooper-Climax cars, but at least he gained some experience driving open-wheeled cars. The team was the Barcelona-based Scuderia Centro Sud. The following year, however, he was part of the ill-fated Aston Martin Grand Prix team who arrived on the Formula 1 scene a season or two too late, their front-engined cars being relentlessly left behind by the technological advances being made by the Coopers and Lotuses. After only four Grand Prix the team was wound up, in complete contrast to their successful sports-car team, which that year provided the high point of Shelby's career with victory at Le Mans, co-driving with Roy Salvadori.

From Racer to Constructor

During 1959 and 1960 an outside influence began to signal the end of Shelby's driving career. Chest pains were eventually diagnosed as a heart complaint and he was advised to stop racing as soon as possible, although it was not until December 1960, aged 37, that he finally hung up his overalls after finishing fifth at a major sports-car meeting in Los Angeles.

Having sold his interest in his sports-car dealership in 1958, he was once more faced with finding a career. However, he knew by this time what it was he really wanted to do - build a low-price, economical V8-powered sports car containing the best elements of European know-how and American horsepower. The idea seemed so utterly obvious that he could not really understand why no major manufacturer had hit upon it. He had been hawking the idea around to anyone of influence that he met on his travels around Europe and America. His first idea was to interest General Motors, but with all the problems they were having with their new Corvette (which was hardly a great success during its first few years), and fear of anything they had not thought of themselves, his idea fell on very stony ground, particularly at board level.

He received the same reaction from companies such as Jensen, Aston Martin, Maserati and de Tomaso and countless other 'experts', who refused to believe that anyone could build what they could only think of as a specialist sports car at anything like the price Carroll Shelby was considering, bearing in mind that many other people had previously tried to build their own cars (particularly the Americans Lance Reventlow and Briggs Cunningham) and had been beset by insurmountable problems, usually of a financial nature.

In order to raise capital for his project he opened the Shelby School of High Performance Driving in 1961, renting the Riverside raceway near Los Angeles, training would-be racing drivers who turned out to be only too pleased to hand over their money in return for instruction from the now-famous Carroll Shelby, although as a long-term project it would never have made his fortune. He was also joined at this time by a brilliant driver and designer called Pete Brock, who was to prove to be a vital part of Shelby American having previously been employed by Chevrolet to work on their 'Sting Ray' project but leaving because of his distaste for large corporations.

In fact Pete Brock soon took over the running of the school, doing much of the instructing and thereby leaving Shelby free to concentrate on running his Goodyear racing tyre distributorship, which involved him in tyre testing and testing for the Champion spark-plug company at the same time.

The AC Connection

It was in September 1961 that Carroll Shelby heard the news that the 2-litre Bristol engine had gone out of production, leaving AC with a problem as to just what to install in its place, although the Ford Zephyr 2.6-litre proved to be a useful alternative. Naturally, with the success of the Ace-Bristol in SCCA racing, this particular lightweight British car was well known to Shelby and at once he saw what he had been looking for - the perfect chassis to turn his dreams into reality.

He wrote to Charles Hurlock, managing director of AC, with his idea and prayed for a good response.

On 4 July that year Shelby was representing Goodyear Tyres at the Pikes Peak Hillclimb, where he met and got to know Dave Evans of the Ford Motor Company, who was responsible for the engines used in Ford racing cars which, at that time, were standard saloons. No mention was made of Shelby's plans at the time but when, in October 1961, he heard of a new lightweight V8 being produced by a new casting process and intended for use in Fairlaines, he had the right contact to approach within the Ford empire.

Having received a favourable reply from Charles Hurlock he quickly contacted Dave Evans at Ford, telling him about his idea and asking whether any racing plans were being formulated for the new V8. Evans liked the sound of Shelby's idea since it seemed to fit in with Ford's future plans and, with characteristic speed of decision, he picked up the telephone and told him to expect delivery of two engines for experimental purposes.

The link was now forged, Shelby had two engines and a potential chassis. The Cobra was about to be born ...

III

THE FIRST COBRAS

Early AC publicity shot of Cobra MkI - note the prototype side exhaust. (Courtesy AC Cars).

The name 'Cobra' was the only one Shelby would use for his car. When the first car was being shipped to California he dreamed of the car with that name on the front. He woke up, jotted it down on his ideas pad beside his bed and the following morning made up his mind that Cobra was the perfect name.

With the passing of the years, the precise details surrounding the timing of the delivery of engines and Shelby's attempts to tie together the various parts of the equation have become clouded by telling and re-telling. However, he did have access to an early example of the 221 motor, which he and Dean Moon were able to examine thoroughly and assess for future use. As soon as Ford had developed their 260 cu in version, one was shipped to AC Cars to install in the prototype which they were developing, whilst two others were sent to Shelby's workshop (XHP-260-1 and XHP-260-8 - the latter being a special, higher compression unit).

Under the direction of Alan Turner, and with suggestions made by Carroll Shelby, AC Cars were preparing their chassis to accept a V8. Being a small company creating a low-volume, hand-made product, they were able to turn their whole attention to the problem and therefore created a new prototype chassis in a matter of weeks, using their own engineering and design department to design a stronger rear axle and driveshaft unit to cope with the huge increase in torque and horsepower.

In choosing the AC Ace for his potential Cobra, Shelby had one piece

of good fortune working for him in that the under-bonnet space was more than adequate to accommodate an American V8; even more fortunate was the fact that the Ford engine benefited from the new thinwall casting technique which kept weight well down compared to earlier iron V8 engines. Ford had begun to design this engine in 1958, deliberately building a lightweight cast-iron block instead of us-

ing aluminium since the graphite in its matrix holds fine particles of oil to assist in more efficient lubrication and hence longer engine life. Iron also has better sound-dampening properties, reducing vibration, and its thermal properties assure proper working tolerances of all reciprocating components at high temperatures. Light weight could always be obtained by using aluminium or special expensive metals, but these units would have spoilt the whole purpose of the Cobra which was to use stock parts which could be easily and inexpensively maintained, offering long-term reliability which, as Shelby realised, was desired by many potential sports car drivers whose budget was limited.

It seems that many people believe Carroll Shelby arrived at the AC factory at Thames Ditton armed with rolls of drawings and blueprints designed to turn their roadster into a road-burning monster. In fact, he supplied the idea, which had already been considered by AC, but, most importantly, be bought the engine, then unknown in England, and a measure of experience gained from racing in Europe (know-

Overleaf: The Ace Ford demonstrates a simple elegance.

25

how gathered by him with just this moment in mind). Shelby is the first to admit that he does not claim to be a talented engineer or designer - he understands what makes automobiles work but readily leaves the finer points to those with the ability to design and construct. His real talent lies in bringing those people together and motivating them to carry his ideas through. In

this respect AC carried out the initial conception and continued to redesign and modify from data sent back from the Shelby works in the USA throughout the life of the Cobra roadster so, although the eventual contract decreed that the responsibility for the installation of the engine and transmission was carried out in California, the car remained very much an AC at heart.

The First 260 V8 Engine

By January 1962 one 260 cu in engine had arrived at Thames Ditton. As it turned out, the Ford V8 weighed only about 15lb more than the old Bristol 2-litre, tipping the scales at around 450lb, and it could be comfortably installed low and well back in the engine bay, which immediately overcame any worries about the handling problems

Above: The original Cobra chassis and tubular frame.
Right: The prototype under construction at Thames Ditton. (Courtesy AC Cars).

The prototype is completed amidst a factory full of chasses, Aces and Greyhounds. (Courtesy AC Cars).

which such an engine could so easily cause. Not surprisingly, the gearbox had to be changed from the Bristol unit to Ford's own Borg-Warner box since the Bristol could handle a maximum of 90lb ft of torque, whereas the Ford could cope with over four times this amount. This substitution was easily carried out since there was no engine/gearbox mating problem and the Ford unit only added an extra 10lb to the weight.

Any increase in weight, however, was more than compensated for by the immediate increase in horsepower -

164bhp with the 260 engine - and, more importantly, a huge increase in torque to 258lb ft. With the prototype now mobile it was taken to the Silverstone motor racing circuit in Northamptonshire where it was put through its paces. Not surprisingly, a number of problems soon came to light, since components designed to handle speeds of 100mph were now having to cope with the stresses of 135mph with all the extra loadings imposed by corresponding increases in cornering and stopping. It was apparent that virtually every part of the car would now

need strengthening. Apart from additional chassis strengthening, the most important redesign job took place at the rear end where a whole new assembly was designed. The rear axle had to be very firmly located, driveshafts strengthened and wheel bearings designed to cope with their new task.

During the rear end redesign the opportunity was taken to experiment with the rear brakes and, probably, one of the most interesting features of this prototype was the use of inboard rear disc brakes designed to give greater stopping power, easier pad changes

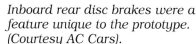

Inboard rear disc brakes were a feature unique to the prototype. (Courtesy AC Cars).

Centre: By the time production began, the '221' V8 had been superseded by the '260'. (Courtesy AC Cars).

Below: The first cars used the Ace steering wheel. (Courtesy AC Cars).

race track. AC would have preferred this inboard application since it was easier and more economical to construct the brakes in this form.

The Salisbury differential, however, was allowed to stay, having been in service for many years in the Ace, since it was found to be strong enough to cope with its new task. Further cross-bracing was added to the Ace chassis, along with an increase in the gauge of tubing used, while the general 'beefing-up' process was employed on the steering components, suspension mounts, wheel bearings and a heavier transverse front leaf spring.

The all-aluminium body was constructed by AC's part-owned sub-contractor in West London, the Brownlow Sheet Metal Company, from aluminium sheets 0.045in thick, the final body weighing only 50lb. Basically, the only visible change made to the Ace body was to produce a slight wheelarch flare front and rear with a shallow, flat 'eyebrow' lip around the edge. Carroll Shelby had rather hoped that the Cobra would be built with a fibreglass body but to change from aluminium

and reduced unsprung weight. These were retained on the prototype but the second and subsequent cars reverted to outboard brakes because of the risk of the pads becoming contaminated by a film of oil carried to them by the cold air ducting which was necessary to ensure that the inboard brakes, mounted out of the airflow, remained cool - particularly when used on the

Below: Outboard rear brakes were used for production models. (Courtesy AC Cars).

Bottom: A MkI Cobra outside the Thames Ditton showroom. (Courtesy AC Cars).

wold seriously delay production and AC had a firm supply-line of aluminium bodies and a workforce used to working in this material, although fibreglass was used for the footwell boxes and sparewheel tray in the boot.

Prototype Flies to California

Within three months the prototype was virtually complete and the engine and transmission were removed before it was flown to California on 16th February 1962 to allow Shelby to study the car at first hand with a new high-compression 260 engine installed.

Although the car was still a long way from being perfect it was at least a mobile basis for what Shelby had in mind and, at this stage of the operation, the biggest problem facing him was to obtain the trust and backing of the Ford Motor Company, since without their interest the supply and cost of engines would create a very real difficulty.

Carroll Shelby had by now invested some $40,000 of his own and his friends' money in producing the prototype, so one can well imagine the excitement as well as the apprehension Shelby must have felt at this stage; his dream was now a three-dimensional reality and the next step would probably be the hardest to bring about - turning a one-off prototype into a serious production vehicle. Had either Ford and even AC lost interest then, or had either company decided that the car did not fit in with future plans and pulled out, the whole project could have easily sunk without trace. From Ford's point of view they had a lot to lose, laying their reputation on the

line in the rather fickle and image-conscious American market, especially backing such an unknown quantity as a very 'English' roadster being built by Shelby American Automobiles, a company with no previous car construction experience. For their part AC could have decided that the arrangement to build bodies and chassis for export only was not in keeping with the kind of car production they had been used to; with their healthy supply of engineering projects from the various government ministries they were not short of orders. However, being enthusiasts they were fortunately more than prepared to undertake the expensive and time-consuming work necessary to make the idea a reality.

The first problem, however, was to get CSX0001 mobile in America. With the engine-less car sitting at Los Angeles airport, a trailer was conscripted from one of Shelby's driving school students and, eight hours after it was rolled into the Santa Fe workshop, the car was drivable, its 260 cu in engine installed and its unpainted aluminium body scoured to a high polish. This car, in fact, became the all-important road test model supplied to the American motoring magazines who were eager to sample the product now that the word had spread about Shelby's latest venture.

US Road Tests
Being the businessman that he undoubtedly is, Shelby ensured that each magazine received the same car sprayed a different colour for every test, thus giving the impression that

more than one car existed and that they were being built by the dozen. In fact, the first road test in *Sports Car Graphic* showed the car in its original unpainted form with the word 'Shelby' painted across the nose and boot. Luckily for all concerned, the magazines were tremendously enthusiastic about the car and its potential. Certainly it lacked nothing with regard to performance and could outrun and out-corner virtually any car on sale in the USA at the time, although the journalists were correct in their assumption that it would not appeal to anybody who valued saloon car comfort, electric windows and air conditioning, which were the accepted norm in America.

Indeed, the concept of a 'traditional' English sports car could have been considered something of a marketing risk, but fortunately there were enough real enthusiasts who were prepared to tolerate removable side-screens and complicated folding hoods, especially since most of them realised the car's potential for weekend racing at their local circuit as a change from the Chevrolet Corvette. (In fact, the Americans found the hood such a challenge that not even Carroll Shelby and his team could figure out a way to erect it, when they eventually got round to that problem. It took the owner of an AC Ace, who lived locally, to provide the answer).

Don Frey & Ray Geddes
As well as the invaluable assistance already received from Dave Evans at Ford, Shelby by now had another

33

A.C. CARS
LIMITED

Registered Offices and Works:
THAMES DITTON, SURREY, ENGLAND

Sales, Service and Repairs Department:
HIGH STREET, THAMES DITTON, ENGLAND

and

SHELBY AMERICAN INC.,
1042 PRINCETON, VENICE, CALIFORNIA, U.S.A.
Tele. EX. 1-6389

FOREWORD

This book was written with the object of enabling the owner to maintain his car in perfect condition throughout its life.

The A.C. Cobra is designed and built at the A.C. Factory, England, and like all other machinery of advanced design needs regular care and attention to give maximum results. A little time spent now and then in this direction will be amply repaid by ultimate performance.

Shelby American Inc. are responsible for the conception of the car, and in America for the fitting of the engine, and gear box, manufactured by the Ford Motor Company of America.

A.C. Cars were happy to co-operate to produce a sports car of outstanding achievement.

This book will enable the owner to have a more intimate knowledge of the car he possesses, a knowledge which will benefit both owner and car alike.

The A.C. Cobra, on leaving the factory, is as perfect as is possible in every detail, through the efforts of the skilled craftsmen producing it, after that it is in the owner's hands to maintain the high standards which have made the A.C. car famous during 60 years of automobile production for quality and efficiency.

PRICE
40s.

Telegrams:
"Autocarrier, Thames Ditton"

Telephone:
Emberbrook 5621

valuable ally at Ford, namely Don Frey, who was in charge of advanced engineering and, unusually for a man in his position at Detroit, a sports car enthusiast. He agreed with Dave Evans' assessment of the Cobra's potential and saw that it could fit in with Ford's 'performance' image. He was to provide Shelby with further backing in the form of sales outlets at specially selected dealers across the country and, even more importantly, provided a key member of Shelby's team by transferring Ray Geddes from Ford.

Ray Geddes was a very astute lawyer who knew exactly how to set up and run a business so that it would be profitable from day one. Indeed, Shelby readily admits that Geddes' talent for co-ordination was a vital link in the whole operation and, although he was there with the objective of safeguarding Ford's 'investment', nobody really objected to his presence and he was soon to become an indispensable member of the team.

By this time CSX0001 had been shown to Dave Evans and his technicians so they could take a closer look at exactly what it was they were backing. Although the prototype need a number of small improvements (as almost all prototypes do) before Cobras were sold to the public, Ford were suitably impressed and an agreement was reached to supply sufficient engines 'on credit' so that Shelby could start selling Cobras in order to repay Ford from the profits. Fortunately, Charles Hurlock went along with this agreement and the chassis/bodyshells were

delivered 'on trust'. This unique arrangement underlines what a shrewd businessman Carroll Shelby is; either that or a very lucky man!

As nobody connected with the project was very sure just how many cars of this nature could be sold (and one has to bear in mind that the Cobra was aimed primarily at the club-racing driver since Ford's aim was to see their name around the circuits of America), it was decided to order the cars in small batches from AC in the first instance just to see how many they could sell and how quickly. However, the first order had to be large enough to satisfy the governing body of world motor sport that the car was being constructed in sufficient numbers to qualify it as a genuine production car and not as a special designed to bend the rules.

What Shall We Call It?
One potential, although relatively minor, problem raised its head at the outset - what exactly was the car to be called? All the parties concerned were naturally eager to see their names used as prominently as possible. Nobody, however, objected to Shelby's suggestion that it should be referred to as a Cobra although this too almost caused difficulties since the name had previously been patented by Crossley Motors, who had built a small engine called Cobra (standing for 'COpper BRAzed') but, since they had gone out of business some years previously, nobody objected to Shelby using the name. Thus the car was provisionally known as the Shelby-Ford AC Cobra.

This rather cumbersome title was shortened later when Ford agreed to have their name shown on the car's front wings and Shelby made up some small plaques saying "powered by Ford". (In fact, Ford purchased the rights to the Cobra name and it was to reappear in future years on various editions of their successful Mustang model). The AC company were naturally eager to see their name displayed on the car since they had played such a major role, but the name Shelby-AC Cobra invariably became shortened in America to Shelby Cobra; although many people decided to refer to it as Ford Cobra. When eventually AC were in a position to build cars for their home market they were sold simply as AC Cobras - understandably, since Shelby played no part in their construction. In fact, AC, who are very proud of their script logo (to the extent of using specially constructed typewriters with an 'AC' key), sent the first bodyshells to California fully painted and with their own badges already in place on the bonnet and boot lid. The Shelby mechanics then removed these, pop-riveted the holes and fitted their own, smaller Shelby Cobra badge (with an even smaller AC logo in the centre) in its place. In time the paint covering these rivets shrank and cracked, to the understandable consternation of proud owners. AC were eventually persuaded to leave the badges off to avoid this problem. However, all Cobras still carry the AC script stamped into the clutch and brake pedals and the only way to remove this (apart from fitting different pedals) is to drive an enormously

high mileage and literally wear the logo away - it is doubtful whether any owner has managed to achieve this.

The First 100 Cars
The first order for 100 cars was fulfilled by AC between December 1962 and April 1963 and AC gave each car a chassis number prior to export. Since chassis CSX0001 was the prototype it did not follow the trend of numbers established by the factory, which began with the first production car bearing the number CSX2001, the letters standing for Carroll Shelby Export. All early cars with leaf-spring suspension began with a number 2 and later models with coil-spring suspension with a 3. Cars not destined for America were given a different prefix, either COX, COB or CSB, and one special car build by AC was given the prefix MA, although this could not be described as a true Cobra. Every chassis constructed was entered into the AC 'bible' which lists every car ever built by them with all relevant details and changes entered alongside including, in the case of the Cobra, the name of the ship which took the car to the USA.

Orders for the car soon materialised as word spread about the amazing performance available for the price - $5995. In fact, the cars were marketed in America for a few hundred dollars less than the superseded AC Ace-Bristol. Very soon Shelby had a small workforce busily turning the rolling chassis into complete cars at a rate of two cars a week at his Santa Fe Springs workshop. The first production chassis was quickly completed and sent to

An AC press release picture from
1964 shows the factory demonstrator
parked alongside the Thames.

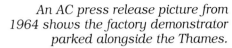

Shelby's newly appointed East Coast dealer, Ed Hugus, whence it swiftly passed into private ownership.

A Hot Problem

The second production chassis was built as a mobile test-bed for future racing Cobras. Not unnaturally, Shelby was eager to find out just how the cars would behave on the circuit - an all-important factor in the success of his venture and the continuation of Ford backing. The original car had already unofficially been driven around the Riverside Raceway where a number of lessons had been learned such as the problem with the carburettor in corners where excessive body lean caused either fuel starvation or flooding, depending on whether it was a right- or left-hand bend, with subsequent loss of control as the engine stalled. The fitting of a more efficient Holley carburettor and anti-roll bars front and rear cured the problem.

Cooling proved to be the Cobra's biggest problem, which was due in no small part to the size of the front air intake. Steps were taken to cure this over the years with two successive redesigns to enlarge the opening. The cars also had problems with radiators and, in fact, early models were fitted with radiators from the 'opposition', the Chevrolet Corvette, which replaced the totally inadequate British Ford Zephyr units installed in Thames Ditton. Shelby personnel were sent incognito to various Chevrolet dealers to buy as many radiators as they could and Chevrolet naturally became suspicious as to where all their spare radiators were disappearing. Before they could put a stop to this unofficial practice Ford came to the rescue by getting the McCord Radiator Company (one of their subsidiary companies) to construct specially designed units in brass, along with more efficient header tanks. These radiators were not constructed in time to be fitted to the first batch of cars, but were fitted with the new 289 engines.

The First Race

Car number 2 was entered in an event at Riverside during October 1962 with Shelby's test driver, Billy Krause, at the wheel. Entered in the Experimental Production class he proceeded to run away from the opposition, Corvettes included, until, with a lead of about 1.5 miles, a stub-axle broke. The race was eventually won by a Corvette (almost inevitably since production sports car racing was at that time totally dominated by 'America's Number One Sports Car'), but for those Corvette owners brave enough to face the truth the writing was now firmly on the wall.

Among those who knew what was about to happen was the man responsible for the Corvette, Zora Arkus Duntov, who admitted at the time that the relatively heavy Chevrolet car was never in with a chance against such a lightweight agile roadster, and from 1963 onwards the few Corvette victories were more often than not gained by default. In fact, from 1964 onwards the SCCA Class A Production Sports Car class which the Corvette habitually won each year was to fall instead to the Cobra and it was not until 1969, some three years after the end of Cobra production, that the Corvette would win this class again.

Many Corvette owners were naturally upset at this turn of events and tried to have the Cobra removed to the Experimental class instead of 'Production', claiming that it was not a true production road car because it was being made in smaller numbers than the Corvette, although how they could expect anyone to accept that is anybody's guess! Carroll Shelby had ensured from the outset that sufficient cars were going to be produced to satisfy all the rules and regulations - the FIA in Paris demanded that 100 cars per annum constituted a production car - so Shelby made sure that the requisite number were built each year (hence the first order of 100 cars given to AC). If it had been feasible, Shelby would have built every Cobra as a race car since all development work was centred on this objective, but he knew that a market for 100 such cars a year was very unlikely so the Cobras sold for road use were virtually 'de-tuned' and fitted out for a little more creature comfort than those sold or retained for racing,

It stood to reason that if every car was strong enough to stand up to racing conditions, then it was unlikely that a customer was going to break the car in any way by using it on the road. (The broken stub-axle suffered at Riverside underlines the usefulness of racing, since the offending part was immediately redesigned and production standardised by AC using a higher

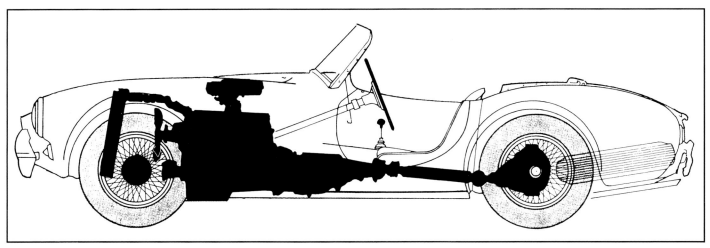

The Cobra's engine was well back in the chassis, giving the car surprisingly good weight distribution.

tensile strength material). The afore-mentioned proposition in fact proved to be the case, the only exception being the engine. On collecting the car, customers were informed that they could drive the car just as hard as they wished and that, short of coming into sudden contact with the scenery, they would not break it but that they should never, under any circumstances, rev it beyond 7000rpm (hardly necessary, anyway, with such a powerful unit with amazing torque in any gear at virtually any speed).

Needless to say, some people just had to find out the hard way that Shelby meant exactly what he said although, in all fairness, most problems were caused when 'junior' was allowed to run the car around the block. Despite the firm denials that he had revved it anywhere near 7000rpm (perish the thought!), the bent valves told another story. This unnecessary problem apart, very few cars were ever returned with any major faults.

The first seventy Cobras were equipped by AC with a Lucas electrical system which, although adequate for most purposes, was incapable of keeping the battery charged when driving for long periods in heavy traffic. So, from chassis number 71 to 200 a higher capacity Ford dynamo was used and from chassis 201 onwards the whole electrical system was made by Ford with an alternator replacing the dynamo.

Experience with CSX0001 in regular daily use threw up a problem with the lack of bumper protection given by the over-riders. The somewhat delicate bodywork was susceptible to modification in supermarket parking lots where parking is traditionally done by the audio method. Thin tubular chrome bars were added between over-riders with an overlapping curved section at the rear, but it was inevitable that body protection would never be the Cobra's strong point. A slightly smaller bootlid was made for production cars to increase the rigidity in the rear body-work, and the fuel tank was removed from its original position beneath the boot to a vertical position above the rear axle and behind the driver; this change improved handling and had less effect on the handling as the tank emptied (important, with racing in mind). It also benefited boot space as the spare-wheel was now able to be positioned in the boot in its own fibre-glass well. A cover placed over it gave it a flat floor.

Virtually all parts of the Cobra which were time-consuming or difficult to install were sent to AC for them to fit as the cars were constructed, leaving the Shelby mechanics with the task of installing the engine/transmission, checking everything over and road testing the car prior to sale. A major reason for AC being in charge of the bulk of the car construction was the simple fact that the labour rates were

so much lower than comparable rates in America, helping to keep the cost of the car down. Shipping a car to America without its engine also saved a great deal of money in customs duty, since it did not then qualify as a 'complete vehicle'.

Early '63 & Sales Grow

By early 1963 sales were increasing at a satisfactory rate as the car's reputation grew. Naturally, performance was its strongest selling point with *Car Life* and *Road & Track* magazines both recording a 0-60mph time of 4.2 seconds; but potential owners were also attracted by the fact that the car could easily be serviced by almost any Ford dealer and that all major mechanical parts were available over the counter of any Ford spares department. No need, as Shelby put it, to wait three months for some 15 cent part to arrive from Italy. Only the occasional modification was necessary to satisfy most customers, most notably the request from owners not fortunate enough to live in a Californian climate for a heater in the car. (It had not actually occurred to anyone in California that it might be needed). Many owners found that the interior of the car was quite hot enough, thank you; with the V8 sited well back in the chassis a great deal of heat found its way through the aluminium footwell walls and even heated the metal pedals! This problem was never totally

eradicated, despite cutting louvres just behind each front wheelarch to help remove engine heat.

The cars were originally offered with a colour choice of red or white, however, in response to customer demand, Shelby soon added black, blue green and burgundy to the range: needless to say, the two most requested colours became red and white.

The interior carried over from the AC Ace, with leather bucket-seats, comprehensive carpeting and a very full dashboard with two main dials (a speedometer and an 8000rpm rev counter) and six smaller gauges ranged in three descending rows of three gauges (ammeter, water temperature, oil temperature), two gauges (fuel gauge, oil pressure) and finally a small electric clock. The ignition switch and various push-pull knobs for lights and wipers completed the rather haphazard arrangement, along with indicator telltale lights, cigarette lighter and small lockable glove box (with a very necessary passenger's grab handle fixed above on the lip of the bodywork which formed the top of the dash). A simple, unframed rear view mirror was also screwed onto the bodywork/dash top and the windscreen fitted into place ahead of this. (The windscreen was simply fitted onto the body in best 'classic' tradition, an almost grudging afterthought with benefit to the 'flow' of the car's styling). The steering wheel fitted to a handful of the earlier cars came directly from the AC Ace but was found (when racing) to lack strength, so a much more attractive three-spoke wood-rimmed wheel was substituted, of generous size and more modern appearance.

Tyres were Goodyear (Shelby was a Goodyear distributor!) Blue Streak fitted to 5 in wide, 15 in diameter 72-spoke wire wheels in silver enamel with chrome as an option. As tyres improved the rim width of the wheels was later increased to 6 in with Goodyear G-8 7.35 x 15 low-profile tyres and, as an option, aluminium alloys were available in various widths, although very few people requested these since the wire wheels were perfectly adequate and were considered more attractive.

Right from the outset the Cobra was a success and cars left the Shelby plant in a steady flow - hardly on the scale of the Corvette, of course, but that was never the intention and never practical since, even at the height of production, AC's maximum output was fifteen complete car per week. It simply fitted into a niche in the American market in much the same way that the Lotus 7, for example, did in the UK. It was a case of if you didn't damn well want one, you didn't damn well buy one. Those customers who were lured away from the only other choice of American sports car, the Corvette, were able to order their Cobra almost as one would buy a suit - in other words, whatever they requested was carried out if at all possible, so it is unlikely that any two Cobras were ever made exactly the same. Many of the first customers, having paid their $1000 deposit, actually dropped by at the Santa Fe workshop to watch their car being finalised.

Cobra

IV

THE COBRA MARK II 289

When the first batch of cars arrived to be united with their engines it became apparent that the Shelby premises at Santa Fe Springs would not be large enough for the task and, after the first thirty cars had been built - at a rate of two per week - the whole operation was transferred to Venice, Los Angeles, occupying the premises where Lance Reventlow had built his ill-fated Scarab racing cars near the Pacific and convenient for access to Los Angeles airport. This gave Shelby the advantage of being able to ship urgent parts in by air and of being only twenty-four hours away from Thames Ditton. The

workforce increased to about thirty-five within a few months, including race mechanics, and five cars could now be worked on at one time under one roof. It also meant more storage space - previously the engines were locked up in an outside shed until they were required.

Mk II Arrives

While Shelby was busy selling and racing Cobras Ford had not been idle. Realising that they had a very solid and powerful engine on their hands they continued its development and, in 1964, introduced its successor, the

These two sporting ACs are separated by almost three decades. The 1936 Alpine Rally-winning AC16/80 stands alongside the 1964 ex-AC demonstrator Cobra.

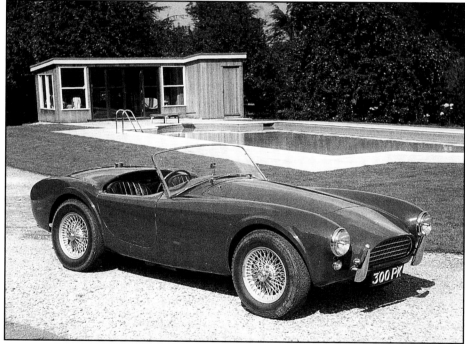

289, possibly the best American V8 engine ever and one which greatly transformed the racing cars. (Later 289 race engines were persuaded to give 380bhp without loss of reliability). This increase in engine size was obtained by enlarging the bore to 4.0 in from the 3.8 in of the 260 which, in turn, had been enlarged from the 221 engine's 3.6 in. Having by now produced some seventy-five 260-engined Cobras, Shelby, who knew a good thing when he saw it, quickly substituted this new engine around the middle of 1963 to create the Mk II. With a few worthwhile Shelby modifications it was offered with a high-lift camshaft, solid lifters and a 460 cfm Autolite carburettor, producing 271bhp. A number of Cobra owners quickly returned their cars for a transplant, while others were offered the new engine when they arrived for routine servicing so a genuine Mk I Cobra is a comparative rarity.

Obviously the Mk II was not a planned change in the model range which had continuously benefited from small changes made to each car as development continued daily. However, the new engine gave Shelby American the opportunity to incorporate more major changes which they felt were necessary, both mechanically and to the bodywork. From chassis number CSX2076 AC began to supply cars with slightly wider wheelarches and side vents in front wings designed to remove engine heat, plus a shorter bootlid to improve bodywork rigidity, a new method of hood fastening and, most importantly, a larger grille cavity to bring in more cooling air.

New wiring-looms, designed with Ford's assistance, were shipped to England for installation to take advantage of the lower labour costs.

Rack & Pinion

Next to the engine change the most valuable redevelopment which took place at this time was the replacement of the old AC Ace worm-and-sector steering with the more modern and efficient rack-and-pinion, which had the desirable advantage of having fewer parts and being a good deal stronger, important for the racing Cobras. Worm-and-sector steering used a long idler arm with two track rods attached to each steering arm, allowing the suspension geometry and toe-in of the front wheels to change during

A line of Cobras in the Thames Ditton works, with a racing bodied car at the rear.

A Cobra MkII exercises at Goodwood.

suspension travel (literally in the middle of a corner on the race track). The effect of all this unwanted movement was to put great stress on the idler arm ball-joints and brackets, resulting in steering failure on many racing Cobras. The rack-and-pinion layout was easier to assemble and service at the race track and transformed both the racing and road cars, making them feel more solid and predictable on the road. Sadly, however, the AC adjustable steering column was sacrificed at this stage since Shelby was worried that a racing Cobra's steering wheel could decide to adjust itself during a race - not very desirable for the unfortunate driver. Short of moving the driver's seat future Cobra pilots had to adopt a more 'arms out' style than was previously the case. However, everyone agreed that the change to rack-and-pinion was a vast improvement, despite the slightly heavier steering at parking speeds and quite a large increase in lock-to-lock from 1 2/3 turns to 2 7/8, but Ken Miles demonstrated the improvement by immediately lapping the Riverside circuit two seconds faster than the best 'worm-and-sector' Cobra time. The change was incorporated from the 126th car (chassis number CSX2126) onwards.

Also at about this time the wider wheels with Goodyear G8 tyres became available, along with a fibreglass detachable hard-top offering less noise and wind buffeting on a long journey. Red and tan leather interiors were offered as alternatives to the standard black of the '260' cars and silver bodywork was added to the range of colours. Chrome luggage-racks became available for those who found the boot space inadequate.

All Mk II Cobras were produced, unless otherwise requested, with a 3.77 differential in place of the earlier 3.54 ratio. This had the effect of lowering the potential top speed from a factory quoted 140mph at 6500rpm) to 132mph but, of course, gave a useful increase in acceleration. It is interesting to note that road tests of the Mk II failed to reproduce the earlier 0-60mph time of 4.2 seconds claimed for the Mk I, despite the increase in power and more accelerative rear axle. Either the earlier timing equipment had been optimistic or the staff of the magazines had been only too pleased to advance the reputation of Shelby American. Another possibility was that a very special differential was fitted although this would never have given the 150mph top speed quoted in the same tests.

The 289 engine, as supplied to Shelby, was a higher performance ver-

Cover of the 1964/5 British sales brochure. (Courtesy AC Cars).

place since the small loss of horse-power was hardly noticed.

Borg-Warner T10 transmissions were housed in aluminium instead of iron casings and contained a different set of gears and stronger input shaft splines. Ford shafts were 1.125in in diameter with 10 splines, while the Cobra used a 1.25in 12 spline shaft which meant using a Chevrolet clutch disc. Inside the Ford housing were Pontiac gears and shafts and ratios were: first 2.20:1, second 1.63:1 and third 1.31:1.

After assembly the cars were checked over using a seventy-five point list, the engines run at 1500rpm in an open area prior to a thirty-mile test drive conducted by the production supervisor, Leonard Parsons, or his shop foreman. Finally, when the car was mechanically complete,, the bodywork and trim were brought up to standard, the chrome and paintwork polished (or, with later Cobras, full painting was carried out) and only when the long checklist was completed was the car handed over to the Shelby American sales department for final delivery.

Busy in Thames Ditton

Meanwhile, some 6000 miles from the Shelby American factory AC Cars Ltd found themselves in the strange position of being busier that ever before, while having nothing to sell to their home market. The large, hangar-like factory with its 100,000 square feet of floor space was full of raw materials and chassis and bodies in various stages of completion; its machine shop was busy producing suspension and steering parts, even the centre-lock hubs for the wire wheels which included the splining of the hubs. In the main assembly area the chassis tubes were arc welded to their cross-members to form the assembly which would carry the mild steel body frames and mounting brackets which were gas welded to the chassis. Body panels were sent to Thames Ditton to be assembled and installed over the chassis frame. Even the radiator grilles

47

Right, below & opposite: The 'Marcewski Special' under construction. The possible Cobra replacement is shown here with 289V8 but it was also designed to accept AC's stillborn flat-six engine. (Courtesy AC Cars).

were hand-made in the factory although they were anodised by an outside contractor. The showroom was used to store completed cars prior to transport to Victoria docks two at a time on the backs of lorries. (Since they were engineless they were loaded onto the side of lorries by fork-lift trucks). Some cars were flown out, usually the urgently required racing 289 bodies which were distinguishable from the road cars by their wide flared wheelarches.

The Marcewski Special

The 289 Mk II was still very much an AC (as opposed to a Shelby) since it carried over a great deal of its Ace ancestry despite the variety of changes made to strengthen the car for its new engine and, of course, changes took place continuously through the experience of the racing programme and customers' road cars in the United States. Although AC planned to build complete Cobras for sale in Britain and Europe as soon as production would allow, they were also looking to the future, since they realised that the Cobras might not have a very long production run, and were busy developing their own potentially more luxurious up-market version of the Cobra. The power, strength and reliability were available, but they anticipated that their traditional customers would demand a softer riding, more civilised Grand Tourer in the European style. To test their ideas they built a prototype (quite early in the production of the Cobra) with a unique space-frame chassis. Within

the factory this was referred to as the 'Marcewski Special', named after its designer, Mr Z.T.Marcewski, and apart from the new chassis it featured strut type rear suspension with wide angle wishbones and needle-roller bearings, along with a steering rack placed above and behind the front suspension. This unique car was intended to be marketed with a 2-litre flat-six engine of AC's own design. It is thought that several of these engines were constructed and

they were a remarkable tribute to the engineering abilities of AC Cars. They were developed to an advanced stage but, sadly, never put into production, even more sadly when one realises that detailed drawings were made for a flat-six mid-engined two-seater sports car with space-frame chassis and alloy bodywork. Remember that this was during the early 1960s ...

However, the flat-six engines proved disappointing during tests, run-

ning rather unevenly and lacking the smooth power delivery of a Porsche. It was thought the unit required more ·main bearings. The whole project was finally shelved when AC realised that the problems would prove either insurmountable or prohibitively expensive to correct. The car itself was used as sales manager Jock Henderson's road car, fitted with a 289 Cobra engine and registered 6000 PE. It was driven to Italy to discuss the possibility of having bodies made in Modena in the future and while there it was photographed by some Americans. Somewhere in the USA an exact copy of the body was later constructed on an unknown chassis and may exist to this day.

Although it proved to be a very relaxed and long-legged car with the V8 installed it had problems with overheating, as well as myriad prototype teething troubles, particularly with the complex suspension which required a great deal of tuning, and front-end float at high speed. Its main advantage over the Cobra was the amount of room offered for the driver and passenger with space behind the front seats for short trips, plus a very generous amount of boot space. The car was built as a convertible although a fastback was sketched on the drawing

board to widen its appeal. For numerous reasons the car failed to replace the Cobra. The space-frame chassis proved expensive to construct although it was stronger than the current Ferrari model, the unusual steering rack position offered no advantage over the conventional layout, and when Ford were approached with a view to supplying the 4.7-litre engine their response was not enthusiastic because of their ap-

proaching involvement with the 7-litre which was about to be installed in all American Cobras.

It is this car which many people believed to be the prototype of the AC428 which it resembles in so many ways, but under the skin it was a very different car. The 428 utilised a lengthened Cobra chassis in an attempt to keep the car as simple as possible, the only notable deviation from the Cobra being the elegant Frua-designed Italian-built bodywork allied to a more comfortable up-market interior.

With AC opting for the more economically viable 428, the 'Marcewski Special' was put one one side and, as with so many prototypes, was destined to be broken up. Fortunately, a Lon-

Left & below: 1966 AC Cobra MkII.

Right: A Cobra shows how to raise dust and pump adrenaline. (Courtesy Mike Fear).

Below right: A MkII poses demurely for the camera. (Courtesy Mike Fear).

don medical student had seen the car a number of times on the road and visited the factory in an attempt to buy it. His visit proved successful once he had established that it was the 'Marcewski Special' and not the prototype 428 that interested him. The car was to remain in his ownership until the mid-1980s when, after his death, it

Cobra

V

EARLY RACING

Make no mistake, the *raison d'être* of the Cobra sports car was to achieve success (and publicity) at racing circuits around America and, in the longer term, to continue the success in the FIA World Championship races which were held in Europe, in addition to the American rounds at Daytona and Sebring. If the Cobra should also succeed in defeating the all-powerful Ferrari equipe in the process, so much the better.

Carroll Shelby was astute enough to realise from the start that out of a projected annual production of 100 cars no more than 20 per cent would ever be raced. To attempt to sell only race cars would be to court disaster as so many other specialist companies had previously discovered. Road cars would serve to provide cash flow, much needed profit, plus extra publicity for the marque in much the same way as Ferrari did, although the Cobra was deliberately aimed at a different sector of the sports car market to that enjoyed by Ferrari.

Throughout the cars' production race cars were offered for sale in various permutations, such as the Dragonsnake Dragster, USRRC Competition Roadster and the Cobra Slalom Snake. The pool of experience gathered together by Shelby meant that

Shelby and AC personnel prepare a racing-bodied Cobra for a Silverstone test session. Fourth from left is Phil Remington and on the right AC's chief engineering designer, Alan Turner. (Courtesy AC Cars).

Bullet-shaped racing mirrors were fitted and when Plexiglass aeroscreens were used these were fitted in the centre of the car, or on either or both wings depending on driver preference. The alloy foot pedals were replaced by larger, stronger steel ones and their location was changed as necessary to suit the driver. All screws were removed from the throttle assembly and were replaced by bolts and self-locking nuts to reduce the chance of failure, since few serious racing drivers ever treat the throttle gently.

Instead of using copper tubing from the clutch master cylinder to the slave on the clutch housing a flexible metal hose was used to ensure that the line wold not pull and fracture as the engine twisted and vibrated under continual acceleration. A double capacity brake fluid reservoir ensured that if a leak should occur in the hydraulic system a driver would have sufficient fluid to cope with the immediate problem until he reached his pit for repairs.

A 37 gallon fuel tank replaced the standard 14 gallon unit and either a Bendix or Stewart-Warner electric fuel pump was fitted below the tank on the rear suspension. A 2 or 3 gallon reserve standpipe was fitted in each tank and a three-way valve installed within the driver's reach allowed him some leeway in deciding when he should refuel. All fuel lines were of aircraft quality armoured tubing of 0.375in diameter, one line from the main tank and one from the reserve, clamped along the chassis tubes. Brackets were also fabricated to prevent the spare-wheel in the boot hurtling forwards

and breaking the fuel lines from the tank. When it was found that fuel was being sucked from the filter tube and carried into the cockpit in the form of a fine mist, a half-moon section of metal was riveted onto the rear body-work next to the fuel filler neck to break up the airflow over the back of the car. This also acted as a safety barrier to prevent fuel spilling over the driver in the event of an overflow during a pit-stop.

Many cars also had an elastic strap looped around securing pins to help hold the bootlid shut after it was found that the body could twist and flex sufficiently to release the catch. Aircraft style Dzuz fastening latches were used to hold the bonnet shut and, being spring-loaded, they also allowed the bonnet to be opened quickly. A stronger catch was used to hold the bonnet stay in place since, on early cars, the rod would often come away from its support and wave around inside the engine compartment. Air pressure built up inside the engine compartment at high speed which caused the bonnet to bulge, so pop-riveting was used to add strength. A scoop was cut into the bonnet (also on some road cars when requested) to bring cold air to the carburettors. To assist in this task a box was fitted around the carburettors above the engine's central vee; when the bonnet was closed the scoop fitted tightly over the box to channel air directly to the intakes.

The radiator had aluminium scoops riveted ahead of it to channel air directly to it for maximum effectiveness, as did the brakes. A unique fea-

ture was a 'shaker' screen which was a heavy wire mesh mounted in front of the radiator on four springs. This not only caught small rocks and debris and stopped them causing damage, but also shook them off at the same time which allowed the air flow to continue uninterrupted. The radiator hoses were discarded and replaced with Shelby's own stronger version - lengths of steel pipe joined at the engine and radiator ends by short lengths of rubber, the whole thing then protected by layers of insulting tape. The problem of rubber hoses splitting was solved in this very effective manner.

Rear wheel hub bearings had to be strengthened to cope with the increase in power by using a large ball in a wider bearing which fitted directly into the hub carrier; this was packed with high temperature grease to cope with increased friction, not just from the extra power but from wider tyres putting more rubber on the road.

So much power was transmitted through the rear wheels that the Halibrand wheel splines which fitted onto the driveshaft hub were unable to cope with the demands made upon them. To avoid stripping these splines the bolts which usually held the disc brakes in place were replaced with six extremely hard machines-steel bolts which were screwed through the disc brake, holding it onto the hub, and the wheel was fitted over these bolts and locked in place. These bolts became responsible for actually turning the wheels with the splines and knock-off spinner acting as extra insurance.

The problem of 'exploding' clutches

Pllp Lewn 1981

and flywheels was countered by the addition of a burst-proof bell-housing, which added 14lb to the car's weight. However, bearing in mind the experience of Skip Hudson whose foot was broken and whose car's steering locked when the clutch exploded, the extra weight was considered worthwhile. Racing Cobras also had a Sunbeam Alpine oil-cooler added above the differential to assist with cooling in long races. With the oil-cooler acting as a small radiator the cars were able, with the assistance of a Bendix fuel pump, to circulate three quarts instead of three pints of oil.

Large racing exhausts were constructed and supplied by Derrington in England and the 4 in diameter pipes were mounted under the car by flexible rubber bushes, terminating under the doors just in front of the rear wheels. With a wide pipe coming from each cylinder allowing a clear uninterrupted flow of gases from the engine the noise was considerable.

By adjustment to the steering rods the front wheels were set with a 0.125in toe-in the same as the rear wheels, although these were adjusted by bending the rear crossmembers. Should more camber be desirable on the front wheels this could be achieved by shortening the front main leaf-spring. Later coil-sprung race cars were much easier to set up. Naturally, anti-roll bars were fitted front and rear, usually 0.75in at the front and 0.625in at the rear, but these were varied widely according to driver preference. In the case of Ken Miles anti-toll bars were rarely fitted at all.

Although the preceding paragraphs list the main additions and alterations necessary to transform a road-going Cobra into a full race car capable of competing against the best cars in American club and national events, they only outline the way in which any such sports car (Corvettes included) would be strengthened to survive a season of competition. It may seem as though the Cobras were radically altered but the owner of a road-going version would still recognise the car as being intrinsically a Cobra once he was installed behind the wheel. Granted it would be somewhat faster, noisier, capable of going through corners more rapidly and offering an even firmer ride, but it still retained the feel and character of a road car.

Shelby offered most of these 'tweaks' to private owners in his racing accessory list either through the factory or Shelby dealers. Many took advantage of at least some of these options so that they could drive their cars on the road during the week and safely compete in slaloms (or sprints) at weekends without worrying about the car's ability to perform either task. Those with a desire to use their cars only in competition were advised to buy a fully built race version, since to completely transform an existing road car would be prohibitively expensive and never as effective as one built from the chassis up. To meet the requirements of amateur and semi-professional races alike Shelby offered the 289 Cobra in 1964 with the three stages of development. The standard road car retailed at $5995, the Stage I car with a small

amount of accessories added was $6275, the Stage II car, still with standard engine but on racing wheels, sold for $7220 while a replica Shelby FIA team car (guaranteed tested by Ken Miles) with full race engine set the lucky owner back $9500.

Cobra in Drag
Never one to miss a gap in the market Shelby also offered the lovers of the quarter-mile drag strip the opportunity to annoy Corvette owners. This car came about when some of his mechanics put the idea to him and he supplied the car while they supplied the labour in their spare time. The pale blue metalflake car set elapsed-time and top-speed National records first time out, using worm-and-sector steering and running massive six-spoke wheels on the rear. Named the Dragonsnake it was later offered in four stages of engine tune from standard 271bhp to a massive 380bhp with Webers, reworked heads and acceleration camshaft, all blueprinted and balanced. Special exhaust manifolds terminated under the doors. With aluminium valve covers and sump, the engine mated to Ford's QK1 aluminium transmission. Standard rear axle ratio was suggested as 4.89:1 but others were available. All Dragonsnake cars (as well as most privately run Cobras) utilised the fibreglass hard top in an attempt to improve aerodynamics and incorporated a hood scoop plus larger wheels to accommodate the dragster 'slicks'. It was also necessary to lengthen the front and rear leaf springs

when the cars were fitted with the special drag racing Cure-Ride shock absorbers. The car was announced in 1964 and only about two or three of these $8995 (in Stage IV trim) Cobras were sold as complete cars. Many owners purchased whatever options they thought necessary from the 23-part Dragonsnake accessory list and prepared their own version of the car. Such cars dominated the sports car classes until 1967 when they finally became uncompetitive.

Slalom Snake

Another Shelby variation on the theme was announced in 1965: the Cobra SS (Slalom Snake) - which was aimed at the weekend competitor - with anti-roll bars, Goodyear Blue Streak tyres on magnesium alloy wheels, front brake air ducts and the familiar chrome roll-over bar with its forward brace. A special feature of the Cobra SS was a double stripe down the centre of the car in the same colour as the interior trim. To decrease weight the sun visors, wind wings and rear bumpers were removed, despite which the price was $1000 more than the standard car. No record was kept of how many such cars were sold but at least one was known to exist, painted white with red centre stripes and red leather interior.

Despite instant success at US club level, with enthusiastic amateurs winning every type of event, Shelby was primarily concerned to see his cars take the FIA World Championship from Ferrari. This, of course, was another ball game. Running his team of cars at european circuits many thousands of

miles from his base, success and experience had to be gained the hard way. Although the Cobras were immediately competitive, Shelby was up against the dominating influence of Enzo Ferrari himself, who was never slow to use his influence to 'persuade' the FIA in Paris to change various rules to suit his ends whenever a rival threatened; Shelby was to suffer from this tactic.

First International

The first serious international event the Cobras entered was the Daytona Continental, Florida, in February 1963. This 24-hour race was also the last event for the 260 Mk I Cobra and, despite the problems encountered during the race, a number of important lessons were learned. Of the three cars entered Skip Hudson's crashed and Dan Gurney's retired with electrical problems and he was transferred to the pit crew, hanging out signals to the remaining driver, Dave MacDonald. A Ferrari GTO won the GT category and even a Corvette finished ahead of the Cobra on that occasion.

The following month saw the World Championship move to Sebring for a 12-hour race. At this event the new 289 cars featured rack-and-pinion steering and Weber carburettors and such driver pairings as Dan Gurney/ Phil Hill. Their car was intended as the team's 'hare', destined to be driven as fast as possible for as long as it held together, while the other team cars followed at a steadier pace. However, a sheared bolt in the steering meant a long stop in the pits and it limped home in seventeenth place behind the

eleventh placed car of Ken Miles/Lew Spencer with Phil Hill also sharing some of the driving. Shelby sat and watched as Ferraris swept the board taking the first six places and 1-2-3 in the GT class.

Le Mans 1963

Probably the most famous and prestigious race for the manufacturers on the World Championship has to be the 24-Hours of Le Mans. This 8.3 mile circuit using public roads was a vital step towards the Championship, with the attendant publicity and unique image built up over many years. It was also an event close to the heart of AC Cars who had entered their own AC Ace in previous years.

Naturally, such an event was too good to miss, particularly since in 1963 they had a much faster car than ever before. Carroll Shelby, himself a Le Mans winner only a few years earlier, was only too keen to be represented at the race in search of Championship points. Because of the comparative inexperience of his newly formed team, not to mention the logistics and cost of shipping the whole equipe to Europe, Shelby decided to approach the problem in another way. Applying the lessons already learned in the USA he assisted AC in the building of three new Cobras specifically for the event, the first purely competition Cobras built by AC. (One was sold directly to a

Overleaf: Le Mans 1963. Two Cobras were entered, one from the USA (white) and one from the AC factory. (Courtesy G. Dempsey).

Le Mans '63. Derek Hurlock pushes his AC Cobra entry from the paddock. Paper plates made high-tech headlight covers!

Le Mans '63. A bearded Stirling Moss in team manager-mode: Phil Remington lurks in the background, directly behind the car.

Le Mans '63. A pit-stop for 39 PH. At right, team manager Stirling Moss, shouts instructions through his megaphone while Carroll Shelby, in white jacket, looks on.

Le Mans '63. Feverish pit work on 39 PH.

customer in South Africa and never ran at Le Mans). AC prepared one right-hand drive car for their own entry wile the left-hand drive car was subsequently prepared and entered by Ed Hugus, a Shelby driver from Pittsburgh who ran as an independent entry. Both cars were registered for road use: the AC car, chassis number CS2131 (the 'X' being deleted since it was not for export), was issued with the registration number 39 PH. The Ed Hugus car was CSX2132.

The Le Mans cars' most distinctive feature was the large, streamlined aluminium hardtop fitted to improve aerodynamics (never a Cobra strong point; to underline the problem the rear windows of these hardtops were prone to be sucked out at high speed), and to increase their speed along the Mulsanne straight. These removable tops necessitated the fabrication of long fuel-fillers which terminated just forward of the top of the rear window. Vents in the side of the roof helped to remove hot air from the cockpit. As a result of the fitting of the long roofs a redesigned bootlid was also necessary and this took the form of a shortened, hinged lid which swung down to take the requisite spare-wheel. These cars also led to the introduction of side vents in the front wings to help remove

Le Mans '63. British Cobra, 39 PH, blasts out of the pits.

Rare in 1963, but a sign of things to come, sponsorship ...

Le Mans '63. Ed Hugus' US entry was unable to complete the race after a major engine blow-up in the tenth hour.

The 1963 Le Mans AC Cobra gleaming under the lights of the Effingham Motor Museum shortly after its restoration.

Below: The ex-Le Mans Cobra at the start of the Brighton Speed Trials in 1978.

engine heat in all race and road cars.

The AC entered car, 39 PH, created a great deal of interest at the time: it was sponsored by *The Sunday Times* and had Stirling Moss as a team manager. It was driven by Peter Bolton and Ninian Sanderson and, despite a comparative lack of top speed (its best practice time was 4 minutes 15.3 seconds), it displayed great reliability, covering 2592 miles at an average speed of 108mph, touching 160mph at 5500rpm on the Mulsanne straight, eventually finishing in seventh place and being beaten only by a gaggle of six Ferraris, winning the over 4000cc class and being the first British car home. Just eleven days later this car was tested by *Autocar* magazine in exactly the same condition as it ran at Le Mans, with the exception of an axle

change from 3.07:1 to 3.77:1 prior to use on British circuits where top speed was not so critical. They recorded acceleration times of 0 to 40mph in 3 seconds, to 60mph in 5 seconds and to 100mph in 12 seconds, crossing the quarter-mile at 107mph, still in third gear. These times were recorded on the well-worn Le Mans Dunlop R6 tyres. Approximate output of the engine was

330bhp with the four double choke Weber carburettors disposing of the content of the 30 gallon fuel tank at around eight miles per gallon during the race. 39 PH was later sold to the John Willment racing team and its green bodywork was resprayed red with white centre stripes.

The Ed Hugus entry was destined not to last the course; the engine suffered fatal injuries when a connecting rod came loose during the tenth hour while the car was in thirteenth place. Both cars were fitted with solid wheels from earlier Jaguar racing cars and tyres specially made by Dunlop.

These Le Mans Cobras were to bridge the gap between the first racing Cobras and the full-race Shelby team cars of 1964, the 'FIA roadsters'. Two further batches of three Le mans replicas were built: the first three were used as Shelby team cars in the 1963 USRRC races and the other three were sold to private entrants campaigning the SCCA A-class Production Sports Car series. (It was one of the Shelby team cars which went on to score the first ever victory for an American car in an international race, with Dan Gurney at the wheel). As the 'replicas' were intended purely for racing they were supplied to Shelby in primer and it was left to him to paint them in his own team's, or customer's colours. Oil coolers, brake ducts and flared arches with small spats to comply with regulations were added at the time of construction, together with full roll cages, racing seats and extinguishers. It is interesting to note that only one replica ever raced with the hardtop in place - Dave MacDonald's example, CSX2138, in one event at the Continental Divide Raceway. The three cars sold by Shelby were purchased without the roofs. (It was rumoured that these had been destroyed since they were superfluous in the SCCA races where the cars used small aeroscreens in place of the full windscreens used in the USRRC events).

It was these cars which marked the change from AC supplying only

road cars which Shelby converted for race use when necessary. They now made a clear distinction between road and race chassis when construction began and completed them accordingly.

Carroll Shelby was present at Le Mans in 1963 although not in his accustomed role. He was representing the Ford Motor Company as a member of a team sent to study all the cars and potential competition against which a possible future Ford team would have to race. Henry Ford II was becoming more enthusiastic about motor racing as a method of publicity and about having the 'glamour' of success rub off onto the whole range of Ford products, in much the same way as the Corvette gave a certain lustre to the Chevrolet range. It was pure chance that during 1963 Enzo Ferrari began to put out feelers among the motor industry to let interested parties know his company would be prepared to allow the right sort of people to buy a major share in the legendary Ferrari name. Henry Ford, quick to realise the potential of such a company with its unique image, its experienced racing team and personnel, sent a team of engineers lawyers and accountants (among them Don Frey) to Modena in May 1963 to negotiate terms. What they had all hoped would prove a straightforward, swift business deal was sunk by the inimitable Enzo Ferrari who began to prevaricate over any number of small details when he realised that his beloved company would soon be swamped by a corporate system larger than he could comprehend. His demands grew continually to a point where Ford could no longer be expected to co-operate. Among these demands were clauses which stated that Ford could never compete in international competition under their own name, only Ferrari's, which would have had the effect of bringing the Cobra programme to a premature close - a point which Enzo would not have overlooked since the feelings between himself and Carroll Shelby were mutual and Ferrari was only too happy to kill any threatened opposition at birth. Finally, it was Ferrari himself who cancelled the negotiations, claiming that he could not work amid such bureaucracy. He later became affiliated to the giant Fiat empire.

Within forty-eight hours of the end of negotiations plans were being hatched within Ford's Dearborn nerve-centre to create a racing programme which would beat Ferrari at his own game and dominate international long-distance racing. Ford, in effect, planned to emulate Carroll Shelby by taking an existing British car (in this case Eric Broadley's advanced mid-engine design called the Lola GT), applying their own skills and massive logistical back-up to complete a metamorphosis and turn the car into a race winner. The result, the Ford GT40, although not strictly relevant to the Cobra story was eventually responsible for the termination of the Cobra racing team when Ford 'requested' Shelby to transform the GT40 from a fast, delicate computer-designed car into a reliable race winner.

Although Carroll Shelby was a key

72

73

figure in Ford's future plans his own Ford-Cobra team were, in 1963, still at the beginning of their international campaign. Throughout the remaining months of 1963 Cobras continued their winning ways in the North American championships and in September Dan Gurney became the first driver to pilot an American car to victory in an FIA international event at the Bridgehampton circuit, Long Island, New York, with Ken Miles in second place.

Corvette Grand Sport

At the end of 1963 the Shelby team headed for the annual party/racing week at Nassau where everyone traditionally went for a holiday and some supposedly less-than-serious racing, but actually hoped to out-psyche the opposition by revealing their cars for the following season. When Shelby arrived he found a potentially serious threat lying in wait for his Cobras - the Corvette Grand Sport. Since Corvette drivers always thought of the Cobra as being a highly modified sports racer disguised as a production car, in order to run in the same class themselves they had always wanted Chevrolet to build a 'special' which could masquerade as a production model and turn the tables on Shelby. Hence the arrival of the Grand Sport which was a classic example of rule bending in an attempt to keep the Corvette competitive.

The Corvette GS was a fascinating car worthy of a chapter of its own and a wonderful example of what can be achieved via some very clever engi-neering carried out by the resourceful Corvette designer, Zora Arkus Duntov, a Belgian expatriate who had been employed by General Motors in 1956 to develop a fuel-injection system for the 1957 Corvette. He attained great status within General Motors by developing the initially troubled car into one of the most successful sports cars of all time and he was given his own laboratory for 'research' purposes, which meant he could do what he wanted as long as it could be labelled research.

During 1962 Duntov began to plan a special limited production of 125 cars which could contest the 1963-1964 championships. Since the FIA decreed that there would be no limit on engine size Duntov considered the possibility of outright wins at the fastest circuits. The one flaw in this plan was that in 1957 General Motors invoked a strict policy of no racing, although private owners could obviously do so if they wished. Word of Duntov's plans reached the ears of the top management at Chevrolet when an attempt was made to have the GS Corvettes homologated as production vehicles. Realising their policy was about to be broken they attempted to ward off the possible bad publicity, which would affect sales and axed the Grand Sports and all performance programmes overnight.

Sufficient parts had been produced to construct only five cars. (Since virtually every part of a Grand Sport had to be designed and built specially for it, there was no chance of any further examples being made), The car which could have taken Chevrolet to the top of international racing was killed be-fore it could show what it could achieve, although the five Grand Sports were smuggled out to people who could be relied on to race them effectively and to keep quiet about where they obtained them. The special 377 cu in engines were capable of delivering 485bhp at 6000rpm and accelerating from 0 to 100mph in 9 seconds.

It was these three cars which appeared at Nassau Speed Week accompanied by an unusually large number of Chevrolet engineers who just happened to be on holiday in the same place at the same time! The GS coupés won all three races in which they were entered while the Shelby team suffered from assorted mechanical problems. The engineers at Nassau used the experience to develop the cars still further and they secretly planned to upset the form book at Daytona and Sebring in 1964, but when pictures began appearing the the national press the management put an end to the matter once and for all. When teh GSs were later sold their wealthy amateur owners planned to race them against the Shelby Cobras. In one such instance, in February 1964, Shelby withdrew his team cars saying that as only five such Corvettes existed they could hardly qualify to run in the Production class and that he would only compete against them when sufficient numbers had been built. Thus a direct clash between Ford and Chevrolet was avoided, the losers, of course, being the paying spectators who would have flocked to the circuits to see such a duel (especially since Shelby had in mind a car

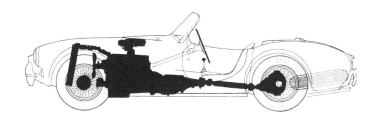

which would do to the GS what the GS could do to the 289 Cobra).

King Cobra

Carroll Shelby not only entered his roadsters at Nassau but also conceived a private project to race in the modified categories. Earlier in 1963 he purchased two British Cooper-Monaco chassis - basically an enlarged Formula 1 chassis with two seats and all-enveloping body with a mid-engine configuration. These cars were purchased with the intention of winning a series of races held on the West Coast each autumn, with valuable purses and equally valuable publicity, and possibly to contest the following year's USRRC Championship as well as being useful test-beds for new engines. (They also kept his mechanics amused, giving them something different to play with). Inaccurately referred to by the media as King Cobras, these cars were run and financed solely by Shelby American and were raced with some success until the Ford GT project took precedence. Driven by Dave MacDonald and Bob Holbert they both failed to finish in their last event, but at the prestigious *Los Angeles Times* Grand Prix at Riverside Dave MacDonald won, lapping the entire field. (The following year the race was again won by a King Cobra with Parnelli Jones at the wheel (Dave MacDonald having been killed during the Indianapolis 500 and Bob Holbert, distraught at the loss of his friend, immediately retired from racing). The King Cobra project was shortlived since, with the loss of its drivers, the approaching Ford GT project and the

rise to dominance of Jim Hall's Chapparal team, the cars were no longer competitive and were sold at the end of 1965.

Brock Creates The Coupé

The most immediate problem of the racing Cobra was undoubtedly its lack of good aerodynamics. The power output from the 4.7-litre engine was impressive (up to 380bhp before reliability failed) but the open, stubby bodywork held it back on the long straights, which was not surprising bearing in mind the age of the design. The Le Mans cars demonstrated the direction in which future Cobras would have to go with their long hardtops helping to raise their top speed along the Mulsanne straight, dictating that a coupé body was required to remain competitive for 1964 . Bodywork design was free in the FIA GT class, so long as the original chassis and engine were used.

It was not deemed practical to have AC design and build the new bodywork. As the British company liked to do things at their own pace, and because of the problems of liaising with a company 6000 miles away about a racing project which was required for the following season. This meant that the task of designing this new car fell to the multi-talented Pete Brock who, although he knew a little about bodywork design (but less about aerodynamics), was not afraid to turn his hand to any new challenge.

Using a clean sheet of paper and the chassis dimensions he drew up his idea of what a coupé should look like,

the final shape being dictated mainly by intuition. In the style of the Ferrari GTO the resulting design kept the frontal area as low as possible and the whole sleek shape kept obstructions to a minimum by recessing the side exhausts, fuel-filler cap and headlights. By lowering the centre of gravity improvements were gained in road-holding, this being achieved by realigning the radiator in a tipped forward position which allowed the nose and whole profile of the car·to be lower and smoother. Headlights were faired in under Perspex covers in the style of the then current E-Type Jaguar and the whole front section built in one piece which could tip forward to allow unimpeded access to the engine and front suspension. The opportunity was taken to lean the rather vertical windscreen further back to improve airflow over the car and over its long, gently sloping fastback which incorporated a top-hinged opening rear window down to the cut-off tail, usually referred to as a Kamm tail.

Somewhat disconcertingly for Pete Brock his initial drawings met with little enthusiasm from the Shelby American team, and even Carroll Shelby was moved to request a second opinion when he called on the services of an aerodynamics expert. He consulted his slide rule and confirmed their worst fears by claiming that such a design would require an engine of at least 450 horsepower just to achieve 160mph. This was bad news as the car was designed to use the 4.7-litre, 380 horsepower unit. The intention of the coupé project was to provide the Shelby

team with a car capable of 200mph to combat the Ferrari GTO which was capable of speeds well in excess of 160mph using an engine almost two litres smaller than the Cobra. However, with time running out and Pete brock quietly confident in his design Shelby crossed his fingers and gave him the green light.

In the tradition of the best Italian designers a full-sized plywood buck was constructed to give an accurate outline of the coupé, over which the aluminium panels were hand-formed and checked for accuracy before being welded into larger panels for fitting to the strengthened roadster chassis

which had been modified by the multi-talented Ken Miles. The first body was constructed at Cal Metal Stampings at Los Angeles with Shelby American completing the job back at base with the addition of inner panels and miscellaneous fabrication prior to installing the engine and electrics. A unique part of the Daytona design was the isolation of the tilted radiator from the engine compartment by surrounding it with a duct which removed hot air upwards and away from the engine. The carburettors were also shielded from engine heat and the large ducts ensured that as much cold air as possible entered the engine compartment. Also unique

to the Daytona was a method of refilling the radiator without removing the radiator cap, the mechanics plugging in a water line via a pressurised nozzle.

To the delight (and relief) of everyone at Shelby American and the consternation of the opposition, the coupé did everything asked of it with only minor modifications such as the later addition of a small GTO style spoiler to negate some lift at 170mph. Some rather un-aerodynamic treatment was necessary to force air into the car's very hot interior and to this end Plexiglass scoops were added behind each side window. The may have disturbed the airflow but helped prevent

Left: Daytona 1964. Dave MacDonald in '14' (CSX2287) prior to the start of the coupé's first ever race. A fire when leading took the car out of the race. Tommy Hitchcock is in Cobra '18' and Dan Gurney in '16'. Car '30' is the Ferrari GTO of Pedro Rodriguez/ Phil Hill. (Courtesy Autosport).

the driver passing out. (In fact, in one race at Sebring in 1964 Phil Remington resorted to driving a screwdriver into the roof to create a crude flap for additional ventilation).

The coupé was sprayed Shelby's favourite colour, Ford's Viking blue, with the oval Kamm tail painted half blue and half white to assist in race recognition. (The following season - 1965 - saw the cars painted the darker Guardsman blue with twin white centre stripes, giving the cars a much more business-like appearance). Interior trim was, of course, non-existent with all-aluminium panels painted matt black and best described as 'functional'. Large holes were punched into each end of the dashboard for ventilation and a substantial fire extinguisher - designed to fill the car with foam at the push of a button, and very necessary when one bears in mind that the 37 gallon fuel load did not have the benefit of a modern bag tank to protect it - fitted to the right of the driver. With the driver's seat mounted low on the floor between the chassis frame tubes it was necessary to fit adjustable pedals to accommodate different drivers.

By the end of the 1964 season four cars had been constructed, followed by a further two for 1965, and representing the entire coupé production prior to the GT40 programme taking prominence. Although the first car was an 'in-house' affair, the remaining cars were entrusted to Italian sheet-metal artisans at Carrozario Gran Sport in Modena and must have been very expensive to construct, bearing in mind their long journeys with the original

Top & above: Sebring 1964. Dave MacDonald/Al Holbert in CSX2287 heading for the coupé's first class win and fourth overall. The second picture shows the car later in the race after the 'installation' of Remington's roof vent. Gurney's Cobra worries a Corvette but, unfortunately, the Cobra was later destroyed in an accident. (Courtesy Autosport).

Overleaf: Carroll Shelby with Daytona Coupé CSX2602.

attempt to stay ahead of the opposition Ferrari pushed his luck to the limit by trying to pass off his mid-engined 250LM as a production model, but not even the FIA would accept that and refused homologation forcing him to continue with the GTO. When Shelby received homologation for his (six) coupés, Ferrari was not pleased.

Shelby kept the usual 289 blueprinted competition engine in these chassis since reliability was paramount in endurance racing and the extra speed was gained by the coupé body. Larger valves were used since it was hoped that these engines would be running at higher revolutions for longer periods than previously, while the 11.5:1 compression ratio was retained in case

chassis being shipped from Thames Ditton to Los Angeles where they were strengthened, back to Europe to the Modena workshop for their bodies and then back to Shelby American.

Coupé Homologation

To homologate the coupé Shelby took a leaf from Ferrari's book by listing the new body as a production variation since it used the same chassis, in the same way that Ferrari had earlier rebodied his stubby 250GT road car with the sleek GTO design and slipped it past the FIA inspectors, although the requisite 100 cars were never planned for production, the final total being in the region of forty cars. For 1964, in his

lower octane European petrol found its way into the tank. The proven 48mm IDA Webers and high-lift camshaft were retained.

The Cobra coupé was completed in time to contest the first round of the World Championship at the Daytona International Speedway on 16 February 1964 and this led to the car being referred to as the Daytona coupé by the press. Although never officially named as such the title was generally liked and it stuck. Driven by Bob Holbert and Dave MacDonald the car qualified well in practice ahead of four Ferrari GTOs and one 250GT, and actually led the race comfortably until the 209th lap when a tragic accident in the pits caused its retirement. Leaking fuel was ignited by burning grease which had been forced out of a seal damaged by severe overheating when the points stuck on the rear oil cooler pump: the car was enveloped in flames, causing serious burns to its mechanic, Jon Olsen.

The damage was too extensive to allow it to continue but it had done enough to prove its worth, and to underline its potential it was to finish fourth overall, winning the important GT class the following month at Sebring. Although other class wins were to follow during 1964 it was not until the 1965 season that the Daytona Cobra succeeded in wresting the World Championship from Ferrari's grasp, fulfilling Carroll Shelby's dream. Bearing in mind that only six cars were ever built, and on a comparatively small budget, they were outstandingly successful racing machines.

The English Coupés

To complete the story of the 'Cobra Coupés' mention should also be made of two further cars constructed in England, one made by AC themselves to contest the 1964 Le Mans race and another by the small but successful team run by John Willment, a Ford dealer and racing enthusiast based in Mitcham who not only campaigned his private Cobra team but also later had a 7-litre Cobra rebodied by Ghia in Turin as a closed road car.

Encouraged by their good showing at Le Mans in 1963, AC decided it would be a worthwhile exercise to enter the 1964 event, although they realised that a coupé body would be essential to raise the top speed along the Mulsanne straight if they were to have any hope of outright victory. Their coupé was designed entirely within the company by Alan Turner, a very talented engineer who could turn his hand to car design in much the same way as Pete brock. The Daytona and AC coupés had much in common but were designed quite independently. Both were built over a stronger 289 chassis and both used the coupé shape to utilise a large square internal roll-over cage with the AC version being even more substantial, and both cars had the driver's seat set low down on the floor on a level with the chassis frames, helping to keep the car's profile down to 41 inches high. The Turner designed (and Maurice Gomm constructed) bodywork was not dissimilar to the Daytona with its forward hinged bonnet section but was, in the view of many people, rather more elegant with

a slightly lower nose and longer flowing fastback roofline leading to a less truncated tail. The windscreen was set back at an even sharper angle, the wheelarch tops were squared off and the front wings incorporated louvres which did not appear on the Daytonas until the 1965 season. The general impression was that the AC coupé looked more like an elegant road car than its stubbier, purposeful American counterpart, and this was indeed the case since the AC was registered for the road.

M1 Madness

It was this car, BPH 4B, which gave Cobras in general and AC in particular more publicity than they could have wished for when the car was tested on the M1 motorway prior to leaving for the race. Unfortunately, somebody happened to mention the forthcoming test to a journalist who wrote a small piece in a national newspaper which, in turn, was picked up by other

"An M.1 two-tonner, Guv! Pulled in to have his brakes tested ... now he's been pulled out to have his brains tested!"

newspapers who were only too delighted to turn a minor incident into a national scandal.

Since no private test road of suitable length existed for driving cars at high speed for any period of time, AC decided to make use of the only stretch of three-lane motorway in the country, the newly-opened M1, by running the Le Mans car during the early dawn when the road was almost deserted. Naturally, great care was taken in choosing the correct time and weather conditions so they would not present a hazard to other traffic, and with drivers of the calibre of Jack Sears and Peter Bolton at the wheel risk was thought to be minimal. Using markers by the roadside and joining the motorway from service areas when sections of the road were judged free from traffic, the car was timed at just over 180mph and the drivers were impressed by the comfort, speed and stability. However, some days later the storm broke with countless self-ap-

"... PALE BLUE LEATHER UPHOLSTERY, INDEX NUMBER GRV 16, TRAVELLING NORTH AT JUST ABOVE THE SPEED OF SOUND!"

Left: The 'Willment Coupé' was powered by a 7-litre Holman and Moody Dual-Quad engine capable of providing 200mph at 6700rpm with a 2.9:1 axle ratio. (Courtesy Nostalgia).

Below left: Another of the M1 incident cartoons.

Below right: The heartbreak of Le Mans - AC's Coupé after the race. (Courtesy AC Cars).

pointed experts (who were not present at the time) pontificating loudly about the dangers of "racing on public roads". The Ministry of Transport, under attack at the time because of the many unpopular policies being introduced by the then current Minister, Ernest Marples, were happy to gain much-needed good publicity by taking the popular stand and attacking AC for their 'irresponsibility' and were relieved to have the press attack someone else for a change. The matter dragged on for quite some time while other manufacturers were quick to point out that they had never used the motorway for testing and would never dream of such a thing! AC were left virtually out in the cold with just about every organization imaginable rushing into print to disclaim any possible involvement, but Derek Hurlock recalls one letter among the many received from the chairman of a major British motor manufacturer voicing the usual opinion of their actions but ending with a small PS which said 'I wish we had thought of it first!'

However, the name of AC was now well known to the British public and the legend of the sheer speed of the Cobra was established. AC went to Le Mans knowing they had a car capable of running at high speed with stability and they were optimistic about their chances. The team was managed by Jeff Uren and the drivers were Jack Sears and Peter Bolton. They were to compete against the usual strong Ferrari entry plus two new Ford GT prototypes, as well as two Shelby American Daytonas and two private American Cobras entered by Briggs

Cunningham and Ed Hugus. Despite a promising display during practice and averaging over 120mph during the first three and a half hours of the race, the AC coupé was soon in trouble with fuel problems, visiting the pits on many occasions in an attempt to make the car run properly. (After the event a quantity of paper was found inside the fuel tank). However, during the 78th lap a tragic accident occurred when a tyre blew causing the coupé to hit a Ferrari which, in turn, spun into a run-off area which three French spectators had illegally entered. Sadly, all three were killed. The AC flew over the guard rails, lopping branches from the trees at a height of twenty feet, coming

to rest as a small crumpled heap in the woods. Peter Bolton emerged with only minor injuries which were soon attended to in hospital, but he was a lucky man and paid tribute to the massively strong roll cage which saved his life. The remains of the car were shipped home and later passed to AC club member, Barry Bird, of Aberdeenshire who undertook the long task of reconstruction with the help of the original wooden bucks over which the body had been formed. Eventually, by the mid-1980s, the long task was completed and the car once again ran under its own power.

The other British coupé was a rebodied Cobra roadster of the John

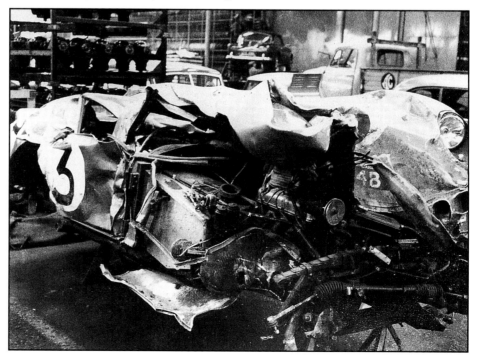

The Willment version of the Daytona Coupé, here at Crystal Palace and temporarily without white centre stripes.

Below and right: The car's whole front end hinged to give access to the engine. Transverse leaf springing gives away the Coupés origins.

Below right: Rear view shows recessed fuel filler, air outlets and small rear window compared to Shelby Daytona Coupé.

Willment team and was built in 1964 to compete in British club meetings as well as international events, even making the trek to the six-hour endurance races in South Africa and being driven

by such people as Frank Gardner. It was basically the team's own interpretation of the Daytona, looking very similar to the Shelby car but with a lower roofline.

It was quite successful, running in company with its fellow team car the ex-Le Mans Cobra 39 PH, and was often driven in British events by Jack Sears who gave the car an inaugural victory in the six-hour race at Oulton Park. Its colour scheme was red with twin white centre stripes and its busy racing schedule continued in club racing in the hands of Amschel Rothschild.

FIA Roadsters

The four Daytona coupés which

competed in the 1964 season were not alone, being competently backed up by a total of five 289 roadsters which were referred to as FIA roadsters and which, as their title implies, were specifically built within the FIA GT regulations. These Cobras were similar in many ways to the Le Mans cars of 1963, incorporating as they did many of the lessons learned during that event. These four cars (a fifth was later built to replace one which was destroyed) are the ones shown so often in motoring books and magazines competing in such events as the Targa Florio, and are well known for their colour scheme of Viking blue with a broad band painted the width of the car over the

The Willment Cobra Coupé in action.

wheelarches and nose, each car bearing a different colour for identification purposes - red, white and yellow with maroon being a later addition. They were among the first Cobras to appear with the soon to be familiar feature of wide flared wheelarches both front and back to accommodate their 6.5in front wheels and 7.5in rears.

A unique feature which appeared only on these cars were small dimples on the bootlid, hammered out from the inside to allow sufficient room to accommodate the regulation FIA suitcase which all cars had to fit inside their boots with the lid closed during pre-race scrutineering. Because of the square-edged rectangular shape of the official trunk the curved sloping boot would not quite close over it without the panel-beating.

Another new feature was the shape of the doors, the rear section of which was concave to follow the curve of the wheelarch, instead of the more usual smooth convex curve of the road car. Wheels were pin-drive, six-spoke magnesium Halibrands and beneath front grille twin scoops were added for additional cooling. A rather unofficial modification appeared to take place to the windscreens during races on long fast circuits when they would mysteriously tilt backwards a number of degrees, only to return to their proper, more vertical position later. (The Cobra's lack of wind-cheating ability dictated that small advantages were to be gained wherever possible).

Instead of the more usual overriders protecting the body the Le Mans style of quick-lift jacking points

was substituted in their place. Dashboards were redesigned to feature a large tachometer ahead of the driver with oil temperature, ammeter, fuel pressure and water temperature to the right and large oil pressure gauge to the left. The glove box was deleted.

Targa Florio '64

Following the first two events - Daytona and Sebring - the following round was a different race altogether, the classic Targa Florio in Sicily, a race originally run in 1906. Held on public roads running around the island made up of countless bends plus assorted hazards of all kinds, each lap lasted 44 miles. To the Americans these roads looked like farm tracks, barely wide enough to accommodate one car in places and running through villages and around unprotected cliff edges with the track surface a mass of pot-holes and loose rocks. Such a race was hardly suitable for the Daytonas with their limited ground clearance so the FIA roadsters made the trip alone with Dan Gurney, Jerry Grant and Masten Gregory heading the four Cobra entries. To add to the difficulties the team could not spare any mechanics, who were busy with the US Championship races, but help was obtained from various branches of Ford's European operations.

The cars built up an early lead in the race, running 1-2-3 at one stage, but proved something of a handful on such a circuit, especially around the tight mountain hairpins and the rough terrain caused a great deal of damage to the hard leaf-spring suspensions.

The Gurney/Grant car managed to claim second in the GT class and eighth overall although they failed to finish (the event was won, to the surprise of many, by the small, nimble mid-engined Porsche 904).

The following two events prior to Le Mans were at the Belgian Spa Circuit and the challenging German Nürburgring event. With little time between the Targa Florio and Spa, practice was short for the team before the event and, as a result, the cars failed to make any impression on the Ferrari GTOs. The Daytonas were once again entered for this race and, as the four cars did not have to make the journey up from Sicily, lack of practice was no real excuse. The GTOs went on to take the first four places in class. The only real lesson learned at Spa was to copy the small spoiler which featured on the GTO tails. This had the effect of adding much needed downforce to increase stability at very high speed, Bob Bondurant and Jochen Neerpasch finished ninth overall and sixth in class followed by Jo Schlesser and Richard Attwood eleventh overall and eighth in class. The FIA roadster's lack of top speed was a serious problem at such a fast circuit.

Nürburgring brought little more joy with GTO first in class and second overall, the twisting, bumpy course again providing the Cobras with many problems as it wound its 14 mile route around the Eifel mountains. Twelfth overall was their only reward since the mechanical gremlins were at work on all the cars - even the private entries - but Shelby's philosophy was to get all

his cars to the finish as long as they remained mobile. It really was just one of those days as far as the Cobras were concerned.

Le Mans '64

Such problematic events were good practice for the team since the next race on the calendar was the all important 24 Hours of Le Mans, where Shelby's Daytonas and roadsters would be joined by the lone AC coupé and the all important car of the future, the Ford GT. The fate of the AC entry has already been documented earlier - three Ford GT cars were entered, two having been constructed in only three weeks to replace cars lost in testing accidents, when the car's aerodynamic qualities were found to be less than perfect. All three cars were too new to be reliable, despite an impressive turn of speed during practice, and they displayed an ability to outrun Ferraris along the Mulsanne straight but the transmissions proved to be their Achilles' heel, the Colotti gearboxes being unable to cope with the continual demands put upon them during a long race. (It was evident to the assembled Dearborn executives that the cars needed attention from somebody with racing experience to transform their promising GTs into genuine race winners, so Shelby's involvement could be said to have stemmed from this event).

Having been left to carry forward Ford's Le Mans involvement, the Daytona car ran well at first with Chris Amon/Jochen Neerpasch running as high as fourth at one stage, but fell foul

original construction and testing. They continued their contract to build the cars since the low labour rates still favoured building small volume cars in Britain, much as Shelby would have enjoyed taking over the job).

Suspension mountings on the road cars were rubber and on the racing versions they were bronze, which gave a very hard ride but proved vital for competition work (later road cars which were used in weekend races were quickly converted to these bronze bushes). Tapered pre-loaded bearings replaced the early roller type in larger hubs along with bigger, strong splined driveshafts which were necessary to cope with the inevitable tyre-burning starts to which many of the cars were subjected. The whole suspension was adjustable for tailoring to drivers' preferences at the race circuit and, importantly, anti-squat characteristics were incorporated along the lines of the new GT40 to counter the enormous engine torque on take-off.

As testified by the Cobra's 0-100-0 time, it not only accelerated like nothing else but stopped as if it had run into a brick wall; just as well, bearing in mind the power on tap and the fact that not all owners were racing drivers. Girling 11.5in discs were fitted to the front and 10.75in to the rear

with, in the case of the race and semi-race cars, large, quick change brake calipers as used on the Daytona coupés and FIA roadsters.

The wheels were Halibrand aluminium; these were specially cast to a Pete Brock design when it was found that Shelby's original choice of wire wheels were not available in the size required, although the Halibrands, in fact, offered a stronger wheel. (Interestingly, the opposite situation occurred with the new Ford GT cars. They were forced to use Borrani wire wheels when suitable lightweight solid wheels couldn't be found). Competition Cobras used lighter magnesium Halibrands. The size of the wheels was 7.5in wide by 15 in and they were fitted with Goodyear Blue Dot 8.15 x 15 tyres.

The smooth, rather elegant style of the original roadster bodywork had, it would seem, found favour with everyone involved in the project as well as with the enthusiasts who bought the cars - somehow the Cobra was always destined to be an open car. The conversion to a fixed-head coupé style would have taken away a great deal of character (as the Le Mans hardtops demonstrated), although the idea of offering the 427 as a coupé was under consideration at one stage. One 427 Daytona

coupé was built in Modena on a longer chassis for potential race analysis but was converted to a normal Daytona to replace a car which was badly damaged when it fell from the front of a transporter. The coupé was never adopted for road use, mainly because it was thought unnecessary with the excess of power now available to overcome the poor aerodynamics of the traditional roadster bodywork. (Carroll Shelby had planned to offer a closed 'Aceca-Cobra' shortly after the car's original announcement but the project never came to fruition).

Mean Machine

At first glance the 427 seemed little changed from its predecessor but when it was looked at more carefully, or seen parked alongside a Mk II, the differences were substantial. Apart from the extra

Detail of the Halibrand alloy wheel fitted to the 427 model. Note wired spinner - more than one Cobra parted company with a wheel after a spinner worked loose ...

Left and far left. Two 427 Cobras. The striped car (COB 6039) has a successful hillclimb history.

Right: A Silverstone paddock awash with Cobras.

Shelby American 427 strikes a dramatic pose.

width and length the car was given a far more menacing and purposeful look with its wide, flared wheelarches extending over the tyres, particularly at the rear where competition cars had even wider flares to accept the massive racing tyres. The other main alteration was around the front of the car with a much larger oval grille cavity which even deleted the 289's steel grille in its attempts to ram as much air as possible into the engine bay, especially when racing. This huge 'mouth' served to enhance an already aggressive appearance. Each side of the intake were chrome overriders and on each

side of these was a vertical oval shaped grille which ducted cool air to the cockpit on road cars and air to the brakes when racing. (They were not, as one Australian journalist claimed, for keeping out low-flying Cessnas).

Bumper protection was again minimal with overriders front and rear or, if requested, a chromed oval guard could be fitted between the front overriders, following the shape of the grille to add a vestige of protection in car parks. When these grille bars were fitted the lower one was used to carry the number plate which was hinged to flip back into a horizontal position when the car was on the move (thoroughly illegal!) Many street cars used racing style wing mirrors and Perspex wind wings fitted to the windscreen

edges. The interiors were virtually un-changed, being trimmed in black to complement the range of six standard body colours. The only significant change in the cockpit was the location of the gearlever. With the longer engine being situated as far back as possible in the chassis a vertical gearlever would have been adjacent to the driver's el-

bow. To overcome this problem a long forward-facing lever was used with the plane of the shift pattern being at about forty-five degrees to the driver - down for first, up and back for second, etc., instead of being in a horizontal plane. It sounds decidedly awkward but owners soon adapted to the idea.

The heart of the matter, however,

lay beneath the bonnet. Shelby's deci-sion to aim for an even larger engine was founded on the all-American prin-ciples of 'there ain't no substitute for cubic inches' and 'if a big engine is good then a bigger engine is better'. With his team cars so tantalisingly close to winning the World Champion-ship at their first attempt with a rela-

A 427 engine with Weber carburettors.

Right and far right: Shelby American's advertising was never afraid to promote the Cobra's staggering performance.

Far right, bottom: Some believe that circular tail lights signify a model fitted with the 428 engine. In fact, Shelby's policy of 'fit what's available' ensures that no such generalisations hold true.

tively small engine, it stood to reason that larger engined cars would give Ferrari even more problems the following season, particularly at Spa (and Monza!) The 427 also had the desirable effect of gaining yet more publicity for his road cars as well as countering the

A right-hand-drive 427 in action at Goodwood.

marketing threat of Chevrolet's own 427 which found its way into the Corvette at about the same time. An equivalent engine in an even lighter car (2150lb, only 250lb more than the Mk II 289) ensured that the status quo would be retained by Cobra owners, who were obviously keen to be one step ahead of competition.

427, or is it 428?

What is not generally realised is that very few 427 Cobras were actually sold with 427 cu in engines - the majority came equipped with Ford 428 Police Interceptor engines. Originally the first four examples were ordered from AC with the intention of installing 390 cu in engines because of a supply problem with the new lightweight 427. Two of the first three chassis (CSX3001 and CXS3003) were destined to use the 390 while CSX3002 was built for a cast-iron 427 with automatic transmission and the fourth was to be

a coupé, again with a 390. CSX3001 was sent to Dearborn for evaluation and 3002 was fitted with a dry sump system for race testing by Ken Miles. These two cars lacked the final 427 shaped bodies, having the correct wide wheelarches but using a widened version of the 289 Cobra nose section, which fitted the wider chassis but lacked the large oval intake.

The first car completed was tested at the Silverstone circuit in its unpainted form in October 1964 (all 427s were supplied unpainted to avoid damage in transit) and the first order for 100 cars requested by Shelby American was for competition versions (CSX3001 to CSX3100) so as to meet FIA homologation demands. Road cars were destined to be built from CSX3101 onwards but Shelby's plans began to go awry when it became obvious that there was little hope of having the full number built and running before the end of 1964 to satisfy the FIA inspec-

tors prior to the start of the 1965 season. The 289 engined cars were therefore destined to do battle with Ferrari for another year.

427 S/C

Because of the prospect of having 100 full race 7-litre cars to sell, a quick change of policy saw the ending of the competition run at chassis number CSX3053 which meant that Shelby

Below: The cockpit of a racing 427. The revised dash panel layout incorporates a 160mph speedometer, large rev-counter and man-sized Hurst shifter.

but no fuel gauge. The massive tank used two fuel pumps, one mounted lower than the other to act as a reserve; when this cut in it was time to visit the nearest forecourt and empty a pump or two. The lucky owner also got the

had fifty-one racing bodied Cobras on his hands (discounting the prototypes). With little chance of selling that number of full race cars a new model was announced - the 427 S/C (meaning 'Semi-Competition' although often referred to as 'Street Competition') - and it is this model which really forged the Cobra's reputation as the fastest car ever offered for sale to the public. Being little more than a thinly disguised 480bhp racer it demanded a skilled driver at the wheel. Only a few additions were made to these cars for road work: a full width windscreen, an attempt to silence the mighty side exhausts and rubber bushes for the suspension. Remove these three items and you had a potential race winner.

The S/C was distinguishable from the standard model by the side exhausts, large fuel filler caps, wide rear arches, an oil cooler opening beneath the front grille, bonnet and brake scoops, front jacking points instead of overriders and a hoop roll bar behind the driver with a rear brace bar fitted to the frame inside the boot, where any remaining free space was occupied by the 42 gallon fuel tank and the huge spare tyre.

The 427 S/C was certainly not a practical road car but as something to stir the adrenalin it was in a class of its own and, indeed, it still is! Unfortunate passengers had to live with a large battery behind their seat and a lack of interior fitments such as glovebox, ashtray, lighter and door pockets, while the driver had a new dashboard layout to admire and memorise with all the items required by the racing driver -

genuine lightweight magnesium alloy wheels fitted, 7.5in at the front and 9.5in at the rear - supplied, of course, with Goodyear Blue Dot tyres at the front and very often racing covers on the rear.

In the following years many 427 owners converted or restored their Cobras to look like the 427 S/C but the genuine article was a unique and formidable machine.

A brace of 7-litres. In the foreground is the ex-John Woolfe race car and behind Rod Leach's car, the registration of which (COB 1) was later transferred to his twin-turbo 427.

Below right: Brands Hatch, May 1967. The Ginetta G4 of Peter Sutcliffe holds the inside line from John Woolfe's 427 as they enter Druid's Bend. (Courtesy Autosport).

Of the fifty cars for sale only sixteen were sold as genuine competition machines. They resembled the S/C model but beneath the bonnet had a 427 high-riser with aluminium cylinder heads, aluminium intake manifolds, 780 cfm 4-barrel Holley carburettor, lightweight valves and a 12.4:1 compression ratio. A 13 quart baffled sump was standard although a 14 quart dry sump system was available. For US club racing the cars were fitted with small aeroscreens, proper bucket racing seats with full harness, quick change brake kits and anti-roll bars front and rear. They retailed in 1965 for $9500 (try buying one for that today!) and went on to dominate the SCCA A-production class for the years 1965, 1966, 1967, 1968 and once more for luck in 1973.

With more than sufficient potential race cars available AC quickly began building road cars with rear wheelarches only large instead of enormous and a fuel tank reduced in capacity to a mere 18 gallons in order to offer a semblance of boot space. The changeover began from chassis CSX3054 although this particular chassis remained in Britain and later became the basis for the ill-fated Daytona Super Coupé. The next chassis, CSX3055, was sent to Italy to be clothed in a coupé body designed by Ghia and commissioned by Cobra team owner John Willment for use as a road car. The next forty-six chassis numbers were never used so the first cars to be sold in America began with CSX3101. At about this time the story of just what found its way under the bonnet becomes cloudy. What is certain is that the genuine Ford 427 NASCAR engine was not being produced regularly or in large numbers.

The 428 Engine

To overcome the engine problem the 428 Police Interceptor engines were used instead. This unit was a well known and proven engine and with a few Shelby modifications, was almost as fast as a genuine 427 with bhp up from Ford's stated 360 to Shelby's claimed 390, although many experts thought the true figure was nearer 355bhp. While people buying the S/C and competition models were guaranteed 427 engines, road cars were sold with 428s (until May 1967 when the genuine 427 became available once again) and very few owners could detect the difference. Even with the standard road exhaust system - which robbed the car of quite a few horsepower as the

105

An AC 289 restored to perfection by Autokraft. (Courtesy Nostalgia).

enthusiast in Denver, Colorado for a fraction of its cost and happily was completed to compete in American vintage races; Cobra pilot, Dick Smith, helped with the development driving.

Pete Brock left Shelby American during the winter of 1965, leaving a company much changed from the one he had joined a few years earlier. Instead of a gang of 'hot-rodders' building cars one at a time it was now virtually an extension of the Ford company, a research and development department looking after their racing programme and busily producing and selling a conversion of their only sports car, the Mustang.

The AC 289
The bad news was that the Shelby Cobra died in 1966 but the good news was that it was alive and well and being built in England, although under a different name.

The AC Cobra Mk II went on sale in England in 1964 when AC were able to find time to construct and complete the right-hand drive versions for a small but impatient band of enthusiasts, who were only too pleased to get their hands on such a fast car in spite of its high price. (The Jaguar E-Type,

its nearest competitor in terms of performance, was always substantially cheaper). Once the initial demand for Cobras was supplied sales settled down to a steady flow to cater for the British and european markets.

Although business was brisk for AC Cars for a number of years the directors knew that the project could not last for long. Progress was already leaving the Cobra behind when it was announced, but when the contract was finally terminated AC still needed a car to sell since their new model was still not complete. When the last Cobra left Shelby American Ford took over all rights to the name, leaving AC with a chassis production line, a number of body panels and a large number of wire wheels from the days of the Mk II. The result was the AC 289 sports car - a car with the assets of the 427 - namely the stronger chassis and coil suspension - but fitted with the smaller and altogether more sensible 4.7-litre 289 V8 engine. It utilised the larger bodyshell with the more efficient intake and wide wheelarches, making the narrow wire wheels which used the Mk II hubs and spindles look even narrower when fitted. The engine was slightly tuned which guaranteed more than adequate

performance, allied to a fuel consumption of about 15 to 16mpg. Inevitably it was still referred to as the Cobra.

The first AC 289, chassis COB 6101, was delivered on 27th April 1966 and was one of only twelve cars purchased during that year. It was soon overshadowed by the announcement of the AC 428, a classic Grand Touring car very much in the traditional european mould but one which used a lengthened Cobra chassis allied to a 428 7-litre engine and elegant body designed in Italy. It was a car which also offered tremendous performance but was deliberately aimed at a different section of the market, although it must have taken a number of sales

Far left and left: With the arrival of the MkIII Cobra, the American market went over to the 7-litre engine while AC kept faith with the 4.7-litre which they thought more suitable for their markets.

from the AC 289. Whereas the Cobra was frantic and hair-raising, the 428 was smooth and dignified, very much in the manner of the Jensen Interceptor, and offered a choice of manual or automatic transmission.

The AC 289 remained available until the end of 1968 when the last complete car was constructed - COX6125 - which was built for export. Two further cars were sold incomplete, 6125 and 6127, to bring the final total to twenty-seven cars. The reason that no more were made was simply that there was no demand for them. With safety legislation being introduced around the world, steadily increasing fuel costs and blanket speed limits appearing overnight, nobody was interested in a car from another era - virtually a modern vintage car, still determinedly using a fold-up soft top and steadfastly refusing to be seen dead using such modern niceties as wind-up windows - removable Perspex sidescreens were still good enough (and still as easily scratched). Driver and passenger comforts rightly took second place; the engine still produced as much heat as ever and drivers arrived at their destination with toasted feet, and an unframed rear-view mirror was still used instead of the nice, safe plastic framed ones used in all other cars. Seatbelts were fitted, of course, but only, one suspects, because the law demanded it.

So the car disappeared - even the famous Morgan company saw a drop in the sales of their equally traditional models around this time - and AC Cars either sold or scrapped the jigs, tools and dies needed for production. Seeminingly leaving no chance of resurrection at a later date.

Quick reflexes and a clear road are needed when testing the 289's limits. (Courtesy Motor).

Left and below: As well as its traditional British sports car interior, the AC 289 retained wire wheels.

Bottom: The inside of AC's 289 Sports sales brochure. Much is made of the Cobra's sporting successes.

SPECIFICATIONS

Curb weight, lbs.	2282
Distribution Front 51.53 % Rear 48.47 %	
Tyre size	185 x 15
Brake swept area	580 sq. ins.
Twin master cylinders. Girling disc brakes to front and rear wheels	
Engine Type Ford V-8 ohv High performance	
Bore & Stroke	4.00 x 2.87
Displacement c.c.	4727
Cu. in.	289
Compression ratio	11 to 1
Bhp at rpm	270 at 5800
Torque, lb. ft.	314 at 3400
Petrol tank	15 galls.

GEARBOX STANDARD SPECIFICATION

Borg Warner all synchromesh close ratio gearbox

GEAR RATIOS

1st 2.20 ; 2nd 1.66 ; 3rd 1.31 ; 4th 1.00

SUSPENSION

F: Ind., unequal-length wishbones with anti-dive and anti-squat, coil springs.
R: Ind., unequal-length wishbones with anti-dive and anti-squat, coil springs.
Rear axle, Salisbury limited slip 4.HU differential 3.45 to 1
Fuel consumption 18/20 mpg

DIMENSIONS

Wheelbase, in.	90.0
Tread f and r	55 x 54
Over-all length, in.	156
Width, in.	68
Height, in.	49
Ground clearance, in.	5
Turns, lock to lock	2.5
Turning circle, ft.	34
Hip room front seats, in.	22
Pedal to seat back, max.	38
Floor to ground, in.	8
Width between doors, in.	56

289 SPORTS

The A.C. 289 sports car has the same basic chassis, suspension and steering specification as the A.C. 428 Convertible, but is 6 ins. shorter in the wheelbase, and is fitted with a 270 bhp high performance 4.7 litre V.8 engine with mechanical tappets, and a manual all synchromesh 4-speed gear box. The new coil sprung suspension and chassis with 4 in. main tubes provide exceptional stability at high speeds with a comfortable ride on secondary roads at touring speeds.
The chassis and suspension of the A.C. 289 sports is exactly the same as that used in the construction of the 7-litre Cobra, which is also built at the A.C. Factory, Thames Ditton, and shipped to Shelby American in Los Angeles. Both cars owe their origin to the Mk. 1 Cobra, which for two years running was the winner of the coveted and highly disputed Manufacturers Championship competing with the fastest Works sports car teams from both sides of the Atlantic.

Past A.C. victories include :—
Sports Car Championship of America, 1963, with outright wins too numerous to list during that year.
First British car to finish the Le Mans 24 hour race, 1963.
First in the G.T. Class Le Mans 24 hour race, 1964.
First, Second and Third G.T. Class, 1964, T.T. Race. Goodwood.
Manufacturer's F.I.A. G.T. Championship. 1964 & 1965.

The remnants of Geoffrey Dempsey's AC289 (COB6104) are transported home after the car tangled with the Silverstone Armco. (Courtesy G. Dempsey).

Below right: COB6104 undergoes year-long restoration at Thames Ditton. (Courtesy G. Dempsey).

Of the final twenty-seven British Cobras eight were built as left-hand drive export models (hence the use of the COX reference instead of COB); two of these went directly to the USA in 1968 for those who had the missed the fun earlier. One or two cars were 'special orders' fitted with even higher specification engines and suspensions and built for club racing, the most famous of which was Geoffrey Dempsey's car registered GD100.

The final body/chassis unit was sold to Ian Richardson for racing in club events. He originally installed a 5.3 litre Chevrolet engine with which it performed with some success, but in 1971 he converted it back to 289 power and it was later sold and converted to a very fast road car.

AC constructed another five chassis (COX6138 to 6130 and COB6131 to 6132) which were special long chassis destined for Paramount Films Ltd. The first three were used in the film *Monte Carlo or Bust*, fitted with replica vintage bodies (two have since been built into 427 Cobras).

Two AC 289s were later converted to 7-litre specification by their owners, One of these cars being the ex-factory demonstrator, KPD150C (COB6106) which saw much sterling service in the hands of many motoring magazines, not to mention many of AC's potential customers.

The last word on the matter should really belong to the late Ken Miles who did so much development work with the early Cobras and the 427 in the USA. His opinion was that a well tuned, 289 engined, coil-sprung Cobra could prove to be a faster car overall, especially on a twisty road or race track, than the over the top 427. When the AC 289 production stopped the nicest, most effective and arguably the most desirable Cobra of all was gone.

VII

RACING
FROM 1965

With the advantage of hindsight the first (1964) season of international racing seems a remarkably successful one for the Cobra, coming as close as it did to toppling the all-powerful Ferrari marque at the first attempt. But, because it was so tantalisingly close to victory, the feeling at the time was one of understandable frustration, together with a renewed determination to take the fight to Ferrari and beat them fairly and squarely. The 'cancellation' of the Monza race was something that Carroll Shelby would not easily forget. Far from demoralising the Cobra team it served only to strengthen their resolve.

FIA Reject The 427

Although success was to follow it was not gained in quite the manner expected, for not everything went to plan. Shelby had two problems to contend with: first was the rejection by the FIA of his 427 engined cars because insufficient numbers were constructed and second was how to run his Daytona coupés in the GT class without defeating the GT 'prototype' cars of the Ford Motor Company. Ford were happy to underwrite Shelby's racing expenses and to assist with equipment and technology, but the Cobra's place in the scheme of things was to act as back-up to the theoretically faster factory prototypes and to either follow them home or take up the running if they failed. They were not intended to beat the Ford GT, only the Ferraris which ran in the same class.

To make life even more awkward Ford approached Shelby with an offer to manage the GT programme and turn their fragile computer designed cars into race winners, a feat which had eluded the motor giant despite the millions of dollars poured into the project. It was the proverbial 'offer you can't refuse' for Carroll Shelby. Although the Cobras were closest to his heart the thought of running a team of potential race winning cars held great appeal.

Ford had, of course, been suitably impressed with the manner in which he ran his Cobra team and the fact that he had won Le Mans only a few years previously carried a lot of weight within Ford, since it was this event they needed to win for the publicity value.

Shelby was not the only one to have trouble with the FIA inspectors prior to the 1965 season, for Ferrari was determined to have his 250LM model recognised as a road car and to run it against the Daytonas in the GT class instead of against the Ford GT in the prototype category. He knew that it would run rings around Shelby's coupés but, like Shelby, he had not built the necessary 100 cars to qualify. The only other Ferrari available for 1965 (the GTO being considered uncompetitive) was the 275GTB4A, a true road car which existed in sufficient numbers but which was at the centre of a strange argument concerning its true weight, at which it had to be homologated.

The debate continued for so many months that it became too late for Ferrari to prepare the car for international racing the following season. Ferrari and his followers claim that he was dealt with harshly by the FIA,

The Shelby publicity caravan which toured the USA after the team won the 1965 World Championship for makes. The forty-foot trailer carried a 427, GT40, Daytona Coupé and Mustang GT350R to most major US cities, handing out photos and decals. (Courtesy SAAC).

while his rather more cynical detractors were of the opinion that he never intended to enter his GTB against the Daytonas since he felt he stood little chance of success (although ironically a private GTB finished ahead of the decimated Shelby entries at the all-important Le Mans event). Whatever the truth of the matter Ferrari officially withdrew from the GT category of the World Championship for Constructors, laying the blame at the door of the FIA. Thus Shelby was offered an excellent opportunity to win the title, although he would still have to face stern opposition from the many GTO models in the capable hands of private teams, many of which employed the services of top rank drivers.

With the large amount of extra work and development to be undertaken by Shelby American the mechanics had only enough time to refettle the existing Daytona coupés and to construct a further two for the coming season. Thus 1965 began where 1964 left off. It was all down to the Daytonas to win the World Championship since the roadsters could no longer be considered competitive in international events, nor could the busy mechanics cope with GTs, Daytonas and roadsters at the same race. (Roadsters were en-

tered in various Championship events but in the hands of private owners; the 427 Cobra raced in National SAAC championship events in the USA).

1965 Season Opens

Once again the season opened at the

The Schlesser/Bondurant Daytona at Sebring 1965. Note the shielding for the carburettors. (Courtesy Autosport).

Daytona Speedway with two Shelby-prepared GTs and four Daytona coupés. Two private Cobras were also entered. To the relief of all concerned success was immediate, thanks to efficient preparation and team management. A Ford GT won the race driven by Ken

Miles and Lloyd Ruby, followed by a Daytona doing its job to the letter by coming home second and, importantly for Carroll Shelby's aspirations, winning the GT class. Jo Schlesser and Hal Keck were the drivers. Another Ford GT was third while Daytonas took fourth and sixth, split only by a Porsche 904. One of the private Cobras came home a creditable tenth.

The 12-hour race around the airport runways of Sebring, Florida, followed but the climate proved to be the talking point of the race. The event began in hot and humid conditions but an approaching storm cloud unleashed a downpour of tropical proportions. To the credit of all concerned the race continued although the circuit was more suited to boats. Daytonas shipped in great quantities of water but kept splashing round despite being embarrassed by their excess of power in the conditions. Suddenly the cars in the smaller classes were proving as fast or faster, provided their electrics were not drowned, and drivers of Austin-Healey Sprites found themselves capable of lapping the big cars who discovered that a top speed of 30mph on massive racing rubber to be dangerously fast! Sebring became a lake, waist-deep in places, with a torrent of water pouring down the pit road washing away equipment and spare wheels. An unlucky Cobra mechanic was found just in time in a deepening pool of water, having trodden on a live cable carrying power to a trailer. One driver stepped unharmed from one half of a Grifo GT when it sailed into a bridge and was cut neatly in two.

Eventually the rain abated and the status quo was restored, but the Ford GT had to accept second best on this occasion to Jim Hall's effective Chapparal, although the Miles/ McLaren GT came home second ahead of David Piper's LM Ferrari. The Jo Schlesser/Bob Bondurant Daytona won its class by finishing fourth overall - the GT Ferraris all failed to finish - to give Shelby American two maximum scores with which to begin the season. Shelby went on to Europe with 28.8 points to Ferrari's 4.8.

Alan Mann

The European campaign brought the introduction of a new approach to preparing the cars so far from home. With guidance from Ford, Carroll Shelby combined resources with Alan Mann, who became responsible for the preparation and entry of three of the Daytona coupés from his base in Byfleet, England. This enabled Shelby American to concentrate on the all-important Ford GT cars and lessened the workload on the mechanics although, when possible, the team did enter its own Daytonas and drivers, for example at Le Mans.

Alan Mann was a relatively young (29 in 1965) but astute engineer whose team of mechanics built up a formidable reputation in England for their ability to construct fast and reliable saloon cars. Alan Mann himself proved to be a team manager to be reckoned with, capable of preparing his cars to comply with the letter of the regulations, even if they went a little beyond the spirit. If he could spot a loophole he knew how to use it to his advantage without falling foul of the scrutineers.

The first project which brought him to the attention of Ford of Great Britain was his preparation of the Ford Cortina MkI which was transformed within his workshops into the fastest saloon car in the country. Impressed by his obvious ability and standard of preparation he was asked to prepare a Ford to send to the 1963 12-hour Marlboro saloon car event in Maryland. It was at this event that he came into contact with John Holman, one half of the famous Holman and Moody engine tuning company. This later led to an unexpected offer from Holman to prepare the Ford Falcon team cars due to enter the RAC Rally. Naturally, he jumped at the opportunity, despite never having been to a rally, and managed to make the large cars reasonably competitive, which was no small achievement.

He also prepared the same cars for the following Monte Carlo rally and, despite failing to take an outright win, the resulting publicity helped to boost falling sales of the Falcon back in America.

Despite this interesting diversion the Alan Mann team kept plugging away with the faithful Cortina, taking a joint victory in the European Touring Car Championship in 1964. They also prepared and homologated Ford Mustangs for a works assault on various European road rallies, taking a class win in the Tour de France. Generally, the American sports and saloon cars were not suited to the style of European events but Ford were suitably

impressed by Alan Mann's abilities; so much so that they included him amongst their team of experts to help sort the GT40.

Monza 1965

Entrusted with three Daytona coupés he also brought in his 'own' drivers from England who were used to working with his team and his cars. When the European part of the season began, ironically it was at the Italian banked circuit of Monza, the first occasion that the Daytonas had raced there. The rather rough circuit made driving the cars a handful at high speed but they managed first and second in class, eighth and ninth overall, driven by Bob Bondurant/Allen Grant and the British pairing of Sir John Whitmore/Jack Sears. Ferrari took third in the GT class in front of their own *tifosi*, so a certain amount of revenge was gained for the previous season's suspect cancellation. Beating any Ferrari on home ground always adds to the

sweetness of the victory but the Italian fans were doubtless more than pleased that Ferrari prototypes took first and second overall, beating the Bruce McLaren/Ken Miles GT40 back into third. A British Shelby Cobra roadster entered by Radford Racing came home in twelfth place, It was an impressive debut for the Alan Mann team despite having to run the coupés below their normal pace for much of the event in order to get to the end safely and win their class.

One week later - May 1st - saw the Daytonas again take a class victory at the Tourist Trophy held at the beautiful Cheshire circuit of Oulton Park. The race was run, for some strange reason, in two parts and saw six Cobras entered, only one of which was a Daytona for Jack Sears wile the other Alan Mann entry was a roadster for Sir John Whitmore. Radford racing had two roadsters for Allen Grant and Neil Dangerfield/John Sparrow. Roger Mac drove the Chequered Flag car (GPG 4C)

while Australian Frank Gardner drove the Willment team's 'Daytona-replica' coupé (39 PE). Sears' Daytona refused to start on the grid and immediately incurred a two lap penalty for a push start and began the race from the back. With Roger Mac's car losing a wheel and John Whitmore stopping for a new rear tyre, the best placed Cobras in the first heat were Frank Gardner's Willment coupé in seventh place followed by Whitmore and Grant with Sears back in fifteenth place.

Heat two saw Sears finish third ahead of Mike Salmons' GTO to take seventh overall, while Whitmore's sixth place netted fourth overall with Allen Grant sixth. Gardner dropped to eleventh place and took tenth overall. The race saw a disputed victory for Denny Hulmes' Brabham BT8 over the Lola T70 of David Hobbs. No Ford GT40s or works Ferraris were entered since only the GT category counted towards the World Constructors Championship. On this occasion a Cobra roadster had

won title points instead of the Daytona.

Ahead of Ferrari

At this stage the Cobras had taken maximum scores from the first four events and led Ferrari by 52.2 to 17.8 points. Ferrari narrowed the gap at the next round, the Targa Florio, by winning their class in the absence of the Cobras: it was thought wise to give the event a miss following their experience the previous year. It was also considered wise to avoid the problems of shipping the Daytonas from England to Sicily and then to Belgium for the next race at Spa all within two weeks, during which time the cars would require virtually a full rebuild after the pounding they would receive at the Madonie circuit.

Even though the Chequered Flag Cobra had a tiger in its tank, it failed to start at Spa. Here it's in the transporter. (Courtesy Autosport).

The GTOs proved very fast on the long Belgian circuit, especially in the hands of Peter Sutcliffe, but Sir John Whitmore caused a sensation during practice by taking the Alan Mann Daytona round half a second faster

than the time achieved by the eventual race winner, Willy Mairesse in his Ferrari prototype 250LM. Both Whitmore and Bondurant seemed certain of victory in their class but fate intervened when Whitmore collided with an errant private Cobra which moved into his path, forcing his eventual retirement. One lap later the engine of the Bondurant car went onto seven cylinders but he continued almost as quickly, even closing on Sutcliffe's GTO at the end, but the Ferrari driver held on to cross the line five seconds ahead. To the surprise of all parties, however, both Ferraris and Cobras were beaten in their class by the Dutch driver Ben Pon who drove an inspired race in a Porsche 914GTS. The Cobra-Ferrari score had now closed to within sixteen points with the next round being held at the long, tortuous Eifel mountain circuit of Nürburgring.

Alan Mann entered two Daytonas for Bob Bondurant/Jochen Neerpasch and Jack Sears/Frank Gardner while a third Daytona appeared in the colours of Ford France and was driven by Jo Schlesser/André Simon. After recording promising times in practice the Cobras at one stage fell behind the GTO of Mike Salmon until he had a halfshaft break as he entered the pits. After his retirement the Cobras ran out comfortable class winners once again

with Bondurant first (seventh overall) and Sears second (tenth overall). The Ford France car finished in twelfth place. Overall victory went to the Surtees/Scarfiotti Ferrari 330P2 as the Ford challenge was decimated by unreliability, the Phil Hill/Bruce McLaren car being the sole surviving GT40 in eighth place.

As was the case during 1964 the Rossfeld hillclimb also counted towards the World Championship and once again Bob Bondurant demonstrated his mastery of this type of event with another comfortable victory, collecting another nine points. However, the next event was the big one and a world apart from any hillclimb - the 24 Hours of Le Mans.

Le Mans '65

The 1965 event had a fantastic line-up with eleven Ford powered cars facing a total of twelve Ferraris. Five of the six existing Daytona coupés were entered, two under the Shelby American banner for Dan Gurney/Ronnie Bucknam and Bob Johnson/Tom Payne, one Alan Mann prepared car entered by AC Cars Ltd for Jack Sears/Dick Thomson (a Corvette expert), the Ford France car for Schlesser/Grant, one Scuderia Filipinetti car for Peter Harper/Peter Sutcliffe and finally the Willment coupé for Frank Gardner/Alan Rees. The main

interest with regard to overall victory lay in the two formidable GT40 models which appeared with 7-litre engines (6982cc) and were known to be capable of over 210mph. Phil Hill achieved fastest lap in the race, no less than 11.7 seconds quicker than his record set the previous year in a 4.7-litre model. Despite their speed the two month old cars lacked sufficient race preparation and the whole Ford effort collapsed, the only surviving car being the Alan Mann AC entered Daytona of Sears/Thomson which finished in eighth place some 600 kilometers behind the winning NART Ferrari 250LM of Masten Gregory/Jochen

Canadian Cobra driver Tom Payne was one of the last of the 'gentleman' drivers taking part in races wearing shirt, tie and sports jacket. (Courtesy Autosport).

Below: Reims, 1965. The Schlesser/ Bondurant Coupé en-route to yet another class victory. It was this event which sealed the World Championship for Shelby American. (Courtesy Autosport).

Rindt. Another 250LM was second but most importantly the third placed car took the GT category from the Cobras, not on this occasion a GTO but the 275GTB of Willy Mairesse/Beurlys - a very impressive result.

The Sutcliffe/Harper Cobra lost a rod through the side of the engine along the Mulsanne straight and the Gurney/Grant car finally broke a crankshaft damper after a troubled run. Johnson/Payne retired with the temperature off the clock and all six of the Ford GT40s retired. It was a major victory for Ferrari despite the fact that success was gained by private entries following the failure of their own works-supported cars, but the Cobra still led the Championship by 95.4 to 66.7 points.

Appropriately for the Shelby American effort the next race was held on 4 July at the French circuit of Rheims. The GT40s were withdrawn

from this round And the Americans shipped the cars home to concentrate on ironing out the problems and trying to find some sort of reliability. It also heralded an even more determined attack on Le Mans the following year. With a change of rules to allow a car to be classified as a GT Production model when only 50 examples had been built, as opposed to the 100 examples previously required, Ford decided to use the GT40 to win the World Championship in 1966 by building the requisite number of cars. The necessary dollars were made available.

An overall victory for Ferrari at Rheims was inevitable, barring a major disaster, while in the GT class three Cobra coupés faced three GTOs, one of which failed to start. Piloting the Alan Mann coupés were Bondurant/ Schlesser and Sears/Whitmore while Frank Gardner/Innes Ireland drove the Willment coupé. The 12-hour race began in darkness at the unsociable hour of 11pm and at the first refuelling stop the Willment car refused to start, despite an hour spent trying to coax it into life.

The Sears/Whitmore car led the other Daytona for much of the race until it threw a rod; drastic surgery in the Alan Mann pit saw the offending rod and piston removed and the car rejoined the race to rumble and bang

round for another five hours to take ninth place at the flag. The long, fast circuit was well suited to the Daytonas but they could not live with the prototype Ferraris which took the first four places, although the Bondurant Cobra was fifth and comfortably won its class, with Sears second and the GTOs failing to last the distance. This result meant that the Shelby American cars had taken the World Manufacturer's title at only their second attempt, being the first American team to win such a Championship. That it was achieved on the Fourth of July helped to make the victory that much sweeter.

Only three rounds remained; the *Coppa di Anna* in Italy, which was run for GT cars only as a curtain-raiser for the Mediterranean Grand Prix. After leading the field Bob Bondurant had a spin plus two pit stops which put his Daytona third behind two Ferrari 250LMs (these cars running as GTs, thanks to a specially formulated category found only in Italy). Jack Sears finished fourth ahead of three GTOs.

The penultimate event was another hillclimb, the Swiss Ollar-Villars climb in the Rhone valley, but the only works backed cars came from Alfa-Romeo, Alpine and Porsche although another private Ferrari collected another nine points.

Cobra Takes '65 Championship

The season closed as it had begun, in America, this time at the Bridghampton circuit where Bob Johnson took a final class win for the Cobra, although without any Ferrari opposition. He took fifth overall but was two places behind a 427 roadster driven by Skip Scott/ Dick Thomson which, not being homologated, was unable to qualify for any points but certainly demonstrated the larger engine's potential.

The final tally was 133.2 points for the Cobra against Ferrari's 80.9, although the Championship was decided on the best seven results, making the official score 90.3 to 71.3. Thus the FIA-sanctioned *Championnat des Constructeurs* Division III crossed the Atlantic for the first time. Carroll Shelby considered this success to be the highlight of his career to date, surpassing even his own Le Mans victory.

In retrospect the victory was devalued a little by the withdrawal of the official Ferrari works entry in the GT class which left the door open for the Cobra assault.

On the credit side of the Shelby American success was the fact that they scored a major victory with a car and team which had only been in existence for a little over three years: added to which was the fact that the car in question was hardly the most sophisticated on the circuit. To build a car which went as fast as the Cobra did, yet with a transverse leaf suspension design (virtually a museum piece by the mid-sixties), was major feat in itself. Full credit must go to Carroll Shelby, Phil Remington, Ken Miles and

The victorious 7-litre Chequered Flag Garage Cobra of Bob Bondurant/David Piper laps the Sunbeam Tiger of Unett/Calcutt in the 1966 Ilford Trophy race at Brands Hatch. The Hobbs/Salmon Ferrari 250LM follows. (Courtesy Autosport).

the rest of the team for producing such a rapid piece of machinery from what most people saw as such an unpromising beginning. While the credits are being handed out a word should be said for the heroes who actually drove the Daytonas to the World Championship. These were not the easiest of cars to handle, requiring a large dose of sheer talent and courage to hurl around a circuit for an hour or more. The track shots of the time illustrate the angles of drift required to push these cars through corners at competitive speeds, with large amounts of power applied to hang the tail out at the required angle.

Finally a word of credit should go to Alan Mann Racing Ltd of Byfleet, England who were responsible for entering and preparing the coupés for eight of the eleven rounds of the Championship. Regrettably, the extent of Alan Mann's involvement seems to have been overlooked since that time but, without doubt, he played a crucial role in this American success. The following year he was given an assembly contract for the GT40 and continued to dominate British and European saloon car racing for a number of years with his Cortinas, and later the Ford Escort.

1966: The Cobra Retires from International Racing

The next season was to be the year of the GT40. The Daytonas were forced to bow to progress and were retired, having achieved their objective, so the age of the Cobra was over as far as international racing was concerned.

The early death of the 427 Super Coupé project also serves to demonstrate the speed at which progress was being made in racing car design for, by now, the front-engined sports car was a thing of the past on the race track. In the same way that Formula 1 cars changed the position of their engines, so sports cars followed their lead.

The Snake still ruled the circuits at club level, however, as well as continuing its domination of the American National Championships. Although Shelby American no longer contested the SAAC events some factory support found its way to competent private entrants who proved capable of keeping the 427 Cobra ahead of the opposition in general and the Corvette in particular. (Ford money for the Cobra had long since dried up for the simple reason that they had been so successful. Having served their purpose of promoting Ford's sporting image around the USA, there was no point in spending any further money on them and, as of May 1965, the Ford Motor Company officially withdrew their support of the Shelby American 289 roadsters).

During the 1967 season the Cobras continued as before, to the frustration of General Motors, who by now felt obliged to lend some weight to teams who raced Corvettes, most notably the Owens-Corning team of Jerry Thompson and Tony DeLorenzo (Thompson was a Chevrolet engineer and DeLorenzo the son of a GM vice president, while Owens-Corning sup-

plied the fibreglass from which the Corvette was built). These partly works-supported cars gained some success against the unsponsored Cobras but at the end of the season it was still the Cobra which took the National titles. At the end of each season the Sports Car Club of America held a national event which brought together the winners of each geographical division in each respective class at one venue to decide the overall champion. This event was known as the American Road Race of Champions and in 1967 it was held at Daytona. Ed Lowther from Pennsylvania qualified his 427 on pole and led the race until a flat tyre cost him a lap, whereupon Dick Smith of Fresno, California, took up the fight with the Owens-Corning Corvette and, after a long, high-speed battle, crossed the line a nose ahead to win the title, with Ed Lowther fighting back to third.

1968 saw a repeat performance of the preceding year. In spite of the best efforts of the Owens-Corning team the lighter Cobras always proved just a shade faster and, at the season's end ARRC championship, a 427 driven by Peter Consiglio again defeated the Corvette with two more Cobras taking third and fourth. A 289 Cobra driven by Don Roberts comfortably won the event for smaller engined sports cars, once again ahead of an Owens-Corning Corvette.

In 1969, however, the trend was to be reversed. The Corvette was at last able to return to the winners' circle with the Thompson-DeLorenzo car win-

David Purley (in sheepskin coat) began his racing career in this Modsports Cobra which was later destroyed at Brands Hatch. Note the unorthodox wheelarch extensions and Pearce alloy wheels.

Below: Before Cobras became super-valuable collectors' items, owners used them in all manner of motorsport. Here, Martin Hilton takes part in a production car trial in 1971 - attempting to climb as far as possible up a muddy hill before traction is lost.

genuine 427 engine retailing in excess of $2000 - a lot of money in 1970. There was no hope of any factory support via the 'back door' since there was no longer any factory and therefore no back door for special parts to find their way to private owners. To add to their problems Cobra drivers now faced another Corvette devotee who appeared on the scene in 1970 with his legendary lightweight Corvettes and who was to dominate the national scene for many years to come - the innovative John Greenwood.

Despite this reversal in fortunes and the understandable reluctance of many owners to risk damaging their prized race cars, the occasional 427 would be prepared for an expensive season of racing and would remind the Corvettes what a 7-litre Cobra could achieve. In 1973 an eight year old 427 driven by Sam Feinstein once again took the ARRC title at Road Atlanta to revive memories of the classic battles of a few seasons before. Sam even contested the 1976 events but without the same success.

Naturally, Cobras also contested club races on the other side of the Atlantic around the British circuits and also appeared regularly in sprints and hillclimbs. One of the first cars campaigned by former Grand Prix driver David Purley was a 289 Cobra which he raced as part of a two-car Cobra team with his cousin Derek Ridler. He campaigned the cars in modsports events until a foggy end of season club event saw the car reduced to scrap metal at the foot of the notorious Paddock Hill bend at Brands Hatch,

ning its class at the ARRC finals, although it was challenged only by two 427s, one of which did not finish and the other cold only manage a lowly sixth place. Matters could only get worse since by 1970 Shelby was completely out of racing and the company was about to close. Ford's attention was fixed elsewhere to the extent that they were attaching the Cobra name (which they owned) to all manner of un-Cobra like vehicles. Racing a 427 in national events was rapidly becoming a very expensive proposition with a

Brighton Speed Trials 1977. The ex-Le Mans Cobra (39 PH) waits its turn for a run along Madiera Drive. On the right, in car '136' is Brain Angliss with the ex-John Woolfe full-race 427.

John Woolfe endeavours to keep his 427 ahead of a GT40 in a 1966 club event. (Courtesy Autosport*).*

following an unsuccessful attempt to overtake another car round the outside. David escaped serious injury despite being thrown about in the car.

British modsports races were dominated in the early seventies by Shaun Jackson driving the Gurney-Weslake engined ex-Chequered Flag Cobra and he enjoyed many dices with

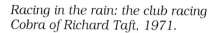
Racing in the rain: the club racing Cobra of Richard Taft, 1971.

The dangers of British club racing: at this 1971 event the Cobra assaulted a Ginetta from the rear, leaving sump (oil pan) marks on the Ginetta driver's helmet!

the similar car of Richard Taft. They both gave the effective Jaguar E-types and some indecently quick MG Midgets a good run for their money. Later, Mick Smith took over the Chequered Flag car and, once accustomed to the power, carried on with the good work. He was frequently joined by the much newer Cobra of Ian Richardson who purchased the last AC 289 body/chassis unit built by the factory in the last months of 1968 (COB6127). With a 5.3-litre Chevrolet engine installed (!), this immaculate blue 289 was a joy to watch and brought a touch of glamour to many an otherwise dull event. The ex-Willment coupé was another car rarely away from the racing scene and it seems never to have left the circuits, appearing regularly in the hands of

Amschel Rothchild prior to its sale at the end of 1982.

In the USA the main purpose of historic races is to show the cars to the public and allow owners to stretch the legs of their 'investments' above the soporific 55mph speed limit. However, racing in the strict sense of the is not encouraged and any form of body contact between 'competing' cars is total anathema. Not so in the UK and Europe, however. To attend a race meeting in England, especially a round of the Inter-Marque Challenge (a closely contested series of races pitting a team of ACs against teams of Aston Martins, Jaguars, Ferraris and Porsches) is to witness committed sports car racing at its best. To stand close to the action during the opening laps is to appreci-

ate that the owners of these valuable machines are not there to pose; in the vast majority of cases the commitment is total, and even above and beyond the call of duty!

As previously mentioned the two most campaigned Cobras in British club racing were the Mk II cars of John Atkins and Martin Colvill. COB6058, the mount of John Atkins, remained victorious during 1983, winning 9 out of 10 races entered but losing the overall Championship by one point. 1984 was the year when age began to tell in the form of reliability problems: 7 starts but only 3 victories. It was time for a winter rebuild and in 1985 both owner and car rolled up their sleeves and sorted out the opposition with a 10 out of 10 score. The problem with such dominance is that it spoils the party for the rest of the players - the Cobra went into semi-retirement during 1986 although the occasional outing brought the almost inevitable victory. The combination was discouraged from further participation (the duo had nothing else to prove). The only other route was to modify (and ruin) the car by entering other Championships, but this was never going to be allowed to happen mainly because this was still a 370bhp road car used for at least 5000 road miles per year, and almost always driven to and from events. In 5 years and 88 races it scored 36 victories, 6 seconds and 7 class victories, with 29 pole positions, 14 lap records and 2 Championships.

In December 1984 car and driver headed out to the Bahamas to take part in a series of invitation races

and classic vehicles started at Tower Bridge in London and headed out to Italy and back, using many of the famous roads of classic rallies of years gone by such as the fantastic Stelvio Pass, a road comprising 48 bends climbing an Alpine pass. A wide range of vehicles entered - Mini Coopers, Lotus, Cortinas, E-Type Jaguars and any number of sedate saloons whose crew members were more intent on sampling every restaurant and watering hole en route than in setting competitive times. Somebody forgot to tell John Atkins that this was meant to be a gentle cruise around Europe: the Cobra headed off into the distance and was never heard (and hardly seen) again by the following competitors. AC Cobras were never intended to go around winning rallies so, while the Atkins entry was accepted the following year, it was on the condition that he could drive any car he wanted apart from a Cobra. He did start, in a Triumph TR4A, and drove the route with a leg in plaster, the legacy of a skiing holiday.

Martin Colvill campaigned his ex-

against European and American opposition around the streets of Freeport, reviving the famous 'Speed Week' last held seventeen years previously. The clash of two cultures became apparent and the Americans were treated to a first-hand view of a Cobra being driven with total commitment. The experience was not one that many of them relished as they had not witnessed this

type of racing before. It was an interesting experience (and a week long party) but in the interests of car preservation the experiment was not repeated.

With a great circuit career behind it COB6058 had one more surprise up its exhaust: suddenly, in 1988 it became a historic rally car. The first run of the 'Pirelli Marathon' for historic

A one-time road car, the Bell and Colvill Cobra was developed over several seasons into a very fast race winner. In this picture it's still fitted with wire wheels.

Below: Moving off the line is a matter of keeping wheelspin under control ...

Bottom: Cobra combat: COB6040A holds off CSX2269.

road car CSX2131A (built as s spare race chassis for John Willment Racing, although never used) and continued his programme of modification. He began the car's racing career with 271bhp under the bonnet and retired it from racing in December 1985 with the engine giving 452bhp. Mathwall Engineering took care of the Gurney-Weslake V8 and in nine years and 6000 miles of competition motoring it did not suffer any engine problems. Out of 107 races it finished on 102 occasions, collecting 44 class wins and 12 outright victories. It should be pointed out that in its racing life it was usually pitted against far more mod-

Martin Colvill in action at Brands Hatch. (Courtesy Mike Fear).

John Atkins fights off a Porsche at Druids Bend, Brands Hatch.

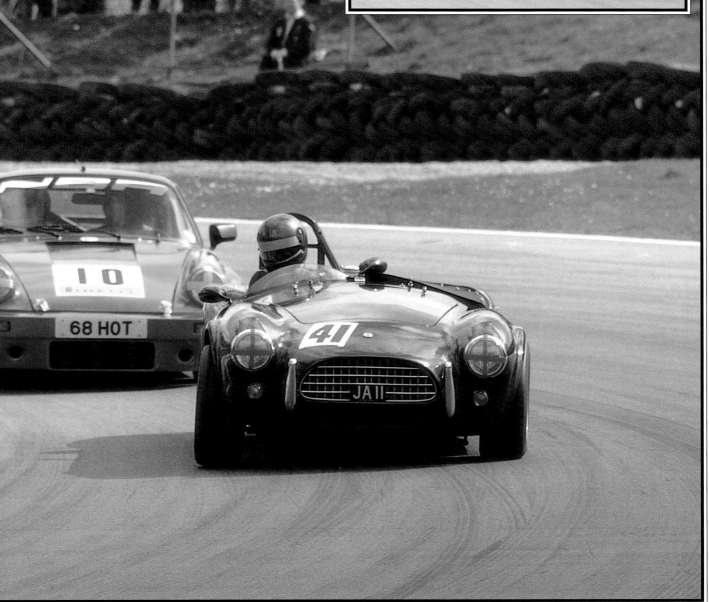

Cobra

VIII

AFTER
THE
ORIGINAL
COBRA

Philip Lemm 1983

The Shelby American operation was a two-tier business dealing with road and race cars, both sections overlapping to a large extent since the company generally sold the public a de-tuned but closely related vehicle to that which they raced.

The GT40 Era
With the demise of the Cobra the purely racing GT40 programme continued and took overall victory at Le Mans in 1966. Ford returned the following year to underline that it was no lucky, one-off success. The GT40 was in a continuous state of development with the huge operation handled by many outside contractors as well as Shelby in an attempt to keep one step ahead of the opposition, who were not sitting idly by and watching. The next variation was known as the J-car and was intended as a leap forward in aerodynamics and race car construction utilising aircraft style aluminium honeycomb structures held together by glue instead of the usual welded monocoque. Its critics were silenced to a certain extent when A.J.Foyt set fastest lap in a prototype J-car at the 1966 Le Mans test days but the car failed to live up to its early promise. Worst of all Shelby's most valuable test driver and engineer, Ken Miles, lost his life while testing a J-car at Riverside in August 1966. The loss of Ken Miles was probably the blackest moment in the successful story of Shelby American.

With the GT cars failing once more at Daytona in 1967 Ford again called in Shelby's best men to revise and improve the race cars; within one month

Phil Remington and his team built a revised J-car which went on to take victory at the Sebring event. Another chassis was constructed to incorporate the lessons learned. Fitted with revised bodywork and the massive 7-litre engine, this model was referred to as the Ford GT Mk IV and represented the high point of GT40 development. No less than seven cars were entered at Le Mans in 1967, Shelby American taking charge of two Mk IVs and one Mk II, the Mk IVs eventually finishing first and fourth. Thus Shelby gave Ford its second successive victory at Le Mans.

Cooper Cobra
As Ford was now retiring from international sports car racing following their massively expensive campaign (and the FIA quickly banning the Mk IV from competition by setting a 5-litre engine limit), Carroll Shelby decided to do likewise. He knew only too well how expensive such racing was and to field a competitive team on his own was a risk which outweighed the potential reward. An acceptable alternative, since he was still as eager as ever to go racing, was to build a car for the popular and successful Canadian-American Challenge Series (Can-Am) which now dominated North American racing, overshadowing the USRRC series. A car which resembled the old 'King Cobra' Cooper-Monaco car, the 'Cooper Cobra', was constructed by Len Terry in England, with a unique suspension design featuring transverse coil springs running across the rear suspension. It was hoped that this would make up in

The ultra-successful Ford GT40 MkII.

Below: A GT40 for the road - the MkIII version. Note the lengthened rear section for extra luggage space.

Bottom: Twin headlights identify the GT40 MkIII from the front.

handling for what the car lost in power, since Shelby proposed fitting a 'small block' 351 cu in Ford engine with Gurney-Westlake heads into this lightweight car.

Regrettably, it proved a major disappointment with terminal handling problems and was never competitive, even with such a determined driver as Jerry Titus at the wheel. To add further problems to Shelby's efforts he walked into Can-Am just as the Bruce and Denny show was getting underway, with Bruce McLaren and Deny Hulme sweeping all before them with their almost total domination of the series, their McLaren M6As proving fast and reliable.

Can-Am & Trans-Am

Determined to rediscover success in American racing, Carroll Shelby purchased a Lola T70 Can-Am car for the 1968 season and hired Peter Revson for the driving duties. After a third place in the season's opening USRRC race in Mexico City the early promise flattered to deceive. By the opening race of the Can-Am series at Elkhart Lake, Shelby had acquired a McLaren M6A (McLaren now had their new M7s) and Revson came home fourth. However, history was to repeat itself with a string of poor results which were mainly due to mechanical problems. The Shelby rise to fame had peaked during the 1965-67 racing seasons and the momentum faltered. Winning with somebody else's car was not to Shelby's liking - failing with somebody else's car was unacceptable too. Expensive forms of racing such as Can-

141

Am were also a massive drain on resources without a major sponsor to pay the mounting bills.

Not only was Shelby involved in sports car events he also found himself preparing Mustangs for the Trans-American Sedan Championship (Trans-Am). Unfortunately the 'fastback' Shelby GT350 Mustangs were not eligible to race in this important manufacturers' championship so Ford prepared and entered their own standard hardtop (or notchback) model. This version was eligible since it had four seats as opposed to the fastback's two. Shelby originally helped private Mustang owners in the first year of Trans-Am (1966) but later withdrew his support since there was little 'product identification' with his own GT350. However, the last race saw Ford in with a chance of victory in the series so a Shelby tuned Mustang suddenly appeared with Jerry Titus at the wheel. Success and the overall championship saw Ford committed to a repeat performance and the following year, 1967.

So with their sponsorship Shelby American fielded a two car team throughout the thirteen race series. Despite some stern opposition from Mercury Cougars (part of the Ford group!) and Chevrolet Camaros, the team accumulated enough points over the year to take the title for Ford once again.

For 1968 the Shelby Racing Co won the opening Trans-Am event as well as the ninth, but the seven races in between saw the blue Sunoco sponsored Camaro of Mark Donohue/Roger

SHELBY G.T. 350

142

Probably the fastest Ford of all - the GT40 MkIV.

Bottom left: There's a very period feel to the Shelby sales catalogue of 1965.

Below: A pair of GT350s with the competition car on the left. Note the remarkable similarity to the road model. (Courtesy SAAC).

Penske take the chequered flag and the Championship.

The 1969 season saw the arrival of the new Mustang model, the Boss 302, as well as even more flexible rules: acid-dipped bodies, massive tyres, spoilers and phenomenally powerful engines. The cost of competing rose in proportion to the importance and popularity of the series. Peter Revson and Horst Kwech drove Shelby's two Boss 302 racers against some equally competent opposition. Revson won the second race at Lime Rock but that was to be the team's only victory and Shelby American's last. At Riverside, on 4th October 1969, Carroll Shelby officially announced his retirement from all motor racing.

Shelby Mustangs

With the last 427 Cobra being constructed in March 1967, the only remaining Shelby American product was the Mustang conversion in GT350 and GT500 form.

During 1965 the Shelby GT350 was announced as Ford's answer to the Corvette in the sports car section of the market. In Ford's opinion the Cobra had by that time fulfilled its role in promoting their new sporting image, therefore, a model was sought which could be constructed in much larger numbers (Ford could construct fifty Mustangs each day) and would appeal to a wider market than the spartan AC. Breathing performance into sports cars was what Shelby enjoyed and the early GT350 was a real no-compromise performance vehicle, stripped of unnecessary embellishments and not unlike a Cobra with a hard top. Fast, hard-riding and noisy it could give Corvette owners the run-around on both road and track although, being heavier than the Cobra, it did not meet with such instant success on the circuits.

An immaculate example of a 1966 GT350 owned by Rick Kopec of SAAC. (Courtesy SAAC).

A multitude of Mustangs at the Shelby works in LA Airport in 1966. (Courtesy SAAC).

This restored 1966 GT350 took part in the 1982 Brighton Speed Trials.

Jerry Titus undertook the arduous task of slalom testing new Mustangs. (Courtesy SAAC).

Left: A 1966 GT350 Mustang poses at Lime Rock race track. (Courtesy SAAC).

Right: At a SAAC convention you might be lucky enough to spot a Mustang, or two ... (Courtesy SAAC).

The prime function of the Mustang was to be the breadwinner for the Shelby company and, almost inevitably, the cars changed during 1966 and especially 1967 as Ford accountants put pressure on Shelby to save money here and there, using less expensive parts wherever possible to improve the company's financial performance. The 1967 models showed the changes most dramatically - gone was the all-out performance car and in its place was a larger, heavier, up-market vehicle with a civilised interior, although a genuine roll cage was still installed. This was the year of the big-engined Mustangs; when Ford offered the 390 cu in Shelby dropped the 428 unit into the GT500 with a handful receiving the genuine 427 just to make life interesting. With the Cobra out of production and the Mustang appealing to a wider section of the market, the Shelby plant was able to produce 3225 cars in 1967 in comparison to the total of 562 Mustangs built in 1965.

Carroll Shelby with GT350 and GT500 Mustangs.

By adding a convertible to the range for 1968 Shelby American reached an all-time high in that year, producing 4450 cars in three guises - the GT350, GT500 and, later in the year, the GT500KR, each in fastback or convertible form. However, by 1968 the Mustangs were moving ever further from their original concept. The lease had also expired on Shelby's Los Angeles plant and his aircraft hangars were to revert to their original use, which resulted in all car production being transferred to the A. O. Smith assembly lines near Detroit at Iona, Michigan, where Shelby parts were fitted to production line Mustangs. The single hood louvre was replaced by ugly twin scoops which ran the full width of the bonnet and the rear of the car featured sequential turn signals from the 1965 Thunderbird. Engineering changes were few, primarily because Ford saw that the 1967 models sold well enough and were therefore content to keep to purely cosmetic alterations, even to the extent of incorporating a tilt away steering wheel to assist driver entry. Shelby's influence was obviously diminishing - Ford were demanding more cars to sell throughout their massive dealer network and their wishes had to be obeyed. With Shelby models now being built so close to Detroit it was inevitable that Ford would have more control over production. (The Los Angeles plant was too small to accommodate the planned increase in output so production would have been transferred regardless of the lease expiring).

Fortunately the 1968 Shelbys were far from emaciated. Midway through the year, in an effort to steal some of the Camaro's thunder with its forthcoming big-block model, the GT500 became the GT500KR ('King of the Road'), which incorporated the 428 engine mated to 427 heads and manifold with a 735 cfm Holley four-barrel carburettor. This machine proved to be the ideal weapon for drag-strip enthusiasts in production car classes.

By 1969 Carroll Shelby was no longer a household name and the Cobra was now history. Ford's ever alert accountants were only too ready to point out to top management that despite a 37 per cent increase in output, the entire production was still so small that to market such cars was to lose money. With no international racing programme requiring money to be 'lost' on specialist vehicles, and their own Boss 302 model about to be launched, plus the Mach One in the pipeline, the Shelby models were no longer necessary to the Ford range. However, Ford were still prepared to honour their contract and continued to offer a GT350 and GT500 model for 1969. These cars benefited greatly from the new restyled basic Mustang model. Gone were the tacked-on hood scoops and unattractive wheels: instead, the new Shelbys became probably the sleekest and most attractive cars the company had offered since 1965, having dispensed with most of the unnecessary embellishments with the exception of the plethora of assorted badges and side strips.

At the same time as Carroll Shelby was winding up his involvement with motorsport he also approached Ford's executive vice-president, Lee Iacocca, with the request that the Shelby models be discontinued. Ever the realist, he could see that with each passing year 'his' cars would change further from their concept as market requirements changed and government intervention grew. Although the performance car market would survive for a few more years, he saw the writing on the wall: his time had come and gone. Even so, to take such an irrevocable step must have been heartbreaking, not to say extremely brave, but it was best to leave before his name appeared on cars with which he had no wish to be associated. The major manufacturers were now in full swing with their own 'muscle cars', building them in quantities which Shelby American never could.

The original Shelby era closed in 1970 with the final Mustangs in the pipeline from the 1969 production schedule being slightly modified and marketed as 1970 models. These 601 vehicles would be the last to carry the Shelby name for a number of years.

So the ambitious dream of one man had come, flourished and was now seemingly gone, but left behind were the fruits of his labour in the tangible form of a wide variety of sporting machinery to gladden the heart of any motorist who enjoys driving cars built by enthusiasts for enthusiasts. Although the company lasted for less than a decade, an enormous amount was achieved in this time for, apart from the Cobras, Mustangs and GT40s, Shelby was also involved in development work on vehicles such as the other Anglo-American hybrid the Sunbeam Tiger, which also used a Ford V8 engine in a British sportscar body. Shelby also produced and marketed Cobra parts with Tiger logos substituted, which all helped to pay the rent.

Nor was the end accepted without a fight. Carroll Shelby always hoped to have a car which could fill the gap left by the Cobra, and both he and the Ford styling department designed and built prototypes with this in mind. Shelby's own hopes were pinned on a sleek mid-engined (289, of course) coupé named 'Lone Star' in deference to his Texan heritage. One fully operational aluminium bodied targa topped car was actually constructed by J. W. Automotive Engineering Ltd in 1967. The speci-

The 1970 Shelby Mustang sales brochure.

1970 Shelby GT 350/500 Specifications

Below: Shelby at the end of one era in his life. The 1970 Mustang was overweight and a far cry from the '65 GT350 - the end of production was in sight. (Courtesy SAAC).

fication of this model was not unlike that of the GT40 which they were building and racing from their Slough workshops, but as a road car the Lone Star received a mixed reception. The biggest cloud on the car's horizon was the ever increasing tide of government restrictions and regulations. The hoped for exemptions for low volume cars were not forthcoming and, rather than face a future arguing with bureaucracy, the coupé project was shelved. The one and only car was consigned to the show car circuit before being sold in October 1968.

As for Carroll Shelby, he now had time to divert his energies to some of his many other interests although, naturally, he maintained close ties with the motoring industry through a company building magnesium alloy wheels and even pioneering the use of such wheels for motorcycles. As well as retaining his successful Goodyear tyre agency he also diversified into marketing 'Original Texas Chili', the hot, spicy Mexican dish so popular in the southern states.

GT350 Convertible Reborn

With a ranch in east Texas where he bred Appaloosa horses and exotic birds, land interests around Lake Tahoe and an interest in an African game reserve, he had plenty to occupy his days. By the early 1980s he was also involved in the world-wide sale of water purifying plants and plasma-ignition systems. In his spare time he found the opportunity to return briefly to the car construction business by undertaking a new project in 1981 to build a further

twelve examples of his own favourite Shelby model, the 1966 GT350 convertible. Only six of these cars were ever built .The idea, therefore, was to purchase twelve normal production 1966 convertibles from California, where rust is less of a problem, and totally strip each car. With advice from ex-Shelby personnel - Phil Remington, projects manager Al Dowd and production manager Jack Khoury - plus further assistance from a Mustang specialist in Beverley Hills who could locate the hard-to-find parts, each car

was rebuilt mechanically and bodily as a genuine Shelby GT350 with all worn parts replaced. The first example retained only one bumper. Naturally, improvements were incorporated wherever possible, the biggest advance over the intervening years being in tyre technology. Eight cars were scheduled as automatics. Each Mustang remained as faithful as possible to the original 1966 model and, indeed, the Shelby American Automobile Club added them to their official register of genuine cars, the chassis numbers carrying on where the final 1966 convertible left off. The original intention was to build just one more car for Carroll Shelby's own use but, of course old habits die hard and the chance to construct a few more cars was too good to miss. Shelby, of course, retained one car to add to his collection which includes, among various European sports cars, the first and last 289 Cobras, a mint 427 roadster, a Daytona coupé and various Mustangs.

Shelby Moves To Chrysler

History, it is said, has a tendency to repeat itself. Take another adage such as 'You can't keep a good man down', throw in a certain set of circumstances and within a matter of months you can easily find the Shelby name stamped on a new range of cars. Not, on this occasion, on Ford cars but on a range from Chrysler, another of the giants of the American automotive industry but in the early 1980s a crumbling empire shored up by billions of US government dollars.

To explain how a dedicated Ford man such as Shelby switched camps one has to return to 1961 when Ford and their advertising agency, J.Walter Thompson, promoted their new range of cars for the sixties under the heading 'Total Performance'. Tied into their new approach to capture the increasingly affluent young motorists the Shelby Cobra provided a vital link, promoting Ford's name by winning on the race track. Such a marketing approach required a high-ranking Ford director to give the whole project the green light and to fight for its survival. In this case it was a man who rose to be the second most powerful figure within the Ford empire, Lee Iacocca. Without his efforts behind the scenes the whole Cobra/Mustang/GT40 era may never have happened. Fortunately he proved to be one of the relatively few high-ranking managers who saw the value of motor racing and the connections between race cars and those sold in thousands to the man in the street.

The one thing that the man who is number two in a company should never do is to fall out with the man who is number one. However, the personalities of Henry Ford II and Lee Iacocca finally clashed. On 30th October 1978 Iacocca left Ford - by 2 November he was appointed President of Chrysler. It was not all good news for he joined what proved to be a sinking ship, but by ruthless management he slimmed the company dramatically and turned the massive losses of 1980 into a small profit in 1982. Many risks had to be taken to revamp a disastrous range of vehicles. Among these was the brave decision to relaunch the convertible, which was non-existent among American car producers by 1976, and also to revive a marketing ploy which had worked so well in the 1960s - the 'performance' image.

Enter the man whose name was still synonymous with fast cars - Carroll Shelby. A deal was quickly reached by which Shelby was granted his own 'research and development' department where he could work his magic on various models from the Chrysler range. The first of these was to be the Dodge Charger which appeared with a tuned engine, revised suspension, improved interior and Shelby's traditional metallic blue paintwork. That was a start but what had not escaped his attention, however, was a promising modern mid-engined sports car then being built in small numbers in a place called Thames Ditton. It used a rather unexciting stock Ford engine and suffered from under-exposure. What Chrysler had was a range of engines, access to turbochargers, development time and money and a need for an instant sports car to liven up their steadily reviving image ... *deja vu?*

AC Cars Ltd

By the mid-1990s, AC had undergone a considerable transformation since the end of Cobra production. The company found itself under new management and in a new factory located just a few miles from the original Thames Ditton base. AC had struggled bravely on for a few more years with the Cobra, renamed the 'AC 289', but demand waned for an unfashionably vintage car which, in Britain and

Convertibles are fine if you like travelling fast in an
open car, but for those who like a permanent roof
over their head, the AC428 wears one of the
most stylish hats in the world.
When you're travelling at speeds of 140-plus, aerodynamics
matter a lot. The Fastback is streamlined to perfection
for optimum airflow as well as for style and comfort.
And there's plenty of behind-seat space for storage too.
In every other respect, of course, it is the same car as
the famous 428 Convertible, with the same superlative
power and performance.

The AC428 Fastback puts a streamlined, aerodynamic roof over your head.

Europe, was considered expensive to buy and maintain as well as somewhat exotic with its American V8 engine. Although the Cobra, or to be more accurate the chassis and suspension, clearly still had great potential, it was the uncompromising style of the car which deterred many traditional AC customers. What AC needed was a vehicle capable of delivering sports car performance in a more refined manner allied to higher levels of driver comfort. Thus, the AC 428 became the car to take AC Cars into the 1970s.

AC 428

In the same way that Shelby had an eye open for a Cobra successor, so AC quietly developed prototypes for future consideration. One car in particular demonstrated a potential path for them to follow. The 'Marcewski Special', built originally to accommodate a flat-six engine, had a longer, more elegant body giving better accommodation for passengers and their luggage, along with a Grand Touring style of motoring. Such a body could easily be adapted to fit a lengthened 7-litre Cobra chassis which, by 1965, had been thoroughly developed. Various drawings were made for consideration and at this stage the Swiss AC agent and enthusiast, Hubert Patthey, introduced the company to the Italian styling house of Frua, with whom he had close associations. By mutual arrangement a chassis was sent to Italy onto which

A.C. CARS LIMITED, THAMES DITTON, SURREY				
RETAIL CAR PRICES				
A.C. 428 Convertible, 4-Speed Gear Box ...	Basic Price	£3750 0 0
	Purchase Tax	782 13 1
	10% P.T. Surcharge ...	78 5 4
		£4610 18 5
A.C. 428 Convertible, Automatic Gear Box ...	Basic Price	£3865 0 0
	Purchase Tax	806 12 3
	10% P.T. Surcharge ...	80 13 3
		£4752 5 6
A.C. 289 Sports Car	Basic Price	£2400 0 0
	Purchase Tax	501 8 2
	10% P.T. Surcharge ...	50 2 10
		£2951 11 0
Prices October, 1966.				

Frua constructed an aluminium panelled prototype convertible body, which was displayed at the London Motor Show of 1965. Initially referred to as an AC 427, the elegant 7-litre car was well received by the press although some naturally made comparisons between the new AC and the Maserati Mistral, which had also been designed by Frua. AC were satisfied, since they now had the type of car they sought and an order was placed with Frua to construct further bodies.

With Ford of America supplying the 428 Galaxie engine the model's name was changed to the AC 428, which also served to avoid any confusion with Shelby's 427 Cobra model. (AC did, at one stage, plan to sell 7-litre Cobras in the UK as well). The price for the new car quoted at the Motor Show was £4250 as against £2732 for the Cobra 289, the latter being in the expensive sports car bracket, so the 428 had to appeal to a very different section of the market from the outset.

A small number of changes were made from the prototype, chiefly the addition of side vents to help relieve under-bonnet heat, and by 1967 the first cars were offered for sale. Although a very swift car against the

The AC 428 sales brochure.

Below left: AC Cars' official price list 1966.

The AC 428 Convertible. (Courtesy AC Cars).

clock with 345bhp to propel it, it was far removed from its Cobra origins with a luxurious well trimmed leather interior and all the refinements one could wish for. Its ride was softer but with its long travel coil suspension it fortunately had adequate reserves of road-holding to help the unwary driver.

Despite having much to its credit on the debit side was the 428's tendency to boil its oil on a long fast run, because of excessive engine heat. Another factor not in its favour was its high price in relation to comparable machinery of the time, although there is always a market for a 'bespoke' hand-made vehicle. The price was forced on AC mainly because of the need to send the bare chassis across Europe to northern Italy where Frua's workmen fitted the body, now made of steel instead of the aluminium of the prototype. The complete assembly was then transported back to Thames Ditton for painting and trimming. Another problem appeared with the passing years - notorious Italian steel which many people claim had in-built rust. Although never a very serious problem some unlucky owners suffered paintwork troubles.

Difficulties also arose in Italy with Frua having labour relations trouble so that the supply of bodies became erratic to say the least. To fill the need for a fixed-head car a fastback coupé was later built which, with its thick window pillars and large rear window, was to prove even more popular than the convertible. In 1970 the vast array of gauges scattered around the dashboard was redesigned into a more readable group; almost the only redesign in the model run.

AC were unhappy about the uncertain Italian arrangement but a search for a British supplier proved fruitless, since the few concerns that were interested demanded a guaranteed large run of bodies which would have placed a big financial burden on the small car company. Then a new problem loomed in the shape of the 1973 Middle East oil crisis which saw an inexorable rise in the cost of fuel. Suddenly, the day of the 7-litre leviathan was over. Despite the initial promise of the AC 428 the final production total was only 80 cars (51 fastbacks and 29 convertibles). Orders were still unfilled even in 1973, mainly because the supply of bodies had dried up. It was hoped to build further examples at a later date but, as fuel prices and inflation increased, so any hope of selling further 428s at a competitive price faded.

Behind the scenes a redesigned 428 was constructed to give increased accommodation for four people. Looking reminiscent of Monteverdis of the time, this elegant saloon featured the

usual well appointed leather trimmed interior, power steering and de Dion rear suspension with inboard rear disc brakes. Such a car would have given such marques as Jensen, Bristol, Aston Martin and Rolls-Royce some interesting competition but it failed to reach production. Another prototype was designed to incorporate concealed headlights, along with a general 'clean up' of the car's already attractive contours, particularly around the rear. Regrettably, it appeared on the scene too late although, with a smaller engine installed, it might well have proved very successful.

AC 3000ME

By 1974 AC had no cars to sell. Not wishing to throw in the towel, however, particularly with such a long and fascinating history behind them, they bravely made public a prototype which was intended to put them firmly at the forefront of sports car manufacture, incorporating, as it did, the now fashionable mid-engine layout. Other companies were rapidly developing mid-engine cars for future release but,

with the notable exception of the Fiat X1/9, there were very few models available with this racing derived configuration at a reasonable price, which discounts the more 'exotic' Ferrari Dino and Lamborghini Urraco. A lucrative market seemed to await anybody who could fill this gap at the right price.

This new AC, designated the '3000ME' (3-litre Mid-Engine), came about in much the same way as did the original Ace of 1953, by taking over and developing an existing design. In this case it was a one-off exercise called Diablo, built by Peter Bohanna and Robin Stables and shown at the 1972 London Racing Car Show, where it created a great deal of interest and received critical acclaim. Ironically, it was AC themselves who sowed the initial seed when they saw another small sports car built by the two designers around a BDA engine. AC ordered two prototypes but later cancelled the deal; fortunately, Bohanna and Stables carried on and finished one car using BMC components and a transverse Maxi 1500cc engine, Sta-

bles put every penny he had behind the project, even to the extent of selling his own AC Cobra to raise money.

At the racing car show financial backing was found which was sufficient to construct further examples at a projected rate of twenty a week. Just when success seemed certain a telegram from BMC promptly cancelled the arrangement for the supply of components, effectively killing the whole project. By this time AC were aware of what a potentially successful car the Diablo was and they took over the project. Bohanna and Stables went to AC in 1973, along with their car, to help with the task of turning it into a production model. With AC's engineering resources they could design and make any necessary components inhouse, and AC's close association with Ford assured a supply of 3-litre engines.

Thus began one of the most protracted public gestation periods of any car. The proposed launch date of June 1974 came and went, with enquiries from potential owners piling up on the sales manager's desk. Each year one

154

The AC 428 that never was. Commissioned in 1973 from Frua, this elegant design featured concealed headlights. The car was not completed until some ten years after production of the 428 ended.

Below: The AC 3000ME.

or two cars appeared at the Earls Court Motor Show but continuing development problems meant that disappointment once again for the public.

The development programme proved more complex than anyone at AC had imagined. Initially the chief designer, Alan Turner, sat down and revised the whole car to turn it into a practical vehicle for production but without losing the original concept. Since AC lacked the massive resources of the giant motor companies the whole process was inevitably slow, especially when one realises how many parts had to be designed and constructed by AC themselves to avoid the many potential difficulties caused by having to rely on outside contractors. To the eternal credit of AC they were not about to appease their critics - they continued until the job was completed to their satisfaction, and at the end of the day they built a good, solid vehicle. By using a strong chassis construction, plus huge side intrusion barriers designed to spread shock loads into the chassis, plus a roll cage built into the roof, the 3000ME was one of the safest fibreglass bodied cars.

The biggest problem encountered proved to be the drive train, particularly the gearbox which eventually used specially made Hewland internals fitted into AC's own gearbox/sump alloy casting located beneath and slightly to the rear of the Ford V6 engine. The expensive Ministry of Transport crash testing also took a great deal of time, money and prototypes.

However, in 1979 the first cars found their way from the factory into

Inside the then new AC factory in Summer Road, Thames Ditton. New cars are constructed alongside earlier ACs which have returned for repair or maintenance. On the left an AC 428 convertible and, centre, a 428 fastback.

private hands, but some five years of inflation had taken the 1974 price from £3000 into the £10,000 bracket and two years later to over £13,000.

Various dealers around the country were happy to sell the car but the arrangement proved disappointing, and by 1982 sales and service of the car were once again handled directly by the factory. Production was slowed for a while when AC moved from their traditional premises in the High Street to a smaller industrial unit on the edge of Thames Ditton. While the company, with its many diverse engineering operations, had been showing a reasonable net profit during the development of their new car, by 1979 the previous year's pre-tax profit of £206,000 had become a £224,950 deficit. In 1980 the loss was £203,000.

The large amounts of money poured into development work (possibly as much as £1 million) and a general recession in the engineering industry were having their effect. Action was necessary to reverse the trend, since the market for the 3000ME was also depressed with only one car a week being sold, although by selling direct to the public the price was able to be reduced from £13,000 to the £11,000 bracket; inflation increased this to £12,600 by mid-83. The company's biggest asset was its 100,000 sq.ft. of factory space which was a prime site and by now too large for their needs. Production was transferred to the new, smaller factory and the old premises sold for £1.2 million. The Unipower company, acquired in 1977 to produce aircraft tenders, was sold along with a general programme of cost-cutting and redundancies. The more profitable

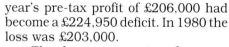

A 3000ME keeps a Greyhound company in the AC service bay.

156

A 3000ME slowly takes shape in the factory.

Below: On the AC 'production line', a 3000ME has its driver's door fitted.

Bottom: The Ghia 3000ME displays a stylish profile. (Courtesy FoMoCo).

project was doomed to remain a styling exercise as the world sportscar market was then at a relatively low ebb and

subsidiary companies, such as a specialist trailer and bodywork building concern on the south coast, were retained.

The AC 3000ME, however, failed to live up to its potential. The cost of its development drained AC's resources to the point where they couldn't afford to develop the model further, much to the frustration of dedicated AC enthusiasts. A small ray of hope lightened the gloom when two chassis were sent to Ford's Ghia styling studios in Italy where Filippo Sapino clothed them in a more modern version of the AC body. The AC Ghia was shown at the Geneva Motor Show in 1981 and naturally created a great deal of media and public interest, giving AC's own model spin-off publicity. Sadly, the Ghia

157

Ford dealers, particularly in the USA, were apathetic: preferring high volume cars to ring their cash tills more often.

The hope of turning the car into the basis for a new Ford rally car was dealt a blow by the appearance of the ground-breaking new Audi Quattro which signposted rallying's move to four-wheel-drive. Ultimately, AC preferred their own in-house body style to the Ghia creation - and from some angles you could see their point.

The 3000ME also surfaced as a lightly restyled car with a certain tall Texan standing beside it in a Chrysler advertisment. This strange turn of events came about when an ME was purchased by Chrysler, via AC's American importer, the Panteramerica company. Shelby, in his role as performance consultant to Chrysler, installed a turbocharged Chrysler engine and improved the model's rear styling by smoothing out the rear wheelarch flares. A photograph of the modified car and Shelby - with tuned Dodge saloon and AC Shelby Cobra in the background - together with the rumour of a launch for this new car in September 1983. AC were bemused as they'd had no communication with Chrysler and, eventually, the whole matter sank without trace.

AC cars continued as best they could but, having lost their lucrative Ministry of Transport contract to build invalid cars, the company's business began to falter and losses were recorded for the first time since the 1930s. In 1984, the rights to build the 3000ME were granted to a newly-formed company - AC (Scotland) - when AC sold its large Thames Ditton site. Sadly, this too, proved to be a blind alley for the ill-starred ME model. The development funding the car needed was certainly not forthcoming in Scotland and the under-financed company produced the last of its 30 AC cars in September 1985, finally closing down the following month with the loss of 28 jobs. The company's prototype ME, fitted with an Alfa Romeo 2500cc V6 engine, was dismantled. The AC/Alfa was an intriguing project, particularly as Alfa had offered to market the car through Alfa Romeo dealerships.

Hurlock Sells Up

AC Cars Plc eventually changed ownership when Derek Hurlock, faced with mounting losses, sold his shares in the company to a stockbroking company in the city and thereby ended fifty seven years of Hurlock management at AC Cars. In retirement he purchased a Surrey farm and renewed his great love of the land. Sadly, Derek Hurlock died in 1992: a cavalcade of AC automobiles escorted his funeral cortege. I shall always hold fond memories of our talks together, for he was a gentleman of the 'old school'.

Angliss Takes Over AC

When Derek Hurlock sold his shares, a number of motoring journalists pondered the idea of Brian Angliss of Autokraft taking over the mantle of AC Cars Plc since his was then the only company actually making an AC at the time. Eventually, Autokraft was able to purchase a majority of shares in AC Cars Plc and Brian Angliss became Managing Director of both companies.

Ford Buys In

In addition to building its modern Cobra Autokraft were busy during the 1980s undertaking construction and development of a number of prototypes for outside clients, with Ford as their main customer. One of their projects had been the development of a two-seater sports car utilising Ford Cosworth power and four-wheel-drive. In 1986 the AC Ace was unveiled at the NEC Motor Show, Birmingham, scheduled for a 1988 launch as a fully developed production car to be built in Autokraft's and AC's new 90,000 sq ft factory on the Brooklands estate. The future for AC was looking assured and this impression was given further credence when, in October 1987, Ford purchased 49 per cent of the shares of AC Holdings and a further 1.96 per cent from Brian Angliss (at a total cost believed to be around £1.3 million) to give the small company the protection of a major producer. AC and Ford were together again, albeit without Carroll Shelby in the picture, but despite that the future looked promising for all concerned.

However, 1988 came and went and no Ace appeared. The prototype had disappeared into 'redevelopment' mode and words were written about 'major re-styling' exercises. On April 22nd 1990, Ford moved to have AC Cars put into liquidation: for motoring enthusiasts who had looked forward to a healthy future for Britain's oldest car manufacturer, this was a bombshell.

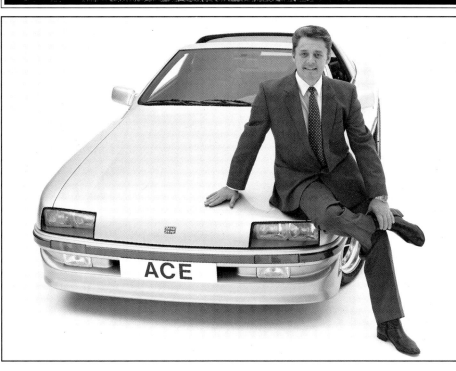

Below: The 1986 AC Ace - prior to restyling - and Brian Angliss, Managing Director, AC Cars. (Courtesy FoMoCo).

Brian Angliss had come across the same type of problem that had caused Carroll Shelby to walk away from Ford in 1969: small manufacturing businesses run by an entrepreneur find it virtually impossible to operate under the stifling oppressions of huge corporations, the two management styles mixing like oil and water. AC developed the Ace in their own way but Ford, with its totally different approach to automotive development, could not tolerate a situation in which they appeared to be bypassed when quick decisions were needed. Things were happening with the Ace which Ford senior management knew nothing about. This could not be tolerated. Liquidating a wholly-owned company is one thing, but liquidating a company which is 48 per cent-owned by another party is not quite so straightforward and, fortunately, Brian Angliss was in no mood to see AC disappear into the history books: he was tenacious in his opposition. Fighting the Ford empire through no less than seven court attempts to sink AC. he finally succeeded in buying back the Ford shareholding in 1992.

Ford Bows Out/Ace Débuts

Peace was declared, Ford wished AC well for the future and, in 1993, the all-new Ace was launched. Under the newcomer's bonnet, what else but a Ford engine? Even better, it was a 5-litre V8 with SVO parts built to AC's specification and producing a comfortable 280bhp. An earlier prototype featured Ford Cosworth mechanicals allied to four-wheel-drive but, finally, AC went for simplicity,

favouring the effortless performance of a big V8 allied to rear-wheel-drive, producing a sports car in the Mercedes SL mould. The Ace for the 90s featured air-conditioning, power steering and ABS brakes as standard: a far cry from its namesake in the 50s. This model is destined to be joined by another all-new AC sports car, lighter and cheaper, and based around General Motors mechanicals.

When these new models are in place, AC will once more be a serious producer of sporting machinery. The Cobra will be the flagship, the Ace its modern mid-range counterpart and the smaller, lighter, sports model will hopefully create volume sales. AC Cars Ltd, appear to have a future once more.

Cobra Goes East ... Almost

As an interesting aside, the Cobra almost disappeared to the Far East for 5 years, for a Japanese conglomerate signed a deal with Autokraft to take the entire 1991 to 1995 Cobra production to fulfill the demand it saw in its home market. However, after just 12 cars had been exported to Japan, the importers fell foul of the worldwide recession and the contract was cancelled. Although AC probably benefited from the small print in the contract insuring them against cancellation, they still had the problem of having a number of Cobras on their hands. Luckily, during 1992, the Cobra was granted full EC certification to allow it to be sold throughout Europe having met all the emission, noise and other regulations that various governments could throw at it. In addition, in 1993, North American

Left: Mk IV Lightweights under construction in the Byfleet factory.

Below left: Completed MkIVs under wraps.

Right: A quick polish for a MkIV prior to delivery.

Below: A 1992 left-hand-drive MkIV awaits export.

certification was granted allowing the car to be sold in 49 states. Quite an achievement, since putting a 1965 design through 1990s red tape is not the work of a moment: that the Cobra has come through all this is a minor miracle.

Cobra Lightweight

The AC Cobra MkIV underwent a noteable transformation at the end of the 1980s. Brian Angliss let it be known that a small number (rumoured to be around 18) of Cobras could be purchased in 'lightweight' form. Many owners of earlier MkIV Cobras had not been greatly impressed by the car, finding the V8 down on power and the heavier overall model lacking the performance and handling of the original 60s roadsters. The Lightweight was a different story! Under the bonnet was a well-tuned V8 pumping out (allegedly and approximately) 345bhp compared to the standard 225bhp.

Detail shows quality of craftmanship in MkIV (note wired spinner).

Opposite right: The superb MkIV Lightweight.

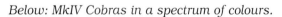

Below: MkIV Cobras in a spectrum of colours.

Insets: Looking like sculptures, unpainted alloy front and rear body sections await further assembly. Quality of traditional workmanship is evident.

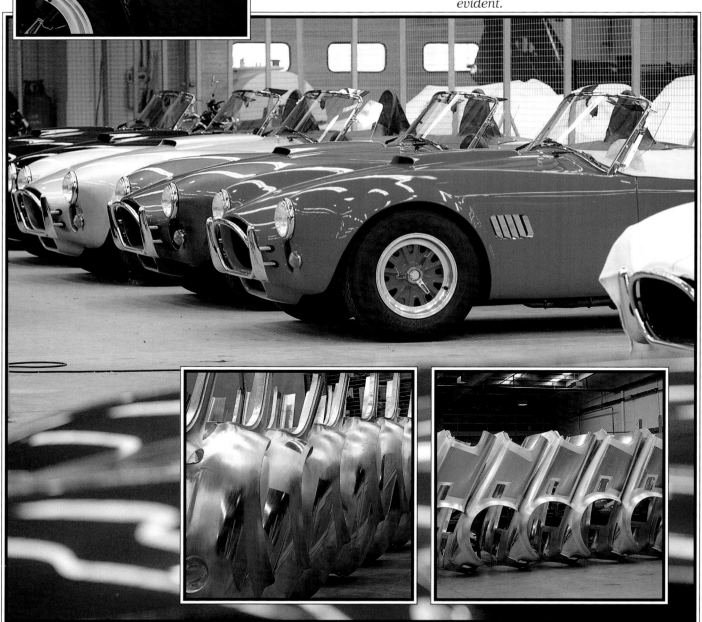

recognised this model as the finest incarnation of of the marque yet.

Thereafter the production Cobra for the 90s was named the AC Cobra MkIV Lightweight and combined the best of the original MkIV with many of the 'Lightweight' revisions. The 5-litre Ford Mustang 90 degree V8 still sported an iron block - with aluminium heads - but could be relied upon to deliver 320bhp and 330Ibf.ft of torque.

After the Japanese deal fell through and the Cobra was openly back on the market, journalists beat a path to the AC factory to road test the cars. The general concensus of opinion was that the Autokraft/AC MkIV was a credit to its predecessor. Whilst it could not pretend to pass itself off as a genuine 60s automobile, it still retained the essence of the original car not unduly compromised by the modifications necessary to allow it to be sold in the 1990s. A major plus point was the improvement in build quality: most journalists were impressed by the fit and finish, noting that the chrome and paintwork were to Rolls-Royce standards.

Having driven and closely examined a number of original cars the author feels that the improvement in build quality achieved by Autokraft is something that cannot be overstated.

The Autokraft car is of such high quality that it borders on being a work of art (especially when painted silver!) Naturally, there is a price to be paid for such workmanship (in excess of 2000 skilled man hours on each car) and in early 1993 this worked out at an awesome list price of £99,578: quite a sum of money for a relatively simple sports car. In fact, in the recession-riddled early-90s, this price proved to be rather an embarrasment as the value of original Cobras plummeted to the point where the new car was considerably more expensive than an original classic. AC addressed the problem and, in November 1993, cut the list price dramatically to £67,995 due to 'reduced overheads'. Today, small boys (of all ages) can visit Piccadilly in central London and press their noses against the window of a showroom containing a brand new 1960s monster sports car and dream that maybe one day .... Grab one while you can!

Carroll Carries On

Meanwhile, on the other side of the Atlantic the originator of the Cobra, Carroll Shelby, is as busy as ever, packing more into one eventful lifetime than many could manage in two or three! Not even a heart transplant in 1990 has slowed him and, once again,

he is a welcome sight at automobile meetings around the world and is ever in demand for autographs, interviews and colourful recollections of his time with Cobras and Mustangs - not to mention winning Le Mans.

His Chrysler association continues with development and conversion work being carried out from the California base to add the 'performance' factor to Chrysler's range of vehicles. In his role as consultant he had the privilege of overseeing the creation of another sports car which owed much to his own original concept some thirty years earlier. For American sports car fans the years since the Cobra disappeared from the scene have been somewhat downbeat, with a long, slow decline in a world of low speed limits, environmental considerations and growing safety legislation. As in the years prior to the Cobra, the Corvette carried the American sports car flag virtually singlehanded. Many years passed, however, before even the Corvette re-discovered true performance with the advent of the late eighties ZR1 model, the 'King of the Hill'.

Dodge Viper

The Carroll Shelby/Lee Iacocca/ Chrysler combination always threatened to create something interesting on the performance car scene; warming over small saloons was one thing, but what was really required was a headline-grabbing show car to create some interest. Added to the mix was Bob Lutz, Chrysler president and genuine Cobra-owning car enthusiast.It was he who initiated a

challenge to his design and engineering chiefs to create a sports car in the traditional style with the Cobra as their yardstick. With the shackles removed, a raid on a huge parts bin, together with two-seater bodywork in the 'coke bottle' style which echoed the Cobra shape of yore, and with Carroll Shelby acting as consultant and advocate of throwing out unnecessary modern 'junk', the 1989 Detroit Motor Show saw the launch of the Dodge Viper RT/10.

This blood-red sports-car-on-steroids instantly created the publicity Chrysler craved but, more importantly,

Left: Carroll Shelby with his creations the Cobra and Shelby Mustang. (Courtesy SAAC).

Something to smile about! Shelby poses with the Dodge Viper at Indianpolis Speedway. (Courtesy SAAC).

the public response was such that they were deluged with orders from motorists desperate for a modern Cobra. Dodge had hit a yawning gap in the market right on target! From show car one moment (with Chrysler insisting that no production cars were planned) the green light was rapidly given and a

90 strong team of engineers got to work under the macho bodywork to turn a dream into reality.

One of the great selling points of the car was undoubtedly its engine - an 8-litre V10 originally intended for truck installation which gave 400bhp at 4600rpm and a huge 450lbf.ft of

torque at 3600rpm, overshadowing even the mighty Dodge Hemi 426 muscle cars of the 1960s. This monster engine went to Chrysler-owned Lamborghini to replace its cast iron heads and block with aluminium, which succeeded in reducing its weight by 100lbs. Despite rumours that the

The Cobra body panels are formed by hand on original wooden bucks using traditional coachbuilding skills.

V10 was to be replaced by a V8, the modified truck motor fortunately proved equal to the task of powering the Viper in its effort to dethrone the mighty Corvette ZR1. Within thirty months of the Detroit show the Viper team brought the car onto the market as a fully sorted production vehicle and an order book overflowing with people happy to part with $50,000 for the privilege of owning a modern American sports car, albeit one caught in a time warp.

At the car's press release early examples were timed at 0-60mph in 4.8 seconds, 0-100 in 12.0 and 0-100-0 in 15.8 seconds. Fast by any standard but still not the equal of the Cobra 427; the claimed top speed of 165mph was considered academic due to the severe cockpit buffeting at around 85mph. The beauty of the Viper, however, lies in the fact that it appeared at a time when all seemed lost for such vehicles. In one sense its timing could not have been worse; theoretically, this is the one car the world should not need, but for those fortunate enough to occupy the lunatic fringe (Cobra enthusiasts understand ...) this is an unexpected gift from an unexpected source. This 'snake' for the nineties appeared at the 1991 Indianapolis 500 as the official Pace Car. The man behind the wheel leading the field was Carroll Shelby.

Shelby v. Ford

Sadly, Carroll Shelby, in common with AC, has crossed swords with the Ford empire when Shelby management initiated litigation against the Ford

Motor Company over Ford's unauthorised use of the GT350 trademark during the 1984 Mustang 20th Anniversary promotion. Ford retaliated by suing Shelby over the use of the Cobra badges on the limited edition of GT350 Mustang convertibles built during 1980-82. In defending the Ford counter-claim Shelby took the opportunity to prove that Ford had abandoned use of the Cobra trademark due to its failure to take action against transgressors and also the lack of use by Ford itself, the term now being generic and 'in the public domain'.

Whilst Shelby still holds copyright to the GT350, GT500, 289 and 427 titles, the Cobra name was sold for one dollar as part of a deal over a loan, fully repaid, but the name remained with Ford (who were rather slow in taking action over the misuse by kit car/replicar companies who cheerfully slapped original badges on their fakes).

Shelby v. Angliss

Shelby has no ill-will toward Autokraft who put the modernised version of the

Cobra back into production using original Thames Ditton equipment, but he was less pleased that Derek Hurlock sold this equipment to Brian Angliss since he considered that it was not AC's property to sell in the first place. He still has paperwork to prove that Shelby American paid in full for their construction and they were his guarantee that the Cobra would not go back into production. Naturally, he is greatly concerned that the 'investments' made by owners of original cars should be protected and promised, at the 11th Shelby American gathering, too sue Ford should they ever allow the Cobra name to be granted to any Cobra-shaped car.

The reality of the situation was that neither Shelby American, nor AC Cars Ltd, owned much of the original Cobra tooling. AC had contracted outside suppliers to produce forgings for suspension and other parts and, as is so common in such cases, the contractor retained 51 per cent ownership of the tooling to ensure continuity of the contract. When Brian Angliss tracked

Following this success, a number of races for kit-built replica automobiles was organised with RAM-constructed cars often comprising around half of the grid. RAM became the the first such company to supply all the cars for a one-make series when the organisers of the French Bardahl Trophy series of races for 1992 ordered a full grid of RAM SECs to NCA specifications. The cars were to full race specification with roll cages, full harnesses, safety fuel tanks and fire-extinguishing systems. All were powered by 5.7-litre Ford Windsor V8 engines developing 400bhp at 5800rpm and 390Ibf.ft at 3500rpm. The series attracted drivers from many other formulae including the World Sportscar Championship, Formula 3 and Porsche Carrera cup. The series grew rapidly in popularity and by 1994 races were also held in Germany and the UK.

Shelby American's official endorsement, dated January 6th 1994, crowned the first 10 years of Adrian Cocking's RAM company, this being the first time any such endorsement had been applied to a 'replica' car - obviously the Bardahl series contributed.

To underline his commitment to the RAM product, Carrol Shelby flew to the UK to help launch the first Shelby American Cobra replica at the *Autosport* Race Car Show at the Birmingham (England) National Exhibition Centre (NEC), where he added his now-famous signature to the glovebox of the first RAM Shelby 427 S/C replica (CSX-R4001 - the new run of chassis numbers being added to the Shelby American Automobile Club records). The proud new owner, John Ashbourne of Cambridge (England), specified a car finished in classic deep metallic blue with white centre stripes and an interior courtesy of Wilton carpets and Connolly leather. Under the bonnet was a Ford 302 V8 with four Weber IDA carbs and Cobra valve covers. The driveline featured a Top-loader transmission and 3.11:1 PowrLok rear axle.

At the same Race Car Show, Carroll Shelby was also able to launch another project of equal importance and of great personal interest: The Shelby Transplant Trust, the European offshoot of his USA-based Shelby Heart Fund, a charity set up to encourage organ donation, sponsor research and to assist people, especially children, in need of organ surgery. Having undergone heart transplant surgery himself and experienced a remarkable improvement in the state of his health, Shelby realised that he could do a great deal to assist other people who suffer in the manner he once did. At the show he was joined by Stirling Moss, Tony Brooks and Roy Salvadori to help launch his trust which is based at the Addenbrooke's Hospital in Cambridge, England. If you'd like to make a donation or get more information, contact: The Shelby Transplant Trust, Addenbrooke's Hospital, Box 163, Hills Road, Cambridge CB2 2QQ, England. As well as financial support, the Trust needs assistance in spreading the word about its existence and to create awareness amongst people about the importance of organ donation. Naturally, many people in the motor racing world pledged support along with HRH Prince Michael of Kent, HRH The Duke of Kent and King Gustav of Sweden.

Protecting The Cobra Name

Understandably, Carroll Shelby has often expressed concern about the rampant spread of kit car replicas (counterfeits with glassfibre bodies made up from 'junk parts'), a view shared by Brian Angliss. Indeed, in 1985 AC Cars Plc of Thames Ditton issued a statement to the press stating that, in their opinion, anyone producing a Cobra-shaped car (other than Autokraft currently building the Mk IV) was in breach of copyright since the kit car market was taking advantage of the 'goodwill, rights and representation derived from this shape'. All unlicensed copiers of the style of the car were leaving themselves open to prosecution, as were any company adding the AC logo or Cobra badge to a kit car.

Whilst AC Cars were on safe ground regarding the use of copyrighted logos, the problem they faced was that the Cobra shape was never registered for copyright. One could sympathise with their attitude towards the copiers but they were not able to prevent anyone using the shape of a vehicle which had, strictly speaking, been out of production for more than fifteen years. Had the vehicle stayed in unbroken production, the huge replica Cobra market might never have come about. Ford, however, lent their considerable weight to the matter and issued a clear warning to all manufacturers stating exactly who owned the Cobra name

Left and below left: MkIVs at Goodwood.

Right: One of the most popular colour schemes for MkIVs.

Below: The Shepherd brothers' Cobra, highly modified for race work.

Thirty skilled craftsmen were employed and production began during 1981, but the biggest problem was what to call the car: it was not an AC and the Cobra name belonged to Ford. Negotiations with AC proved fruitful: Derek Hurlock was impressed with the whole operation and, in February 1982, very generously gave permission for Autokraft to use the famous curved AC logo on the car and to market it as a genuine AC, with the legend 'Mark Four' sufficing in the (current) absence of the Cobra name. Fourteen years after its death the car was once again available to the public. The whole of the production was initially scheduled for export to America; the first right hand drive car being constructed in August 1983.

In the same way that Ford supplied Shelby with engines, so they supplied Autokraft with 5.7-litre 351 Windsor V8 iron block units. When news broke that Angliss was considering installing a Rover V8 (based on a General Motors design), an unexpected phone call from America put matters right. The official car should at least have the official engine. It's nice to know that someone within the Ford empire still cared.

The completed cars were shipped to America where the engine was forced to use power-sapping, anti-smog equipment which reduced power to around 170bhp.

One of the main departures from the original Cobra concerned the tyres with the Mk IV using the ultimate in road rubber, Pirelli's remarkable low-profile P7, the 255/275 section 15 in tyres filling the huge wheelarches. The other main departure was the addition of four fibreglass mouldings between chassis and body which improves the finish by protecting the inside of the wheelarches from stone chips, as well as improving the weatherproofing. As before, Borg Warner supplied the gearbox and Salisbury the 3.3:1 differential, but the luxurious Connolly leather interior and superb paint finish would have been more familiar to Rolls-Royce owners than to those who purchased original Cobras.

With the right to carry the famous AC logo and a 25-year license to build Cobra-shaped cars, the Autokraft car lacked was the right to be called 'COBRA' due to Ford owning the right to use that name on its own products. However, even the senior management within Ford were sufficiently impressed by the Autokraft product to eventually relent and allow the Mk IV to carry the coveted Cobra title, but not including those cars destined for the American market because of the legal minefield of lawsuits and liability insurance. In some cases senior Ford management even purchased examples for themselves and Carroll Shelby bought four! Thus, as we head toward the twenty first century the AC Cobra Mk IV continues to contribute to the history of motoring.

Indeed, a small band of eighteen fortunate devotees have in their possession an even more coveted version of this beautifully constructed instant classic: the Mk IV 'Lightweight'. At the end of the 1980s the Mk IV underwent a form of automotive diet (in Formula One parlance 'adding lightness') and, along with a host of subtle engineering tweaks, shed over 300lbs. Allied to a re-work of the 302 engine to raise the power (345 being the quoted figure against that of the 'standard' engine output of 225bhp), the Lightweight represents a new high point in Cobra construction and will assuredly be one of the most desirable and sought after sports cars in years to come (or for as long as the internal combustion engine has a market!).

In effect, this model replaces the 427 as the tyre-burning 'brute' but is altogether more civilised and usable than its 1960s relative, despite performance well into the Supercar league. 0-60 in 4.6 seconds, 0-100 in 10.8 seconds are facts which tell their own story, but a revision of the suspension geometry by Len Bailey means that such power can be used on the public road without the driver running the risk of experiencing the sort of difficulties that certain owners of original 7-litre Cobras encountered when least expected! Add to this the unquestioned quality of Autokraft's workmanship and you have the definitive red-blooded sports car. The fact that the Mk IV has never needed to be advertised demonstrates the desirability of the modern Cobra and the loyalty of its countless admirers worldwide. Sadly the asking price continues to place the car firmly in the supercar league. During the mid-sixties, the Cobra was comparible in price to the equally immortal Porsche 911 and this remains the case in the mid-nineties (temporarily even competing on price with the top end of the

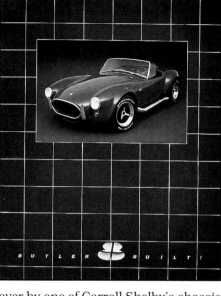

Butler catalogue cover from the early 80s.

Below: Contemporary Cobras await completion. (Courtesy Contemporary Classic Motor Co.).

Ferrari range!) Although the Cobra seems expensive for a relatively simple vehicle, a trip to the factory shows where the money goes: it takes sixty Autokraft employees around 2500 hours to build each of the grand total of four to five cars a month.

AC Cars Plc eventually changed ownership when Derek Hurlock, faced with mounting losses, sold his shares in the company to a stockbroking company in the city and thereby ended fifty seven years of Hurlock management at AC Cars. In retirement he purchased a Surrey farm and renewed his great love of the land but, sadly, died in 1993.

When Derek Hurlock sold up a number of motoring journalists pondered the idea of Brian Angliss of Autokraft taking over the mantle of AC Cars Plc since his was the only company actually making an AC at the time. Eventually, Autokraft was able to purchase a majority of shares in AC Cars Plc and Brian Angliss became Managing Director of both companies.

Early replicas

At the beginning of the 80s potential 'Cobra' owners had not one maker's version to choose from but *twelve* ! Although only the superb Autokraft cars carried the AC logo, many kit-car builders produced replicas, all of which keep faith with the original. No other car has attracted such a wealth of replicas, which must prove something.

Almost inevitably the first copies began to appear in California, where homemade 'alternative' vehicles have a ready market. The cult of customising old cars and vans has its founda-tions on the West Coast ad from this industry grew the necessary expertise to build cars such as Cobra replicas to a high standard and meet the demand from those Californians who loved the original but found the high purchase and maintenance costs beyond their pockets.

Among the first to market a Cobra in kit form was Steve Arntz of San Francisco. Customers could purchase the fibreglass car in three stages, from a rolling chassis to a complete car requiring simply the final assembly of a few items, to avoid the problems of registering his company as a car manu-facturer. The Arntz Cobra was a 427 copy capable of taking any V8 engine and it came fitted with massive side exhausts. Given a suitable paint job the result was a very purposeful look-ing car to say the least. However, vari-ous problems brought production to an end and the operation was taken over by one of Carroll Shelby's chassis specialists, Ron Butler. Ron built the chassis/body units in Culver City with the customer supplying the engine, transmission, suspension and wheels.

The advantage of buying a 'Cobra' in bits is that the owner becomes the production line, bolting the parts to-gether and saving on the high cost of labour, although many owners have their cars constructed by an expert, especially if money is not a great prob-lem. However, the main fabrication work is carried out by experts so, with care, the final result can be a car arguably as good as an original Cobra. Another advantage is that parts can be purchased over a period of time as

necessary finances, however, it was now possible to fool even the experts with your 'genuine' fake.

Replicas were also constructed in places as diverse as Brazil and Switzerland, the latter's Cobra Automobile Jurg Weinem producing another 7-litre copy with side exhausts and wheelarches full of Pearce-style wide alloy wheels. Jaguar mechanicals were used, only with this particular car the brave owner could specify the Jaguar 5.3-litre V12 engine: with all that power beneath the bonnet performance was spectacular in such a lightweight car.

The Brazilian replica was produced in São Paulo by a company called Glaspac. Their main line of business was in fibreglass; and they produced virtually anything which could be made from that material. Naturally, the automotive world was a regular source of work and they were often involved in fibreglass repairs for the Formula 1 teams when the Grand Prix circus was in town.

Because of the vast legislative and financial problems of importing AC Cobras into Brazil, Glaspac decided that a logical solution was to build their own copy. This would also act as a mobile advertisement for their company. Needless to say, great attention

was paid to the quality of the car's bodywork and each car received thirty-six man hours of sanding and polishing before any paint reached it. The same attention to detail ran throughout the car and it certainly looked as a Cobra should, although some artistic licence was taken with the rear wheelarches which had to be widened to incorporate the only rear axle available in Brazil which was from the huge Ford Galaxie. However, the temptation to add embellishments such as external door handles or wind-up windows was resisted and the exhaust pipes were sensibly routed under the car. To make the whole package move as it should the Ford Galaxie again supplied the power plant, a 4950cc V8 of some 199bhp and 287lb torque in untuned form. The Glaspac Cobra weighed in at some 2240lb and could reach 60mph in under seven seconds and then go on to a top speed of around 130mph with the standard 3.07:1 rear axle.

In 1983 Glaspac felt sufficiently confident to begin exporting their product and, within the first three months, received orders for over fifty cars from the United States alone. At a cost of about $25,000 each, the orders bore testimony to the quality of the Brazil-

ian product and the demand for Cobras.

Apart from the official AC Mark Four there were three other replicas under development in England in the early 80s. Metaline Ltd of Ascot had been steadily evolving their replica over the past few years using a very strong and corrosion protected chassis with crushable front and rear zones and a rigid GRP bodyshell (aluminium was available as an option). The body shape was based on the the 427 and featured side exhausts. The well proven Jaguar XJ6 suspension was complimented by XJ12 ventilated brake discs at the front. It has been developed to be sold in various stages of completion, from a rolling chassis up to a fully finished car built to concours standard, with the customer's choice of V8 engine installed, painted in any colour and with the interior fully trimmed in Connolly leather and Wilton carpet.

Another early British replica was being developed by Unique Autocraft of Harlow, Essex, a custom car specialist dealing in all manner of American autoparts and undertaking various forms of customising. They had a desire to build a car of their own and when the opportunity arose with the growth of the 'alternative' car scene, it was decided that the car they wished to build was an updated version of their favourite sports car, the AC Cobra. A very helpful owner allowed then to take moulds of his genuine AC car's body shape but, unfortunately, they had to spend a great deal of time correcting the rear of the mould when they discovered that the original car's body-

195

work had been badly out of true. Their labours proved worthwhile and the prototype body looked identical to an AC 289.

The chassis itself was a very impressive construction, even to the extent of being over-engineered for the prototype's 351 cu in Ford V8, then running with automatic transmission. An extra two inches added to the wheelbase allowed the use of wider doors for easier entry and exit. Almost inevitably Jaguar XJ6 suspension was used, shortened where necessary and fitted with Spax adjustable dampers. Originally a Triumph Dolomite steering rack was used but this was replaced by a more robust Saab unit. A specially constructed radiator filled the nose and was more than adequate to cope with even the largest engine offered. In fact, the whole construction was very solidly engineered and held great promise.

Probably the one car being built in England during the early 80s which really deserved the 'replica' tag was a kit car called the BRA, constructed by Beribo Replica Automobiles Ltd of Castle Donington, Derby. They offered a GRP bodyshell and tubular chassis which they had designed to utilise the running gear of the ubiquitous MGB. Bearing in mind how many MGBs were built there should have been a plentiful supply of donor cars. Originally the design simply followed the general shape of the Mk II Cobra, featuring a modern flared air dam beneath the nose, but this was later deleted and, with a few other alterations, the result was a car capable of fooling even an experienced Cobra expert at quite a short distance. Anyone wishing to own a sports car with a traditional and more attractive body had only to purchase a used MGB and carry out the necessary conversion. Sadly, the donor's 1800cc engine was incapable of delivering Cobra performance and the Beribo company were therefore unable to resist the temptation of dropping the Rover V8 into a strengthened chassis, thereby offering a genuine performance vehicle for those sports car drivers who are not turned on by four-cylinder engines. A small amount of extra space was required under the bonnet for the alloy V8, but fortunately it was almost the same weight as the iron block MGB unit.

The reason the BRA model looked so like a Mk II 289 Cobra is that the moulds were taken from an original car. The factory prototype featured a rebuilt Rover engine which had been modified with special heads, cams and manifolds to give around 230bhp and a power-to-weight ratio better than that of the contemporary Ferrari Boxer or Lamborghini Countach. With a body/chassis unit and V8 kit with doors, bonnet, boot lid, dashboard and numerous other parts retailing for about £3000, it was possible for a BRA owner to experience Cobra-like motoring for around £6000: a far cry from the £20,000-plus then asked for a good example of an original Cobra.

The BRA bodyshell also found its way across the North Sea to Denmark, where it adorned chassis constructed by Danish designer, Ole Sommer. The car was known as an OScar and then represented Denmark's only production vehicle. Under the bonnet was a Volvo B23 engine tuned by Volvo Rallye Sport of Gothenburg to produce 140bhp. The car was officially launched at the Danish Motor Show in Copenhagen in January 1983. It's nice to know that the popularity of the Cobra also extended to the European mainland.

Replica Development
By 1985 at least 17 companies were offering Cobra-shaped vehicles in the UK, catering for those with a budget of £5000 to £20,000. Since then many companies have come and gone but, overall, their numbers have been swelled by others keen to try their luck. Beyond doubt, the Cobra replica market has grown steadily and, love it or loathe it, it is a well established part of the motoring scene. Of those who fell

With Rover V8 power, the Beribo replica was much more like the real thing.

by the wayside Metaline of Ascot came and went with barely a ripple; apparently, a handful of aluminium bodies were built but their perfectionist creator was more in demand as a piano tuner than an erstwhile Carroll Shelby, so he is probably busy somewhere now tickling the ivories.

I felt tempted not to mention the name, but a company called Cheetah did offer something vaguely Cobra-shaped but rapidly disappeared, to the relief of all concerned: in the author's opinion they were a disgrace to even the bottom end of the market. I had the sad misfortune to see one of their misbegotten efforts moving under its own power - a Reliant Robin suddenly seemed an attractive alternative ...

However, on the positive side, this sad vehicle did lead to a number of other replicas. It first resurfaced under the name of Sheldonhurst Cobra, the builders being a Birmingham (England)-based company who were amongst the first to utilise the Ford Granada as a mechanical base. The quality of these cars was vastly better than their predecessor, so it came as a surprise when the company failed. Goodbye Sheldonhurst, Hello Brightwheel, courtesy this time of Granada and Jaguar donor cars. These were well finished replicas whose builder used the services of some competent engineering companies to supply components but, due to some dubious managerial guidance - which included a futile public argument with their competitors - they launced a Cortina-based vehicle at a price somewhat below the cost of its components.

Smart move. Farewell Brightwheel, Greetings Cobretti. As former Brightwheel agents, Cobretti Engineering took over the jigs and moulds to create the Viper (you follow so far?) Guess what happened to Cobretti in 1993? Yes, they sank of course, but, oh joy, resurfaced as Autotrak. To liven up this saga, the director of Brightwheel has made a comeback with a company called Classic Sports Cars and is in litigation with Autotrak! Such are the machinations of the kit/replicar market.

Various other companies surfaced and then sank relatively quickly, usually due to poor quality and/or only offering 4 or 6-cylinder engines, such as the KIng Cobra. Others failed because they were hastily thrown together disasters designed to relieve naive punters of their hard-earned cash by means of the disappearing deposit trick: the SCS Cobra launched by Sports Car Services being one such example, together with the highly dubious AD Cobra. The Essex-based AD outfit succeeded in taking a number of 'non-returnable 20% deposits' in return for not very much. I have in my possession a copy of the AD 'brochure' - a mis-spelt concoction complete with a photocopy picture of an American 427 stuck on the front. How such a tacky document could part people from their cash will remain forever a mystery. The AD concern soon ceased trading, but the car resurfaced as the Gravetti Cobra which also sank but not quite without trace as the project was taken over by a company in Somerset, and thus we had the CK Cobra. In fairness, the whole car was redesigned in the hope of producing a worthwhile product, but the model's dubious history sealed its fate and it finally failed.

A number of the early manufacturers of replicas are still going strong in the 90s. Not on the list, though, is the Unique Autocraft Python which departed in 1993, the victim of rising costs and slow sales. In fact, the quality of the Python demanded a higher

Above: B.R.A. (Beribo Replica Automobiles) Cobra replica with Rover V8 power.

Right and below: The DAX Tojeiro Cobra replica offers real wind-in-the-hair motoring. (Courtesy D J Sportscars).

price which was difficult to achieve during a recession. BRA of Doncaster still market their relatively successful MkII-style 289 model, but dropped the 427 version from their range due to slow sales. Developed over a number of years by Gerry Hawkridge, the relatively rare 427 should prove a sound investment for any enthusiast coming across a used example. In 1994 the BRA company was put up for sale as a going concern.

D.J. Sportscars of Harlow in Essex, grew from relatively humble beginnings producing fibreglass mouldings for industry. The company was commissioned to produce a bodyshell for a German-based company which planned to rebody Corvettes with fibreglass, Cobra-shaped shells (surely guaranteed to upset just about everyone imaginable!). Naturally, the project sank without trace leaving DJS with a number of bodies which were sold to anyone who wanted to make an offer. The response to their advertisement demonstrated to DJS that a large market existed for fake Cobras. From such lowly beginnings the 'DAX Cobra' grew inexorably, backed up by regular advertising, a well made demonstrator available for potential clients and journalists and steady development of their original concept.

One master stroke was to sign up John Tojeiro (designer of the original AC chassis) who had sold his company and, with time on his hands, was happy to join the board of DJ Sportscars and lend his name to the renamed 'DAX Tojeiro', affording the vehicle extra publicity and credibility. DJS were the

first company to shoehorn the Jaguar V12 under the bonnet as an interesting alternative to the traditional big block V8. Without doubt, the massive engine endowed the car with huge torque and effortless, smooth performance. I saw one of the first V12s built and can attest to the smooth nature of the vehicle, although the sound was wrong somehow, not fitting the image, but it remains an interesting - and powerful - alternative. They also developed a 289-bodystyle replica but, in direct contrast to BRA, lack of sales led to its demise. The relative success of DJS's Cobra led to the production of GT40 and Lotus 7 copies with other projects 'under development'.

Obliquely, DJS have been responsible for (at least) two other Cobra copies. In 1984, Ian and Brian Nichols were subcontracted to fabricate chassis for DJS but, as often happens, it was felt that their own line of development would produce a better product: a tour around a number of kitcar manufacturers in the USA led to the creation of Southern Roadcraft in 1985. Based near Brighton, on the Sussex coast, the company produces some of the most rapid Cobra copies unleashed on the public roads. Their demonstrator - fitted with a 300bhp 350 cu in Chevrolet engine - recorded 'fifth-wheel' test times of 0-60 in 4.2 seconds and a top speed in excess of 150mph. They are one of the few companies to export to the USA and they run a separate company supplying new or used engines and transmissions to customers building their cars.

Amongst other companies to leap

on the Cobra bandwagon are KD Kit Cars who offer an affordable version of the 289 shape based on the Ford Cortina and using 4-cylinder or V6 engines. A new spaceframe chassis is under development to accept Ford Cosworth or Sierra mechanics. Gardner Douglas offer the GD 427 based on the shape of the MkII AC289, while Magnum Engineering build a race-designed variation on the Cobra theme. The majority of their cars are destined for track use but road versions come fully trimmed with Kevlar bodies. Crendon Replicas aim for a more authentic look, with original-style chassis, 427-style bodywork and replica interior. Motivation is by Ford or Chevrolet V8. A relative newcomer to the market is the KF Premier built by AK Sportscars of Peterborough, using a ladder-frame chassis, Jaguar running gear and a range of V8 engines.

Another Sussex-based company is Pilgrim Cars who entered this competitive market at the bottom by producing Cortina-based models for those satisfied with 4-cylinder power. The range has grown and the demand for more serious power has led to the Sumo model - which has been rapidly improved while keeping pace with demand. The latest version, now Jaguar-based, has recently passed the tough German TUV chassis test which endorses the strength of the product. However, the Sumo has still to overcome its original bottom-of-the-market image.

One of the stalwarts of the British kitcar/replicar scene is Gerry Hawkridge, now of Hawkridge Developments, purveyors of the Hawk. Having been originally associated with Beribo Replica Automobiles as developer of their 289 model and builder of their 427 prototype, he moved on to develop other vehicles, including the Transformer 2000 - a notable copy of the Lancia Stratos. Almost inevitably, he progressed to the production of his own variation of the MkII Cobra copy. Based around MGB mechanics and with Rover V8 engine this is a very desirable sports car. A quick blast around the lanes of Kent will soon melt the cynic's cast iron heart and a lunch stop at a local hostelry will ensure that all resistance is overcome.

Gerry is nothing if not a Cobra enthusiast and has gone one step further in the field of replicars by replicating an individual original Cobra, namely 39 PH of Le Mans fame. In fact 39 PH's owner, Nigel Hulme, was so impressed by the Hawk 289 that he gave permission for a limited run of 10 replicas of his car, complete with hardtop, fuel filler extension, FIA rear wheelarches and cutaway doors, plus split bootlid. Thus the Hawk Le Mans joins the line-up. Never one to sit around (watching his pot-bellied pig grunt around the garden), Gerry has also developed a very passable replica of the AC Ace in two body styles: the original Bristol-engined flat-fronted version and the elegant Ford-engined variation which was to become the Cobra shape when flared wheelarches were added. So, if the overblown 427-look is not to your taste, then Hawk cars may be for you. What Gerry will produce next is anybody's guess.

The replica scene in the USA has inevitably continued to grow as the price of the genuine article climbed steadily out of reach of the new generations of young motorists who, upon gaining their driving licences, look at the modern range of cars and are less than impressed by what is on offer. The lure of a big engined basic sports car at an affordable price - even one they have to bolt together themselves - represents a more exciting alternative. At the time of writing approximately 34 different Cobra-shaped kits are available for the discerning masochist! However, both Contemporary Classics and ERA have been marketing kits for over ten years and their experience is mirrored in the undoubted quality of their products - provided the future owner puts the thing together in a competent fashion, of course! It was almost inevitable that a replica Daytona Cobra would one day find its way onto the market and Contemporary Classics were the first to submit to the temptation. Without doubt they have done a commendable job in creating a vehicle which could easily be mistaken, at quite close range, for one of the six genuine articles. Exactly who would want to drive around in an enclosed Cobra is open to question since the original was so noisy only heavy metal rock stars would appreciate them.

Contemporary Classics also export to Europe and the United Kingdom: although only a handful have crossed the Atlantic they are all well cared for by the Contemporary agents - in the UK this is American Speed Specialists. The latest additions to the Contemporary 427 model means that the final vehicle is now virtually indistinguishable from the original version, even down to its genuine Halibrand wheels. Naturally, such a car does not come cheap - around £25-30,000 for a fully built model depending on engine options. Take heed, however, that anyone hot-footing it to American Speed with the necessary folding money and an idea that an old Rover V8 would fit a treat under the bonnet (hood), can save themselves a trip. Mention the word Rover and they will not sell you a thing - it's a *GENU-INE* American V8 or nothing!

However, should you wish to experience 'Cobra' motoring via the kitcar/replicar route, the choice is wide and varied, both in the USA and Europe and continually expanding (and contracting as some companies are prone to disappear without trace, as in the case of Aurora Cars of Canada). Almost any kit car magazine will be awash with articles and advertisements and you can be sure that 'Cobras' will frequently appear on the cover. The reason for this is simple - a large increase in magazine sales each time. Cobra Replica Clubs have also spring up to cater for the needs of owners and potential owners. Such clubs can be useful as a guide to the difference between kits, where future owners can judge for themselves and speak to people with first-hand knowledge. Reading so-called road tests in the kit car magazines can be somewhat confusing; witness a recent magazine which reviewed a wide range of kits, each test highly complimentary to both car and

Left and below: Time warp motoring: this 1993 Hawk 289 brings back memories of the 60s.

Right and below: A one-off replica shows off its own interpretation of the Cobra theme. Interior trim goes Hollywood and transmission tunnels just get bigger every day!

Airfix and AMT Cobra model kits.

Below right: Like the real thing, but much smaller: Cobra by Revell.

manufacturer. When a good friend (with wide experience of the business) drove one of the vehicles in question to deliver it to a kit car show he found it had a propensity to ground its chassis. When it was not performing this trick it was burning off its tyres by rubbing them firmly into the top of the wheelarches, accompanied by lots of smoke and hot smells! *Caveat Emptor!* Before purchasing a kit, look, listen, think long and hard and buy the best that your finances allow. If you have any doubts whatever, stick your money back under the mattress (or buy a motorbike!).

Miniature Cobras

As desirable as it may be to have a genuine AC Shelby Cobra lurking in the garage, many owners - and even more would-be owners - have a scale model on their coffee table or desk top. As the Cobra legend has grown so has the market in scale models.

The model market was relatively quiet at the time of Cobra production but subsequentt years saw a steady increase in the popularity of plastic and especially metal Cobra kits. Various manufacturers around the world have produced models of Cobras, many being small production batches which have appeared briefly before being withdrawn from the market for a variety of reasons, so it is virtually impossible to collate a truly accurate and complete list, especially since so many models are now unavailable.

The first Cobra model of note was made in plastic by Revell and this kit was aimed at the toy market portray-

ing a racing style 289 similar to the cars used in the 1964 Targa Florio. This followed some years after Cobra production ceased, by a 1/25 scale model of a 289 roadster made by AMT Corporation of Michigan in their Modern Classics series (number T414), which could be constructed as a road, race or 'custom' car. It claimed to be endorsed by the then current Cobra Club (before it was called The Shelby American Automobile Club) despite the kit featuring Firestone tyres! Carroll Shelby may not have approved.

A desirable plastic kit must be the Airfix 1/16 Cobra 427 (series 14 number 14401) which could easily be constructed to a very high standard. It is worth noting that the kit can be finished either with the Halibrand or the Pete Brock designed Sunburst alloy wheels - buy two, if you can, and

produced, although one of the more interesting ones, the Tenariv Daytona coupé, is no longer in production. However, examples may still be available through specialist model shops and dealers. A 1/43 scale 427 kit was available through Grand Prix models in the UK and this road/race version could also be purchased fully built. Auto Replicas offered a 289 Mk II road car which the skilled modeller could convert to race trim. Having seen one built as a Targa Florio team car I can say that the extra time and patience required is well rewarded. For the dedicated Cobra collector an essential addition must be the Mikansue example of AC's own 1964 Le Mans Coupé, BPH4B, of M1 test session fame. Finally, John Day Models produced a 289 kit for road or race trim and this could also be purchased fully built.

In recent years, the scale model scene has seen an enormous increase in the number of mini Cobras. Available in resin, metal and plastic as Daytonas, 289s and 427s, and even individual models such as the two 1963 Le Mans cars and the first race car all of these models are highly collectable.

To complete a collection one should not overlook the fact that, in the 1960s, Scalextric produced a slot-car racing 289 complete with driver and exhausts, although it is no longer in production.

build one of each! This American model was exported.

Monogram produced a small and not very detailed kit of the Daytona coupé (they also offered a Shelby Mustang GT350), but this model was aimed at the toy market rather than collectors.

For lovers of metal or resin based kits a number of examples have been

Caveat Emptor

Cobras, both real and totally fake, have appeared in many forms since the end of the original production run. As values have soared, so the temptation to create

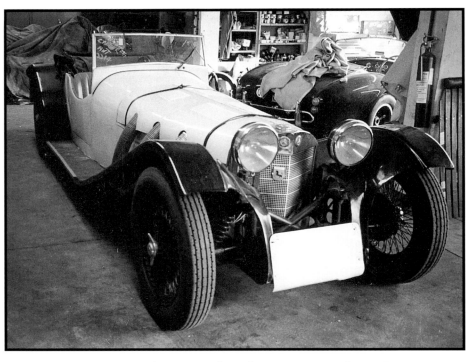

a car which is not quite as it seems has proved too much for many people. As a result of some ungentlemanly behaviour and great confusion caused to would-be buyers of a great piece of motoring history, the Shelby American Automobile Club attempted to define the descriptions which should apply to Cobras coming onto the market - they ended up with seven categories -

1) **Original**- *refers to the fact that the main frame tubes and pieces carrying the serial numbers have not been replaced or altered.*

2) **Original/restored** - *a car having less than 50% of its original substructure or bodywork replaced, but not the main frame tubes or pieces carrying serial numbers.*

3) **Original/rebodied** - *a car having more than 50% of its original substructure or bodywork replaced, but not the main frame tubes or pieces carrying serial numbers.*

4) **Replica** - *a car that has been rebuilt substantially to original specifications (including the replacement of the main frame tubes), but where some part of the original car existed prior to the rebuild; also documental paperwork exists (i.e. traceable bill of sale, title, registration, etc.).*

5) **Air Car** - *a car built from scratch, starting out with no frame tubes or pieces carrying the original serial numbers and with no legitimate paperwork.*

6) **Kit Car** - *any car with a body which approximates the original Cobra shape, using any kind of frame, suspension, brakes or driveline.*

7) **Mk IV** - *the updated version of*

the Mk III coil-spring Cobra currently being built in England by Brian Angliss' CP Autokraft from the original AC jigs and body bucks. These cars do not fit into any of the foregoing categories.

That so few Cobras were ever constructed during their production run is remarkable when one considers the following these cars have generated. The search is always on for an unrestored 'find' or a chassis from the original production days. Forgotten Cobras are as rare as hens' teeth but once in a while an example will surface. Rod Leach of Nostalgia had the good fortune to uncover just such a vehicle, a 289 Mk III built in 1966 and with only 31,994 miles on the clock. It was buried away in a barn in the wilds of Norfolk, untouched for over five years. Rod was amazed to find this genuine Mk III, still resplendent in its Guardsman Blue paintwork, sitting on totally flat tyres and covered in dust, but nevertheless free from any serious deterioration. At its owner's invitation Rod was persuaded to try the engine - it started first time after five idle years! All that was required then was a brake and suspension overhaul, plus cosmetic tidying, to restore it to its former

glory. It now resides in Japan.

However, chassis with genuine Cobra production numbers still come onto the market as fully built Cobras; the five Paramount chassis are still a source of some contention (chassis numbers COX6128 to 6132). Strictly speaking these cars are outside the true production run from the 1960s and, in 1991, COX6129 was completed as a modern 427 Cobra on an old chassis, having been stripped of the pseudo-1930s aluminium bodywork used during the filming of *Monte Carlo or Bust* The important point about such vehicles is that, when changing hands, their provenance should be clearly documented since the chassis were never intended for use as Cobras. In the case of COX6129 it was sold by Nostalgia and naturally accurately described.

Air Cars

This brings us to the subject of 'Air Cars' and the sudden appearance of a previously 'untraceable' Cobra chassis. Once again, money is the root of the problem, the lure of relatively easy money being too much to resist. The only difficulty is obtaining a 'title' of a vehicle, but once that has been

chassis complete with the even more important chassis number (COB6131) and, as such, it has been registered as the genuine article by the Shelby American Automobile Club. Since virtually no two Cobras are truly identical, few people could argue against the validity of this 427's many special features - it really is that much more special than other Cobras since it incorporates a good deal of modern technology.

Such a creation borders on being a work of art and one can imagine many fastidious owners locking such a beautiful machine away from the ravages of road work and sticky fingers. Fortunately, Rod is less narrow-minded. Although my visit was timed during some very wet weather, the skies were clear when I arrived and, for a change, the roads mainly dry. Quite unexpectedly Rod suggested a quick (very quick!) drive in the Hertfordshire countryside, and there can be no finer experience for any admirer of the Cobra than a ride in such a machine. Words can hardly describe the sensations that are experienced when such a car is unleashed on the open road: the deafening roar of the side exhausts, even the tremendous feeling of inherent safety and controllability when the massive brakes haul the speed down so effortlessly. Indeed, one has to hang on to avoid sliding off the leather seats and into the footwell when the brakes clamp on, so the seatbelts serve a very useful purpose. Despite, at the time, having only 400 miles on the odometer and the engine still 'running in', it was patently obvious that there was nothing on the roads of Hertfordshire capa-

ble of overtaking us on that day unless, of course, it had a blue light on the roof and, funnily enough ...

Probably the most abiding memory is that of the police patrol car which pulled out of a side turning as we passed. Lights flashing, it pulled us over and stopped; the police sergeant walked back to the Cobra declaring "I think I'm in love!" A wide-eyed glance under the bonnet and he departed, suitably impressed.

Such reactions are familiar to Cobra owners for they undoubtedly own one of the most charismatic sports cars of the sixties, and the car's appeal has been maintained and even grown some two decades later. All that matters is that Cobra drivers know what they enjoy when it comes to motoring, and although today virtually every owner has a more practical vehicle in the garage, nothing can replace the enjoyment gained by occasionally slipping behind the wheel of a traditional, powerful, uncomplicated sports car.

Sadly, the lot of the true exotic vehicle owner can be an unhappy one at times, especially in Rod's case: whilst he was conducting the monster around Brands Hatch, the engine let go in a manner which says 'full rebuild please'. The task of this major rebuild fell to Power Engineering of Uxbridge, England, who spent 15 months redesigning the twin-turbo installation including waste gates and intercoolers and incorporating a combined carburettor/fuel injection system. Prior to being run-in, the power output at 3000rpm - half throttle - was 410bhp at the rear wheels. Estimated maxi-

mum power was in the order of 750bhp, enough to give 0-100mph acceleration in around 7.5 seconds. For those craving more horsepower than they will ever need in a roadcar, at the time of writing, COB 1 was for sale.

AC 289 (COB6121)

Between the months of April and October each year the quiet Sussex village of Lindfield reverberates to the thump of a Cobra V8 engine when, with the coming of spring, Peter Voigt brings his beautiful 289 out of the garage to enjoy whatever sunny days come along as well as to drive the car to various motoring events or simply to do the shopping.

Completed on 23 June 1968, with the chassis number COB6121, this car was originally registered in Jersey (the land of 40mph speed limit!) before returning to the mainland a few years later where it was re-registered ELW72J.

In 1975 it came into the possession of Peter Voigt shortly after he had 'retired' from his favourite sport of hillclimbing. His motor racing interests began with a Lotus 7, used for driving tests and autocrosses until he discovered hillclimbing when it was replaced by a unique DRW Imp; this was followed in successive seasons with a single-seater Ginetta, a disastrous Palliser Repco and, finally, with a one-off, single-seater of his own construction. The road cars he has owned include a Ferrari 330GTC, which left him unimpressed, and a Porsche Carrera 2.7 which he enjoyed a great deal more but which still takes second

place in his affections to the Cobra since, in his opinion, a sports car should be a convertible and the urge of big, multi-cylinder engine is always preferable to a small 'screamer'. When he is not involved with this motoring interests he is to be found carrying on the family tradition, dating back to the eighteenth century, of restoring musical instruments of the violin family - in fact, the business of E.R.Voight & Sons is the oldest of its kind in the world.

His first job after purchasing the car was to replace the carpets which were literally falling to pieces, and to sweep out what appeared to be a quantity of Jersey sand from the interior, although the car itself was generally rust free. Any work on the car is generally carried out throughout the winter months and both front and rear suspensions were rebuilt when time allowed, with the addition of Peter Voight's own redesigned suspension settings - a 1/8 in camber on the rear wheels helps to put the power on the road more effectively. A change from wire wheels to a Halibrand pattern set of alloys from a GT40 (correct for the period if not, strictly speaking, for the car), plus a change from original pattern Michelins to B.F.Goodrich tyres meant that the clutch could be dropped at 4500rpm and that all the power is

transmitted to the road. With Michelins and standard suspension the car wasted its potential through massive wheel spin, even with the clutch swiftly engaged at 2500rpm. Standing starts had to be made cautiously and the power had to be fed in progressively when on the move.

It is also interesting to note that the Goodrich tyres were very unsatisfactory when new, particularly in the wet, and despite many road miles they failed to show any sign of wear until a few quick laps of Goodwood scrubbed them in properly and literally transformed the car.

A home made detachable roll bar was fitted behind the driver's seat and paintwork given attention - racing numbers sometimes pull off the top layer of paint and the flexing of the aluminium body panels can actually produce cracks in the paintwork. In fact, when the car was being driven across France one summer visible cracks appeared on the wings while on the move, only to disappear after it had been standing for a while.

The original engine was replaced by another 4.7-litre in a higher state of tune having seen service, it is believed, in a GT40. A dual pump Holley was fitted on a high-rise manifold and has, like the gearbox, been a model of reli-

ability. To add the final touch the registration 289 COB was purchased from Jamesigns, purveyors of so many 'COB' registrations and owned by the former secretary of the Cobra Register, John Atkins.

As Peter Voigt admits, he can think of no sports car with which to replace the Cobra, nor one he would prefer to drive, which says it all really.

AC Cobra Le Mans (CS2131)

Built by AC Cars Ltd specifically for the Le Mans 24-Hour event, 39 PH is a special part of British sports car racing and, as part of the Willment racing team, was a common sight at racing circuits from 1964 until the early seventies.

As detailed elsewhere its Le Mans performance was impressive: despite the fact that it was handicapped by a relatively under-powered engine, it came home seventh and won the over 4-litre class behind a procession of Ferraris. A unique feature was its detachable streamlined aluminium hardtop, designed to improve top speed along the Mulsanne straight. This necessitated a redesign of the bootlid fro top to bottom hinges and a long fuel filler hose to the tank which resulted in the filler cap being located in the roof.

After the race it was sold to the John Willment racing team as one of their three Cobras for a busy and successful career in club and international meetings. It was resprayed from its original green to the team colours of red with white twin centre stripes, while the Le Mans hardtop was permanently removed since it was consid-

217

Right and below: The 1963 Le Mans Cobra (CS2131) in Willment Team colours.

ered not to serve any useful function. 39 PH found most success in the capable hands of Willment team driver, Jack Sears, with a second place overall in the 1964 Sussex GT Trophy race at Goodwood, beaten only by Graham Hill's Ferrari GTO, second at Oulton Park, winning the GT class at

from its appearance, despite the occasional stone-chip and ill-informed people leaning on the aluminium bodywork. It still fires at the turn of the key and at 120mph sings along without fuss or drama. The Hulmes have owned many desirable road and race cars but 39 PH will remain as a permanent part of the family.

Shelby-AC Cobra (HEM6)

Of all the Cobras to feature on these pages this one could probably lay claim to having seen the most competition mileage; its long history could almost be the subject of a book itself.

Originally constructed in 1964 for C.T. (Tommy) Atkins, it first appeared at the British Grand Prix meeting of

into the hands of the Chiswick sports car dealers, The Chequered Flag, who were also campaigning a Formula 3 Brabham during 1965. Graham Warner's team installed a modified Holman & Moody engine and thoroughly sorted the car for their drivers, Roy Pike, Roger Mac, Chris Irwin and occasionally Bob Bondurant. The green paintwork was resprayed in the team colours of white with a large black centre stripe.

Its first victory soon followed in the Sussex Trophy GT race at Goodwood where Roger Mac fought off a determined challenge from Peter Sutcliffe's GTO and Peter Lumsden's lightweight E-type Jaguar. Four other major victories or class wins followed as well as numerous victories in club racing. The car was registered for road use at the beginning of the year which is why a 1964 car carries a 1965 number plate.

For 1966 'The Flag' added a 7-litre Cobra to their team leaving GPG 4C out in the cold, although it was entered in the 500 miles Ilford Films race at Brands Hatch where it ran second behind its larger-engined team mate until it dropped a rod.

In 1967 the car was entered in occasional club events and hillclimbs by its new owners, Keith and Wendy Hamblin. It was painted a silver-grey. A new colour scheme was adopted in 1970 by its next owner, Shaun Jackson, who campaigned the red and gold car now fitted with a hardtop for two very busy seasons, scoring a number of victories in Modsports events. The engine was a 5-litre Gurney-Weslake giv-

that year where Roy Salvadori finished third in the GT event in the still unpainted car. Chris Amon drove it to second place behind Jack Sears at the August Bank Holiday meeting while, at the Tourist Trophy, Salvadori initially led the Shelby Daytona coupés before having to retire.

At the end of 1964, following the death of Tommy Atkins, the car passed

This page & overleaf: Shelby Cobra 427 (CSX3035) has a great racing history in the USA.

world; he also has the good fortune to own one of the fastest Cobras in the world. The two together are formidable as their record proves and as I was fortunate enough to witness for myself.

In September 1981 a trip to California coincided with the annual Ferrari Owners Club hillclimb near Carson City, Nevada, and the Shelby American Automobile Club had been invited to attend. A quick change of plans and a 500 mile drive resulted in a day spent standing in the middle of nowhere photographing the only Cobra to attend the meeting. But what a Cobra! The most successful example of the marque racing in America and still in the hands of its original owner, ex-test pilot and SAAC Champion, Dick Smith, of Fresno, California (a member of the SAAC Advisory Board).

The hillclimb course was impressive - a five mile public road (closed for the day) climbing steadily up to Virginia City with massive drops disappearing far below the narrow ribbon of tarmac. Among the host of Ferraris

233

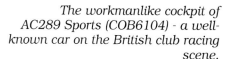

(Daytonas, Dinos, 250LM, a beautiful 250GTO) one car was visibly faster than the opposition: its driver set the car perfectly for the bends with no sound of the throttle being feathered and not a trace of the right foot lifting. Dick Smith and his 427 collected their traditional Fastest Time of the Day.

The following year a Californian tyre dealer decided to end Mr Smith's supremacy. He prepared a brand new Porsche 930 Turbo shod with suitable rubber and installed motorcycle ace, Randy Mamola, in the driver's seat. On the first run he equalled the Cobra's record for the hill. Always one to enjoy a challenge, Dick Smith proceeded to set Fastest Time of the Day and a new hill record on his second run, putting the shiny new Porsche firmly in its place.

So the long list of victories continues for this 427 and it has almost certainly won more races than any other Cobra. In the course of winning the National ARRSC Championships at Daytona in 1967 it went through the speed traps at 198mph along the straight and joined the '100 Club' by averaging over 100mph for a full lap. Indeed, in 1980s it was still recording speeds of 190mph at Sebring and is still capable of beating full race GT machines even now. All this with a car which can be driven on the road, as was proven when it was driven to a race meeting in Monterey from its Fresno base.

As well as the 1967 SCCA A/P National Championship and North Pacific Division Championship, other national victories were gained in 1965

and 1966, plus various successes too numerous to list around the country. (The 427 was then painted in its original colours of silver with a yellow nose section).

Because of his great knowledge of the Shelby cars Dick Smith's Cobra is outstanding - as his concours awards prove. He put this experience to good use by sorting out and test driving the 7-litre Daytona Super Coupé.

AC 289 Sport (COB6104)

To the British club racing fan the number plate of this AC is probably more famous than the car which carries it although, during the 1980s, the car made a very welcome return to the circuits in the hands of its new owner.

A word of explanation: GD 100 was the personalised number plate of amateur racing enthusiast and AC stalwart, Geoffrey Dempsey, who was a familiar figure at the circuits during the late fifties and early sixties with his AC Ace. A true enthusiast, he raced for fun as often as his budget would allow. In a sudden urge for more power he sadly parted with his well-used but still immaculate Ace and ordered an AC 289 from the Thames Ditton factory in 1966, specifying a few modifications to the engine and suspension to improve matters for circuit work. A 715 cfm Holley carburettor was fitted along with a high rise induction manifold and eight-branch exhaust manifold with a stainless-steel system.

Sadly, after only a few months of ownership the combination came to grief shortly after rounding the very fast Woodcote bend at Silverstone (in

pre-chicane days) and the car crossed the finishing line backwards, demolishing its front and rear bodywork against the banking opposite the pits.

Although thankfully not seriously injured Geoffrey Dempsey decided to retire from racing. GD 100 returned to Thames Ditton for a full and painstaking rebuild; a new body plus the addition of Halibrand wheels, along with some better tyres than those which had let the car down at Silverstone. Destined for summertime road use, plus the occasional sprint such as the Brighton Speed Trials, it only covered some 800 miles in the last five years of Geoffrey's ownership and, in 1982, had a total of 36,000 miles on the clock.

During 1981, however, it changed hands. Des Cassidy proved fastest to the phone when the advertisement appeared in *MotorSport* and he set about preparing the car for a return to club racing. With a new roll-over bar, brake servo and a thorough overhaul, GD 100 made a very welcome addition to the ranks of racing Cobras and both car and driver gradually became more competitive with each race. The road going Bridgestone tyres proved an embarrassment at first and a change to more suitable rubber made a great improvement to the extent that the 289 was able to turn in lap times comparable to those of the well sorted Cobra Mk II of post Historic Champion, John Atkins, although the earlier car still held on to cross the line first.

After a few seasons of excitement around the UK circuits, Des parted company with GD 100 in favour of a

Left & below: AC 289 Sports (COB6104).

239

return to the Ferrari marque. The Cobra remains in private hands in the UK.

Shelby Cobra 427 (CSX3234)

As the number plate - 427 COB - says 427 cubic inches (7-litres) of Cobra power. Although this particular 427 may not have a particularly fascinating history - no major racing victories, nobody has ever driven it off a cliff - it is nevertheless a wonderful example of the true racing-bodied 7-litre Cobra with its massive rear wheelarches and, even more unusual, it featured 'sunburst' design alloy wheels. These were created by Pete Brock at Shelby American when supplies of the usual six-spoke Halibrands virtually dried up. (Many 427s were later converted to these Halibrands by their owners).

This particular Shelby Cobra was re-imported to England by Brian Classic in 1973 and was purchased soon

240

These two pages & overleaf: Shelby Cobra 427 (CSX3234) is fitted with Pete Brock Sunburst pattern alloy wheels.

afterwards by John Stevens, who had been impressed by American V8 power after test drives in both of the AC factory demonstrators, the 428 and 289 Cobra. At that time the 427 was considered the ultimate Cobra to own since its straight line performance was by then almost legendary. However, this example was not in the best of health when it arrived in England. To cut a long story short it was almost falling apart and had suffered frontal damage. Since it was to share its new home with a collection of beautifully restored classic Bentleys it was given back to the AC factory for a complete rebuild which took a full year. A larger

capacity sump was fitted, along with a twin-fan installation to improve the inevitable cooling problems and, as the photographs show, was converted to right-hand drive. The interior was retrimmed in a non-standard cream leather by an outside contractor.

From completion of the work, in 1974, up to the time the accompanying photographs were taken (nine years later) the car had travelled just over 1300 miles. Although its owner was greatly impressed by its effortless power and 'Grand Touring' abilities, a trip around the Silverstone circuit proved what a handful an excess of power can be and, along with many owners of

427s in England, John Stevens is sure that a 4.7-litre Cobra would be a more practical proposition around country lanes.

During the 1980s the car was sold to a Swiss collector, Klaus Dechslin, but returned to the UK where it was resprayed silver and changed its number plate to COB 3. It has appeared twice in *Classic & Sportscar* magazine; originally in 1984 when in the hands of Rod Leach's company Nostalgia and prior to its sale to Switzerland and again in January 1990, as COB 3, under the heading 'Too Much is Just Right'. The car took overall honours at the ACOC concours in 1989.

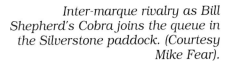

Inter-marque rivalry as Bill
Shepherd's Cobra joins the queue in
the Silverstone paddock. (Courtesy
Mike Fear).

APPENDIX
CLUBS, DATA
ROAD TESTS
&
PHOTO PRINT
OFFER

Philip Lemon 1983

244

Clubs

For devotees of the marque two clubs exist to cater for the needs of both owners and enthusiasts. In England the AC Owners Club is divided into registers for each model constructed since the 1950s. The Cobra register is currently in the charge of Thames Ditton resident, John Atkins, who regularly races his Mk II Cobra and always drives it to and from events. (Both John and his car are improving each season and in 1982 he won the Post Historic Sports Car Championship and is proving just as invincible in 1983). Regular meetings are held and newsletters are sent to members to keep them up to date in all things 'Cobra'.

The AC Club also enters teams of up to six Cobras in the Robin Hamilton Inter-Marque Challenge each season which fare with considerable success against strong opposition from the Aston Martin, Jaguar and Porsche teams at circuits around the country.

Naturally, with only a relatively small number of Cobras in the United Kingdom, the Cobra Register is not a large 'organization', but anyone fortunate enough to be able to join its ranks will be assured of sound expert advice and sympathy when any problems arise.

Inevitably, the largest club exists within Shelby territory - the United States. Based in Connecticut, the Shelby American Automobile Club (SAAC) is a club on a massive scale, numbering its members in thousands around the world. This complex network is handled by directors Kenneth Eber and Richard Kopec, and their advisory board is a 'Who's Who' of Shelby history: Pete Brock, Phil Remington, Bob Bondurant and Dick Smith. It is headed, not unnaturally, by Carroll Shelby.

Within the headquarters of the SAAC lies every piece of information you could wish to know about the history of Shelby American from day one; even Carroll Shelby admits that the club knows more about him and his company than he ever did! Its detective work has been prodigious, to say the least, and the efficient running of the club is no less impressive. For anyone remotely interested in this fascinating period of American motoring, or in the cars themselves - Mustangs, Cobras, GT40s etc - then the SAAC is a must. Its excellent magazine, *The Shelby American*, appears five times a year and is well worth the subscription. The annual Shelby Convention is a motoring mecca which draws enthusiasts from around the world for days of lectures, discussions and, of course, circuit races and parades which feature all manner of desirable machinery. Throughout the year the various regional centres around America hold their own meetings and conventions.

Underlining the wealth of information that the SAAC has at its disposal is a massive directory it has published called *The Shelby American Guide* which lists all the chassis numbers of every Cobra and Mustang built, along with all the information available about each car - quite an undertaking by any standard, especially as the factory records were initially not

very well documented.

Addresses

AC Owners Club,
Membership Secretary,
E.C.Clark,
The Flint Barn,
Upper Wooten,
Near Basingstoke,
Hants RG26 5TH,
England.

AC Owners' Club,
Cobra Registrar,
W.Shepherd,
c/o Royston Road,
Byfleet,
Surrey KT14 7PB,
England.

SAAC HQ,
PO Box 788,
Sharon,
CT 06069,
USA.

PRODUCTION FIGURES

Cobra Production Totals

1962-1965 Cobra

260 cid cars	75
289 cid cars	579
TOTAL	654

1965-1967 Cobra

427, 428 cid cars	348
TOTAL	348

GRAND TOTAL   **1002**

Shelby Production Totals

1965

Mustang GT-350 street model	525
Mustang GT-350 competition model	37
TOTAL	562

1966

Shelby GT-350	1438
Shelby GT-350 Hertz model	936
Shelby GT-350 convertible	6
TOTAL	2380

1967

Shelby GT-350 fastback	1175
Shelby GT-500 fastback	2050
TOTAL	3225

1968

Shelby Cobra GT-350 fastback	1253
Shelby Cobra GT-350 convertible	404
Shelby Cobra GT-500 fastback	1140
Shelby Cobra GT-500 convertible	402

Shelby Cobra GT-500KR fastback	933
Shelby Cobra GT-500KR convertible	318
TOTAL	4450

**1969

Shelby GT-350 fastback	1085
Shelby GT-350 convertible	194
Shelby GT-500 fastback	1536
Shelby GT-500 convertible	335
TOTAL	3150

**1970

Shelby GT-350	315
Shelby GT-500	286
TOTAL	601

GRAND TOTAL   **14,368**

** These figures are from Ford and are likely to be incorrect. In fact, SAAC records indicate that probably a total of 3350 1969-1970 Shelbys were built. Because no accurate records have been found the above Ford figures should be used only as approximations.

SHELBY FORD COBRA (1964 MODEL) - DATA

Dimensions

Wheelbase	90"
Overall length	167"
Width	61"
Height to top of windshield	45"
Tread, front	53.25"
Tread, rear	52.75"
Ground clearance	5.5"

Engine specifications

Type - High performance Ford Fairlane V8

Displacement	289 cu in
Bore & stroke	4.00 x 2.87"
Compression ratio	10 to 1
Basic carburation	single 4v
Bhp	271 @ 5800rpm*
Torque	269lb @ 4800 rpm

*Optional versions up to 370hp

General

Curb weight	2100lbs
Weight distribution	49/51
Steering wheel turns lock to lock	3
Turning circle	33'3"
Tyre size, front	7.35 x 15
Tyre size, rear	7.35 x 15
Brake lining, swept area	550sq in

Transmission: 4 speed, close ratio

First	2.36-1
Second	1.61-1
Third	1.20-1
Fourth	1-1

Differential

4.56	110mph
4.26	115mph
3.77	132mph
3.54	140mph
3.31	150mph
2.72	180mph

Speeds quoted = top speed at 6500rpm with stock equipment.

Features

All aluminium hand-formed body; genuine leather upholstery; individual bucket seats; limited slip rear end; rack & pinion steering; 72 stroke wire wheels with knock-off hubs; full independent suspension front & rear; alternator; replacing generator; wide based wheels for better handling; Le Mans type 12 inch Girling disc brakes on all four wheels with dual master cylinders; choice of final drive ratios from 2.72:1 through 4.56:1. Road equipment: safety glass windshield; folding top & side curtains; turn indicators; full lighting.

Colours available: red, maroon, white, black, bright blue, princess blue, silver.

Price: P.O.E. Los Angeles, $5995.00

Factory installed optional equipment & accessories
(As of January 8, 1964. Prices and specifications subject to change without notice)

Group A
Tuned air cleaner, chrome: $4.00
Aluminium rocket arm covers: $52.35
Front grille guard, chrome: $39.50
Rear bumper guard, chrome: $42.50
Exhaust pipe tips, chrome: $5.00
Adjustable wind wings: $22.50
Tinted sun visors: $19.50
Smiths heater: $95.00

Competition seatbelts (each): $16.50
White sidewall tyres: $42.50

Group B
Wheels, chrome (5): $150.00
Aluminium 4v intake manifold: $71.00
Outside rear view mirror: $6.00
Dual 4v carburettor and manifold: $243.00
Custom AM radio & antenna: $58.50
Competition oil pan: available soon
Oil cooler: $128.25
Competition vehicles and related high performance equipment (prices available on request.

COBRA 289 (COMPETITION VERSION) - DATA

Tread (track), front	52"
Tread (track), rear	53.5"
Wheelbase	90"
Overall length	151.5"
Overall height	49"
Overall width	67"
Weight	1912lbs

Construction - Large diameter steel tube frame of simple ladder construction, body of aluminium panels over light gauge steel tube formers.

Engine
Type - Ford V8 high performance; capacity 289 cid

Firing order	1,5,4,2,6,3,7,8
Bore	4.00"
Stroke	2.87"
Cylinder block	cast iron
Cylinder heads	cast iron

Crankshaft - cast iron, supported in five main bearings with external counterbalances

Bearings	copper-lead
Main bearing diameter	2.25"
Rod bearing diameter	2.125"

Valve operation - pushrod from cam in block

Valve diameter, inlet	1.88"
Valve diameter, exhaust	1.63"

Valve springs - 1 and 1 damper spring per valve

Valve lift	0.490"
Carburation	4 x 2v Weber 48IDA
Compression ratio	11.5:1

Ignition, coil - Ford; voltage, 12
Exhaust system - Nassau type tuned header system with large diameter mufflers & tailpipes

Gearbox

Type	Borg Warner T10
Case material	aluminium
Ratios	
High	1:1
3rd	1.20:1
2nd	1.62:1
1st	2.36:1

Clutch

Type	Ford
Disc diameter	10.5"

Rear Axle Centre Section
Salisbury hypoid mounted to chassis frame by three large diameter rubber sleeve type mounts. Open half shafts, universally joined at each end, transmit power to wheel spindles. Limited slip differential standard. Ratio, standard, 3.77:1, optional, 3.07, 3.31, 3.54, 4.09, 4.27

Suspension
Anti-sway bars fitted front and rear. Koni shock absorbers standard equipment

Brakes
Girling disc brakes front and rear

Front	11 5/8"
Rear	10 3/4"

Wheels & Tyres
Front - 6.70 x 15 stock car specials on 6 1/2" rim x 15" magnesium centre lock pin drive wheels
Rear - 8.20 x 15 stock car specials on 8 1/2" rim and 15" magnesium centre lock pin drive wheels

Capacities

Radiator	12 quarts
Engine	8 quarts
Fuel tank	18 gallons

Oil cooler, large capacity steel oil pan, rear axle cooler and circulating pump, special racing bucket seats, roll-over protection hoop, seat belts, shoulder harness, special instruments are standard equipment on competition cars.

Options

Fuel tank	37 gallon

Cobra Competition Cars

Stage 1
A dual purpose machine for the man who wants something a little better than stock, suitable for slaloms, autocrosses and mild club racing events. Fitted with roll bar, anti-sway bars, front and rear, seatbelts, otherwise as street specifications with standard 289 cid, 271 horsepower engine; $6275.00

Stage II

For the man who takes his racing seriously. As above but fitted with centre lock magnesium wide rim wheels with Goodyear racing tyres, fenders modified to accept wide tyres, special steering arms, hood air scoop. With standard 289 cid, 271 horsepower engine: $7220.00

Stage III

A team car replica. Identical in every way to the famous Shelby-American team cars which won the Manufacturers' Championship, the SCCA Class A Championship and the Drivers' Championship. Each car is tested personally by Ken Miles at Riverside and guaranteed to equal the best lap times established by a factory team car (the GT lap record). Complies with SCCA Production Class A requirements and homologated with the FIA as a GT car, Class III.

Fitted with roll bar, sway bars front and rear, wide base magnesium centre lock wheels on special hubs, strengthened chassis, Koni shock absorbers, special steering arms, heavy-duty brake pads, engine oil cooler, rear axle cooler, hood air scoop, brake air scoops, racing windshield, racing seats, quick lift jack pads, long range fuel tanks, supplementary electric fuel pump, special instruments, special brake fluid, Goodyear racing tyres, choice of axle ratio. Available only with option IV, full race engine: $9500.00.

Either Stage I or Stage II cars may be fitted with any of the following options, the price of which is in addition to the base cost of the car.

Option II-R

Standard engine but equipped with dual quadruple choke carburettors and aluminium large capacity oil pan, polished valve covers: $254.75

Option III-R

Full racing engine, magnafluxed, balanced, crankshaft reworked, pistons modified, heads ported and polished and fitted with larger valves, special camshaft, degreed crankshaft damper, reworked distributor, large capacity steel racing oil pan, two four-throat carburettors on an aluminium manifold: $1907.71

Option IV-R

As above but fitted with four two-barrel Weber carburettors and associated linkage: $2905.42.

427 COBRA (STREET VERSION) - DATA

Engine

428 cid Special Police Interceptor engine with modifications by Shelby-American. Water cooled, cast iron block with 5 main bearings. Bore 4.13"; stroke 3.98"; displacement 428 cubic inches; 7014cc; compression ratio 10.0:1; carburation 1-4v Ford; horsepower 390 @ 5200rpm; torque 475 ft/lbs @ 3700rpm; electrical system 12v battery, alternator, valve train, pushrod, O.H.V.; mechanical lifters; mileage 9-12mpg; premium only recommended.

Chassis

Tread (track), front	56"
Tread (track), rear	56"
Wheelbase	90"
Wheels	7.5" x 15" alloy

Tyres - 8.15 x 15 Special Goodyear Blue Dots

Overall length	156"
Overall height	49"

Construction - large diameter steel tube frame carrying suspension mounts, body of aluminium panels formed over lightweight steel tube formers.

Overall width	68"
Curb weight	2529lbs

Drive Train

Clutch - 11.5" single dry plate, hydraulic release.

Transmission - 4 speed, all synchro

Gear	Ratio	Overall	mph/1000 rpm	Max mph
Rev	2.32	7.68	10.86	69
1st	2.32	7.68	10.86	69
2nd	1.69	5.59	14.98	95
3rd	1.29	4.26	19.62	126
4th	1.00	3.31	25.12	162

Rear axle centre section - Salisbury, limited slip differential standard equipment; final drive ratio, 3.31:1

Suspension

Independent front and rear using large coil spring. Hydraulic shock absorber units incorporated in a highly developed design which virtually eliminates dive and squat.

Brakes

Type	Girling disc
Front disc diameter	11.625"
Rear disc diameter	10.75"

427 COBRA (COMPETITION VERSION) - DATA

Tread (track), front	56"
Tread (track), rear	58"
Wheelbase	90"
Overall length	156"
Overall height	49"
Overall width	70.5"
Weight	2150lbs

Construction: large diameter steel tube frame carrying suspension mounts, body of aluminium panels formed over lightweight steel tube formers.

Engine
Type - push rod operated, overhead valves. Operated from camshaft in block

Cylinder block	cast iron
Cylinder heads	aluminium
Bore	4.24"
Stroke	3.788"
Displacement	427 cu in
Crankshaft	steel forging
Main journal diameter	2.750"
Crank pin diameter	2.439"
Bearings	copper-lead
Valve size, inlet	2.085" diameter
Valve size, exhaust	1.650" diameter
Valve springs	coil, 2 per valve
Carburettor	Holley 4v
Ignition: coil	Ford.
Voltage	12

Gearbox

Type	Ford
Ratios (standard) -	
High	1:1
3rd	1.29:1
2nd	1.69:1
1st	2.32:1
Ratios (optional) -	
High	1:1
3rd	1.19:1
2nd	1.54:1
1st	2.32:1

Clutch
Ford, single plate, 11.5" diameter

Rear Axle Centre Section
Type   Salisbury
Ratio - standard 3.77:1; optional 3.09, 3.31, 3.54, 4.09. Limited slip differential standard equipment

Brakes

Type	Girling disc
Diameter, front	11.4"
Diameter, rear	10.75"

Wheels
Front 7.50 x 15; rear 9.50 x 15 pin drive magnesium alloy

Capacities

Radiator	20 quarts

Engine oil - wet sump 13 quarts; dry sump 14 quarts

Fuel tank	42 gallons

Sway bars front and rear; special tuned exhaust system, roll-over protection; seatbelts; rear axle oil cooler and pump; engine oil cooler; all standard equipment on competition model.

Optional equipment
Special racing bucket seat; shoulder harness; quick change brake pad kit; mechanical chronometric tachometer; dry sump kit.

427 COBRA DRAGONSNAKE - DATA

The 427 Cobra Dragonsnake is equipped as follows:
• Heater
• Seatbelts
• Drag headers, located outside front fenders; exhaust flow is directed through front fenders, ouside & parallel to body lines
• Koni front shocks (reworked to up-lock action
• Koni rear shocks (50-50 down-lock action)
• Two (2) Goodyear Drag Slicks
• Three (3) Goodyear Blue Dot Tyres
• Rear end ratio: 4.54
• Hood air scoop
• Two (2) electric fuel pumps
• Battery has been relocated behind passenger seat

• Heavy duty half shafts equipped with AN nuts & bolts to prevent shearing and/or loosening under high torque loads
• NHRA approved scattershield
• NHRA approved roll bar

The engine in the 427 Cobra Dragonsnake has been competition prepared to exact factory specifications. Every clearance and dimension has been checked and set to minimum specification. Clearances of all bearings in the lower end of the engine have been set for high rpm.

All moving parts of the engine assembly have been balanced, including the cam followers, pushrods, rocker arms and the valves and spring retain-

ing washers. The cylinder heads are cast aluminium and have lightened competition valves installed. The ports and combustion chambers are not polished, to comply with NHRA rules for Stock Sports Classes. The cam can be either advanced or retarded to customer specification. The rear and front spring assemblies are modified slightly to create better ground contact on the rear spring and better lift characteristics on the front springs. A hood scoop is also added to ensure cool, efficient air intake to the carburettors.

Shelby-American will soon offer as an option hardtop and aluminium framed side curtains. No price has been established on this option to date.

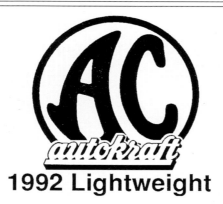

1992 Lightweight

SPECIFICATIONS

Two seat, two door sports convertible of 4 inch diameter x 14 gauge solid drawn tube, lightweight superstructure "ladder" spaceframe construction with internal diaphragm. Stainless steel tubular bumper bars on telescopic struts, chrome plated overiders. Original short nose bodywork with brake cooling ducts, hand rolled in 16 gauge aluminium alloy, seam welded using parent metal. MKIV size cockpit. Seats, facia and door panels trimmed in Connolly hide. Deep pile wool carpeting bound in leather. Convertible top and tonneau cover in Everflex. Aluminium bonnet scoop. Windshield wipers, windwings and sunvisors. Chrome roll over bar. Lockable fuel filler cap.

Ancillary equipment

Original type dashboard with chrome bezel instruments including speedometer and tachometer. Gauges for oil pressure, oil temperature, water temperature, fuel level and battery condition. Warning lights for low fuel level, indicator/hazard lights, oil pressure, handbrake/brake fluid level, headlamp main beam and ignition. Heater. Adjustable steering column and woodrim steering wheel. Full safety harness for driver, lap and diagonal for passenger.

Engine

5.0 Litre Ford V8 302 EFI GT40 High Output Dual stainless exhausts with tubular headers. Roller camshaft, aluminium valve covers and intake manifold.

Transmission

Borg Warner T5 - 5 speed. Salisbury limited slip differential.

Suspension - front and rear

Independent by unequal length wishbones with coil springs and concentric shock absorbers.

Steering

Rack and pinion. 3.6 turns lock to lock. 24 foot turning circle kerb to kerb.

Wheels and tyres

Halibrand pattern aluminium alloy with peg drive - 7.5 x 15 in. front and 9.5 x 15 in. rear. Front tyres 225-65-VR15 Pirelli P7R. Rear tyres 275-55-VR15 Pirelli P7R. Three eared bronze wheel spinners supplied, wheel nuts fitted.

Brakes

Four wheel disc brakes, with 11.56 in. diameter ventilated front and 10.75 in. diameter rear. Dual independent servo-assisted hydraulic circuits. Mechanical parking brake.

Electrical equipment

12 volt negative earth, fully fused. 75 amp. alternator, 60 amp./hr. battery. Two 60 watt sealed beam main headlamps with combined 45 watt dip headlamps. Parking and indicator lights at front. Parking, indicator and stop lights at rear. Hazard warning system. Windscreen washers with two-speed wipers and delay.

Dimensions

Wheelbase	90 in.
Track (front/rear)	56 in./60 in.
Length	162 in.
Width	68 in.
Height	49 in.
Weight	2520 lb.

Autokraft Ltd, Vickers Drive, Brooklands Industrial Park, Weybridge, Surrey KT13 0YU England.
Telephone 0932 355222   Facsimile 0932 343444
In view of its policy of constant improvement, Autokraft reserve the right to change specifications without prior notice.

A.C. Cobra 4,726 c.c.

Autocar Road Test

NUMBER 2053

MANUFACTURER:
A.C. Cars Ltd., Thames Ditton, Surrey

PRICES:

Basic	..£2,260	0s 0d
Purchase Tax	£472	4s 9d
Total (in G.B.)	£2,732	4s 9d

EXTRAS (inc. P.T.)
Fog and sport lamps, each
(Carello iodine vapour) £6 19s 6d

PERFORMANCE SUMMARY

Mean maximum speed ..	..	138 m.p.h.
Standing start ¼-mile ..	..	13·9sec
0-60 m.p.h.	..	5·5sec
30-70 m.p.h. in 3rd	..	6·8sec
Overall fuel consumption	..	15·1 m.p.g
Miles per tankful	..	226

AT A GLANCE: Thoroughbred sports car with powerful American vee-8 engine. Terrific acceleration with high gearing, but noise level high. All-independent suspension gives firm ride; handling generally good. Powerful brakes. Stark body with rather primitive weather protection. Exciting performance.

FEW readers indeed will get this far before turning to the data page which follows, for the name of A.C. Cobra is synonymous with performance. There they will have seen the steepest acceleration graph we have ever plotted, with a 0 to 100 m.p.h. time of only 14sec and an elapsed time for the standing quarter-mile of 13·9sec.

Largely due to some sensational newspaper stories of testing on M1 prior to Le Mans last year, the Cobra already has a fast public image. Too fast perhaps, for in its ordinary road form as sold here and in the United States particularly, the Cobra is barely a 140 m.p.h. sports car. It is geared for lightning step-off and electrifying acceleration, not high-speed record breaking.

There is nothing new about the Cobra we have been testing. Over three years ago Carroll Shelby suggested to A.C. that their Ace sports two-seater might benefit from being fitted with an American Ford V8 engine. At that time the supply of 2-litre Bristol engines was drying up, and the Zephyr 6 power unit used in the Ace 2·6 was a less powerful substitute, so the idea was tried with tremendous success. Arrangements were made for body-chassis units to be shipped out to California for engine installation, and soon all A.C. production was turned over to Cobras. There was intense demand from the home market, so at intervals small batches of right-hand-drive models were made and snatched up eagerly.

Because of this situation there has never been a press demonstrator available for road test. However, it would not be right for such a car to escape us completely, so when Ken Rudd offered us his own personal machine with no strings attached, we gratefully accepted.

This car, in fact, is over 12 months old and does not have the latest coil-spring and wishbone suspension. But it is still very much a Cobra, and as the new chassis will not be avail-

c →

251

Autocar Road Test 2053

MAKE: **A.C.**

TYPE: **Cobra**

TEST CONDITIONS

Weather   Dry and cloudy with 10-15 m.p.h. wind
Temperature ..   ..   13 deg. C. (55 deg. F.)
Barometer ..   ..   29·4in. Hg.
Surfaces..   ..   ..   Dry concrete and tarmac

WEIGHT

Kerb weight (with oil, water and half-full fuel tank):
         21·7 cwt (2,315lb-1,050kg)
Front-rear distribution, per cent   F. 48·7; R. 51·3
Laden as tested   ..   24·7 cwt (2,651lb-1,202kg)

TURNING CIRCLES

Between kerbs   ..   L, 32ft 9in.; R, 33ft 9in.
Between walls   ..   L, 33ft 4in.; R, 34ft 4in.
Steering wheel turns lock to lock   3.0

PERFORMANCE DATA

Top gear m.p.h. per 1,000 r.p.m.
(Pirelli Cinturato) ..   ..   21·3
(Dunlop R.6) ..   ..   23·8
Mean piston speed at max. power 2,745 ft/min.
Engine revs at mean max. speed   ..   5,800 r.p.m.
B.h.p. (gross) per ton laden   243

OIL CONSUMPTION

Miles per pint (SAE 30)   500

FUEL CONSUMPTION

At constant speeds

30 m.p.h.	32·0 m.p.g.	70 m.p.h.	22·2 m.p.g.
40 m.p.h.	30·8 m.p.g.	80 m.p.h.	19·6 m.p.g.
50 m.p.h.	27·8 m.p.g.	90 m.p.h.	18·2 m.p.g.
60 m.p.h.	24·7 m.p.g.	100 m.p.h.	17·0 m.p.g.

Overall m.p.g.   ..   **15·1 (18·7 litres/100km)**
Normal range m.p.g. 14-20 (20·2-14·1 litres/100km)
Test distance (corrected)   ..   ..   659 miles
Estimated (DIN) m.p.g. 20·2 (14·0 litres/100km)
Grade ..   ..   Super Premium (100·3-101.8 RM)

Speed range, gear ratios and time in seconds

m.p.h.	Top (3·54)	Third (4·99)	Second (6·30)	First (8·35)
10—30	—	4·2	2·6	2·3
20—40	4·6	3·6	2·5	1·9
30—50	4·3	3·4	2·5	1·8
40—60	4·2	3·4	2·4	2·2
50—70	4·1	3·4	2·4	—
60—80	4·3	3·8	3·0	—
70—90	4·8	4·1	—	—
80—110	5·4	4·5	—	—
90—110	6·1	6·8	—	—
100—120	8·3	—	—	—

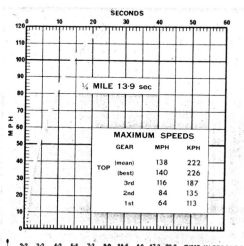

¼ MILE 13·9 sec

MAXIMUM SPEEDS			
GEAR		MPH	KPH
TOP	(mean)	138	222
	(best)	140	226
3rd		116	187
2nd		84	135
1st		64	113

BRAKES	Pedal load	Retardation	Equiv. distance
(from 30 m.p.h.	25lb	0·17g	177ft
in neutral)	50lb	0·35g	86ft
	75lb	0·56g	54ft
	100lb	0·81g	37ft
	125lb	1·0g	30·1ft
Handbrake		0·47g	64ft

CLUTCH: Pedal load and travel—65lb and 4·5in.

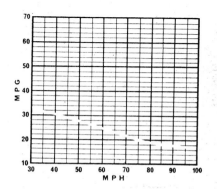

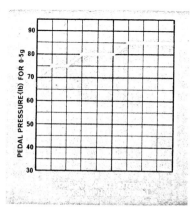

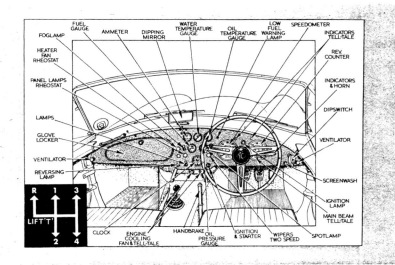

able here until the middle of 1966 we feel there is sufficient interest to warrant the full road test treatment.

Superficially the Cobra looks little different from the Ace-Bristol we tested exactly seven years ago. It has the longer, more elegant snout introduced on the Ace 2·6, and there are square-sided lips to extend the wheel-arches over the extra-fat section tyres. Under the skin there has been a lot of re-inforcing and beefing-up of chassis members, hubs, drive shafts, brakes, bearings and mountings. Substituting a cast-iron vee-8 for an aluminium six is partly responsible for a 4cwt weight increase, but a good deal of this comes from lenient stressing and the hard lessons learnt in the early competition days of the new model.

Nevertheless, with a 4·7-litre Mustang engine tuned to deliver 300 b.h.p. gross there is still an impressive 243 b.h.p. per ton laden, the most we have ever handled. This kind of vigour is bound to produce exciting performance in a class difficult to match, even by out-and-out racing cars. In the Cobra the power is well tamed and we suffered few embarrassments from its abundance.

Climbing into the cockpit, one recalls vivid memories of the old Ace, and very little seems changed. There is rather less footroom because of the wider transmission tunnel, with nowhere to rest the left foot, and one is faced by a very full instrument panel. There is an automatic choke and the engine always bursts into life at the first turn of the key. Mechanical tappets on this engine rattle rather noisily and there is a deep and very potent throb from the dual exhausts.

The compound carburettor has four barrels with two primary butterflies and two large secondaries coming in progressively. The accelerator pedal has a long and sensitive movement which helps in controlling

the vast amount of power; the two stages of carburation are felt more in what they do than as a resistance under one's foot. Stabbing the throttle at rest produces a crisp staccato crackle with the characteristic vee-8 beat and a violent surge in revs. The same procedure with first engaged and the clutch home sends the car rocketing forward like a missile from a steam catapult, accompanied by a racket akin to 10 motorcycles and three pneumatic drills all working at once.

Road holding

On dry surfaces there is remarkably little wheelspin in a straight line (on the Dunlop R.6 racing tyres we used for all performance testing never once was adhesion lost) as a Powr-Lok limited-slip differential is a standard fitting and there is more than 50 per cent of the weight over the back wheels. On corners taken sharply the tail can be kicked round under power when required, but at a

steady throttle the handling is virtually neutral.

In the wet the whole picture changes and a lot of restraint is needed to prevent great snaking slides all over the road. It is not that the Cobra is particularly unmanageable, but even with wide-section Pirelli Cinturatos it is not easy to transmit 285lb. ft torque through a pair of contacts loaded only to about 5cwt each. In fact, the car is not difficult to control and it behaves no more wildly than its driver. However, one soon learns to respect it in these conditions by slowing early for all turns and making up the leeway afterwards by a short burst of power.

While the graph and full table of acceleration figures speak well for themselves, it is important to realize just how phenomenally fast these are. First gear, for example, gives over 60 m.p.h. without exceeding 6,000 r.p.m., and around the peak of the torque curve a 20 m.p.h. increase takes less than 2sec. Corresponding
→

The Ford V8 engine is mounted well back behind the front suspension and accessibility is good. The dipstick fits into a tube high up by the dynamo

Left: Bucket seats are leather covered, and there are big pockets in the doors. The sidescreens are plastic with sliding panels

Below: The large wrap-round rear window prevents any blindspots with the hood erected. At speed the fabric billows out and creates gaps round the sidescreens

A.C. Cobra . . .

times for the same band in second take only ½sec or so more, and even by using third they are barely lengthened by another 1sec. For all practical purposes in traffic it does not matter which gear is engaged and there is never any lack of overtaking power.

On a distance rather than time basis it takes only a quarter-mile to accelerate from rest to 100 m.p.h. through the gears, and even when trickling away from 20 m.p.h. in top, 80 can be reached in the same distance. Speed differentials with other traffic are therefore much more marked, and one spends a lot of time slowing down. The problem on most roads is not finding gaps in the on-coming traffic stream to pull round the car in front—this barely takes more than two or three seconds—but finding gaps in one's own stream to tuck back into.

The purposeful front of the Cobra helps a lot here, and all kinds of drivers reacted with surprising courtesy when they saw it in their mirrors. A large proportion, of course, never saw it at all and are no doubt still puzzled by the thunder in their ears.

Gearbox

Although a little stiff when cold, the Borg-Warner gear box has un-beatable synchromesh and extremely well-chosen ratios. It is worked by a short, stubby lever with a lift-up cross-tree to guard reverse. All the gears are silent, and the movements between them sweet and positive.

Being a privately-owned car, this Cobra was fitted with Pirelli Cin-turato tyres which are limited to speeds of about 120 m.p.h. because

of their construction. Pirelli recom-mend their slightly larger-section HR type for faster driving, but these do not offer the same grip and for normal road running the ones we had were adequate. Standard tyres on new cars are now the high-speed Dunlop SP 41 HR, but for all our performance measurements we fitted Dunlop R.6 racing tyres for our own peace of mind and in anticipation of a maximum higher than 140 m.p.h.

These tyres are larger than the others, which raised the gearing about 10 per cent (our fuel figures have been corrected accordingly). On maximum speed runs we were not able to run beyond the peak of the power curve against the wind, so the car may even be a fraction faster on a smaller size. Above about 80 m.p.h. the fabric hood billows taut like a drum skin and pulls its edges clear of the sidescreens. After a mile or two

at maximum speed we noticed the screen rail had lifted off the glass along its top edge, indicating the need for a central tie strut like that fitted on several other sports cars.

At these three-figure speeds there is a tremendous roar of wind noise superimposed on a high-pitched mechanical "busy-ness" from be-yond the bulkhead. Conversation is impossible and we had to communi-cate by hand signs and lip reading. Water temperature and oil pressure remain normal (although the electric fan windmills as a generator and lights its warning lamp), but the oil temperature creeps up steadily to as high as 115deg. C.

Stability is generally good, unless the surface is damp or one lifts off the accelerator suddenly, when the torque reaction causes a sudden lurch to the left. Rack and pinion steering is used, with no lost motion, little

A lot of felt has been added to the test car to reduce the noise level but the carpet in the boot is standard. The spare wheel fits in a well in the floor and the jack is clamped in a corner

CPO 681B

Caught in a rare moment at rest, the Cobra could accelerate to 100 m.p.h. before the first bend shown here. Despite the extensions over the wheel arches the tyres at the front still stand proud

feed-back from bumps to the driver's hands, and positive response to guidance and correction. The gearing feels right for the car, and even when manœuvring in tight spaces the load is not heavy.

Disc brakes front and rear provide the Cobra with stopping power to match its tremendous engine. Without the benefit of a servo pedal loads are quite high, but 1g stops from 30 m.p.h. are easy to achieve and there is only a slight degree of initial fade during repeated braking from 70 m.p.h. The handbrake is exceptionally powerful when used in an emergency—0·47g—but only just held on a 1 in 3 gradient.

The suspension of the Cobra is very firm, with a distinctly Vintage harshness and a lot of jolts and jars. Rough patches of road taken slowly cause parts of the body structure to creak and groan, and we found the rear suspension bottomed when charging over the familiar subsidences on M1. There is no scuttle shake nor visible signs of flexing anywhere, however, and the tubular chassis is tremendously rigid. This can be demonstrated by jacking a corner and watching the whole car lift evenly. Incidentally, only a simple screw type is provided for inserting anywhere under the chassis; this can be a dirty and intricate task when a flat tyre has reduced the ground clearance and one we would not like to attempt on a dark, wet night in a good suit.

Several other aspects of the Cobra seem dated and even rather crude by today's standards. For example, the doors have no outside handles and cannot be locked. Plastic side-screens form part of the weather protection, with the rear half sliding forwards for ventilation and access to the door handles from outside; these become scratched and misty all too easily.

The hood is a fairly flimsy affair which does not look particularly rainproof—we never had the car in a downpour to check this—and there are gaps in places where it fits the body and screen.

But the Cobra is essentially an open car, and it is a very quick operation to unclip the roof, fold it and put it in the boot. There is then no sign, apart from a row of studs, that it even exists and the smooth curves of the body flow uninterruptedly. A wind deflector is fitted on the outside edge of each screen pillar to reduce draughts and prevent buffeting.

The pedals are hinged on the floor and have swivelling pads to pivot with one's feet. They are mounted quite close together and narrow shoes without welts are safest. Just the other side of the toeboard are the exhaust pipes, on each side, and consequently it gets very hot in this region. Cold-air vents are provided for a forced

→

HOW THE A.C. COBRA COMPARES:

TOTAL PRICE		MAXIMUM SPEED (mean) M.P.H.	STANDING-START ¼-MILE (secs.)
£2,732	A.C. Cobra		
£1,934	Jaguar E-type		
Not available	Chevrolet Sting Ray		
£3,679	Jensen C-V8		

	0-60 M.P.H. SECONDS	M.P.G. Overall
A.C. Cobra		
Jaguar E-type		
Chevrolet Sting Ray		
Jensen C-V8		

A.C. Cobra ...

draught, but they had been sealed off on the test car presumably because they let in water.

Tucked away in the centre above the gearbox is a simple recirculating heater with three little trap-doors to direct the air in different directions. It has a rheostat for its booster fan and provides a good blast of hot air in the right direction, even with the roof off. The two demister slots are very narrow, however, and cannot cope with the wide screen in damp conditions.

The engine cooling fan is mounted ahead of the radiator and is driven by an electric motor. There is a thermostatic switch to cut this in automatically at about 90 deg. C. but very little pitch on the blades so that during long traffic stops the temperature goes on climbing. If the car keeps moving all is well, but even by over-riding the control and switching the fan on very early at 70 deg., we could not prevent the engine overheating to 105 deg. C. at times. The system is pressurized at 13 p.s.i., so boiling cannot occur until even higher temperatures.

There can be no denying that the Cobra is an extremely exciting car to drive, or even passenger in. The acceleration is sensational and very similar to taking off in a piston-engined aircraft with open cockpit. In much the same way, nearly all creature comforts must be sacrificed for performance—a condition which is worth it most of the time, but very occasionally not. It is a fine-weather car for clear skies, open roads and a life away from it all. Part of its sorcery lies in its ability to instil the same exhilaration from a short run up the road on a Sunday morning, but most of it comes from that aggressive thrust of power that is always more than enough for any situation. ∎

SPECIFICATION : A.C. COBRA FRONT ENGINE, REAR-WHEEL DRIVE

ENGINE
Cylinders .. 8 in 90 deg. vee
Cooling system .. Water; pump, electric fan and thermostat
Bore .. 101·6mm (4·00in.)
Stroke .. 72·9mm (2·87in.)
Displacement .. 4,727 c.c. (289 cu. in.)
Valve gear .. Overhead, pushrods and rockers
Compression ratio 11-to-1
Carburettor .. Single 4-choke Holley
Fuel pump .. Mechanical
Oil filter .. Full-flow, renewable element
Max. power .. 300 b.h.p. (gross) at 5,750 r.p.m.
Max. torque .. 285 lb. ft. (gross) at 4,500 r.p.m.

TRANSMISSION
Clutch .. Single dry plate, 10·5in. dia.
Gearbox .. Borg-Warner, 4-speed, all-synchromesh
Gear ratios .. Top 1·0; Third 1·41; Second 1·78; First 2·36; Reverse 2·36
Final drive .. Salisbury Powr-Lok, hypoid bevel 3·54 to 1

CHASSIS AND BODY
Construction .. Separate tubular steel chassis, aluminium body on tubular frame

SUSPENSION
Front .. Independent, transverse leaf spring and wishbones, telescopic dampers
Rear .. Independent, transverse leaf spring and wishbones, telescopic dampers

STEERING
Type .. Rack and pinion. Wheel dia. 16in.

BRAKES
Make and type .. Girling disc front and rear
Servo .. None
Dimensions .. F, 11·7in. dia.; R, 10·75in. dia.
Swept area .. F, 320 sq. in.; R, 260 sq. in. Total 580 sq. in. (470 sq. in.) per ton laden

WHEELS
Type .. Centre-lock, wire-spokes 5in. wide rim
Tyres .. Pirelli Cinturato fitted, Dunlop SP41HR standard, Dunlop R.6 Green Spot used for performance testing.—size 185—15in.

EQUIPMENT
Battery .. 12-volt 57-amp. hr.
Generator .. Lucas C.40, 22-amp
Headlamps .. Lucas 50/40-watt
Reversing lamp .. Extra
Electric fuses .. 3

Screen wipers .. 2-speed, self parking
Screen washer .. Standard, electric
Interior heater .. Standard, recirculating
Safety belts .. No provision
Interior trim .. Leather seats, p.v.c. hood
Floor covering .. Carpet
Starting handle .. No provision
Jack .. Screw pillar
Jacking points .. Anywhere under chassis
Other bodies .. None

MAINTENANCE
Fuel tank .. 15 Imp. gallons (no reserve) (68 litres)
Cooling system .. 20 pints (including heater) (11·4 litres)
Engine sump .. 10 pints (5·7 litres) SAE 30. Change oil every 2,000 miles. Change filter element every 4,000 miles
Gearbox .. 2·25 pints SAE 80. Change oil every 4,000 miles
Final drive .. 2·5 pints SAE 90. Change oil every 4,000 miles
Grease .. 4 points every 500 miles; 6 points every 1,000 miles; 14 points every 2,000 miles
Tyre pressures .. F, 32; R, 26 p.s.i. (normal driving). F, 38; R, 38 p.s.i. (fast driving).

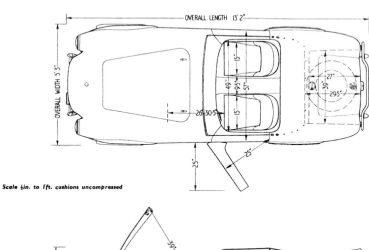

Scale ¼in. to 1ft. cushions uncompressed

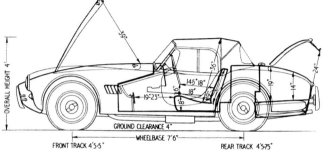

The driver sits well up with a good view across a long shapely bonnet; there is surprisingly little buffeting behind the screen.

The power game

A spectacularly fast car in a grand if dated tradition.

I F IT WERE not for the fact that the term Vintage is inextricably tied up with dates, one would be able to say with absolute truth that the A.C. 289 is the most splendid vintage sports car, a car that is characteristic of the image of the true masculine fun car. If you don't actually own one of the modern brand of sports car, whether it be a sophisticated Lotus or basic BMC, you may well think that they are all as stark and hairy as the A.C., but the 289 (the one-time Cobra) stands on its own as a car whose tremendous performance and roadholding is for ever a joy. Unfortunately the drawbacks are there too: it has a ride which many would consider poor; a primitive hood which you leave down unless it is actually raining when you are stationary; and little useful luggage space. To some these are the normal attributes of a sports car, part of the appeal of open style motoring.

The story of the sports A.C.s is an unusually long one with a concept which has remained virtually unchanged since 1953. John Tojeiro designed the chassis for the prototype shown in 1953; it used twin tubes with cross bracing, plus body tubes around which the aluminium panels were wrapped. Suspension at both ends was independent by transverse upper leaf springs and lower wishbones. The original Ace engine was the overhead cam six that had first been designed in the mid-1920s; the 2-litre Bristol engine was offered later in 1956. In 1961, still with basically the same chassis, a further option became available with the six-cylinder

Continued on the next page

Price: £2,400 plus £551 11s. 0d. equals £2,951 11s.

The whole shape of the car must be regarded as a classic.

257

A.C. 289 **Sports** *continued*

Ford Zephyr unit in varieties of tune from Rudds of Worthing. It was in 1963 that Ford of America, in conjunction with Carroll Shelby, were looking for a race-worthy chassis for the 4.7-litre Fairlane engine; they chose the A.C., called it the Cobra, beefed up the chassis and went racing.

By 1965 the 380-odd bhp was not enough, and Shelby began to drop the 7-litre Ford engine into an even further revised chassis. The basic twin tube frame remained but the tubes grew bigger; still more important was the introduction of twin wishbone and coil-spring suspension at each corner replacing the transverse leaf springs. With Ford brain power behind Shelby, the installation was successful, but few were sold in Europe. With the termination of the A.C./Shelby contract and the sale of the name Cobra to Ford, A.C. were left with a more than adequate chassis for the 4.7-litre engine; the same chassis, lengthened, provides the basis for the Frua bodied 428 convertible, a superb car in the luxury tradition of A.C.

From 1953 to the present day, the two-seater body has remained basically similar with a revised nose coming with the Zephyr engine option and ever wider wing flares along with an ever wider track.

With 271 bhp in 21cwt of car, the 289 is the fastest car to 100 mph that we have tested, by just 0.1sec from the TVR Tuscan with the same engine. The unit is extremely tractable and it has an excellent gearbox. Although the cornering attitude of the car is largely dictated by the throttle at road speeds, the way the power is put through to the road, particularly on wet surfaces, is quite remarkable. At high speeds, around the 100 mph mark, it did not seem quite as stable as expected, but this was possibly due to worn rear wishbone rubbers on a two-year old demonstrator.

At £2,952, the 289 is an expensive toy if you are going to use it as a second car, but it is such fun to drive that it would probably get promoted to first car very quickly; it is not too impractical but a 15 mpg thirst and frequent servicing might put one off using it as a

Performance

Performance tests carried out by *Motor's* staff at the Motor Industry Research Association proving ground, Lindley.

Test Data: World copyright reserved; no unauthorized reproduction in whole or in part.

Conditions

Weather: Dry with little wind 0-8 m.p.h.
Temperature: 59°-70°F. Barometer 29.53 in. Hg.
Surface: Dry concrete and tarmacadam.
Fuel: Super premium 101 octane (RM) 5-star rating.

Maximum speeds

	m.p.h.
Mean of opposite runs	134.9
Best one-way run	135.3
3rd gear	98½
2nd gear } at 6,000 r.p.m.	77½
1st gear	58½

Acceleration times

m.p.h.	sec.
0-30	2.5
0-40	3.4
0-50	4.4
0-60	5.6
0-70	7.2
0-80	9.0
0-90	11.3
0-100	13.7
0-110	17.9
0-120	22.8
Standing quarter mile	14.4

m.p.h.	Top sec.	3rd sec.
10-30	—	3.7
20-40	3.9	3.6
30-50	4.2	3.6
40-60	4.2	3.4
50-70	4.3	3.5
60-80	4.4	3.8
70-90	4.7	3.9
80-100	5.0	4.7
90-110	6.1	—
100-120	8.0	—

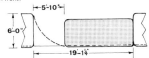

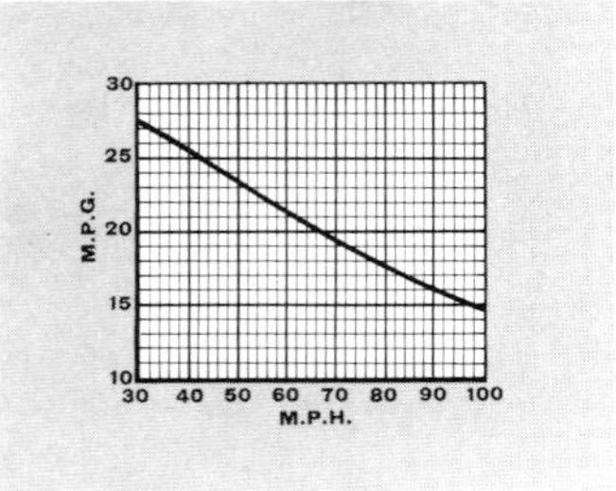

Fuel consumption

Touring (consumption midway between 30 m.p.h. and maximum less 5 per cent allowance for acceleration) . . . . 16.3 m.p.g.
Overall . . . . 15.2 m.p.g.
(•18.6 litres/100 km.)
Total test distance . . . . 1,648 miles
Tank capacity (maker's figure) . . . . . . 15 gal.

Brakes

Pedal pressure, deceleration and equivalent stopping distance from 30 m.p.h.

lb.	g	ft.
25	0.19	158
50	0.40	75
75	0.60	50
100	0.83	36
120	0.93	32
Handbrake	0.30	100

Fade test

20 stops at ½g deceleration at 1 min. intervals from a speed midway between 30 m.p.h. and maximum speed (= app. 85 m.p.h.)

	lb.
Pedal force at beginning	62
Pedal force at 10th stop	74
Pedal force at 20th stop	75

Steering

	ft.
Turning circle between kerbs:	
Left	33¾
Right	34¼
Turns of steering wheel from lock to lock	2.9
Steering wheel deflection for 50 ft. diameter circle	1.0 turns

Clutch

Free pedal movement	= ½ in.
Additional movement to disengage clutch completely	= 2¾ in.
Maximum pedal load	= 62 lb.

Speedometer

Indicated	30 40 50 60 70 80 90 100 110 120
True	31 41 52 61 71 80 89 98 108 117
Distance recorder	4% slow

Weight

Kerb weight (unladen with fuel for approximately 50 miles) . . . . 21.0 cwt.
Front/rear distribution 50/50
Weight laden as tested . . . . 24.7 cwt.

Hill climbing

At steady speed		lb./ton
Top	1 in 4.0	(Tapley 550)
3rd	1 in 3.2	(Tapley 670)
2nd	1 in 2.3	(Tapley 895)

Parkability

Gap needed to clear a 6 ft. wide obstruction parked in front:

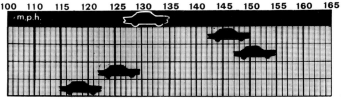

AC 289 £2,952		
Jaguar E fhc. £2,068		
TVR Tuscan £2,364		
Porsche 911 £3,000		
Lotus Elan plus 2 £1,923		

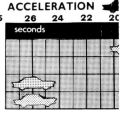

KPD 150C

20,000-mile-a-year car. As lovers of controllable high performance we soon became attached to the 289 particularly with the roof down to reduce engine noise and hood flap. As we said earlier it has this splendid Vintage character which is not everyone's cup of tea.

Performance and economy

There are two ways of starting the big V-8; you can either pump twice on the accelerator or pull the choke out. The engine seems quite happy to idle straight away at less than 500 rpm and pulls without hesitation long before the temperature gauge moves off its bottom stop after some two miles. There is some tappet noise, mainly audible when the hood is up, but otherwise the engine is fairly unobtrusive. In normal road use you won't use more than 4,000 rpm and with the hood down you never hear the exhaust unless you accelerate past a wall, when the tremendous blast of sound conjures up all sorts of racing memories; if you wind on beyond 5,000 rpm towards the maximum around 7,200 rpm on this seemingly unburstable engine it becomes more frenzied but never alarmingly so. During our acceleration tests we used up to 6,500 rpm, reaching 60 mph in just 5.6 sec (still in first gear), 80 mph in 9.0 sec and flashing past the quarter mile at over 100 mph—almost dragster levels.

If the sheer power is impressive so too is the smooth torque delivered throughout the range from under 1,000 rpm. From 20–90 mph each 10 mph increase only needs between 2.1 and 2.5 sec; 0–100 mph using only third gear takes less than 20 sec.

For our maximum speed we had to retire to foreign parts; the mean 134.9 mph represented 6,300 rpm which was ear shattering with the hood up. With no oil cooler the oil temperature rose rapidly during these runs from its normal 80–100 deg C to over 140 deg C, and it might be an idea to fit a thermostatically controlled cooler if really fast work is contemplated. Fuel consumption over that 640 mile trip worked out at 16.3 mpg with a lot of cruising in the 80–100 mph range, but the previous 900

Continued on the next page

A touch of opposites to show how controllable the 289 is; it can be balanced at will on the throttle give or take a few feet of road space. Chrome bumper bar does not detract in any way from the purposeful aggressive appearance.

A slightly cluttered dashboard provides all the necessary information; the gearlever is offset to the left but still falls to hand easily. Tall people found splayed knees fouled the handbrake.

Cast pedal pads carry the A.C. insignia and rubber buttons top and bottom stop the foot slipping off. Steering wheel has its wooden rim reinforced with aluminium. Rear view mirror is unframed.

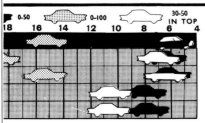

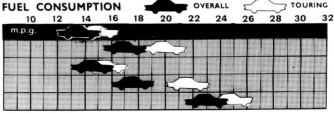

0-50		0-100			30-50 IN TOP	FUEL CONSUMPTION			OVERALL			TOURING
18	16	14	12	10	8	6	4	10	12	14	16	18	20	22	24	26	28	30	32

m.p.g.

Rear bumper bar obstructs the boot handle. Brake cooling air outlets are behind the front wheel arch. The hood looks well tensioned but gets noisy around 70 mph. Side screens are removable and fit in a pocket behind the seats. Visibility is good with the hood up.

A.C. 289 Sports *continued*

miles in this country with a lot of town use and a fair amount of exhilarating blasting through the countryside only returned 14.5 mpg. You are unlikely ever to get better than about 17 mpg which gives a usable range on the 15-gallon tank of about 220 miles. Five star fuel is recommended but there was no pinking on four-star.

Transmission

When you have such tremendous torque a close ratio box tends to pass unnoticed until you come to do the standing start accelerations; for most manoeuvres out of town you could comfortably stay in top gear, and we frequently did when pottering through towns at 25 mph, but the gearbox has such excellent ratios and the short stubby gear lever is so pleasant to slide around that we all often used the box as if the car were a Mini with "...nothing below 3,500 rpm, old boy". The pedals are well placed for heel-and-toeing and there is room for the left foot beside the clutch, resting on a piece of floor which gets uncomfortably hot at times. The clutch itself grips smoothly and well but its long travel more or less dictates the seating position, and it is certainly the heaviest we have met for a very long time. With the seat adjusted for comfortable clutchwork the gearlever becomes well placed too; it requires very little practice to make smooth "family saloon" changes.

Since our test model was produced (since chassis No. 6120, in fact) these cars have been fitted with a 3.31 final drive instead of 3.54. This raises the gearing from 21.5 mph per 1,000 rpm to 23.0, and might add a few mph to maximum speed. Both final

drives are Salisbury 4HU with limited-slip differential which contribute a lot to the confidence with which one can blast off past a line of cars for a quick overtaking burst in the wet; without it, life would be difficult. On standing starts we were able to get just as much wheelspin as we needed by controlled throttle use; we *could* have sat there with the accelerator on the floor and the wheels spinning helplessly, but with the clutch dropped in at about 2,500 rpm and the accelerator floored only when the speed of the car had caught up the rear wheels, we established our best times.

Measuring the Tapley pull in second gear sent the drum revolving to a record high, which worked out at the ability to climb a 1-in-2.3 hill. Small wonder then that the 289 romped away from rest on the 1-in-3.

Apart from a little gear whine in the indirects, and the occasional clonk from the limited-slip differential in parking manoeuvres the transmission was unobtrusive.

Handling and brakes

It takes a little time to be able to use the 289 chassis and power to best advantage; you start by coming into the corners too slowly and then blasting out too quickly. The tail is unlikely to unstick even so, but there are smoother ways of getting round. It pays to get the braking done beforehand, particularly as the rear brakes lock first, then go round the corner under more or less constant power until the exit is in sight. You can then use more throttle keeping the tail just in check, or let it come out a fraction lined up ready to squirt down the next straight (we tried all this out on a closed track). If the tail comes out a little it is easy to keep under control with a little less throttle and a bit of correction; but if it comes out a lot, and we had it up to an outrageous 60 deg attitude angle in the course of our experiments, it is difficult to bring back cleanly without a self steering lurch as the car comes back on the right keel. However, we still caught it, emphasizing what an extremely controllable car the A.C. is; with all that power it is quite a tribute that it handles so well and of course at very high cornering powers.

On wet roads we learnt to be careful having at one point lost the tail while pulling out to overtake. It came back as soon as power was eased but we developed the habit of using one gear higher than we would on dry roads; this reduced the torque suitably without sacrificing too much of the phenomenal acceleration. We discovered shortly after the first excitement that the rear tyres had reached the throwaway level of 1½—2 mm; with new tyres, Dunlop SP41HRs as before, wet road holding was rather better but staying a gear high was still a good maxim; with all that power you develop motorcycle sensitivity to road conditions.

This is all helped by the excellent steering which gives just the right kind of feel for safe fast driving. There is kickback on bumps

Safety check list

Steering assembly

Steering box position	In front of axle line
Steering column collapsible	Yes with 2 UJs
Steering wheel boss padded	No
Steering wheel dished	No

Instrument panel

Projecting switches	Yes
Sharp cowls	No
Padding	Covered facia with rounded metal top

Windscreen and visibility

Screen type	Laminated
Pillars padded	No
Standard driving mirrors	Interior only
Interior mirror framed	No
Interior mirror collapsible	No
Sun visors	None

Seats and harness

Attachment to floor	Sliding runners fastened to floor
Do they tip forward?	No
Head rest attachment points	None
Safety harness	Attachment points provided

Doors

Projecting handles	No
Anti-burst latches	No
Child-proof locks	No rear doors

The boot takes a reasonable 3.9 cu-ft., of our luggage. The width is 37" with longest diagonal 49¼". The toolkit is usefully comprehensive. Copper ended hammer is used for the knock-off wire wheels. Grease gun it used every 2,000 miles.

14" X 11" X 5"

17½" X 13" X 6"

21" X 15" X 7"

through the rack-and-pinion mechanism, but it is nicely geared and surprisingly light at parking speeds. At high speed very little movement is required and you are hardly conscious of doing more than vary the pressure on the steering wheel to get round quite a noticeable 100 mph corner. This extreme sensitivity at speeds around the 100 mph mark leaves no room for heavy hands or feet; we were also a little peturbed at the tendency to veer to the right when power was eased after a full throttle blast at high speed. We hadn't really noticed this on the road, but during our acceleration tests on MIRA's narrow horizontal straight it was very evident, and it meant that the third to top change at over 100 mph had to be rather smoother than our normal rushed changes.

This directional variation is due to rear wheel steering; we suspect that newer cars or cars that haven't had a long spell as demonstrators, would not exhibit this feature, since it is almost certainly a sign of worn wishbone bushes; the wishbones are fairly wide-based but not comparable with modern racing designs which have to cope with the same power. Lifting off from steady speeds rather than full throttle makes less difference, and the car feels impressively stable and firm on the road even in strong side winds.

Looking back through the road tests of previous A.C. sports cars, we have recorded in each one that the rear wheels lock first which rather limits the maximum stable braking. With the 289 this is still true, and we could only get 0.93g using a high 120lb pedal pressure. On the road the brakes feel heavy (no servo is used) but firm and fade-free, but during our fade test stopping from about 82½ mph there was a steady pressure rise from 62lb to 75lb, although no loss of feel; the water splash produced a slight pressure rise for the first two stops but we only dared to make one trip as the water gushed in through the floor. The handbrake,

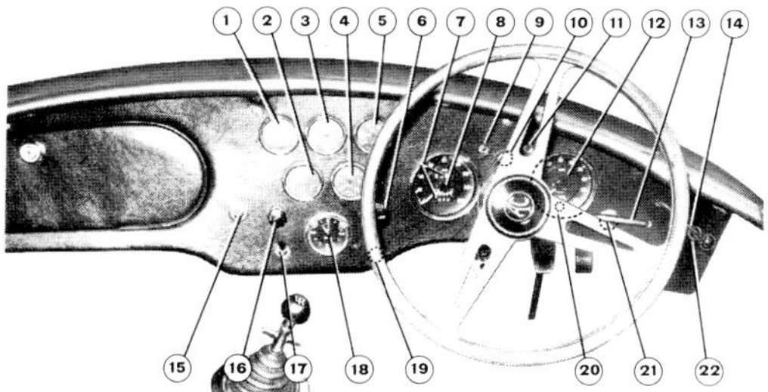
1
2
3
4
5
6
7
8
9
10
11
12
13
14
15
16
17
18
19
20
21
22

1, ammeter. 2, fuel gauge. 3, water temperature gauge. 4, oil pressure gauge. 5, oil temperature gauge. 6, two-speed wiper. 7, trip and total mileage recorders. 8, speedometer. 9, left indicator tell-tale. 10, dynamo warning light. 11, right indicator tell-tale. 12, rev counter. 13, indicator/horn stalk. 14, flasher/dipswitch. 15, two speed heater blower. 16, panel light rheostat. 17, side/headlight switch. 18, clock. 19, ignition/starter key. 20, main beam tell-tale. 21, choke. 22, washer button. Right hand fresh air control is obscured behind wheel rim at 4 o'clock.

which has a separate caliper, held the car on a 1-in-4 hill but did not have enough adjustment to hold it nose down on a 1-in-3, although the potential was there.

Comfort and controls

With the track increased from 4ft. 2in. in 1953 to 4ft. 6in. now, the springs stiffened and the dampers made firmer there is very little roll; the ride is firm round town, though with little

Continued on the next page

Specification

Engine

Cylinders	V-8
Bore and stroke	101.6mm x 72.9mm
Cubic capacity	4.727 c.c.
Valves	Pushrod ohv
Compression ratio	11.0:1
Carburetter	Ford 4-barrel
Fuel pump	Ford mechanical
Oil filter	Ford by-pass
Max. power (gross)	271 bhp at 6,000 rpm
Max. torque (gross)	312 lb.ft. at 3,400 rpm

Transmission

Clutch	10½in. s.d.p.
Top gear (s/m)	1.00
3rd gear (s/m)	1.31
2nd gear (s/m)	1.66
1st gear (s/m)	2.20
Reverse	2.20
Final drive	Hypoid bevel 3.54—Salisbury limited slip
Mph at 1,000 rpm in:—	
Top gear	21.5
3rd gear	16.4
2nd gear	13.0
1st gear	9.8

Chassis

Construction	Twin tube frame with hoops and cross bracing—aluminium body

Brakes

Type	Girling disc brakes
Dimensions	11 11/16in. dia. front, 10¾in. dia. rear
Friction areas:	
Front	27.6 sq. in. of lining operating on 249.4 sq. in. swept area of disc
Rear	21.1 sq. in. of lining operating on 195.8 sq. in. swept area of disc.

Suspension and steering

Front	Independent: wishbones and coil springs
Rear	Independent: wishbones and coil springs
Shock absorbers:	
Front	Armstrong telescopic
Rear	Armstrong telescopic
Steering gear	Rack and pinion
Tyres	Dunlop SP41HR 185-15
Rim size	6½L-15

Coachwork and equipment

Starting handle	None
Jack	Screw type
Jacking points	Chassis tubes and wishbones
Battery	12-volt negative earth, 45 amp hrs capacity
Number of electrical fuses.	4
Indicators	Self-cancelling flashers
Screen wipers	Lucas two-speed
Screen washers	Lucas electric
Sun visors	None
Locks:	
With ignition key	ignition/starter only
With other keys	Boot and glove locker
Interior heater	Recirculatory with two-speed blower
Extras	Detachable hard top, chrome wheels, radio
Upholstery	Leather
Floor covering	Carpet
Alternative body styles	None

Maintenance

Sump	6½ pints SAE 30
Gearbox	2½ pints SAE 80 or 90EP
Rear axle	2½ pints Shell 6721A
Steering gear	SAE 140 hypoid
Cooling system	24 pints (2 drain taps)
Chassis lubrication	Every 2,000 miles to 8 points
Minimum service interval	2,000 miles
Ignition timing	10° b.t.d.c.
Contact breaker gap	0.018—0.021 in.
Sparking plug gap	0.028—0.032 in.
Sparking plug type	Autolite BF 32
Tappet clearances (hot)	Inlet 0.020in.; Exhaust 0.020in.
Valve timing:	
inlet opens	46° b.t.d.c. } at 0.008 clearance
inlet closes	84° a.b.d.c. } at 0.008 clearance
exhaust opens	94° b.b.d.c. } at 0.010 clearance
Exhaust closes	36° a.t.d.c. } at 0.010 clearance
Front wheel toe-in	1/16in.
Camber angle	Front 0°, Rear 2° negative
Castor angle	3°
King pin inclination	11°
Tyre pressures:	
Front	26 psi
Rear	30 psi

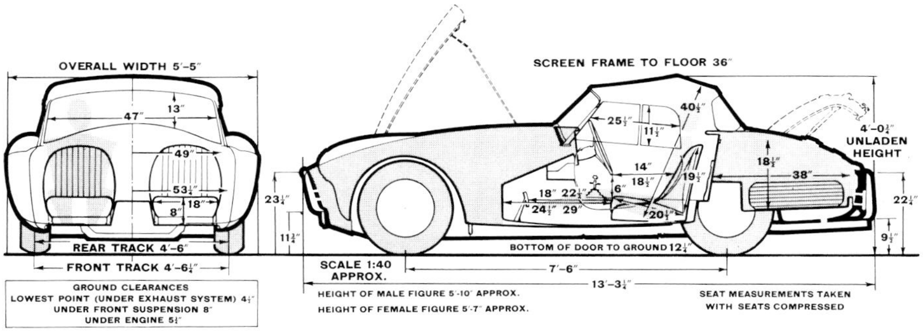
OVERALL WIDTH 5'-5"
13"
47"
49"
53¼"
18"
8"
23¼"
11¾"
REAR TRACK 4'-6"
FRONT TRACK 4'-6¼"
GROUND CLEARANCES
LOWEST POINT (UNDER EXHAUST SYSTEM) 4½"
UNDER FRONT SUSPENSION 8"
UNDER ENGINE 5½"
SCREEN FRAME TO FLOOR 36"
25½"
11½"
40½"
14"
18½"
19½"
18" 22½"
6"
24½" 29"
20½"
18½"
38"
4'-0¾"
UNLADEN
HEIGHT
22¼"
9½"
BOTTOM OF DOOR TO GROUND 12¼"
SCALE 1:40
APPROX.
7'-6"
13'-3¼"
HEIGHT OF MALE FIGURE 5'-10" APPROX.
HEIGHT OF FEMALE FIGURE 5'-7" APPROX.
SEAT MEASUREMENTS TAKEN
WITH SEATS COMPRESSED

A.C. 289 Sports *continued*

or no radial thump, and the car follows the road contours faithfully. At speed on main roads it is comfortable. On poorly filled-in roadmenders' holes you get the odd rattle from the rear suspension, but otherwise the car feels rigid and free from scuttle shake on surfaces which might be expected to produce it. Out of town, the ride remains firm but gives that reassuring feel of the road that is essential in fast cars; you get jerked in the slightly bouncy seats on sharp bumps, but on wider spaced undulations it just follows the road with no wallowing and no discomfort for that type of car.

On the Belgian pavé the car behaved fairly well; on good sections it would maintain 80 mph or so with only a loud rumble to show you were on a different surface, but on worse sections with potholes the speed was dropped to 50 mph for fear of using up all the rather small ground clearance. On typical French secondary roads with steep cambers and fairly ridged surfaces the wheels stayed on the road but there appeared to be some bump steering which occasionally spoilt the line into corners.

The driver's seat seemed to be a little more comfortable than the passenger's which had less lumbar support; both backrests were too upright but no one found them uncomfortable and they have good side support. The pedals are slightly offset with respect to the wheel, but the seat is angled so that you don't get the spinal twist of some offset layouts. The pedal pads are metal with rubber inserts and pivot through a small angle range to adapt to the angle of the foot, a pleasing feature of A.C.s for some time; those with shoes of size 9 or so occasionally jammed their clutch foot on the toe-board—a piece of untrimmed glass fibre; there is an adjustable steering column.

The soft hood doesn't appear to have changed in design since the first of this line; it is held on top of the screen by two pins in the centre which slide into a channel, and at the edges by over-centre clips. Press studs hold it down round the base of the hood, and there is a rubber sealing strip inside; tensioning is provided by a hoop hinged to the main arch.

Insurance

A group rating	7
Lloyd's	On application

1, starter solenoid. 2, battery. 3, radiator filler. 4, washer reservoir. 5, distributor. 6, oil filler. 7, coil. 8, dipstick.

MAKE: A.C. MODEL: 289 Sports MAKERS: A.C. Cars Ltd., Thames Ditton, Surrey, England.

The fabric and the side screens fit into the bag behind the seats. It takes about two minutes for one practised person to put up, but two could probably halve the time. Once up it is rather primitive for this day and age; you get leaks coming in round the side screens, and the noise is rather less bearable than the lesser buffetting when the hood is down. It is with the hood down that we all had our best memories of A.C. motoring; it is quite acceptable up to 110 mph or so and only at 120 mph does it get really uncomfortable.

Visibility is unusually good with the soft top; the screen pillars are thin and there is plenty of clear sheet in the fabric. With the speed limit, we found the lights good enough in this country where we either knew the road or were guided by Cats-eye studs, but in France, where neither condition existed, we felt that they could have penetrated further; as it was they limited the speed to around 80 mph.

With the hood up there are few draughts until you move the sliding sidescreen forward, which is necessary in traffic when the interior can get a bit warm. On the move you can get cold air in by ram effect at foot level; this is controlled by knobs at either end of the facia. For hot air you have to use the two-speed fan since the system is a recirculatory one; there are flaps at foot level and the screen outlets demist the screen quite quickly.

Fittings and furniture

There is a splendid number of instruments on display, but their layout is hardly ideal. The wheel spokes obscure the lower edges of the speedometer and rev-counter so that 30 mph is largely guesswork and taller people with the seat right back found the oil pressure gauge also hidden. We liked the horn operation, a bar in the back of the indicator stalk, but didn't like the flasher/dipswitch stalk on the facia with its two-plane movement. There is no padding on the painted metal facia top and its flat surface reflects overhead trees on to the screen.

There is a glove locker on the facia and you can get a brief-case behind the seats, but the rest of the luggage has to go in the boot on top of the spare wheel. In fact the boot took 3.9 cu.ft. of our luggage, or rather more than either the Mini or the long tailed Hornet. Maps can fit in either door pocket.

Carpets are fitted to the floor and transmission tunnel and the seats are upholstered in leather; the door locks at the rear of the panel are operated by a simple leather pull-strap and you have to open the sidescreen and pull the strap to undo the door from the outside. No safety belts were fitted to our test car but anchorage points are provided behind the seats.

Servicing and accessibility

The bonnet is retained by two top catches at the rear and hinges at the front end; it is easy to lift and is propped open by a single rod with a rubber tipped end. There must have been a lot of room around the original six-cylinder engine because all the parts on the V8 are easily accessible.

The 289 needs servicing every 2,000 miles for which the handbook gives reasonable instructions to the owner mechanic. There aren't many dealers in the country, but A.C. retain a personal contact with all owners and can arrange the nearest suitable agent; there are in fact fewer than 30 of the coil sprung V8 engined cars in this country and only 60 leaf sprung ones, since the vast majority went to America.

As can be seen from the boot picture a comprehensive toolkit is provided. The jack has to fit under the chassis tubes or under the wishbones, but with a flat tyre there is little room to get it under; you need to spread the tonneau cover out on the ground, lie down and grovel underneath.

M

Maintenance summary

Every 2,000 miles: change engine oil, grease drive shaft joints, grease drive shaft splines, grease prop. shaft joints, check master cylinder reservoirs.

Every 4,000 miles: change differential oil, change gearbox oil, grease steering pinion bearing, oil distributor, oil accelerator shaft, grease handbrake nipples, oil carburetter linkages.

Every 10,000 miles: inspect front and rear hub bearings and grease sparingly, oil dynamo front bearing, grease steering gaiter ends. Occasionally oil wiper arm pivots, grease battery terminals, oil locks and hinges.

COBRA 427

Not long ago, the Cobra 427 would have been the hot setup on any race track. Now it's a civilized street machine!

S everal years ago, the manufacturers of a posh British grand touring car got a fair amount of mileage out of the claim that their vehicle could accelerate from 0-100 mph and brake to a complete stop in less than 25 seconds.

This was indeed an impressively brief period of time during which all that change of velocity happened, but automotive development has come a long way since then and today perhaps half a dozen production cars of one kind or another can perform on that level. What's more, there are several automobiles being produced in the United States that will break through that arbitrary 25 second barrier like the Germans through the Maginot Line. One is the 427 Sting Ray (see page 49); another, most certainly, is the new 427 Cobra from Shelby American.

Alright, you say, if 25 seconds from 0-100-0 isn't so hot anymore, what the hell is? Twenty seconds?

Forget twenty seconds.

How about 18 seconds?

Not too bad, but the Cobra can do better.

How much better, wise guy?

How about maybe 14.5 seconds? Get that, 14.5 seconds to accelerate to 100 miles an hour and then stop

CONTINUED
37

263

again. Until something better comes along, that may have to stand as some sort of high water mark in performance for cars that are readily available to the general public. That figure, mind you, is obtainable by the average Cobra driver with the regular 8.15 x 15 Goodyear Blue Dot street tires. Cobra test driver Ken Miles has done the job in as little as 13.8 seconds, and who knows how much improvement could be made with racing tires that would nullify some of the tremendous wheel spin?

The 427 Cobra does accelerate and decelerate at unbelievable rates, as the above figures should imply. What's more, it is a more civilized machine than the original 289 Cobra that brought the fabulous Shelby organization into being four years ago. It handles properly, thanks to a completely new all-independent suspension system that is traceable to the deft hand of Klaus Arning, the Ford Motor Company genius responsible for the impeccable handling of the Ford GT.

Everyone at Shelby is more than candid about admitting that the handling of the original Cobra was considerably less than optimum. In fact, *C/D* was once informed by a Shelby lieutenant that the old tubular AC chassis had considerably less torsional rigidity than the rail frame of a Model T! Coupled with this flexible frame was an antiquated suspension system, designed in the post-war years, that utilized leaf springs and lower wishbones. One staff member recalls a particularly painful day in southern California when he was outrun down a bumpy orange grove lane by an MG 1100. "There I was, with all that Cobra horsepower, and the rear wheels were bouncing and leaping around so badly that I could barely keep the beast on the road, much less catch up to the MG. It was terrible!"

He should try the same trip in the 427. The new frame, still fabricated at AC Cars in England—but to Shelby specifications—is as stiff as a Redwood trunk and permits the equally-new coil sprung suspension to operate at maximum efficiency. Arning has designed the same anti-dive and anti-squat characteristics into the 427 Cobra that he used so successfully on the Ford GT and they contribute immensely to the 0-100-0 times the car is able to record. Under heavy acceleration, the car tracks nicely for a machine with such power, and its braking manners are magnificent. The massive Girling discs haul the car down from 100 mph-plus speeds like you've suddenly run into a sand bank, and much of this is due to the suspension's anti-dive capability. The only defect we found in the Cobra's acceleration-deceleration performance was a nasty little habit of trying to dog track when the throttle is wide open. The car will break traction to speeds beyond 100 mph and imprudent applications of power will send the tail-end slewing sideways. This apparently is an inbred trait in all front-engine automobiles with power-to-weight ratios in the 6:1 range and no amount of suspension work can eliminate it entirely. Certainly wider-base racing tires will reduce the problem, but the fact remains that the Cobra 427 is not an automobile for novices.

Unlike the 427 Sting Ray, the Cobra has retained its identity as a raw-boned, wind-in-the-face sports car. While the Sting Ray is a completely civilized vehicle, available with everything from multiplex FM radio to air conditioning, the Cobra comes across the counter with the same kind of side curtains that English sports cars have carried since Sir Henry Seagrave first turned an ignition key. Another feature designed to delight the Purist is the hand-operated

PHOTOGRAPHS: JESSE ALEXANDER

top, the erection of which may rank second only to folding up a road map for sheer, brain-addling complication. Some of the staff complained about these archaic fittings, claiming loudly that any automobile that lays claim to being contemporary should at least have roll-up windows and a power-operated top. Others defended the Cobra, arguing that its raw power, the great brakes and the advanced suspension create a vehicle with such unabashed appeal and excitement that the owner plain won't give a damn about creature comfort. He *might* object if he knew that at any moment an automobile could invade his chill, wind-buffeted world and blow his Cobra into the nearest ditch. But that just simply ain't going to happen. The driver of a 427 Cobra, at the moment this is written, has about as much fear of being passed by

38   **CAR** and **DRIVER**

a herd of stampeding Water Buffalo as he does by a faster automobile, and *that* alone can make up for a lot of uncivilized traveling.

We tested the Cobra during the same Los Angeles heat wave that contributed to the tragic race riots and found the big car to be amazingly tractable. It refused to heat up, despite several hours of chuffing along on clogged freeways, and this was a welcome contrast to the old 289s, whose temperature gauges were inclined to rise clean off the scale at anything under maybe a sustained 80 miles an hour. The installation of a thick-core, 20-quart radiator, and a bigger grille opening aid greatly in keeping things cool, but the biggest safeguard against overheating is a small fan mounted ahead of the radiator that is thermostatically actuated whenever the water tem-

perature reaches 70 degrees Centigrade.

Heat is a factor in the cockpit, however. With that great brute of a powerplant thumping away just inches ahead of the firewall, a substantial amount of heat is bound to penetrate even the best insulated flooring, and we found that temperatures around the feet were inclined to get awfully uncomfortable after a few hours running. Shelby American engineers are attempting to correct this problem with the use of more insulation, but we wonder if there simply just isn't too much heat to overcome.

Being about seven inches wider than the old 289, the 427 is a more comfortable car; about that there should be no question. The same basic Cobra layout remains essentially unchanged in the new car, includ-
(Text continued on page 76, Specifications overleaf)

427 COBRA

Manufacturer: Shelby American Inc.
6501 W. Imperial Highway
Los Angeles, California

Price as tested: $7000 (approx.)

ACCELERATION

Zero to	Seconds
30 mph	3.2
40 mph	3.6
50 mph	3.9
60 mph	4.3
70 mph	5.5
80 mph	6.2
90 mph	7.3
100 mph	8.8
Standing ¼-mile	118 mph in 12.2

COBRA 427

Top speed, observed .... 165 mph
Temperature .... 72° F
Wind velocity .... 4 mph
Altitude above sea level .... 50 ft
In 4 runs, 0-60 mph
times varied
between 4.2 and 4.6 seconds

ENGINE

Water-cooled V-8, cast iron block, 5 main bearings
Bore x stroke .... 4.24 x 3.78 in, 107 x 96 mm
Displacement .... 427 cu in, 6998 cc
Compression ratio .... 10.4 to one
Carburetion .... Two 4-bbl Holley
Valve gear. Pushrod-operated overhead valves, mechanical lifters
Power (SAE) .... 485 bhp @ 6500 rpm
Torque .... 480 lbs-ft @ 3500 rpm
Specific power output .....1.14 bhp per cu in, 69.29 bhp per liter
Usable range of engine speeds . 500–7000 rpm
Electrical system ... 12-volt, 70 amp-hr battery, 55A alternator
Fuel recommended .... Premium
Mileage .... 9–12 mpg
Range on 18-gallon tank .... 162–216 miles

DRIVE TRAIN

Clutch .... 11.5-inch single dry plate
Transmission .... 4-speed, all synchro

Gear	Ratio	Over-all	mph/1000 rpm	Max mph
Rev	2.32	8.21	-9.86	-69
1st	2.32	8.21	9.86	69
2nd	1.69	5.98	13.54	95
3rd	1.29	4.57	17.71	124
4th	1.00	3.54	22.91	160

Final drive ratio .... 3.54 to one

CHASSIS

Wheelbase .... 90 in
Track .... F 56, R 56 in
Length .... 156 in
Width .... 68 in
Height .... 49 in
Ground Clearance .... 4.35 in
Dry weight .... 2354 lbs
Curb weight .... 2529 lbs
Test weight .... 2890 lbs
Weight distribution front/rear ... 48/52%
Pounds per bhp (test weight) 5.95
Suspension F: Ind., unequal-length wishbones with anti-dive and anti-squat, coil springs.
R: Ind., unequal-length wishbones with anti-dive and anti-squat, coil springs.
Brakes ... discs, 11.63-in front, 10.75-in rear, 580 sq in swept area
Steering .... Rack and pinion
Turns, lock to lock 2.5
Turning circle .... 36 ft
Tires .... 8.15 x 15 Goodyear Blue Dot
Wheels .... 7½ x 15 Cast alloy

CHECK LIST

ENGINE

Starting	Good
Response	Excellent
Noise	Good
Vibration	Good

DRIVE TRAIN

Clutch action	Excellent
Transmission linkage	Excellent
Synchromesh action	Excellent
Power-to-ground transmission	Good

BRAKES

Response	Excellent
Pedal pressure	Good
Fade resistance	Excellent
Smoothness	Excellent
Directional stability	Excellent

STEERING

Response	Good
Accuracy	Good
Feedback	Good
Road feel	Good

SUSPENSION

Harshness control	Good
Roll stiffness	Excellent
Tracking	Fair
Pitch control	Good
Shock damping	Excellent

CONTROLS

Location	Good
Relationship	Good
Small controls	Good

INTERIOR

Visibility	Excellent
Instrumentation	Good
Lighting	Good
Entry/exit	Good
Front seating comfort	Good
Front seating room	Good
Rear seating comfort	—
Rear seating room	—
Storage space	Fair
Wind noise	Fair
Road noise	Fair

WEATHER PROTECTION

Heater	Good
Defroster	Good
Ventilation	Poor
Weather sealing	Good
Windshield wiper action	Good

QUALITY CONTROLS

Materials, exterior	Good
Materials, interior	Good
Exterior finish	Good
Interior finish	Good
Hardware and trim	Good

GENERAL

Service accessibility	Excellent
Luggage space	Poor
Bumper protection	Poor
Exterior lighting	Good
Resistance to crosswinds	Good

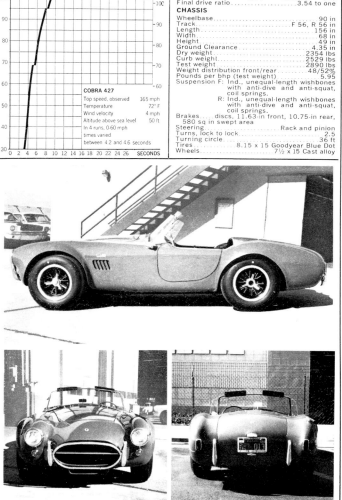

ing those hilariously antique metal brake and clutch pedals with the art nouveau "AC" emblem, but everything is simply a bit roomier. The seats are deep, comfortable leather-covered buckets that would accommodate even Goose Tatum without great difficulty. We found that a six-footer sticks a good distance up over the doors, but he's still well protected by the windshield and any vulnerability he might feel is purely psychological. The steering wheel is perfectly positioned, though the shift lever comes out of the tunnel about three inches too far aft to be described as ideal. Although this causes no real upset, a reasonably tall driver will

find that he has to bend his elbow as if he was getting ready to let fly with a bowling ball whenever he wants to engage first gear.

For a car that lays valid claim to being the fastest production machine in history, the 427 Cobra is amazingly simple. Its powerplant is the standard big Ford of the type that be purchased in any Galaxie at any local dealership. "It's a big cooking engine, with a rather peaky torque curve that produces a great horsepower reading for the customer and is ideal for flexible road driving. But we tune the competition 427s much differently, with a flatter curve," says Ken Miles.

One might expect a Cobra with an

engine displacing 427 cubic inches to be an absolute beast on the street. It is utterly to the contrary, with a positively placid disposition at low speeds. This faked us out completely because we expected to find a machine with a vicious, bear-trap clutch and an engine that idled something like a Double-A fuel dragster. We found the 11.5 inch Ford clutch to be no more challenging than a normal domestic unit and the engine ticked off a 700-rpm idle with style and grace. In fact, the smoothness of the Cobra at low speeds completely belies its breathtaking performance, and only when the throttle is cracked does the driver realize the reservoir of power is practically a bottomless pit. A top speed of 165 mph is possible with the car's standard 3.54:1 final drive ratio, and that should be sufficient for travel on any thoroughfare except the Mulsanne Straight.

Like the engine, the transmission is a standard Ford four-speed unit that operates like all the other domestic all-synchros on the market today. Lest there be any misunderstanding, that means we love it.

The 427 Cobra is bulkier looking than its forerunner, and if anything, looks meaner. It utilizes the same wild fender flares that first appeared on the 289 racing versions, and based on pure subjectivity, we think the 427 Cobra is maybe the toughest looking car on the road.

Everybody knows wire wheels are out and Shelby American is supplying the 427 with Halibrand knock-off, magnesium wheels as standard equipment. They are specially fabricated for the car and are painted black, save for a polished rim and highlights around the air slots. It is possible that special Shelby-manufactured magnesium wheels will replace the Halibrands later on in the year, but the latter will remain as an option throughout the expected production run of about 200 automobiles.

Nearly a year has passed since the 427 Cobra was announced, and skeptics can still be found who will tell you there ain't no such thing as a production 427 Cobra. This is nonsense. There were at least 50 of the machines at the Shelby plant when we ran our test and more were arriving from England on a daily basis. The new Cobra is a reality and only approximately $7000 cash and the insatiable desire to own the fastest car in four counties stands between you and owning one. If you can scrape up the dough, we recommend that you take the plunge. Like they say, it'll never hurt you. Or at least it shouldn't. **c/D**

Road test - 7-litre AC Cobra (Autosport 1967).

JOHN BOLSTER tries

A 7-litre AC Cobra

THE AC ACE was originally designed to take 80 bhp or so from the old AC 2-litre engine. I have just been proving that what is recognizably the same vehicle can absorb over 500 bhp from a "hot" 7-litre Ford V8 engine, and that in this guise it is a superb touring car!

This car was one of a pair built for a wealthy American driver. The other one was purely a track car, but the present machine has all the road equipment of a standard 4.7-litre Cobra. However, the 7-litre engine has Shelby aluminium racing cylinder heads and it also has a "full race" bottom end, including special connecting rods at £30 each. It differs from the 550 bhp racing unit in having a gentler camshaft for road use, and in fact its characteristics are ideal, for it will creep through London traffic in top gear or, with a bellow of rage, swing the rev counter needle past 6000 rpm in the same gear in a few seconds—and that means 144 mph on the 3.54 to 1 rear end which is at present installed.

With all that torque available, normal tyres would be quite incapable of transmitting the power to the road. However, this is one of 50 special Cobras which were built to give body clearance for immense racing tyres on wide light-alloy wheels. These are almost unbelievably effective, and all the power can be used all the time, except from a standing start.

The present owner, John Woolfe, has had the car converted to right-hand drive. This is not supposed to be possible with the 7-litre engine, owing to the position of the starter motor, but some modification of the bulkhead and pedals has allowed the standard British steering gear to be adopted. An effective hood with detachable sticks came with the car, but to enjoy it to the full I drove the machine in open form.

Driven slowly, this Cobra seems a real heap! The huge tyres make the steering feel sloppy and the rear end kicks about over bumps, with apparently no directional stability at all. When one releases a few hundred horses, the car instantly comes alive. At 150 mph it runs absolutely straight and true with no correction from the driver, who can relax with one hand on the wheel. In spite of its short wheelbase and wide track it is well balanced on corners, accepting a great deal of power when leaving a bend without getting sideways. On the wide open spaces of Snetterton I was surprised at the cornering power and controllability.

The acceleration is simply tremendous, and bears no relationship to that of any other road-equipped car. It is not only that the Cobra is light and has 500 bhp but, even more important, all that power can be transmitted to the road. Any sports car that one happened to encounter could be overtaken without bothering to change down.

My first attempt at the standing quarter-mile produced a time of 12.8 s which, with a little practice, I reduced to 12.4 s. This was achieved by using only moderate wheelspin at the start but keeping just appreciable wheelspin going for a considerable distance. It was found best to change up relatively early, employing no more than 6000 rpm on any gear, and I did not snatch the changes with an open throttle. The clutch is perfectly happy to handle all that torque and the gearbox gives light, fast changes. For my fastest standing quarter-mile I used top gear for quite a distance towards the end of the run. From a standing start, 100 mph comes up in 9.8 s, using the three lower gears.

With the special racing bottom end, the engine is safe up to 7000 rpm, but I am too much of a mechanical purist to let an engine with nearly a litre per cylinder run that fast. With a really wild camshaft, it might pay to use such extreme revs, but with a road camshaft there seems no reason to do so. The final drive ratio fitted suits the average circuit very well and gives an easy 150 mph without over-revving. With a higher gear (lower numerical ratio) and a hard top on the body, extremely high speeds would certainly be possible, but the present gear ratio is a very good compromise for normal use.

The car takes a bit of stopping from high speeds. The brakes are there all right, and they do not fade, but a strong right leg is required for emergency retardation. However, when a corner rushed towards me and I realized that I had left it a bit late, my fear lent extra strength to my muscles and I did not enter the *décor*. A lady driver, for whom this car is otherwise perfectly suited, would want a bit more servo assistance on the pedal.

No better town and shopping car could be imagined. It is immaterial whether one uses first gear or third for starting from the traffic lights, as in either case the rest of the traffic just melts out of sight. The engine idles absurdly slowly and completely evenly, the typical V8 exhaust note smoothing out into quite a high-pitched scream as the big engine attains full revs. Apart from the exhaust, the engine is remarkably quiet mechanically and the gearbox and final drive are quite inaudible. At reasonably high speeds the ride is very comfortable, and the seats give good location. The handling is far better than that of other Cobras I have driven, the suspension obviously having been set up correctly for the enormous racing tyres. Unfortunately the stupendous performance must be paid for at the rate of 10 mpg or worse.

John Woolfe is very fond of his Cobra, as he has good reason to be. However, he is deeply involved in other racing projects and may find little time to make full use of this delightful machine. Anybody wishing to own a Lamborghini-eater might do worse than try tempting him with a cheque book.

Photographic Print Offer

The publishers are pleased to be able to offer a series of photographs from the pages of this book which are suitable for collecting or framing to liven up the walls of your study/office/boudoir or wherever ...

Our offer means that you can purchase a black and white photograph printed and signed by the author, Trevor Legate, and produced from the original negative. The prints may be purchased in two sizes: 16" x 12" with a one inch white border all round (image size 14" x 10") and 10" x 8" with a half-inch border all round (image size 9" x 7"). We can offer the 16" x 12" print mounted on card ready for framing should you prefer. All prints will be carefully packaged and despatched as quickly as possible.

10" x 8"	**£ 5.00**
16" x 12"	**£15.00**
16" x 12" mounted on card	
	£19.50

The photographs found on the following pages are available -

2 & 3, 40, 70 & 71, 92 & 93, 132 (top), 141 (bottom), 160 (bottom), 161 (bottom), 164, 165 (top), 165 (bottom), 182, 185, 209, 242 & 243, 247, 269.

Send your order - giving page number and location, number of copies required and your name and mailing address - to Veloce Publishing Plc, Godmanstone, Dorset DT2 7AE, England. Enclose a cheque drawn on a UK bank or an international money order made payable to Veloce Publishing Plc: alternatively give your access/visa/mastercharge card number, expiry date and billing address. Add £2.00 for postage and packing to each order. All payments must be in Sterling.

Note prices were correct at the time of publication but are subject to change without notice. The publisher may withdraw the photographic print offer at any time.

INDEX

Dear Reader,
We hope you enjoyed this Veloce Publishing
production. If you have ideas for books on
this, or other marques, please write and tell
us.
Meantime, Happy Motoring!

THE END